Systematic History Fund,

Instituted in 1896.

VITAL RECORDS

OF

ATHOL,

MASSACHUSETTS,

To the end of the year 1849.

WORCESTER, MASSACHUSETTS:
PUBLISHED BY FRANKLIN P. RICE,
Trustee of the Fund.
1910.

Notice

In many older books, foxing (or discoloration) occurs and, in some instances, print lightens with wear and age. Reprinted books, such as this, often duplicate these flaws, notwithstanding efforts to reduce or eliminate them. The pages of this reprint have been digitally enhanced and, where possible, the flaws eliminated in order to provide clarity of content and a pleasant reading experience.

Originally published:
Worcester, Massachusetts
1910

Reprinted:
Janaway Publishing, Inc.
2011

Janaway Publishing, Inc.
732 Kelsey Ct.
Santa Maria, California 93454
(805) 925-1038
www.janawaygenealogy.com

ISBN: 978-1-59641-105-0

Made in the United States of America

Publisher's Note.

THE list of Athol Births, Marriages and Deaths comprised in this volume includes all that were found in the Town Books covering the period from the earliest date there recorded to the end of the year 1849. Some additions have been made from other sources, and these are indicated in each instance by proper reference.

All of the records are condensed in print as much as is consistent with intelligibility, accuracy, and completeness of information. Differences in duplicates, and explanatory or other matter which seemed necessary or desirable, appear in brackets.

Marriages and intentions of marriage are printed under the names of both parties, but the full information concerning each person is given only under his or her name. An asterisk after a marriage indicates that the intention is not found recorded, and in many cases this is accounted for by the fact that neither party belonged in Athol, and consequently publishment was made elsewhere.

When places other than Athol and Massachusetts are named in the original records, they are given in the printed copy.

ABBREVIATIONS

a. — age
b. — born
bap. — baptized
ch. — child
C.R. — church record
d. — daughter; day; died
Dea. — Deacon
dup. — duplicate entry
G.S.1. — gravestone, Highland Cemetery
G.S.2. — gravestone, Mount Pleasant Cemetery
G.S.3. — gravestone, Old Cemetery
G.S.4. — gravestone, Cemetery, Pleasant Street
G.S.5. — gravestone, Cemetery on Conant Road
G.S.6. — gravestone, Cemetery on Adams Road
h. — husband
inf. — infant
int. — publishment of intention of marriage
Jr. — junior
m. — male; married; month
P.R. — private record
s. — son
Sr. — senior
w. — wife
wid. — widow
widr. — widower

The age given in the Deaths is in years unless otherwise indicated.

Athol,

Worcester County.

ESTABLISHED March 6, 1762, from the plantation called "Payquage." A part was included in the District of Orange, Franklin County, October 15, 1783, and another part in the new town of Gerry, now Phillipston, October 20, 1786. Parts annexed to Royalston February 26, 1799, and March 7, 1803. A part of Gerry was annexed February 28, 1806, and a part of Orange February 7, 1816. Certain Common Lands were annexed June 11, 1829. A part of New Salem in Franklin County was annexed February 5, 1830, and another part of New Salem called "Little Grant" annexed March 16, 1837.

Population at different periods: 1765, 359; 1776, 848; 1790, 848; 1800, 993; 1810, 1,041; 1820, 1,211; 1830, 1,325; 1840, 1,591; 1850, 2,034.

Population in 1905, 7,197.

Number of Births printed	3,529
Marriages . . . . 1,138 =	2,276 names
Deaths	1,470
	7,275 total

ATHOL RECORDS.

ATHOL BIRTHS.

To the year 1850.

ADAMS, Achsah, d. Timothy and Laura, Oct. 26, 1832.
Augusta, d. Franklin and Samantha, June 11, 1845.
Benjamin, July 21, 1805. G.S.6.
George T., s. Timothy and Laura, March 13, 1835.
Gustin, s. Timothy and Deidamia, Jan. 15, 1810.
Jane, d. Franklin and Somantha, Nov. 22, 1842.
Josephine Ellen, d. Franklin and Samantha, Jan. 17, 1848.
Mary, w. Benjamin, April 21, 1809. G.S.6.
Rosannah, d. Timothy and Laura, Jan. 11, 1831.
Silvia, d. Timothy and Deidamia, Feb. 10, 1812.

AINSWORTH, George M., Aug. 27, 1849. G.S.1.

ALLEN, Aaron, s. Aaron and Lucy, bap. Jan. 8, 1776. C.R.
Anna J., —— —, 1839. G.S.1.
Elishah, s. Aaron and Lucy, bap. March 1, 1778. C.R.
Fanny R., w. William P., —— —, 1823. G.S.2.
Francis Maria, d. James and Roena, Feb. 23, 1844.
Gideon, s. John and Lucy, bap. June 25, 1780. C.R.
James Andrew, s. James and Rowena, Feb. 25, 1847.
John, s. Aaron and Lucy, bap. March 1, 1778. C.R.
John Frederick, s. John and Elvira Eunice, April 30, 1840.
Lucretia, d. Aaron and ——, bap. Aug. 21, 1785. C.R.
Seth S., —— —, 1839. G.S.1.
William P., —— —, 1819. G.S.2.

AMSDEN, Cora L., d. Warren H. and Lois S., Aug. 6, 1845.
Frederick H., s. Festus and Mary L., Nov. 1, 1847.
Warren H., —— —, 1817. G.S.2.
——, d. Warren H. and Sarepta, May 26, 1846.
——, s. Festus F. and Mary, Aug. 19, 1846.
——, s. Festus F. and Mary L., Dec. 29, 1849.

ANDREWS, Alonzo, twin s. Collin and Hannah, March 8, 1828.
John Nichols, s. Collin and Hannah, Sept. 28, 1829.
Lorenzo, twin s. Collin and Hannah, March 8, 1828.

ATWOOD, Emma C., —— ——, 1847. G.S.2.

BABBIT (see Babbitt), Anne, d. Nathaniel and Mary, May 24, 1773.
Seth, s. Nathaniel and Mary, Nov. 23, 1769.

BABBITT (see above), Alfred, s. Stillman and Jane, July 25, 1841.
Francis Fairbanks, twin s. Pliny H. and Lydia P., Jan. 1, 1844.
Franklin Phinney, twin s. Pliny H. and Lydia P., Jan. 1, 1844.
Harriet Augusta, d. Thomas and Nancy W., Jan. 14, 1837.
Harriet Newell, d. Thomas and Nancy W., July 11, 1833.
Levi, June 26, 1780. G.S.2.
Lyman Dwight, s. George W. and Susan A., Sept. 5, 1838.
Maria M., w. Maro F. ?, —— ——, 1832. G.S.2.
Maro F., —— ——, 1829. G.S.2.
Nancy W., w. Thomas ?, July 26, 1812. G.S.2.
Polly L., w. Levi, April 27, 1781. G.S.2.
Sally Cellista M., d. Thomas and Nancy W., May 2, 1831. G.S.2.
Spencer Stockwell, s. Stillman and Jane, May 30, 1840.
Thomas, March 12, 1807. G.S.2.

BACON, Henry B., Aug. 5, 1829. G.S.1.
Mary A. Farr, w. Henry B., Feb. 24, 1830. G.S.1.

BAGLEY, Moses, —— ——, 1839. G.S.2.

BAKER, Adaline, d. Marshal and Elizabeth, Nov. 25, 1796.
Almira, d. Marshal and Elizabeth, Oct. 20, 1801.
Eliza, d. Marshal and Elizabeth, Jan. 27, 1800.
Mary H., w. Milton ?, May 5, 1821. G.S.2.
Milton, July 28, 1812. G.S.2.
Uri, s. Marshal and Elizabeth, May 15, 1798.

BALCOM, Susan A., —— ——, 1831. G.S.2.

BALL, Abraham, s. Moses and Susanna, Nov. 15, 1764.
Adonijah, s. Moses and Susanna, Dec. 5, 1762.
Adonijah, s. Adonijah and Mary, July 12, 1791.
Adonijah, s. Isaac Jr. and Hannah, Nov. 20, 1778.
Almira Hill, d. James and Maria, Aug. 29, 1828.
Ann Sophia, d. Adonijah Jr. and Anna, March 30, 1822.
Charles Hervey, s. Adonijah Jr. and Anna, April 19, 1820.
Charles Hervy, s. Adonijah Jr. and Anna, Aug. 19, 1821.
Francis Augustus, s. James and Maria, Feb. 3, 1823.
George Elliot, s. James and Maria, April 21, 1835.
Grace Cachran [Cothrane in bap.], d. Moses and Susanna, Aug. 18, 1773.

BALL, Isaac, s. Moses and Susanna, Nov. 15, 1769.
Jacob, s. Moses and Susanna, May 18, 1771.
James, s. Adonijah and Mary, Aug. 27, 1797.
James W., s. James and Maria, Oct. 6, 1820.
Jane Maria Goodhue, d. James and Maria, Aug. 13, 1825.
Mary Ann, d. Adonijah and Mary, June 14, 1805.
Mary Ann, d. James and Maria, March 13, 1838.
Moses, s. Adonijah and Mary, Oct. 3, 1793.
Moses Phillips, s. Adonijah and Mary, July 26, 1795.
Samuel Collins, s. Adonijah and Mary, Oct. 10, 1799.
Sarah, d. Moses and Susanna, Oct. 5, 1767.
Susanna, d. Moses and Susanna, April 22, 1776.

BALLARD, Abigail, d. Joshua and Anne, Sept. 28, 1784.
Ann, d. Elijah and Polly, Oct. 12, 1828.
Anna, d. Joshua and Anna, June 20, 1795.
Daniel, s. Joshua and Anne, Feb. 21, 1786.
Edward, s. Joshua and Anne, March 14, 1783.
Elijah, s. Joshua and Anne, July 22, 1789.
Elizabeth, d. Elijah and Polly, April 21, 1822.
Franklin, s. Joshua and Anne, April 21, 1797.
Hepsibah, d. Joshua and Anne, March 28, 1779.
James, s. Joshua and Anne, April 16, 1793.
Jane, d. Elijah and Polly, March 4, 1826.
John, s. John and Hepzibah, Oct. 13, 1759.
John, s. Joshua and Anne, April 23, 1777.
John Cutting, s. Elijah and Polly, Sept. 14, 1820.
Joshua, s. John and Hepzibah, April 14, 1754.
Joshua, s. Joshua and Anne, Jan. 18, 1781.
Marion, d. Elijah and Polly, Sept. 21, 1833.
Mary, d. Elijah and Polly, Aug. 31, 1823.
Molly, d. John and Hepzibah, April 19, 1762.
Molly, d. Joshua and Anne, July 1, 1787.
Stephen, s. Joshua and Anne, April 26, 1791.
Stephen, s. John and ———, bap. June 12, 1791. C.R. [Probably same as foregoing.]
William Morse, s. Elijah and Elizabeth, May 22, 1815.

BANCROFT, Charles, ———, 1801. G.S.I.
Charles Otis, s. Charles and Nancy, ———, 1827. G.S.I.
Elizabeth Foster, w. Charles Otis, ———, 1828. G.S.I.
Harriet Sarah, d. Esther and Samuel, July 3, 1838.
Hiram A., Dec. 21, 1847. G.S.2.
Nancy Dike, w. Charles, ———, 1797. G.S.I.
———, d. Samuel and Esther, June 22, 1844.

BARBER, Emily, d. John P. and Ellen, May 6, 1841.
Esther Oliver, d. John P. and Ellen, March 24, 1839.
George N., s. John P. and Ellen, Oct. 9, 1847.
———, s. John P. and Ellen, Oct. 9, 1844.
———, d. Chauncey, ——— —, 1847?

BARNS, ———, ch. ———, Jan. 31, 1846.

BARRETT, Alice George, d. John and Naomi, Nov. 1, 1810.
Benjamin Baily Hale, s. John and Naomi, May 22, 1813.
Henry Rice, s. John and Naomi, Feb. 6, 1793.
John Ross, s. John and Naomi, Nov. 8, 1804.
Lydia, d. John and Naomy, March 14, 1798.
Nancy, d. John and Naomy, Aug. 4, 1802.
Nancy, d. John and Naomi, Dec. 21, 1807.
Oliver Baley, s. John and Naomy, March 11, 1800.
Polly, d. John and Naomy, April 21, 1796.
Rosanna C., d. Benjamin and Eunice, Dec. 17, 1841.

BARRUS, Mary S., w. William J., ——— —, 1846. G.S.2.

BARRY, Adaline, d. Thomas and Lucinda, March 28, 1837.
Ellen Maria, d. Thomas and Lucinda, May 29, 1833.
Emily, d. Thomas and Lucinda, Dec. 19, 1841.
George Henry, s. Thomas and Lucinda, Aug. 3, 1839.
Laura Jane, d. Thomas and Lucinda, April 19, 1835.
Lucinda Elisabeth, d. Thomas and Lucinda, Jan. 5, 1831.
Luthera, d. Thomas and Lucinda, Dec. 25, 1824.
Mary Ann, d. Thomas and Lucinda, July 14, 1826.
Thomas Gardner, s. Thomas and Lucinda, March 3, 1829.
William Francis, s. Thomas and Lucinda, Sept. 25, 1846.
———, father, ——— —, 1799. G.S.1.
———, mother, ——— —, 1804. G.S.1.
———, d. Thomas and Lucinda, April 15, 1844.
———, d. Thomas and Lucinda, April 15, 1845.

BARTLETT, Chauncey, s. John and ———, bap. Aug. 4, 1811. c.r.

BARTON, Caroline C., w. Hiram ?, ——— —, 1810. G.S.2.
Charles Henry, s. Hyram and Caroline, Nov. 18, 1841.
Elisabeth Warren, d. Hyram and Caroline, Jan. 4, 1835.
Emily Smith, d. Hyram and Caroline, Dec. 19, 1838.
Everlena J., w. Charles H.?, ——— —, 1843. G.S.2.
Hiram, ——— —, 1809. G.S.2.
Sarah Jane, d. Hyram and Caroline, May 26, 1837.

BASSET, Celia French, d. Jacob and ———, bap. Dec. 17, 1816. c.r.
Cloe, d. Jacob and ———, bap. June 1, 1817. c.r.
Cyrus, s. Jacob and ———, bap. Dec. 17, 1816. c.r.
Electa, d. Jacob and ———, bap. Dec. 17, 1816. c.r.
Harriet, d. Jacob and ———, bap. Dec. 17, 1816. c.r.
Lois, d. Jacob and ———, bap. Dec. 17, 1816. c.r.

BATCHELDER, Charles Harvey, s. Joseph and Mary T., Sept. 5, 1824. At Greenwood, N.Y.
Daniel, ——— —, 1792. g.s.2.
Huldah T., w. Daniel, ——— —, 1797. g.s.2.
Huldee Maria, d. Lysander and Martha, Feb. 12, 1845.
John Humphrey, s. Joseph and Mary T., July 21, 1820.
Joseph Mayo, s. Joseph and Mary T., Sept. 23, 1822. At Greenwood, N. Y.

BATES, Caleb, s. William and Marcy, bap. Sept. 7, 1775. c.r.
Dolle, d. William and Mercy, bap. July 27, 1771. c.r.
Joseph F., Dec. 15, 1821. g.s.5.
Susan W., w. Joseph F., Oct. 15, 1828. g.s.5.
William, s. William and Marcy, bap. Sept. 7, 1775. c.r.
William, Junior, s. William and Marcy, bap. June 11, 1776. c.r.

BATTLES, Naaman, ——— —, 1801. g.s.5.
Polly, w. Naaman, ——— —, 1802. g.s.5.

BEARD, George W., Feb. 10, 1818. g.s.2.
Porter, s. Edmund and Hannah, Oct. —, 1849.
Roswell, Aug. 30, 1824. g.s.2.
———, s. Edmund and Hannah, Aug. 27, 1846.

BEMAN, Franklin, s. Josiah and Martha, July 16, 1841.
Henry, s. Josiah and Martha, Dec. 11, 1834.
Sarah, d. Josiah and Martha, June 9, 1837.

BEMIS, Huldah G., w. Samuel A. ?, ——— —, 1825. g.s.2.
Samuel A., ——— —, 1835. g.s.2.

BIGELOW, Abel, s. David and Louis, May 29, 17[87].
Abigail, d. William and Elizabeth, July 26, 1814.
Betsy Almira, d. William and Elizabeth, Feb. 6, 1818.
Charles William, s. William and Elizabeth, Jan. 15, 1810.
Daniel, s. David and Louis, June 8, 1800.
David, s. William and Margaret, Aug. 30, 1754.
David, s. David and Louis, May 9, 1790.
Esther, d. William and Margaret, Nov. 30, 1757.

ATHOL BIRTHS.

BIGELOW, Esther, d. Abel and Hannah, March 8, 1817.
Esther, d. Abel and Hannah, Nov. 27, 1821.
Fanny, d. Abel and Hannah, Jan. 4, 1819.
George Alven, s. William and Elizabeth, Nov. 1, 1823.
Hannah Lucina [twin ?], d. Abel and Hannah, Aug. 25, 1825.
Hannah Lucinda [twin ? or dup. of above], d. Abel and Hannah, Aug. 25, 1825.
Harriot Maria, d. William and Elizabeth, April 17, 1820.
Henry A., s. Abel and Eunice, Feb. 10, 1834.
Lois, d. David and Louis, March 17, 1793.
Lucretia, d. David and Louis, Nov. 16, 1795.
Mary Ann, d. William and Elizabeth, March 10, 1812.
Patty, d. David and Louis, Dec. 19, 1784?
Persis [Perses in dup.], d. David and Louis, May 29, 1782.
Rhoena Ellinwood, d. Abel and Eunice, Jan. 27, 1830.
Richard Sautell, s. Abel and Eunice, Nov. 17, 1831.
Sarah E., d. Abel and Eunice, Aug. 22, 1836.
Solon, d. Abel and Eunice, Nov. 29, 1838.
William, s. David and Louis, Jan. 21, 1780. Dup.
William, s. Abel and Hannah, Aug. 25, 1825.

BILLINGS, Abigail R. E., w. Erastus, —— ——, 1805. G.S.2.
David E., s. Erastus and Abigail R. E., —— ——, 1837. G.S.2.
Erastus, —— ——, 1798. G.S.2.
Sarah Ann, d. —— and Mary Ann, May 20, 1842.

BLACKBURN, Charles F., —— ——, 1841. G.S.2.
Hattie A., w. Charles F. ?, —— ——, 1840. G.S.2.

BLAKE, Ebenezer Deane, s. Timothy and Julia, Dec. 5, 1803.
Warren, s. Timothy and Julia, April 14, 1801.

BLANCHARD, Elezebeth, d. Moses and Azubah, Feb. 20, 1789.
Prudence, d. Moses and Azubah, Oct. 4, 1786.

BLISS, Emily Ann, d. Stephen W. and Persis, Oct. 18, 1834. Dup.
Joseph W., s. Stephen W. and Persis, Aug. 3, 1838.
Mary Jane, d. Stephen W. and Persis, Sept. 17, 1836. Dup.
Sarah Abby, d. Stephen W. and Persis, Nov. 3 [9 and 19 in dups.], 1843.
Sarah Elizabeth, d. Perrin and Persis Ann, Jan. 19, 1838.

BLODGET, Alonzo, s. Amos and Phebe, July 14, 1814.

BOUTELL, Adelia Sophia, d. John and Maria, Feb. 21, 1837.
Emma Francis, d. James and Martha H., May 13, 1849.
Martha Ann, d. John and Maria Ann, March 26, 1844.

ATHOL BIRTHS. 15

BOUTELL, Mary Elizabeth, d. John and Maria, Dec. 27, 1840.
———, d. James and Martha, March 5, 1847.
BOWEN, John. s. John and Sabrina, Sept. 5, 1849.
BOYCE, Robert F., ———, 1828. G.S.2.
BOYDEN, Ellen Louisa, d. Elbridge and Louisa, May 10, 1835.
George Elbridge, s. Elbridge and Louisa, Aug. 29, 1837.
BOYNTON, Elizabeth R., w. John, formerly w. Stillman Simonds, Dec. 11, 1807. G.S.2.
BRAG, Joab, s. Abial and ———, bap. June 15, 1760. C.R.
BRIDGE, Aden Jones, s. Aden and Luana, April 20, 1834.
Luana Caroline, d. Aden and Luana, Dec. 4, 1840.
Rebeccah Catharine, d. Aden and Luana, Feb. 17, 1843.
BRIGGS, Albert D., s. Sylvanus B. and Lucinda B., Feb. 7, 1847.
Betsy, d. Isaac and Polly, Nov. 28, 1794.
David, s. Isaac and Polly, April 8, 1799.
Elvira, d. Sylvanus B. and Lucinda, ———, ——— [1845 ?].
Esther, d. Isaac and Polly, July 21, 1808.
Francis N., s. Nathan G. and Betsey, July 28, 1840.
George Nixon, s. Sylvanus B. and Lucinda, Feb. 7, 1849.
Isaac, s. Isaac and Polly, Feb. 6, 1790. At Tanton.
John, s. Isaac and Polly, March 7, 1797.
Levi, Aug. 20, 1767. G.S.3.
Levi, s. Isaac and Polly, July 19, 1803.
Marilla, d. Nathan G. and Betsy, Jan. 27, 1847.
Martha W., ———, 1835. G.S.2.
Moses, s. Isaac and Polly, Dec. 23, 1805.
Nancy, d. Isaac and Polly, Oct. 10, 1793.
Polly, d. Isaac and Polly, Nov. 9, 1786. At Tanton.
Rhoda, d. Isaac and Polly, Feb. 16, 1792. At Tanton.
Sally, d. Isaac and Polly, April 2, 1788. At Tanton.
Sophronia, d. Isaac and Polly, May 19, 1800.
BRIGHAM, Sophia, d. Aaron and Comfort, Jan. 17, 1815.
William Henry, s. Artemas and Mary Ann, Aug. 18, 1831.
BROCK, Abby Fidelia, d. David S. and Fidelia, March 2, 1849.
Albert Elliot, s. Isaac Z. and Esther, Nov. 12, 1847.
Anderson LeRoy, s. Isaac and Esther, June 5, 1842.
Caleb Mortimer, s. David A. and Fidelia, June 29, 1847.
Caroline H., w. Ebenezer ?, June 28, 1821. G.S.2.

BROCK, Charles Flavel, s. Ebenezer and Caroline, July 30, 1842.
Cordelia Celia, d. Henry and Mary A. Rogers, March 7, 1848.
David H. H., s. David S. and Elizabeth B., Jan. 25, 1840.
Ebenezer, Aug. 8, 1816. G.S.2.
Esther, w. Isaac Z., Feb. —, 1811. G.S.6.
Esther L., d. Isaac Z. and Esther, Jan. 24, 1846.
George S., —— —, 1826. G.S.1.
Hannah E., d. David S. and Fidelia, June 12, 1845.
Henry Davis, s. David S. and Elizabeth B., Nov. 18, 1842.
Isaac Z., —— —, 1814. G.S.6.
Leonard H., s. Isaac Z., April 9, 1838.
Mary E., d. David S. and Elizabeth B., Feb. 12, 1837.
Mary L., May 24, 1814. G.S.6.

BRONSDON, Ellen, d. William and Phebe, Sept. 7, 1835.
Sumner, s. William and Phebe, Oct. 3, 1831.
Susan Rebeccah, d. William and Martha, Feb. 21, 1840.
William Tingley, s. William and Martha, June 27, 1842.
———, s. William and Martha, Oct. 25, 1844.

BROOKHOUSE, Eliza H., —— —, 1848. G.S.2.

BROOKS, Hannah, d. Jonas and Joanna, June 25, 1786.
Phebe, d. Jonas and Joanna, Dec. 10, 1782.
Polly, d. Jonas and Joanna, Aug. 1, 1784.
Sally, d. Jonas and Joanna, Nov. 19, 1781.

BROWN, Abner G., s. Israel and Polly, Sept. 29, 1834.
Benjamin, s. Isreal and Polly, March 15, 1819. In Manchester, N. H.
Cyrus, s. James and Dulcenia, May 5, 1824.
Dolly R. G., d. Israel and Polly, Sept. 24, 1836.
Dulcenia, d. James and Dulcenia, Feb. 21, 1811.
Elizabeth, May 9, 1820. G.S.1.
Elizabeth, w. Oliver E., —— —, 1831. G.S.2.
Fanny M., w. Jesse, Oct. 11, 1825. G.S.2.
Harriot, d. James and Dulcenia, Jan. 17, 1813.
Henrietta Agnes, March 28, 1844. G.S.1.
Isaac, Dec. 13, 1785. G.S.1.
Israel, s. Isreal and Polly, Dec. 2, 1829.
James, s. James and Dulcenia, Nov. 14, 1814.
Jane Agnes, July 29, 1845. G.S.1.
Jane Agnes Elizabeth, d. Samuel S. and Elizabeth, Aug. 30, 1845.
Jesse, Dec. 30, 1815. G.S.2.
———, d. John G. and Lydia, June 30, 1846.

ATHOL BIRTHS. 17

BROWN, John Groves, s. Isreal and Polly, Jan. 10, 1817. In Manchester, N. H.
John Henry, s. John G. and Lydia S., Sept. 20, 1840.
K. Maria, Nov. 12, 1844. G.S.?.
Lois, d. James and Dulcenia, Aug. 14, 1821.
Lucy, d. Isreal and Polly, Oct. 14, 1823.
Lydia Mariah, d. John G. and Lydia S., June 25, 1839.
Oliver B., s. Isreal and Polly, Sept. 19, 1831.
Philander, s. Isreal and Polly, June 12, 1821.
Rebeccah, d. Isreal and Polly, Nov. 9, 1825.
Serenia, d. James and Dulcenia, Dec. 24, 1816.
Susan Elizabeth, d. [b. or d. ?] May 12, 1841. G.S.1.
Susan Hale, w. Isaac, Oct. 9, 1784. G.S.1.
Col. S. S., s. Isaac and Susan, June 26, 1810. G.S.1.
William, s. James and Dulcenia, April 19, 1819.
Williby C., s. Isreal and Polly, July 26, 1827.
———, d. Samuel Somes and Elisabeth, March 27, 1844.

BRUCE, Charles Eli, s. Charles and Cynthia, Aug. 11, 1832. At Wardsboro, Vt.
Charles R., s. Charles and Lucretia, Feb. 20, 1847.
Cynthia Sophia, d. Charles and Cynthia, Dec. 27, 1833. At Brighton.
Elmira Lydia, d. Charles and Cynthia, July 31, 1836. At Phillipston.
Marcus Rich, s. Charles and Cynthia, June 22, 1842.
Martha Ann Gates, d. Charles and Cynthia, Sept. 24, 1830. At Phillipston.
———, d. Charles and Cynthia, May 1, 1844.

BRYANT, Calvin T., s. Clement and ———, June 11, 1830.
Eliza Ann, d. John W. and Ellen, May 15, 1845.
George Q. A., s. Clement and Rachel, Jan. 9, 1819.
Jonathan W., s. Clement and Rachel, Feb. 4, 1827.
Mary Ann, d. Clement and Rachel, March 26, 1817.
Rachel, d. Clement and Rachel, Oct. 26, 1832.
Richard S., s. Clement and Rachel, Feb. 9, 1822.
Silence L., d. Clement and Rachel, June 29, 1824.

BUCKLEY, Robert Broadbent, s. William and Abigail, June 28, 1808.
William Broadbent, s. William and ———, bap. July 3, 1808. C.R.

BUCKMON, Joel, s. Stephen and Sarah, March 11, 177[8].

BUCKNAM, Abner, s. Joseph and Hannah, bap. Sept. 7, 1766. C.R.
Amzy, s. Josiah and Hannah, bap. Oct. 23, 1768. C.R.

BUCKNAM, Asa, s. Joseph and Hannah, Junior, bap. Feb. 7, 1762.
C.R.
Elisabeth, d. Amos and Mercy, Aug. 2, 1771.
Hannah, d. Joseph and Hannah, bap. May 29, 1774. C.R.
Jacob, s. Joseph and Hannah, bap. Oct. 7, 1764. C.R.
Mary, d. Amos and Marcy, bap. Oct. 22, 1769. C.R.
Reuben, s. Joseph Junier and Hannah, bap. July 20, 1760. C.R.
Rhoda, d. Joseph and Hannah, bap. Oct. 30, 1776. C.R.
Robert, s. Joseph and Hannah, bap. Feb. 24, 1771. C.R.

BULLARD, Amos, s. Amos and Polly, July 19, 1809.
Daniel, s. Ebenezer and Elisabeth, May 9, 1766.
Daniel, s. Amos and Polly, April 15, 1807.
Daniel Franklin, s. Daniel and Polly, Feb. 8, 1839.
Daniel Franklin, s. Daniel and Polly, April 30, 1843.
Ebenezer, s. Ebenezer and Elisabeth, Oct. 31, 1768.
Elisabeth, d. Ebenezer and Elisabeth, April 9, 1759.
Elizabeth, d. Dea. ——— and ———, bap. June 16, 1822. C.R.
Lydia, d. Ebenezer and Elisabeth, April 8, 1761.
Mary, d. Amos and Martha, Nov. 15, 1816.
Mary Ann, d. Daniel and Polly, April 14, 1837.
Molle, d. Ebenezer and Elisabeth, May 27, 1771.
Sarah, d. Ebenezer and Elisabeth, Dec. 11, 1763.
Seth, s. Ebenezer and Elisabeth, Aug. 18, 1773.

BULLOCK, Hiram, s. Welcome and Grace, Nov. 16, 1801.

BURBANK, Betsy, d. Thomas and Abigail, Nov. 25, 1784.
Daniel, s. Thomas and Abigail, Dec. 13, 1781.
Eliza, w. Stephen A., June 15, 1806. G.S.1.
Luke, s. Thomas and Abigail, Jan. 30, 1792.
Nabby, d. Thomas and Abigail, Jan. 4, 1790.
Polly, d. Thomas and Abigail, Jan. 30, 1787.
Stephen A., March 13, 1804. G.S.1.

BUTLER, Cornelia, w. Henry S., ——— —, 1839. G.S.2.
Henry S., ——— —, 1835. G.S.2.

CADA, Daniel [Daniel Cadey in C.R.], s. Ephraim and Mercy, April 18, 1771.
Luse [Lucy in C.R.], d. Ephraim and Mercy, Dec. 4, 1772.

CADEY, Aaron, s. Ephraim and Sarah, bap. Jan. 6, 1779. C.R.
Salle, d. Ephraim and Salle, bap. March 6, 1781. C.R.

CAPRON, Abijah, s. Ephraim and Sally, Feb. 8, 1785.
Ephraim, s. Ephraim and Sally, Dec. 19, 1786.

ATHOL BIRTHS. 19

CAPRON, John, s. Ephraim and Lucy, April 30, 1797.
Lucy, d. Ephraim and Lucy, May 9, 1799.
Sally, d. Ephraim and Sally, March 6, 1789.
Sally, d. Ephraim and Lucy, July 5, 1793.
William, s. Ephraim and Lucy, June 2, 1795.

CARTER, Edwin Y., s. Jacob and Arathusa, May 19, 1817.

CARUTH, Amos Ludlow, s. Amos and Anna, Aug. 28, 1815.
Anna Nurse, d. Amos and Anna, Dec. 31, 1813.
Jane Kendall, d. Amos and Anna, July 31, 1811.
Lucy Garry, d. Amos and Anna, Dec. 25, 1808.

CASAVANT, Adaline F., w. Joseph, Dec. 3, 1824. G.S.2.
Joseph, Sept. 24, 1821. G.S.2.

CATLIN, Catharine, March 8, 1783. G.S.2.

CHAPMAN, Charles W., s. Earl W. and Phebe, Oct. 18, 1849.

CHASE, Ambrose Peck, s. Ebenezer and Barsilva, March 5, 1815.
Barsilva, d. Ebenezer and Barsilva, Oct. 7, 1810.
Benjamin, s. Freeman and Adaline, ———, ——— [1845 ?].
Caroline Amelia, d. Freeman and Adaline, July 21, 1843.
Clarisa, d. Ebenezer and Barsilva, April 22, 1801.
Clarissa, d. Ebenezer and Barsilva, Nov. 28, 1806.
Clark, s. Moses and Meriam, Sept. 25, 1802.
Dulcenia, d. Moses and Meriam, May 7, 1811.
Elijah, s. Ebenezer and Barsilva, Dec. 17, 1804.
Elizabeth Ann, d. Freeman and Adaline, Oct. 17, 1835.
Ellen M., d. Freeman and Adaline, Nov. 10, 1846.
Ephraim Fairbank, s. Moses and Meriam, Jan. 9, 1814.
Ephraim Fairbank, s. Freeman and Adaline, May 8, 1840.
Francis Freeman, s. Freeman and Adaline, Dec. 29, 1838.
Freeman, s. Moses and Meriam, Jan. 9, 1805.
Freeman, s. Moses and Miriam, April 18, 1809.
Hannah, d. Moses and Meriam, Feb. 8, 1807.
Mary Jane, d. Freeman and Adaline, Dec. 8, 1833.
Meriam, d. Moses and Meriam, Sept. 1, 1820.
Parney, d. Ebenezer and Barsilva, Feb. 9, 1803.
Royal, s. Moses and Meriam, May 20, 1800.
Sarah, d. Ebenezer and Barsilva, Nov. 13, 1808.
Stilman, s. Moses and Meriam, July 17, 1798.

CHENEY, Amos, s. Amos and Elvira, April 22, 1830.
Charlotte A., d. Dexter and Laura B., Aug. 6, 1847.

ATHOL BIRTHS.

CHENEY, Ellen Holbrook, d. Nathan and Rhoda, Dec. 20, 1829.
Francelia Perkins, w. George S., —— —, 1842. G.S.I.
Frederic Eugene, s. Leander and Lucy, Dec. 10, 1844.
George S., —— —, 1834. G.S.I.
Matthew, —— —, 1821. G.S.2.
Patty, d. James and ——, bap. Sept. 10, 1780. C.R.
Royal Whelock, s. Amos and Elvira, May 16, 1827.
Sarah E., d. James M. and Mary E., Aug. 3, 1847.
Susan G., w. Matthew, —— —, 1825. G.S.2.

CHUBB, Andrew S., —— —, 1820. G.S.2.
Harriet Hoar, w. Andrew S., —— —, 1814. G.S.2.

CHURCH, Esther, d. Paul and Esther, March 26, 1777.
James, s. Mahetabel, the wife of Deacon Paul, bap. Sept. 23, 1798. C.R.
Marcy, d. Paul and Esther, Sept. 25, 1785.
Mehetabel, d. Mahetabel, the wife of Deacon Paul, bap. Sept. 23, 1798. C.R.
Paul, s. Paul and ——, bap. Oct. 11, 1789. C.R.
Phebe, d. Paul and Esther, April 7, 1779.
Sarah, d. Paul and Esther, June 30, 1775.
Thadeus, s. Mahetabel, the wife of Deacon Paul, bap. Sept. 23, 1798. C.R.

CLAPP, Edward Pason, s. Samuel and Nancy B., Sept. 16, 1840.
Harriot Shipley, d. Samuel and Nancy B., March 27, 1831.
Nancy Angelia, d. Samuel and Nancy B., Feb. 5, 1826.
Priscilla Elvira, d. Samuel and Nancy B., Feb. 13, 1820.
Samuel Austin, s. Samuel and Nancy B., Oct. 30, 1821.

CLARK (see Clarke), Alice, w. James, —— —, 1797. G.S.2.
Benjamin, s. Benjamin and Mehitable, March 12, 1780.
Clarence F., s. James E. and Sylvia C., —— —, 1847. G.S.2.
David, s. Benjamin and Mehitable, May 1, 1778.
Eber, s. Benjamin and Mehitable, June 14, 1791.
Edson, s. Benjamin and Mehitable, May 14, 1785.
George W., s. Joseph W., Sept. 5, 1845.
James, —— —, 1789. G.S.2.
James E., —— —, 1822. G.S.2.
James W., s. James E., July 17, 1845.
Jonathan, s. Benjamin and Mehitable, June 3, 1783.
Josiah, s. Benjamin and Mehitable, March 28, 1787.
Lucian E. [twin ?], s. James E. and Sylvia C., —— —, 1846.
Lucius E. [twin ?], s. James E. and Sylvia C., —— —, 1846. G.S.2.

ATHOL BIRTHS. 21

CLARK, Margella, d. James E. and Sylvia C., Oct. 6, 1849.
Mary E., d. James E. and Sylvia C., —— —, 1849. G.S.2.
Polley, d. Benjamin and Mehitable, Jan. 19, 1789.
Samuel, twin s. Benjamin and Mehitable, Sept. 18, 1793.
Servetus W., s. William S. and Pallas E., April 26, 1844.
Susanna, twin d. Benjamin and Mehitable, Sept. 18, 1793.
Sylvia C., w. James E., —— —, 1825. G.S.2.
———, ch. William and ———, April 26, 1845.
———, twin d. James E. and Salva, May 17, 1846.
———, twin d. James E. and Salva, May 17, 1846.
———, d. Samuel and Polly, April 29, 1847.

CLARKE (see above), Mary E. Morse, w. Rev. S. F., June 15, 1826. G.S.2.

CLEVELAND, George Henry, s. Jason and Lucy H., Oct. 29, 1847.

COLEMAN, Samuel, s. John and Martha, bap. March 5, 1771. C.R.

COLLAR (see below), Rev. Hezekiah B., —— —, 1794. G.S.5.
Rhoda, w. Rev. Hezekiah B., —— —, 1798. G.S.5.

COLLIER (see above), Sarah A. B., w. Leonard S. ?, —— —, 1832. G.S.2.
Leonard S., —— —, 1828. G.S.2.

COLMAN, Calvin, s. John and Martha, Sept. 13, 1772.
John, s. John and Martha, Sept. 9, 1762.
Otis, s. John and Martha, Feb. 11, 1765.
Phebe Sprague, d. John and Martha, Dec. 6, 1782.
Rowland, s. John and Martha, Jan. 25, 1769.
Royal, s. John and Martha, March 5, 1778.
Samuel, s. John and Martha, April 5, 1775.
Sarah, d. John and Martha, Sept. 24, 1767.

COMINGS (see below and Cummings), Daniel W., s. John and Sarah, Dec. 27, 1839.
Frederick, s. John and Sarah, Jan. 26, 1842.
Henry Williams, s. John and Sarah, June 18, 1829.
Isabella Relief, d. John and Sarah, Aug. 19, 1831.
John Albert, s. John and Sarah, June 12, 1825. At Keene, N. H.
Lewis Chandler, s. John and Sarah, July 30, 1833.
Samuel B., s. John and Sarah, June 6, 1835.
Sarah Elizabeth, d. John and Sarah, Dec. 14, 1823. At Keene, N. H.
Stillman, s. John and Sarah, Aug. 17, 1837.
Thomas Rhoads, s. John and Sarah, Aug. 8, 1827.

COMMING, Daniel, s. Joseph and Elisabeth, May 20, 1768. Dup.
Nathan, s. Joseph and Elisabeth, April 8, 1771.
COMMINGS (see above), Daniel, s. Joseph and Elisabeth, Jan. 27, 1781. Dup.
Samuel, s. Joseph and Elisabeth, Feb. 2, 1773. Dup.
Susanah, d. Joseph and Elisabeth, Jan. 7, 1778. Dup.
CONANT, A. W., —— ——, 1839. G.S.2.
H. W., —— ——, 1845. G.S.2.
Laura A., d. George W. and Laura, Sept. 20, 1849.
Zerviah, d. Silas and ——————, bap. April 1, 1781. C.R.
COOK, Benjamin Jr., —— ——, 1802. G.S.6.
Betsy, w. Benjamin Jr., —— ——, 1800. G.S.6.
Charity, w. Benjamin, —— ——, 1773. G.S.6.
Charles Elliot, s. Benjamin and Betsey, Sept. 6, 1836.
Eliza Jane, d. Ira and Lucy, Sept. 13, 1838.
George Otis, s. Benjamin and Betsey, Oct. 14, 1834.
Harriet Stratton, d. Benjamin and Betsey, April 23, 1830.
Lorenzo, —— ——, 1819. G.S.6.
Lucy Ellen, d. Ira and Lucy, Dec. 30, 1845.
Mary Elizabeth, d. Benjamin and Betsey, April 30, 1839.
Oscar M., s. Jacob S., May 4, 1845.
Varnam Stiles, s. Ira and Lucy, April 8, 1841.
——————, inf. d. Benjamin and Betsey, March 4, 1829.
CRAWFORD, Albert Barnes, s. Chester and Hannah, March 8, 1838.
Laura Ellen, d. Daniel and Laura, Sept. 8, 1843.
CROSBY, Albert Galliten, s. Jonathan and Anna, Sept. 27, 1801.
Catharght, d. Joseph and Hannah, Sept. 13, 1775.
Catharine, d. Joseph and Hannah, June 23, 1776.
Cynthia, d. Joseph and Rhoda, Jan. 13, 1792.
Dolly, d. Joseph and Rhoda, Dec. 13, 1790.
Emory, s. John and Cendea, Jan. 25, 1805.
Franklin, s. Joseph and Rhoda, Sept. 3, 1803.
Freeman Higgins, s. William and Mercy, Oct. 16, 1791.
John Morse, s. John and Betsy, Aug. 30, 1809.
Joseph, s. Joseph and Rhoda, Aug. 4, 1798.
Joseph Young, s. Charles and Hannah, Jan. 16, 1827.
Lucinda Kendall, d. John and Betsy, Oct. 4, 1812.
Lucy, d. John and Cendea, Dec. 2, 1800.
Lucy Ann, d. Charles and Hannah, Sept. 26, 1825.
Lydia, d. William and Mercy, July 6, 1786.

ATHOL BIRTHS. 23

CROSBY, Maria, d. Jonathan and ———, bap. March 27, 1808. C.R.
Maria Frances, d. Jonathan and Anna, Feb. 15, 1811.
Mary, d. Joseph and Hannah, May 7, 1770.
Nancy, d. John and Cendea, July 12, 1798.
Phebe Stevens, d. Jonathan and Anna, Oct. 17, 1803.
Polly, d. Joseph and Rhoda, March 27, 1794.
Releef, d. Joseph and Rhoda, Jan. 12, 1789.
Reliance Crocker, d. William and Mercy, Jan. 26, 1785. At Orang.
Salvo, s. Jonathan and Anna, Aug. 11, 1791. In Marlborough.
William Morse, s. Charles and Hannah, Dec. 16, 1820.

CROSSMAN, Amy Ann, d. Maltiah and Lucinda, March 13, 1843.
Charles, s. Maltiah and Lucinda, Dec. 31, 1839.
Daniel, s. Maltiah and Lucinda, Nov. 26, 1849.
Fervilla [Ferrilla ?] Josephine, d. Malatiah and Lucinda, April 10, 1847.

CUMMINGS (see Comings, Commings, etc.), Almena J., d. Samuel Jr. and Maria, Dec. 1, 1829.
Charles H., ——— ——, 1828. G.S.2.
Dulcinia Lestima, twin d. John and Sarah, Aug. 29, 1844.
Eliza J., d. Stephen L. and Mary A., Oct. 28, 1846.
Jonathan B., s. Samuel Jr. and Maria, July 22, 1827.
Louisa, d. Samuel and Maria, June 18, 1846.
Lucy A., d. Samuel Jr. and Maria, Dec. 29, 1825.
Mary A., w. Charles H., ——— ———, 1831. G.S.2.
Nancy M., d. Samuel Jr. and Maria, May 7, 1841.
Phylinda, twin d. John and Sarah, Aug. 29, 1844.

CURTIS, Nathaniel, s. Ebenezer and Martha, bap. May 15, 1763. C.R

CUTTING, Dolle, d. George and Lois, bap. Feb. 11, 1778. C.R.
Earl, s. George and Judith, Aug. 21, 1757.
George, s. George and Judith, June 4, 1751.
George, Junior, s. George and Lois, bap. Feb. 11, 1778. C.R.
George, s. George and Lois, Sept. 22, 1794.
Hannah, d. George and Judith, July 29, 1755.
John, s. George and Judith, Jan. 1, 1750.
Judith, d. George and Judith, June 26, 1753.
Mary, d. George and Judith, April 11, 1758.
Oliver, s. George and Judith, Oct. 23, 1763.
Oliver, s. George and Lois, bap. Feb. 11, 1778. C.R.
Polle, d. George and Lois, bap. Feb. 11, 1778. C.R.

ATHOL BIRTHS.

CUTTING, Samuel, twin s. George and Judith, Oct. 21, 1761.
William, twin s. George and Judith, Oct. 21, 1761.

DANFORTH, Augusta Mariam, d. Erastus and Hannah, bap. Sept. 24, 1816. C.R.
Erastes, s. John and Hannah, Dec. 10, 1791. At Clarendon, Vt.
Hara, s. John and Hannah, July 25, 1797.
John, s. John and Hannah, April 11, 1799.
Royal, s. John and Hannah, Dec. 1, 1802.
Salla, d. John and Hannah, July 15, 1795. At Whitehall, N.Y.
Silvester, s. John and Hannah, April 6, 1801.
Sophrona, d. John and Hannah, June 17, 1793. At Clarendon, Vt.

DARLING, Louisa Richardson, d. Wheeler and Sybil, July 13, 1828.

DAVENPORT, Abner B., —— ——, 1827. G.S.4.
Maria N., w. Otis P., —— ——, 1824. G.S.2.
Otis P., —— ——, 1820. G.S.2.
Sereno R., s. David B. and Martha R., June 1, 1845.

DAVIS, Ann Susanna, d. Ezekiel G. and Lydia, Aug. 15, 1828.
Azor Sadock, s. Ezekiel G. and Lydia, Sept. 26, 1830.
Cynthia Ann, d. Norris and Lucy Ann, July 4, 1837.
Eliza Rogers, d. Ezekiel G. and Lydia, Dec. 31, 1832.
Ellen Maria, d. Ezekiel Jr. and Lydia, March 18, 1835.
Erastus Andrew, s. Norris and Lucy Ann, Nov. 25, 1832.
Ezekiel Gardner, s. Ezekiel G. and Lydia L., Jan. 16, 1844.
Fanny Zebiah, d. Ezekiel G. and Lydia, March 7, 1837.
Jenett Josephine, d. Ezekiel G. and Lydia, Jan. 29, 1841.
Lydia E., d. Ezekiel G. and Lydia S., Aug. 29, 1849.
Philetus Ansbury, s. Norris and Lucy Ann, May 25, 1835.
Sally, d. Roswell and Marcy, Feb. 5, 1813.
Thenais Bertha, d. Daniel and Lura W., Feb. 12, 1843.
——, inf. Ezekiel G. and Lydia, Jan. 10, 1842.

DEAN, Rachel, d. Jeremiah and Abagail, bap. Sept. 19, 1779. C.R.

DEATH, Aaron Mors, s. Jotham and Mercy, Feb. 28, 1765.
Ann, d. Jotham and Mercy, Oct. 26, 1757.
Benjamin, s. Jotham and Mercy, Dec. 23, 1751.
Hannah, d. Jotham and Mercy, March 10, 1754.
Jotham, s. Jotham and Mercy, April 7, 1760.
Lusinda, d. Jotham and Mercy, March 17, 1762.
Martha, d. Jotham and Mercy, Feb. 5, 1756.

DENNIS, Cynthia, d. George and Louisa, March 25, 1842.
George, —— ——, 1816. G.S.6.

DENNIS, Louisa, w. George, —— —, 1816. G.S.6.
Mary, d. George and Louisa, Aug. 1, 1846.

DERBY, Harriot, d. Abraham and Demarious, Nov. 3, 1807.
Loisa, d. Abraham and Demarious, Aug. 28, 1805.

DEXTER, Abigail, d. Ichabod and Abigail, bap. March 10, 1765. C.R.
Benjamin Wilkes, s Ichabod and Abigail, bap. April 16, 1775. C.R.
Caleb, s. Joseph and Martha, bap. Oct. 4, 1761. C.R.
Clark, s. Ichabod and Abagail, bap. May 10, 1772. C.R.
Ephraim, s. Joseph and Martha, bap. May 21, 1769. C.R.
Hannah, d. Benjamin and Hannah, bap. June 28, 1772. C.R.
Lemuel, s. Joseph and Martha, bap. May 2, 1763. C.R.
Lucy, d. Ichabod and Abigail, bap. Aug. 1, 1762. C.R.
Lydia, d. Joseph and Martha, bap. April 21, 1765. C.R.
Mariam, d. Jehabod and Abigail, bap. Sept. 28, 1760. C.R.
Rhoda, d. Ichabod and Abagail, bap. May 14, 1769. C.R.
Samuel, s. Ichabod and Abigail, bap. March 1, 1767. C.R.
Simeon, s. Benjamin and Hannah, bap. Dec. 13, 1772. C.R.
Zenas, s. Joseph and Martha, bap. Aug. 14, 1768. C.R.

DIKE, Aurilla Susannah, d. John and Aurilla, Nov. 3, 1830.
Cosive? d. Saml. and Hannah, bap. Nov. 17, 1805. C.R.
Edward, s. John and ——, bap. Dec. 6, 1795. C.R.
George L., s. David and Patty, March 12, 1808.
John, s. David and Patty, bap. Sept. 20, 1801. C.R.
John, s. David and Susanna, Sept. 26, 1799.
John Loren, s. John and Aurilla, Aug. 4, 1829. At Wendell.
John Wood, s. Edward and Susanna, Nov. 15, 1803.
Lucetta, d. Saml. and Hannah, bap. Nov. 17, 1805. C.R.
Lucind R., d. David and Patty, Feb. 2, 1804.
Mary, d. David and Patty, Sept. 29, 1810.
Nancy, d. David and Susanna, May 23, 1796.
Nancy, d. David and Patty, bap. Sept. 20, 1801. C.R.
Patty H., d. David and Patty, March 13, 1806.
Rachel, d. David and Patty, March 4, 1802.
Sally, d. David and Patty, bap. Sept. 20, 1801. C.R.
Sarah, d. David and Susanna, Sept. 15, 1797.

DOANE, Benjamin C., s. Austin and Hannah V., Sept. 20, 1848.
Hannah, d. Harden and Aurelia, Dec. 27, 1820.

DOW, Augusta, w. Moses, —— —, 1831. G.S.2.
Moses, —— —, 1826. G.S.2.

DRAKE, George A., s. Bradley B. and Harriet, Dec. 15

ATHOL BIRTHS.

DREWRY (see Drury), Jonathan, s. Edward and Experience, July 8, 1780.
Olive, d. Edward and Experience, June 2, 1778.
Susanna, d. Edward and Experience, June 26, 1783.

DRURY (see Drewry), Amasa, s. David and Lois, Nov. 13, 1808.
Amos, s. Samuel and Polly, Jan. 19, 1808.
Angelina M., July 19, 1836. G.S.2.
Asa, s. John and Lydia, Dec. 7, 1765.
Asa, s. Joel and Ruth, July 26, 1801.
Asenath, d. Joel and Ruth, Aug. 29, 1797.
Damaris, d. Edward and Experience, March 7, 1774.
David, s. John and Lydia, Jan. 6, 1778.
David, s. David and Lois, Jan. 30, 1821.
Dolly, d. Joel and Ruth, Dec. 8, 1793.
Edward, —— —, 1806. G.S.5.
Elbridge A., July 3, 1826. G.S.2.
Electa, d. John and Lydia, Nov. 21, 1770.
Electta, d. John and Lydia, May 25, 1784.
Elizabeth, w. Edward, —— —, 1807. G.S.5.
Eric, s. David and Lois, June 7, 1810.
Frances Mary Elizabeth, d. George Washington and Sally, March 12, 1829.
George W., s. George Washington, Sept. 7, 1832.
George Washington, s. Joel and Ruth, July 30, 1799.
George Winthrop, s. Edward and Elizabeth, Oct. 14, 1839.
Henrietta, d. David Jr. and Betsey, May 25, 1849.
Joel [Joel Scot in C.R.], s. John and Lydia, March 1, 1768.
Joel, s. Joel and Ruth, July 3, 1806.
Joel Reed, s. Errick and Judith, Aug. 17, 1840.
John, s. John and Lydia, bap. June 9, 1776. C.R.
John, s. John and Lydia, March 22, 1780.
John Sanderson, s. David and Lois, May 1, 1817.
John Smith, s. Joel and Ruth, Feb. 1, 1811.
Lois Young, d. David and Lois, July 22, 1824.
Lucy Emily Sherwin, d. George Washington and Sally, Jan. 25, 1835.
Lucy Luan, d. Joel and Ruth, Nov. 17, 1821.
Luse, d. John and Lydia, March 28, 1773.
   "The first child that was baptized in the New Meeting house by me—— James Humfrey." C.R.
Lydia, d. John and Lydia, Dec. 28, 1788.
Lydia, d. Joel and Ruth, Nov. 10, 1795.
Marietta, d. David Jr. and Betsy, May 19, 1847.

Drury, Olive, —— —, 1802. G.S.5.
Rhoda, d. John and Lydia, Nov. 26, 1790.
Rhoda, d. David and Lois, July 26, 1812.
Ruth, d. Joel and Ruth, June 9, 1808.
Ruth Dorathy, d. George Washington and Sally, Feb. 23, 1840.
Sally, d. Joel and Ruth, Nov. 8, 1803.
Samuel, s. Edward and Experience, April 2, 1776.
Samuel T., —— ——, 1828. G.S.2.
Samuel Young, s. David and Lois, May 10, 1815.
Sarah Amelia, d. George Washington and Sally, July 2, 1831.
Simeon Stockwell, s. George Washington and Sally, Jan. 18, 1837.
Willard Blucher, s. Joel and Ruth, Aug. 17, 1817.
——, s. David and ——, Aug. 31, 1844.

DUNMORE, Eliza, d. Silvenus and Jaine, Sept. 14, 1806.
Eliza, d. Silvenus and Jane, April 10, 1809.
Ezra, s. Silvenus and Jaine, April 26, 1804.
Lucy, d. Silvenus and Jane, April 19, 1811.

DUNTON, Hannah, w. Ebenezer, bap. Nov. 1, 1778. C.R.
Hannah, d. Ebenezer and Hannah, bap. July 2, 1781. C.R.
John Cummings, s. Ebenezer and Hannah, bap. Oct. 5, 1783. C.R.
Naba [Naby, in C.R.], d. Ebenezer and Abbigail, Aug. 18, 1771.
Nehemiah, s. Joseph and Abigail, bap. June 9, 1771. C.R.
Nehemiah, s. Ebenezer and Hannah, March 28, 1779.
Rebekah, d. Ebenezer and Abbigail, March —, 1773.

DYER, Abigail, d. Shebna and Mary, Dec. 3, 1783.
Ambrose, s. Shebna and Mary, Dec. 1, 1782.
Eames Humphreys, s. James and Polly, May 28, 1819.
Emeline, d. James and Polly, Sept. 30, 1825.
Hannah, d. James and Polly, July 31, 1820.
Horatio Nelson, s. James and Polly, April 13, 1817.
James Franklin, s. James and Polly, Feb. 21, 1815.
Loisa, d. James and Polly, Aug. 16, 1808.
Marcy, d. James and Polly, Nov. 15, 1830.
Mariam Blanchard, d. Molly, Jan. 20, 1802.
Olly, d. Shebna and Mary, June 23, 1787.
Sarah, d. Shebna and Mary, April 25, 1786.
Theodore Jones, s. James and Polly, July 3, 1822.
Thomas, s. Shebna and Mary, April 6, 1791.
William Holt, s. James and Polly, Feb. 25, 1811.

EARLS [Earle ? in C.R.], Hezakiah, s. Stephen and Mary, Feb. 15, 1784.
Lydia, d. Stephen and Mary, June 2, 1786.

EATEN, Ann, d. Maltiah and ———, bap. Sept. 17, 1780. c.r.

EATON, Huldah, d. Maltiah and ———, bap. July 11, 1784. c.r.
Sophia, w. Otis, April 14, 1837. g.s.2.

EDDY, George P., Dec. —, 1839. g.s.2.

ELLENWOOD (see Ellinwood), Cynthia, d. James and Rebecca, March —, 1809. At Eden, Me.
Daniel, s. James and Rebecca, Sept. 13, 1814.
Daniel W., s. Daniel and Dulcina, Feb. 21, 1847.
Edwin, s. Daniel and Dulcinea, March 30, 1845.
Edwin Otis, s. James and Rebecca, Feb. 28, 1817.
Eliza Crombie, d. James and Rebecca, Nov. 21, 1812. At Boston.
Elvira, d. James and Rebecca, Sept. 3, 1807. At Eden, Me.
Frederick T., s. Thomas and Persis S., May 31, 1827.
Lucy Ann, d. James and Rebecca, Oct. 16, 1838.
Lusaby, d, James and Rebecca, June 17, 1819.
Nelson, s. James and Rebecca, Aug. 27, 1810.
Rebecca, ———, 1785. g.s.2.
Tilden Bradley, s. James and Rebecca, Oct. 31, 1821.

ELLINWOOD (see Ellenwood), Abigail, d. Daniel and Lucy, June 11, 1789.
Abigail Fay, d. Daniel and Dorothy, April 13, 1812.
Alfred Clarence, s. Benjamin and Almena, Aug. 14, 1842.
Alphonso, s. Benjamin and Almena, Nov. 14, 1843. Dup.
Austin, s. Daniel and Dorothy, Nov. 10, 1814.
Austin, ———, 1817. g.s.5.
Austin F., ———, 1848. g.s.5.
Austin Farnsworth, s. Austin and Eliza Farnsworth, May 5, 1842.
Belinda, d. Daniel and Dorothy, Nov. 9, 1804.
Benjamin, s. Daniel and Dorothy, May 2, 1819.
Daniel, s. Daniel and Lucy, May 11, 1776.
Daniel Austin, s. Daniel and Dorothy, Dec. 6, 1816.
Eliza Maria, d. Daniel Austin and Priscilla, June 16, 1849.
Emily A. Homer, w. Laroy, March 24, 1843. g.s.2.
Harriet [Hannah in dup.] Maria, d. Daniel and Dulcena, July 31, 1843. At Springfield.
James, s. Daniel and Lucy, Oct. 23, 1781.
Justus [Justin in c.r.], s. Daniel, and Lucy, Feb. 25, 1784.
Laroy, Dec. 4, 1840. g.s.2.
Lucy, d. Daniel and Lucy, April 12, 1786.
Maria, d. Daniel and Dorothy, July 2, 1802.
Priscilla A. [Mann ?], ———, 1826. g.s.5.

ATHOL BIRTHS. 29

ELLINWOOD, Rhoena, d. Daniel and Dorothy, April 13, 1807.
S. Maria, w. Daniel, June 8, 1823. G.S.2.
Senaca, s. Daniel and Lucy, Jan. 18, 1779.
Thomas, s. Daniel and Dorothy, Sept. 13, 1800.

ELLIS, Chester, s. Clark and Mary Ann, Aug. 29, 1842.
F. Maria, w. Seth C., —— —, 1819. G.S.2.
George G., ——·—, 1844. G.S.2. [Probably s. Clark and Mary Ann.]
Louisa F., w. Seth C., —— —, 1829. G.S.2.
Maria L., d. Seth C. and Louisa F., —— —, 1848. G.S.2.
Seth C., —— —, 1814. G.S.2.
——, s. Clark and Mary Ann, June 8, 1844.
——, d. Seth C. and Louisa, Nov. 24, 1849.

ESTABROOK (see Esterbrook), Rev. Joseph, March 4, 1759. G.S.2.
[Estabrook ?], Lucia, a child under the care of Joseph and Lucy Estabrook, bap. July 2, 1815. C.R.
Lucy Cushing, w. Rev. Joseph, June 23, 1764. G.S.2.
Nathaniel C., s. Nathaniel C. and Mehitable, Nov. 28, 1824.

ESTERBROOK (see Estabrook), Benjamin, s. Rev. Joseph and Lucy, Nov. 23, 1803.
Fidelia, d. Rev. Joseph and Lucy, May 8, 1801.
Joseph Hubbard, s, Rev. Joseph and Lucy, Oct. 15, 1797.
Lucy, d. Rev. Joseph and Lucy, Jan. 19, 1793.
Marcia, d. Rev. Joseph and Lucy, May 8, 1799.
Nathaniel Cushing, s. Rev. Joseph and Lucy, April 9, 1795.
Turner, s. Rev. Joseph and Lucy, April 18, 1790.

FAIRBANK (see Fairbanks), Asa, s. John Jr. and Fanne, Sept. 9, 1784.
Assenath, d. Jonathan and Arsenath, March 30, 1820.
Benjamin, s. John and Releef, Aug. 1, 1759. Dup.
Benjamin Franklin, s. Reuben and Lucinda, July 11, 1807. At Champlain, N.Y.
Calvin Warren, s. John Jr. and Fanne, Sept. 15, 1801.
Dolly, d. John and Releef, May 14, 1761.
Doritha, d. John and Releef, May 14, 1761.
Ephraim, s. John and Releef, Nov. 2, 1765. Dup.
Fanne, d. John Jr. and Fanne, Oct. 27, 1796.
Hannah, d. Benjamin and Hannah, Aug. 25, 1798.
Harriot, d. Reuben and Lucinda, April 23, 1809.
Harriot, d. Jonathan and Arsenath, June 11, 1816.
[Farbank in dup.], John, s. John and Releef, May 6, 1755.

ATHOL BIRTHS.

FAIRBANK, John 3d, s. John Jr. and Fanne, July 27, 1798.
Lecte, d. Thomas and Hannah, July 16, 1767.
Levi, s. Benjamin and Hannah, Oct. 13, 1793.
Loisa, d. Jonathan and Arsenath, March 28, 1809. In New Salem.
Loranzo, s. John Jr. and Fanne, Jan. 4, 1804.
Lydia, d. John Jr. and Fanne, April 25, 1787.
Lyman, s. Benjamin and Hannah, May 13, 1796.
Mahitable, d. Thomas and Hannah, June 11, 1774.
Meriam, d. Jonathan and Arsenath, July 12, 1812. In New Salem.
[Farbank in dup.], Nahum, s. John and Releef, Aug. 24, 1753. In Sterling.
Olive, d. Thomas and Hannah, Sept. 14, 1769.
Orator, s. Jonathan and Arsenath, April 25, 1806. In West Boylston.
Parnee, d. John and Releef, July 10, 1771. Dup.
Patty, d. Benjamin and Hannah, April 21, 1807.
Philemon, s. Jonathan and Ruth, bap. June 10, 1759. C.R.
Phillimon, s. Phillimon and Sally, March 16, 1782.
Polly, d. Phillimon and Sally, May 21, 1780.
[Farbank in dup.], Releif, d. John and Releef, Nov. 24, 1751.
Reubin, s. John Jr. and Fanne, Sept. 20, 1780.
Rhoda, d. John and Releef, May 11, 1768. Dup.
Ruth, d. Jonathan and Ruth, bap. March 17, 1765. C.R.
Samuel, s. John and Releefe, Feb. 21, 1757. Dup.
Silas, s. Benjamin and Hannah, Feb. 25, 1790.
Stephen, s. Benjamin and Hannah, June 21, 1788.
Wilder, s. Jonathan and Arsenath, Jan. 12, 1814.
Zelinda, d. John Jr. and Fanne, Aug. 21, 1791.

FAIRBANKS (see Fairbank), Asel, s. Jonathan and Ruth, bap. March 12, 1775. C.R.
Jonathan, s. Jonathan and Ruth, bap. Oct. 12, 1766. C.R.
Pamelia, d. Jonathan and Ruth, bap. April 6, 1760.
Zuba, d. Jonathan and Ruth, bap. Aug. 16, 1772. C.R.

FARNSWORTH, John B., s. Asa and Surphila, Aug. 6, 1833. At Ware.
Phebe O., d. Asa and Surphila, Jan. 4, 1825. At Enfield.

FARR, Albert, s. Amariah and Clarissa, April 8, 1824.
Amariah, June 1, 1791. G.S.I.
Andrew E., s. George and Emily M., April 29, 1849. Dup.
Charles, s. Amariah and Clarissa, April 15, 1817.
Clarissa Farnsworth, w. Amariah, Nov. 15, 1794. G.S.I.
Clarissa, d. Amariah and Clarissa, Sept. 1, 1841. At Westmoreland, N. H.

ATHOL BIRTHS. 31

FARR, George, s. Amariah and Clarissa, March 6, 1821.
Hollon ?, s. Amariah and Clarissa, Feb. 13, 1819.
Jane Annette, d. Charles and Cynthia, June 16, 1841.
FAY, Abby Ann, d. Jonathan Ward and Mary L., Jan. 31, 1837.
Abigail, d. Joseph and Abigail, Oct. 20, 1785.
Adaline, d. Josiah and Molly, April 7, 1811.
Adoniram Judson, s. Lysander and Priscilla E., June 24, 1831.
Anna, d. Solomon and Mary, March 17, 1771.
Artemas, s. Solomon and Mary, May 5, 1767.
Benjamin, s. Joseph and Abigail, Sept. 14, 1783.
Beriah Ward, s. Jonas and Anna, Dec. 2, 1820.
Betsy, d. Josiah and Molly, Jan. 27, 1814.
Celestina Miransa, d. Emerson and Nancy A., May 2, 1831.
Charles Pratt, s. Jonas and Anna, Oct. 24, 1817.
Cinda, d. Joseph and Abigail, Sept. 28, 1797.
Deborah Maria, d. Lysander and Priscilla E., July 22, 1841.
Dorothy, d. to Joseph and Abigail, Dec. 14, 1778.
Elizabeth, d. Solomon and Mary, April 16, 1780.
Emerson, s. Artemas and Delight, July 11, 1801.
Emona Jane, d. William G. and Sarah E., Dec. 28, 1848.
Esther Ward, d. Josiah and Molly, May 28, 1799.
Capt. F. F., Feb. 19, 1833. G.S.2.
Freeborn Raymond, s. Jonas and Anna, Jan. 16, 1827.
Grace, d. Solomon and Mary, Aug. 25, 1774.
Hannah, d. Joseph and Abigail, Feb. 12, 1794.
Hattie A., w. Capt. F. F. ?, Jan. 14, 1837. G.S.2.
James Humphreys, s. James S. and Mary B., Feb. 1, 1839.
James Sullivan, s. Josiah and Molly, May 18, 1808.
Jasper White, s. Nahum and Sarah, Dec. 20, 1804.
Jonas, s. Solomon and Mary, March 25, 1788
Joseph Frederick, s. Jonathan Ward and Mary L., Oct. 3, 1830.
Josephine Aravilla, d. Lysander and Priscilla E., Aug. 13, 1838.
Josiah, s. Joseph and Abigail, March 16, 1774.
Josiah, s. Jonathan Ward and Mary L., July 22, 1834.
Levi Benjamin, s. Jonathan Ward and Mary L., April 14, 1843.
Lovinia Elsimena, d. Lysander and Priscilla E., Aug. 14, 1836.
Lucy Raymond, d. Jonas and Anna, Oct. 11, 1815.
Lysander, s. Artimas and Delight, May 3, 1805.
Martha Clement, d. Jonathan Ward and Mary L., Jan. 12, 1839.
Metilda, d. Joseph and Abigail, July 7, 1781.
Minerva, d. Josiah and Molly, Dec. 11, 1803.
Molly, w. Josiah, March —, 1773. G.S.4.
Nabbee [Nabby in C.R.], d. Solomon and Mary, April 16, 1762.

ATHOL BIRTHS.

FAY, Nahum, s. Solomon and Mary, Nov. 12, 1777.
Nancy Maria, d. Jonas and Anna, March 18, 1831.
Nehemiah, s. Joseph and Abigail, Dec. 1, 1776.
Othello A., s. Lysander and Priscilla E., Oct. 14, 1844.
Polly, d. Solomon and Mary, Aug. 25, 1785.
Polly, d. Josiah and Molly, March 16, 1806.
Priscilla Elvira, d. Lysander and Priscilla E., Sept. 19, 1847.
Rebeccah Leonard, d. Jonathan Ward and Mary L., June 22, 1832.
Sabra, d. Solomon and Mary, July 2, 1783.
Sabra, d. Artemas and Delight, Oct. 27, 1797.
Sarah, d. Joseph and Abigail, July 17, 1788.
Sereno Edwards, s. Lysander and Priscilla E., Sept. 12, 1833.
Seth, s. Joseph and Abigail, July 1, 1791.
Suse [Susa in c.r.], d. Solomon and Mary, April 20, 1765.
Vieney [Viena in c.r.], d. Solomon and Mary, March 13, 1769.
Ward, s. Josiah and Molly, April 25, 1801.
William Jenerson, s. Jonas and Anna, May 10, 1822.

FELTON, Daniel, s. Daniel and ———, bap. Oct. 3, 1791. c.r.
David, s. Daniel and Lois, Sept. 5, 1777.
Lloyd, s. Daniel and Lois, May 5, 1779.
Lois, d. Daniel and Lois, Aug. 15, 1781.
Lucy, d. Daniel and Lois, June 22, 1776.
Lydia, d. Daniel and Lois, July 5, 1783.
Lyman, s. Daniel and ———, bap. May 8, 1791. c.r.
Polley, d. Daniel and Lois, March 9, 1785.
William Webber, s. Daniel and Lois, July 4, 1775.
Zeruiah, d. Daniel and Lois, April 19, 1780.

FIELD, Charles, s. Zachariah and Abigail, June 9, 1815.
Frederic, s. Spencer and Carissa, Feb. 23, 1830.
Lucius Hubbard, s. Lucius and Lucia, bap. April 18, 1815. c.r.

FINLEY, Mary Ann, adopted d. and grandchild of Mr. Kedges, bap. April 2, 1843, (a. 1 y.). c.r.

FISH, Betsy, d. Samuel and Betsy, May 25, 1805.
Esther, d. Samuel and Betcy, Jan. 21, 1812.
Ezra W., s. Henry and Sally, Sept. 20, 1836.
Francis, s. Samuel and Betcy, Nov. 16, 1800.
Frederick Appleton, s. Jason and Sophia, Oct. 11, 1819.
Harriot Young, d. Moses and Ann, March 28, 1827.
Henry K., s. Ezra and Chloa, May 15, 1805.
Horatio Kingsbury, s. Samuel and Betcy, Oct. 22, 1818.
Jason, s. Samuel and Betcy, Feb. 14, 1796.
Joseph, s. Samuel and Betcy, Dec. 21, 1793.

ATHOL BIRTHS.

FISH, Lucia, d. Samuel and Betcy, July 20, 1814.
Lucinda, d. Samuel and Betcy, March 26, 1803.
Lucy, d. Ezra and Chloa, Nov. 12, 1802.
Maria Ann, d. Moses and Ann, Oct. 3, 1828.
Moses, s. Ezra and Chloa, Aug. 18, 1799.
Nancy, d. Samuel and Betcy, April 28, 1798.
Sally, d. Samuel and Betcy, June 9, 1807.
Samuel, s. Samuel and Betcy, Oct. 25, 1809.
Samuel 2d, s. Henry and Sally, Nov. 27, 1840.

FISK, Braddyll, s. Jonathan and Mary, Jan. 18, 1777.
David, s. Jonathan and Mary, Oct. 18, 1792.
Lusenda, d. Jonathan and Mary, Oct. 18, 1786.
Mary Ann, d. Benjamin and ———, bap. June 18, 1816. c.r.
Polly, d. Jonathan and Mary, Dec. 31, 1775.
Sarah, d. David and Sarah, Oct. 23, 1770.
Sarah, d. Jonathan and Mary, Feb. 27, 1785.
Simeon, s. Jonathan and Mary, Oct. 2, 1780.
Sucah, d. Jonathan and Mary, Jan. 21, 1782.

FITTS, Caroline, d. George and Sally, June 23, 1810.
Mariette, d. George and Sally [Nancy, c.r.], May 3, 1821.
Sally Luann, d. George and Sally, July 21, 1812.
Sally, Lu Ann, d. George and Sally, Nov. 24, 1815.

FLETCHER, A. Florentine, s. William and Betsey, March 28, 1839.
Amaracus V., s. William and Betsey, Oct. 24, 1835.
James Sullivan, s. William and Betsey, Feb. 25, 1843.

FLINT, Abigail Hill, d. Josiah and Elizabeth, Feb. 13, 1833.
Cyrus Frank, Sept. 25, 1843. g.s.2.
Eliza Ann, d. Josiah and Elizabeth, April 27, 1831.
Elizabeth, w. Josiah, Jan. 1, 1803. g.s.2.
Elizabeth Ann, d. Josiah and Elizabeth, April 16, 1829.
George Isham, s. Josiah and Eliza, Nov. 20, 1845.
Hannah Elizabeth, twin d. Josiah and Elizabeth, Jan. 15, 1828.
Jane Augusta, d. Josiah and Elizabeth, Dec. 1, 1836.
Josiah, March 10, 1802. g.s.2.
Josiah Willard, s. Josiah and Elizabeth, Nov. 4, 1839.
Mary [Polly, c.r.] Goddard, twin d. Josiah and Elizabeth, Jan. 5, 1828.
Rebekah Sibly, d. Josiah and Elizabeth, Sept. 26, 1834.
———, s. Josiah and Elizabeth, Sept. 25, 1843.

FORD, Benjamin Beaman, s. Joseph and Jemima, bap. May 29, 1774. c.r.

ATHOL BIRTHS.

FORD, Fuller, s. Josiah and Jemima, bap. Aug. 2, 1775. C.R.
Hannah, d. Josiah and Jemima, bap. Nov. 17, 1782. C.R.
Mercy, d. Josiah and Jemima, bap. Nov. 14, 1779. C.R.
Thomas K., —— —, 1834. G.S.2.
Zerviah, d. Josiah and Jemima, bap. Nov. 2, 1777. C.R.

FOSGET, Esther, d. Ebenezer and Abigail, bap. April 7, 1779. C.R.

FOSTER, Abby Elmira, d. Asa W. and Elmira, Feb. 13, 1839.
Akins, s. John and Rebakah, Feb. 7, 1788.
Ebenezer, s. John and Rebekah, Oct. 19, 1780.
Hiram S., July 12, 1821. G.S.1.
Hopstill, s. Edward and Deborah, bap. May 2, 1773. C.R.
James, s. Edward and Deborah, bap. Oct. 12, 1777. C.R.
James, s. John and Rebkah, Sept. 22, 1778.
John, s. John and Rebeckah, Sept. 3, 1776.
Leroy, s. John W. and Dorinda, July 17, 1846.
Lucy S., —— —, 1821. G.S.2.
Lydia, d. John and Rebeckah, Feb. 10, 1772. At Rochester.
Lydia, d. Edward and Deborah, bap. June 11, 1775. C.R.
Madison H., s. Samuel W. and Parna S., Sept. 6, 1846.
Martha How, d. Asa W. and Elmira, June 26, 1827.
Martha Jane, s. Asa W. and Almira, July 24, 1843.
Nathaniel, Jan. 26, 1795. G.S.1.
Rebekah, d. John and ——, bap. March 13, 1791. C.R.
Shadrack, s. John and Rebeckah, March 20, 1783.
Simeon James, s. Asa W. and Elmira, March 8, 1832.
William, s. John and Rebkah, Oct. 17, 1769. At Rochester.
William Henry, s. Asa W. and Elmira, Sept. 15, 1828.

FRENCH, Mary, —— —, 1799. G.S.2.

FRY (see Frye), Elizabeth Ann, d. Job and ——, Feb. 28, 1835.
George Dexter, s. Job and ——, Nov. 14, 1842.
George M., s. Silas and Susanna R., Oct. 13, 1848.
Job Warren, s. Job and ——, Aug. 30, 1837.
Joseph H., s. Silas and Susanna K., July 20, 1843.
Martha Jane, d. Job and ——, Aug. 14, 1840.
Susannah Ellen, [d. Job and Florella ?], July 29, 1833.

FRYE (see above), Clara B., —— —, 1848. G.S.2.
Florella Arvilla, d. Job and Florella, April 25, 1831.

FULLER, Fanny Bigelow, w. Leonard C., Jan. 4, 1819. G.S.2.
Leonard C., March 13, 1814. G.S.2.
William, s. Leonard C. and Fanny Bigelow, Feb. 23, 1847. G.S.2.

GAGE, Amanda A., —— —, 1829. G.S.2.
Charles Henry, s. Dennis and Ellen E., May 24, 1849.
Dennis, —— —, 1825. G.S.2.
Ellen E., w. Dennis, —— —, 1828. G.S.2.
Màuro Fernando, s. Edmund J. and Mary, Jan. 22, 1849.

GAIL, Judith, d. Jemima Kimpland, bap. July 25, 1761. C.R.

GARFIELD, Sarah M., d. George R. and Eunice, Nov. 1, 1847.

GATES, John Fay, s. John and Betsey, Sept. 25, 1841.

GAY, David Daupheus, s. Alanson and Mary S., April 13, 1838.
Lucy Amelia, d. Alanson and Mary S., May 7, 1843.
Mariah Emerancy, d. Alanson and Mary S., Aug. 20, 1840.
Nancy Lodema, d. Alanson and Mary S., Feb. 6, 1836.

GIBBS, Warren P., —— —, 1832. G.S.2.

GILES, Elmira Stratton, w. Prescott, —— —, 1807. G.S.1.
Marcia, d. Hiram B. and Charlotte, July 17, 1848.

GILLET, Gertrude, d. Daniel W. and N. M., May 13, 1846.

GILMORE, Seneca Allen, s. William and Sarah, April 19, 1845.
Zenas Allen, s. William and Sarah A., April 19, 1844.
——, d. Phelps P. and A. A., Oct. 8, 1848.

GODARD (see Goddard), Alfred, s. David and Sally, Oct. 19, 1840.
Cynthia, d. Ephraim and Huldah, Nov. 11, 1798.
David, s. Ephraim and Huldah, Jan. 16, 1801.
Dorinda, d. Joseph and Lucy, 2d wife, July 27, 1805.
Edward, s. Ephraim and Huldah, Nov. 19, 1812.
Elijah, s. Elijah and Mahitable, April 16, 1804.
Elmira, d. Luther and Polly, Feb. 14, 1817.
Ephraim, s. Ephraim and Huldah, Jan. 2, 1817.
Franklin, s. Walter and Hannah, Jan. 14, 1809.
Hannah, d. Elijah and Mahitable, Oct. 23, 1805.
Hannah, d. Elijah and Mehitable, June 20, 1812.
Harriot, d. Luther and Polly, Jan. 30, 1820.
Harvey, s. Ephraim and Huldah, Aug. 10, 1810.
Hiram, s. David and Sally, March 8, 1836.
Hollis, s. Elijah and Mehitable, June 8, 1814.
Jane, d. David and Sally, Oct. 18, 1830.
Joseph Wilson, s. Joseph and Lucy, 2d wife, March 13, 1807.
Julia, d. Ephraim and Huldah, April 6, 1808.

ATHOL BIRTHS.

GODARD, Lucinda, d. Luther and Polly, May 5, 1815.
Lysander, s. Luther and Polly, Oct. 8, 1818.
Mary Ann, d. Luther and Polly, May 26, 1813.
Mason, s. David and Sally, Dec. 7, 1833.
Polly, d. Walter and Hannah, Aug. 19, 1810.
Ruth, d. Ephraim and Huldah, Jan. 22, 1803.
Susan, d. Ephraim and Huldah, Sept. 2, 1805.

GODDARD (see Godard), Abby Ann, d. Joseph W. and Abigail D., May 3, 1837.
Abigail, d. Ebenezer and Sibbil, bap. June 12, 1761. c.r.
Abigail D., w. Joseph W., —— —, 1806. g.s.2.
Anna, d. Nathaniel and Mary, bap. Feb. 4, 1767. c.r.
Anne, d. Nathaniel and Mary, Jan. 24, 1767.
Ashbel, s. Josiah and Ruth, Dec. 13, 1788.
Bailey, s. Elijah and Mahitable, Oct. 13, 1798.
Benjamen, s. Ebenezer and Hannah, July 7, 1779.
Betsy, d. James and Betta, July 4, 1780.
Bette, d. Moses and Unice, bap. June 6, 1779. c.r.
Catey, d. David and Margit, Nov. 31, 1762.
Charles Loring, s. Ephraim Jr., Aug. 6, 1845.
Clara, d. Edward and Ruth, Sept. 14, 1773.
Daniel, s. Josiah and Ruth, May 14, 1793.
David, s. Edward and Ruth, June 27, 1777.
David Goodell, s. Harvey, Sept. 29, 1845.
Dennis, —— ——, 1832. g.s.2.
Dorothy, d. Edward and Ruth, May 12, 1779.
Ebenezer Jr., s. Ebenezer and Anna, bap. April 7, 1779. c.r.
Eber, s. Josiah and Ruth, April 27, 1791.
Edward, s. Edward and Ruth, Feb. 8, 1791.
Electa, d. Joseph and Lucy, Aug. 20, 1798.
Electa, d. Luther and ——, bap. Oct. —, 1821. c.r.
Elijah, s. James and Betta, Oct. 9, 1771.
Elijah Dexter, s. Eber and Melinda, Jan. 5, 1843.
Elisha, s. Nathaniel and Mary, April 4, 1764.
Ella, d. Ephraim and Laura, —— ——, 1848. g.s.2.
Elmer, s. Joseph and Lucy, 2d wife, Oct. 22, 1822.
Ephraim, s. Edward and Ruth, Nov. 22, 1771.
Francis, s. Eber and Lucinda, March 31, 1824.
Goodale, s. Elijah and Mahitable, May 1, 1797.
Hannah, d. Simon and Mary, March 12, 1775.
Hannah, d. James and Betta, April 26, 1778.
Henry, s. Josiah and Ruth, March 5, 1778.
Hezekiah, s. David and Margit, Nov. 10, 1757.

ATHOL BIRTHS. 37

GODDARD, Hollis, s. Elijah and Mahitable, Jan. 12, 1795.
Jacob Williams, s. Joseph and Lucy, 2d wife, Feb. 14, 1820.
James, s. Elijah and Mahitable, Jan. 22, 1800.
John, s. David and Margit, April 20, 1768.
Jonathan, s. David and Margit, Dec. 23, 1755.
Joseph, s. Edward and Ruth, June 24, 1775.
Joseph M., s. Joseph W. and Abigail, Nov. 8, 1835.
Jotham, s. Ebenezer and Hannah, March 15, 1781.
Laura, w. Ephraim, ———, 1825. G.S.2.
Lois, d. Nathan and Dorithy, Dec. 31, 1762.
Lucy, d. David and Margit, June 19, 1760.
Lucy, d. Joseph and Lucy, July 6, 1800.
Lydia, d. David and Margit, Dec. 2, 1764.
Luther, s. Edward and Ruth, Oct. 24, 1783.
Mahitable Burnett, May 21, 1802.
Manassa, s. David Jr. and Sarah, Sept. 25, 1772.
Marcy, d. David Jr. and Sarah, July 27, 1774.
Marcy, d. Ebenezer and Hannah, Nov. 8, 1777.
Marcy, d. Edward and Ruth, Oct. 23, 1785.
Martin Luther, s. Luther and ———, bap. Oct. 5, 1823. C.R.
Mary, d. Eber and Lucinda, Oct. 24, 1828.
Mary Jane, d. Joseph W. and Abigail D., Jan. 6, 1841.
Mercy, d. Edward and ———, bap. Dec. 1, 1816. C.R.
Miranda, d. Joseph and Lucy, 2d wife, Dec. 11, 1814.
Molly, d. James and Betta, Dec. 1, 1774.
Moses, s. David and Margit, July 25, 1754.
Nabby, d. Josiah and Ruth, Nov. 30, 1797.
Nathan, s. Josiah and Ruth, June 22, 1780.
Persis, d. Joseph and Lucy, March 21, 1802.
Phebe, d. David Jr. and Sarah, Nov. 23, 1770.
Polley, d. Simon and Mary, July 21, 1783.
Rebekah, d. Simon and Mary, April 15, 1773.
Rhoda, d. Josiah and Ruth, June 17, 1795.
Royal, s. Moses and Unice, bap. March 7, 1780. C.R.
Royal M., s. Joseph W. and Abigail D., Feb. 22, 1834.
Ruth, d. Edward and Ruth, June 14, 1781.
Sally, d. Josiah and Ruth, March 4, 1784.
Sally, d. Edward and ———, bap. Dec. 1, 1816. C.R.
Sarah, d. David Jr. and Sarah, Nov. 12, 1776.
Sarah, d. Edward and Ruth, Nov. 14, 1787.
Silas, s. Simon and Mary, May 21, 1780.
Simon, s. Simon and Mary, July 19, 1777.
Sophia W. w. Dennis, ———, 1840. G.S.2.
Susanna, d. Josiah and Ruth, Dec. 1, 1781.

ATHOL BIRTHS.

GODDARD, Walter, s. James and Betta, Sept. 15, 1769.
——, s. Ephraim Jr. and Laura, April 22, 1848.
GOODELL, Timothy Justis, s. Timothy and Sarah, Dec. 29, 1788.
Wyman, s. Jonathan and Almira, March 23, 1848.
GOODNOUGH, Henry Williams, s. Samuel and ——, bap. April 18, 1822. C.R.
Laura Emily, d. Samuel and ——, bap. April 18, 1822. C.R.
Lucy L., d. Samuel and ——, bap. April 18, 1842. C.R.
GOULD, Hiram S., —— ——, 1830. G.S.6.
Jacob Orlando, s. Curtis and Sally, Nov. 22, 1828.
Jacob Orlando, s. Curtis and Sally, June 20, 1834.
John Curtis, s. Curtis and Sally, May 1, 1827.
Lewis Milton, s. Curtis and Sally, March 26, 1830.
Sarah Ellen, d. Curtis and Sally, April 4, 1842.
GOULDING, Harriet Elvira, d. James G. and Elvira P., Dec. 2, 1843.

GRAVES, Abner, s. Abner and Alice, July 8, 1780.
Alice, d. Abner and Alice, Sept. 18, 1772.
Azubah, d. Nathaniel and Hannah, bap. Nov. 4, 1750.
Azubah, d. Abner and Alice, Sept. 2, 1784.
Eleazer, s. Eleazer and Sarah, bap. Sept. 13, 1752. C.R.
Eleazer, s. Eleazer and Sarah, Jan. 10, 1759.
Elijah, s. Eleazer Jr. and Olive, Oct. 17, 1789.
Fanny, d. Nathaniel Jr. and Marcy, Sept. 17, 1790.
Hannah, d. Abner and Alice, May 21, 1770.
Hannah, d. Nathaniel Jr. and Marcy, March 23, 1778.
Ichabod Portor, s. Nathaniel Jr. and Marcy, March 11, 1780.
Jessa, s. Eleazer Jr. and Olive, April 12, 1798.
Laura, d. Eleazer Jr. and Olive, March 19, 1796.
Lois, dau. Eleazer and Sarah, bap. Feb. 2, 1755. C.R.
Lois, d. Eleazer Jr. and Olive, July 20, 1800.
Lucinda, d. Abner and Alice, Sept. 19, 1768.
Lucinda, d. Nathaniel Jr. and Marcy, July 4, 1792.
Marcy, d. Nathaniel Jr. and Marcy, Dec. 21, 1782.
Melinda, d. Nathaniel Jr. and Marcy, Aug. 21, 1794.
Mercy, d. Nathaniel and Mercy, bap. Feb. 11, 1782. C.R.
Nancy, d. Eleazer Jr. and Olive, Dec. 16, 1793.
Nathaniel 3d, s. Nathaniel Jr. and Marcy, May 6, 1783? [1784?].
Richardson, s. Nathaniel Jr. and Hannah, March 16, 1775.
Ruben, s. Nathaniel and Hannah, bap. Sept. 23, 1753. C.R.
Ruben, s. Nathaniel Jr. and Marcy, March 16, 1786.

ATHOL BIRTHS. 39

GRAVES, Sally, d. Eleazer Jr. and Olive, Aug. 6, 1787.
Susa, d. Abner and Alice, Sept. 10, 1775.
William, s. Nathaniel Jr. and Marcy, April 16, 1789.

GRAY, Adaline, d. Thomas and Milley, Sept. 13, 1806.
Adaline, d. Alexander and Elvira, Oct. 18, 1839.
Charles, s. Alexander and Elvira, Nov. 25, 1833.
Charles, s. Alexander and Elvira, Aug. 19, 1841.
Henry, s. Alexander and Elvira, Jan. 16, 1830.
Jane, d. Alexander and Elvira, Nov. 21, 1835.
Lucinda M., w. Henry, —— ——, 1834. G.S.2.
Mary, d. Thomas and ——, bap. April 6, 1828. C.R.
Saphira Allen, d. Thomas and Milley, April 3, 1809.
Sophira, d. Alexander and Elvira, April 14, 1837.
Thomas, s. Alexander and Elvira, Aug. 20, 1827.

GRIFFITH, Emily Ann, d. Samuel and Betsey, Oct. 2, 1842.

HAGER, Cynthia L., d. Jesse S. and ——, Feb. 20, 1836.
Henry S., s. Jesse S. and ——, March 10, 1832.
George W., Aug. 15, 1809. G.S.5.
James L., s. Jesse S. and ——, Aug. 28, 1826.
——, s. Martin and ——, Sept. 2, 1844.

HALE, Amos, s. Samuel and Mary, April 22, 1791.
Edward Simonds, s. Edward and Sally, June 1, 1819.
Ephraim, s. Samuel and Mary, Oct. 14, 1795.
Isaac, twin s. Samuel and Mary, Oct. 29, 1786.
Joel, s. Samuel and Mary, Oct. 14, 1797.
Joel Stearns, s. Saml. Hale, deceased [and Lidea?], bap. April 17, 1810. C.R. [Possibly his name was changed to Stearns.]
John, s. Samuel and Mary, July 30, 1780.
John Rogers Goodnough, s. Edward and Sally, Sept. 25, 1821.
Jonas, twin s. Samuel and Mary, Oct. 29, 1786.
Polly, d. Samuel and Mary, Sept. 12, 1784.
Polly, d. Edward and Sally, Dec. 7, 1814.
Samuel, s. Samuel and Mary, March 13, 1789.
Samuel Drury, s. Edward and Sally, Dec. 7, 1814.
Stephen, s. Silus and ——, bap. Sept. 19, 1779. C.R.
——, s. Sumner P. and Joanna, April 24, 1849.

HAMMOND, George R. P., s. Joseph W. and Abby, Jan. 2, 1848.
Martha Ann, d. Joseph W. and Nabby, Feb. 16, 1846.

HANKS, Eliza A., w. William, —— ——, 1822. G.S.5.
William, —— ——, 1812. G.S.5.

HANSHAW, Albert Green, s. John and ———, bap. Aug. 19, 1284. c.r.

HAPGOOD, Josephine Eliza, d. Lyman W. and Eliza Jane, Oct. 17, 1841.
Sarah Louisa, d. Lyman W. and Elvira J., Oct. 23, 1845.

HARKNESS, Elisha, s. Asa and Esther, bap. Feb. 20, 1775. c.r.

HARRINGTON, Abagail, d. Jason and Abagail, bap. Dec. 1, 1779. c.r.
Allen, s. Joseph and Abigail, bap. June 6, 1781. c.r.
Millisant, s. (sic) Jason and Abagail, bap. Dec. 1, 1779. c.r.

HARRIS, Abel, s. Robert and Mehitable, bap. March 19, 1763. c.r.

HARTSHORN, ———, s. John and ———, Nov. 10, 1844.

HARTSON, John, ——— —, 1818. g.s.2.
Sophronia, w. John, ——— —, 1814. g.s.2.

HARWOOD, Adaline, d. Seth K. and Caroline, April 27, 1835.
Benjamin Bradley, s. Benjamin M. and Harriet, Sept. 1, 1843.
Benjamin M., s. Jonathan and Olive, July 26, 1812.
Caroline, d. Seth Kendall and Caroline, May 11, 1843.
Fanny, d. Jonathan and Olive, Nov. 22, 1809.
George Wilson, s. David and Lois, July 7, 1828.
Harriet, d. Seth K. and Caroline, April 24, 1839.
Harriet Adaline, d. Seth K. and Caroline, April 20, 1841.
Jonathan Williams, s. David and Lois, Dec. 31, 1823.
Lisander, s. Stephen and Elisabeth, April 11, 1815.
Lucinda, d. David and Rebeccah Ann, June 21, 1819.
Mary Jane, d. Jonathan and Olive, Feb. 6, 1834?.
Olive, d. Jonathan and Olive, Sept. 14, 1814.
Oliver Cutting, s. David and Lois, Dec. 17, 1832.
Ozro J., s. Benjamin M. and Harriet, Sept. 16, 1848.
Reuben, s. Stephen and Elisabeth, Dec. 24, 1808.
Ruben, s. Seth K. and Caroline, July 14, 1837.
Seth Kendall, s. Stephen and Elisabeth, Dec. 24, 1808.
Seth Kendall, s. Seth K. and Caroline, Feb. 16, 1846.
Stephen, s. Stephen and Elisabeth, April 6, 1813.
Stephen K., s. Seth K. and Caroline, May 21, 1833.

HASEY, Samuel, s. Samuel and Silence, Sept. 15, 1777.

HASTINGS, Wallie, s. E. C. and A. M., Jan. 5, 1820 ?. g.s.2.

ATHOL BIRTHS. 41

HAVEN, Artemas, s. Simon and Ruth, Oct. 22, 1778. Name changed to Daniel Haven, Feb. 10, 1784.
Asa, s. John Jr. and Martha, Dec. 6, 1792.
Asa Sumner, s. Asa and Lucy R., Dec. 29, 1825.
Bette, d. Simon and Ruth, March 19, 1766.
Chancey, s. John Jr. and Martha, Feb. 24, 1800.
Chloe, d. Simon and Ruth, Oct. 15, 1776.
Daniel, see Artemas above.
Daniel, s. Deacon John and Martha, bap. April 25, 1779. c.r.
Emily Sherman, d. Chauncey and Urania, March 2, 1826.
Eunice, d. John and Susanna, July 20, 1762.
Eunice, d. John Jr. and Martha, Aug. 4, 1795.
Eunice, d. Jotham and Hannah, March 30, 1820.
Ezra, s. John Jr. and Rachel, Dec. 22, 1832.
Grace, d. John and Susanna, Dec. 26, 1747.
Grace, d. John and Susanna, Oct. 20, 1766.
Hannah, d. Jonathan and Hannah, Aug. 19, 1762.
Hannah Maria, d. Jotham and Hannah, Feb. 12, 1829.
Harriot, d. John Jr. and Rachel, March 26, 1811.
John, s. John and Susanna, Oct. 24, 1756.
John, s. Simon and Ruth, June 7, 1762.
John 3d, s. John Jr. and Mather, June 16, 1784.
John Harrington, s. Jotham and Hannah, May 13, 1832.
Jonathan, s. Jonathan and Hannah, May 8, 1767.
Josiah, s. Jotham and Hannah, March 16, 1818.
Jotham, s. John Jr. and Mather, July 11, 1786.
Jotham Franklin, s. Jotham and Hannah, Sept. 13, 1825.
Keziah, d. John and Susanna, Nov. 17, 1759.
Levi, s. John Jr. and Mather, March 18, 1778.
Lidea, d. John Jr. and ——, bap. June 8, 1823. c.r.
Lois, d. Jonathan and Hannah, Jan. 22, 1764.
Luana C., w. Ezra ?, —— —, 1837. g.s.2.
Lucius Sprague, s. Asa and Lucy R., Jan. 17, 1821.
Lucy Smith, d. Asa and Lucy R., Sept. 4, 1823.
Lydia, d. John and Susanna, Nov. 17, 1751.
Lydia, d. Jonathan and Hannah, March 27, 1761.
Lydia, d. John and Susanna, Dec. 23, 1767.
Lydia, d. Simon and Ruth, June 24, 1774.
Lydia, d. John Jr. and Rachel, March 18, 1823.
Lydia, d. John Jr. and Rachel, June 18, 1825.
Martha, d. John Jr. and ——, bap. Aug. 6, 1820. c.r.
Mary, d. Jonathan and Hannah, July 1, 1769.
Mary, d. John Jr. and Rachel, June 18, 1825.
Mercy, d. John Jr. and Martha, June 26, 1797.

ATHOL BIRTHS.

HAVEN, Moses, s. Simon and Ruth, May 22, 1764.
Moses, s. Simon and Ruth, Jan. 5, 1781.
Oramel Taft, s. Jotham and Hannah, May 11, 1814.
Patty, d. John Jr. and Martha, Aug. 5, 1788.
Rhoda, d. John and Susanna, July 10, 1754.
Rhoda, d. John Jr. and Martha, Sept. 24, 1790.
Richard, s. Simon and Ruth, May 12, 1772.
Ruth, d. Simon and Ruth, March 5, 1768.
Sally, d. John Jr. and Rachel, Jan. 16, 1813.
Sally, d. John Jr. and Rachel, Nov. 16, 1827.
Samuel, s. John Jr. and Mather, Jan. 23, 1780.
Samuel Sargent, s. John Jr. and Rachel, June 12, 1816.
Simon, s. Simon and Ruth, April 10, 1770.
Susa, d. Simon and Ruth, Oct. 22, 1783.
Susanna, d. John and Susanna, Jan. 18, 1750.
Susannah, d. John Jr. and Mather, March 25, 1782.
Unice, d. John and Susannah, bap. Aug. 22, 1762. C.R.
Urania Aldrich, d. Chauncey and Urania, May 25, 1827.
William LaRoy, s. Jotham and Hannah, May 24, 1835.
―――― and ――――, twins of Asa and Lucy R., Jan. 17, 1828.

HAYWOOD (see Heywood), ――――, s. Alpheus and ――――, Jan. 30, 1845?.

HEMENWAY (see Hemmenway), Abigail White, d. Benoni and Martha, Jan. 7, 1761.
Anna, d. Benoni and Martha, bap. Sept. 27, 1767. C.R.
Asa, s. Benoni and Martha, March 5, 1763.
Bette, d. Benoni and Martha, bap. May 27, 1770. C.R.
Sophia, d. Benoni and Martha, Jan. 18, 1759.

HEMMENWAY (see above), Martha, d. Benoni and Martha, bap. June 9, 1765. C.R.

HEYWOOD (see Haywood), Betsey R., d. Alpheus and Lucretia, March 3, 1829.
Charles H., s. Alpheus and Lucretia, Dec. 5, 1839?.
George A., s. Alpheus and Lucretia, April 3, 1842.
Hannah F., d. Alpheus and Lucretia, July 12, 1824.
Harriet H., d. Alpheus and Lucretia, July 5, 1827.
Lysander N., s. Alpheus and Lucretia, Nov. 27, 1825.
Myra F., d. Alpheus and Lucretia, June 13, 1840?.
Myra Fairbanks, d. Alpheus and Lucretia, Jan. 30, 1844.
Rosilla B., d. Alpheus and Lucretia, March 1, 1834.

HIGGINS, Ebenezer, s. Zoheth and ――――, bap. Oct. 28, 1781, C.R.

ATHOL BIRTHS. 43

HILL, Aaron, s. Aaron and Hannah, June 25, 1815.
Abigail, d. Aaron and Hannah, Jan. 25, 1818.
Abijah, s. John C. and Dolly, May 7, 1840.
Abijah, s. John C. and Dolly S., Feb. 16, 1847.
Andrew Jackson, s. William and Eliza, Oct. 17, 1842.
Asa, s. Moses and Luce, Aug. 13, 1785.
Augustus Emory, s. Emory and Rhoda, Feb. 11, 1824.
Caleb, s. Moses and Luce, Aug. 28, 1780.
Caroline, d. Aaron and Hannah, April 14, 1821.
Catherine Exva, d. Emory and Rhoda, Jan. 19, 1832.
Charles, s. Emory and Rhoda, Oct. 14, 1830. At Barre.
Charles Harrison, s. William and Eliza, Sept. 26, 1840.
Chester, s. John and Susanna, Dec. 9, 1802.
Daniel, s. Isaac and Miliscent, Dec. 10, 1795.
Dolle, d. John and Dorithy, Oct. 23, 1768.
Elijah, s. Moses and Luce, Feb. 4, 1783.
Eliza Ann, d. William, July 14, 1845.
Elizebeth, d. Aaron and Hannah, bap. June 10, 1817. C.R.
Fidelia, d. Aaron and Hannah, bap. June 10, 1817. C.R.
Frances, d. William and Eliza, July 22, 1847.
Frances Janette, d. Jonathan and Hannah, April 27, 1846.
George W., s. James and Sophia, May 10, 1845.
Hannah, d. Aaron and Hannah, bap. June 10, 1817. C.R.
Hannah Crosby, d. Emory and Rhoda, Nov. 26, 1829. In Barre.
Huldah Maria, d. Danford and Charlotte, Jan. 16, 1828.
Isaac, s. Moses and Luce, Oct. 5, 1769.
Jacob Perminter, s. John and Susanna, Jan. 22, 1811.
James, s. Aaron and Hannah, bap. June 10, 1817. C.R.
James Dwight, s. James and Sophia, April 1, 1841.
John, s. Moses and Luce, May 5, 1774.
John, s. Moses and Luce, June 25, 1789.
John Fisk, s. John and Susanna, July 20, 1797.
John Fisk, s. James and Sophia, June 2, 1838.
Josiah, s. Emory and Rhoda, Oct. 21, 1834.
Lucy, d. Moses and Luce, June 20, 1778.
Lucy, d. Isaac and Miliscent, Aug. 18, 1799.
Lucy Barnard, d. Emory and Rhoda, May 3, 1822.
Mary, d. Moses and Luce, Oct. 4, 1767.
Mary Emerline, d. Jonathan and Hannah, Dec. 5, 1844.
Mary Josephine, d. William and Eliza, March 30, 1838.
Moses, s. Moses and Luce, Dec. 27, 1771.
Moses, s. Asa and Anna, Aug. 15, 1822.
Otis Willard, [s. Emory and Rhoda]. Dec. 23, 1835.
Polly, d. Aaron and Hannah, May 2, 1813.

ATHOL BIRTHS.

HILL, Rhoda Sophia, d. Emory and Rhoda, June 6, 1828.
Roxy, d. Isaac and Miliscent, Aug. 23, 1797.
Ruth, d. John and Dorithy, Jan. 10, 1770.
Ruth Janette, d. John C. and Dolly, Nov. 19, 1841.
Sabra, d. Emory and Rhoda, Dec. 19, 1825.
Samuel, s. Moses and Luce, June 23, 1776.
Sarah d. John and Dorithy, Sept. 26, 1771.
Sarah, d. Emory and Rhoda, June 15, 1833.
Sarah Claraette, d. John C. and Dolly, Jan. 23, 1844.
Sarah Luann, d. Danford and Charlotte, Nov. 5, 1829.
Sophia, d. John and Susanna, July 14, 1805.
Susanna, d. John and Susanna, June 13, 1800.

HINDS, Edwin W., s. Hiram D. and Ellemanda, Feb. 26, 1834. At Barre.
Eliza Ellemanda, d. Hiram D. and Ellemanda, April 26, 1830.
Elmanda, d. Hiram D. and Elmanda, Dec. 15, 1845.
Frederick B., s. Hiram D. and Ellemanda, May 11, 1835. At Orange.
Josephine Ella, d. William L. and Sarah P., Sept. 13, 1842.
Sabrina W., d. Hiram D. and Ellemanda, April 11, 1832. At Hubbardston.
Sarah Adalaid, d. William L. and Sarah P., May 7, 1841. At Winchester, N. H.
William Henry, s. Hiram D. and Ellemanda, Feb. 25, 1838.
William Lloyd Garrison, s. Hiram D. and Ellemanda, March 10, 1837.

HOAR, Addison Dwight, s. Timothy and Lydia, March 28, 1820.
Charles, s. Timothy and Lydia, Aug. 9, 1830.
Christopher Columbus, s. Timothy and Lydia, March 9, 1827.
Lucy Ann, d. Timothy and Lydia, Jan. 18, 1823.
Susannah Graves, d. Timothy and Lydia, Jan. 24, 1825.

HODSKIN, Albert, s. Marshall and Almira, Sept. 10, 1842.

HOLBROOK, Charles Warren, s. Adin and Polly, Feb. 9, 1814. At Keene, N. H.
Laurinda, d. Adin and Polly, Feb. 10, 1811. At Keene, N. H.
Mary Abbott, d. Adin and Polly, Feb. 10, 1819.

HOLDEN, Rozella, d. William ?, —— —, 1843. G.S.I.
William, —— —, 1809. G.S.I.

HOLLAND, Oliver, s. Hugh and Elizabeth, bap. May 17, 1752. C.R.

ATHOL BIRTHS. 45

HOLLAND, Ruben, s. Hugh and Elizabeth, bap. Nov. 10, 1754. C.R.
Sarah, d. Hugh and Elizabeth, bap. Feb. 20, 1756. C.R.

HOLMAN, David, s. Edward and Sally, Feb. 24, 1779.
Hannah, d. John and Sally, June 11, 1796.
John, s. John and Sally, Feb. 6, 1791.
Polly, d. John and Sally, March 28, 1789.
Seth, s. John and Sally, March 2, 1794.

HOLMES (see Holms), Catharine, d. Jacob and Thankful, July 10, 1810.
Elizabeth, d. Jacob and Thankful, July 10, 1813.
Horace, s. Luther and Mary, July 16, 1789. At Chesterfield.
John, s. Luther and Mary, Aug. 24, 1797.
Lucinda, d. Luther and Mary, Oct. 20, 1791.
Polly, d. Luther and Mary, Oct. 8, 1793.

HOLMS (see above), Catharine, d. Jacob and Thankful, Aug. 23, 1816.

HOLT, Aaron H., —— ——, 1825. G.S.2.
Abigail Walker, d. Ebenezer and Arethusa, May 13, 1835.
Sophia T., w. Aaron H., —— ——, 1829. G.S.2.

HORN, Addison D., s. Timothy and Lydia, —— ——, 1820. G.S.2.
Charles S., s. Timothy and Lydia, —— ——, 1830. G.S.2.
Eliza, d. Timothy and Lydia, —— ——, 1832. G.S.2.
Hannah H., w. Timothy, —— ——, 1814. G.S.2.
Lucy A., d. Timothy and Lydia, —— ——, 1823. G.S.2.
Lydia, w. Timothy, —— ——, 1794. G.S.2.
Timothy, —— ——, 1791. G.S.2.
——, s. John and Bridget, July 7, 1849.

HORR, Christopher C., March 9, 1827. G.S.2.
George W., s. Maj. Warren and Sarah P., —— ——, 1829. G.S.2.
Grace H., w. George W., —— ——, 1829. G.S.2.
Lucy F., w. Christopher C. ?, May 23, 1836. G.S.2.
Sarah P., w. Maj. Warren, —— ——, 1800. G.S.2.
Maj. Warren, —— ——, 1804. G.S.2.

HORTEN (see below), Edwin B., —— ——, 1838. G.S.2.
Martha M., w. Edwin B., —— ——, 1840. G.S.2.

HORTON (see above), Alfred M., —— ——, 1813. G.S.2.
Eunice E., w. Alfred M., —— ——, 1816. G.S.2.

HOUGHTON, Benjamin, s. Benjamin and Susanna, Dec. 31, 1817.
Francis T., s. Alvin and Louisa, July 30, 1847.

ATHOL BIRTHS.

HOUGHTON, John, s. Benjamin and Susanna, Jan. 1, 1813. In Fitchburg.
Levi B., s. Benjamin and Susanna, June 2, 1815.

HOW, Abel, s. Perkins and Nancy, May 12, 1808.
Nancy, d. Perkins and Nancy, Feb. 27, 1806.
John Perkins, s. Perkins and Nancy, May 12, 1802.
John Perkins, s. Perkins and Nancy, Nov. 29, 1803.
Susannah, d. Phineus and Susannah, bap. April 15, 1764. c.r.

HOWARD, Artemas, s. Simeon and Lucy, July 1, 1805.
Catharine Allen, d. Simeon Jr. and Mary, June 1, 1848.
Charles, s. Simeon Jr. and Mary, March 31, 1834.
Cynthia Putnam, d. Simeon and Lucy, Oct. 25, 1812.
Dolly Diana, d. Lemuel and Lydia, Aug. 9, 1820.
Emily, d. Simeon and Lucy, Feb. 26, 1820.
Fanny, d. Lemuel and Lydia, July 9, 1811.
Francis Simeon, s. Simeon Jr. and Mary, March 31, 1839.
Hannah Ward, d. Artemas and Susanna, May 3, 1829.
Julia Ann, d. Artemas and Susanna, Jan. 25, 1831.
Lemuel, s. Lemuel and Lydia, Sept. 23, 1807.
Lucy Ann, d. Simeon and Lucy, July 31, 1811.
Lurana, d. Lemuel and Lydia, Nov. 7, 1817.
Lydia, d. Lemuel and Lydia, Sept. 2, 1814.
Mary, d. Lemuel and Lydia, Sept. 6, 1802.
Minerva, d. Lemuel and Lydia, Feb. 8, 1805.
Miranda, d. Simeon and Lucy, Aug. 13, 1823.
Phebe Harriet, d. Simeon and Phebe, Jan. 7, 1831.
Polly, d. Simeon and Lucy, Aug. 12, 1801.
Prudence Putnam, d. Simeon and Lucy, May 7, 1809.
Ruth, d. Simeon and Lucy, June 11, 1803.
Seth, s. Simeon and Phebe, Aug. 10, 1829.
Simeon, s. Simeon and Lucy, Feb. 9, 1799.
Stillman, s. Simeon and Lucy, Nov. 2, 1816.
Sumner, s. Simeon and Lucy, March 11, 1807.

HUBBARD, Annetta M., w. Warren B., ———, 1846. g.s.2.
Warren B., ———, 1837. g.s.2.

HUDSON, Azubah, d. Ezra and Releaf, Sept. 4, 1778.
Ebenezer, s. Ezra and Relief, bap. June 8, 1774. c.r.
Ezra, s. Ezra and Releaf, March 10, 1769.
Liberty, s. Ezra and Releif, bap. Oct. 15, 1775. c.r.
Molly, d. Ezra and Releaf, Sept. 17, 1771.

HUMFREY (see forms below), Calvin, s. James and Esther, Dec. 29, 1763. c.r.

ATHOL BIRTHS. 47

HUMFREY, Lydia, d. Samuel and Lois, Feb. 28, 1766.
Sarah, d. James and Esther, Dec. 20, 1753. Thursday. C.R.
Sarah Evens, d. Samuel and Lois, Oct. 27, 1768.
Susanna Payson, d. Samuel and Lois, Sept. 10, 1764.
Zube [Zuba in C.R.], d. Samuel and Lois, Nov. 3, 1770.

HUMPHERY, Calvin, s. Jaems and Esther, Oct. 6, 1767.
James, s. James and Esther, Dec. 29, 1763.
John, s. James and Esther, Dec. 22, 1755. In Dorchester. [Monday, C.R.]
Lois Wiswell, d. James and Ester, Jan. 8, 1758. [Bap. on day of birth, C.R.]
Royal, s. James and Ester, Sept. 22, 1761. [Bap. on day of birth, C.R.].

HUMPHREY, Anna Richards, d. John and Hannah, June 24, 1799.
Anna Richards, d. John and Hannah, Sept. 19, 1801.
Arethusa, d. Royal and Euseba, Oct. 31, 1791.
Caroline, d. John F. and Betsey, June 28, 1821.
Charles, s. John and Hannah, Oct. 9, 1807.
Clarissa, d. John and Mary, Nov. 25, 1789.
Clarissa, d. John and Hannah, May 27, 1804.
Edwin, s. John F. and Betsey, July 15, 1814.
Esther, d. Samuel and Lois, May 5, 1774.
Esther, d. Royal and Euseba, May 4, 1805.
Eurania B., w. J. Harvey, Oct. 19, 1815. In Putney, Vt. G.S.2.
Frances Wiswill, d. John and Hannah, May 7, 1797.
George Flavel, s. John F. and Cordelia P., May 4, 1847.
Henry, s. Royal and Euseba, Nov. 7, 1795.
James Jr., s. James and Esther, bap. Dec. 29, 1763. C.R.
James, s. James Jr. and Lucy, Feb. 28, 1797.
John Flavel, s. John F. and Betsey, Jan. 29, 1819.
John Flavil, s. Royal and Euseba, Sept. 7, 1788.
John Harvey, s. John and Hannah, Jan. 26, 1813.
John Wiswell, s. James Jr. and Lucy, Aug. 9, 1801.
Jonas, s. Samuel and Lois, Sept. 15, 1772.
Lois, d. Samuel and Lois, Sept. 25, 1780.
Lucy Morse, d. James Jr. and Lucy, Oct. 14, 1794.
Martha, d. Samuel and Lois, Dec. 22, 1778.
Mary Tileston, d. John and Hannah, July 5, 1795.
Otis, s. Royal and Euseba, Oct. 8, 1797.
Otis, s. Royal and Euseba, Aug 10, 1802.
Rebeccah, d. John F. and Betsey, Sept. 15, 1823.
Samuel, s. Samuel and Lois, Dec. 6, 1776.

ATHOL BIRTHS.

HUMPHREYS (see forms above), Elizabeth Hannah, d. John H. and Urania B., Dec. 8, 1847.
Frederick Augustus, s. James Jr., and Sarah, March 8, 1834.
George E., s. John W. and Sophia, March 22, 1836. G.S.2.
George W., s. John W. and Sophia ?, May 4, 1833. G.S.2.
Helen A., d. Henry and Saphronia, Jan. 3, 1844.
Henry Martin, s. Henry and Sophronia, Aug. 10, 1840.
Horatio Willard, s. James Jr. and Sarah, May 8, 1832.
James 3d, s. James Jr. and Sarah, April 1, 1830.
John, s. John H. and Urania, Aug. 29, 1838. Dup.
Lucy Brigham, d. James and Lucy, June 3, 1814.
Maria Antoinettee, d. James Jr. and Sarah, April 15, 1824.
Sophia Smith, w. John W., March 20, 1810. G.S.2.

HUNT, Abigail Pratt, d. Luther and Deborah, Oct. 31, 1823. In Woodstock, Vt.
Andrew P., s. Luther Jr. and Roxy, June 25, 1846.
Ellen Louisa, d. Lewis and Joanna, April 24, 1848.
Gustavus Adolphus, s. Luther and Deborah, Dec. 11, 1820. In Shutesbury.
Hiram Wilson, s. Luther and Deborah, Sept. 27, 1830.
Lewis Brigham, s. Luther and Deborah, Nov. 23, 1826. In Templeton.
Luther, s. Luther and Deborah, Oct. 13, 1818. In Shutesbury.
Mary Roxy, d. Luther Jr. and Roxy, Dec. 5, 1843.
———, s. Luther Jr. and Roxa, June 25, 1846.

JACKSON, Julitta, d. Thomas and Mary, bap. April 19, 1772. C.R.
Nabe, d. Thomas and Mary, bap. June 19, 1774. C.R.
Nathan, s. Thomas and Mary, bap. July 7, 1776. C.R.
Nehemiah, s. Thomas and Mary, bap. March 21, 1779. C.R.

JACOBS, Abel, s. John and Bulah, March 23, 1784.
Asa, s. John and Bulah, Aug. 4, 1787.
Dana, s. John and Bulah, Aug. 26, 1795.
John, s. John and Bulah, March 28, 1782.
Lydia, d. John and Bulah, Dec. 28, 1778.
Mary, d. John and Bulah, Aug. 27, 1792.
Palletiah, s. John and Bulah, Sept. 11, 1785.
Royal, s. John and Bulah, Oct. 23, 1789.
Roxy, d. John and Bulah, Sept. 17, 1797.

JENNINGS, Nathan, s. Lyman and Hannah F., Aug. 31, 1846.

JENNISON, Austin, July 6, 1812. G.S.2.

ATHOL BIRTHS. 49

JOHNSON, Daniel, s. Henry and Lucy, Aug. 27, 1832.
Emily, d. Henry and Lucy, April 14, 1821.
Jonathan, s. Henry and Lucy, Oct. 1, 1825.
Lucy, d. Henry and Lucy, March 11, 1823.
Mary Eliza, d. Rufus and Eliza, Aug. 5, 1849.
Nancy, w. William, —— —, 1795. G.S.6.
Warner, s. Henry and Lucy, Sept. 13, 1830.
William, —— —, 1788. G.S.6.
William Henry, Aug. —, 1841. G.S.6.
———, d. George W. and Hannah F., April 29, 1848.

JOHNSTON, George, s. Jonathan and Rachel, bap. April 2, 1780. C.R.

JOHNSTONE, Aaron, s. Jonathan and Rachel, bap. Sept. 20, 1778. C.R.
Jonathan Jr., s. Jonathan and Rachel, bap. Sept. 20, 1778. C.R.

JONES, Benjamin Orville, s. Theodore and Marcia, May 5, 1835.
Charles Cushing, s. Theodore and Marcia, July 27, 1824.
Edwin, s. Prescott and Jane, July 15, 1811.
Ellen Adelia, d. Theodore and Marcia, Oct. 13, 1832.
Frederick, s. Prescott and Jane, Aug. 31, 1803.
Frederick Eugene, s. Theodore and Marcia, Feb. 17 [15, G.S.], 1828.
Frederick Eugene, s. Theodore F. and Selina, May [June, G.S.2.] 4, 1849.
Isadore, Jan. 2, 1847. G.S.2.
Jane, s. Prescott and Jane, June 16, 1809.
Jerome, s. Theodore and Marcia, Oct. 13, 1837.
Joseph Estabrook, s. Theodore and Marcia, Nov. 11, 1820.
Josiah [Josiah Moar in C.R.], s. Prescott and Jane, Jan. 13, 1800.
Macia Estabrook, w. Theodore, May 8, 1799. G.S.2.
Marcia, d. Theodore and Marcia, March 22, 1843.
Nathaniel Hubbard, s. Theodore and Marcia, March 15, 1830.
Otis, s. Prescott and Jane, June 26, 1807.
Prescott, s. Prescott and Jane, Jan. 27, 1802.
Sarah, d. Amos and Lydia, Feb. 8, 1785.
Theodore, Aug. 24, 1780. G.S.2.
Theodore [Theodore Turner, G.S.2.], s. Theodore and Marcia, Sept. 30, 1822.
William Augustus, s. Prescott and Jane, Oct. 21, 1805.

KELLOG, Chester, s. Dwight H., bap. June 15, 1845. C.R.

KELTON (see Kilton), Almeda Wait, d. John W. and Electa, Sept. 21, 1816.

KELTON, Calvin, s. Calvin and Hepzibah, Sept. 22, 1806.
Calvin Dwight, s. Calvin Jr. and Belinda, May 16, 1843. Dup.
Charles Henry, s. Calvin Jr. and Belinda, Oct. 7, 1830.
Cornelius Washington, s. John W. and Electa, April 12, 1821.
Edward Ellinwood, s. Calvin and Belinda, July 22, 1845.
Ellen Maria, d. Calvin Jr. and Belinda, May 25, 1835.
Frances Ann, d. Calvin and Hepzibah, Aug. 14, 1819.
Hannah Fairbank, d. John W. and Electa, May 22, 1819.
Hannah Lucas, d. Calvin and Hepzibah, Dec. 19, 1800.
John Morton, s. John W. and Electa, Aug. 30, 1826.
Lutheria Diana, d. John W. and Electa, Nov. 22, 1822.
Margaret, d. Calvin and Hepzibah, March 19, 1803.
Margaret Lucenia, d. Calvin and Hepzibah, May 24, 1816.
Salley White, d. James 2d and Polley, Feb. 11, 1798.
Sucar, d. Calvin and Hepzibah, bap. Aug. 7, 1803. c.r.

KENDAL (see Kindall), Rebeca, d. Timothy and Rebeca, May 17, 1776.

KENDALL, Abigail, d. Calvin and Abigail, Aug. 29, 1810.
Abigail B., d. Calvin Jr. and Lydia, July 5, 1833.
Abigail Balch, d. Joel and Sall, Aug. 23, 1799.
Abigail Balch, d. Lyman and Hannah, Jan. 17, 1829.
Andrew, s. Jesse and Elisabeth, April 17, 1766.
Angeline, d. Calvin Jr. and Lydia, Jan. 12, 1844.
Ann H., w. John L., —— ——, 1819. G.S.2.
Anna, d. Jesse and Elisabeth, May 4, 1775.
Anna, d. Joel and Sall, Aug. 16, 1794.
Anna, d. John and Susanna, Oct. 17, 1803.
Anne [Anna, in c.r.], d. Jonathan and Anna, March 16, 1774.
Anstis, d. Calvin and Abigail, Dec. 25, 1798.
Calvin, s. Jesse and Elisabeth, July 15, 1770.
Calvin, s. Calvin and Abigail, Feb. 19, 1803.
Charles Lyman, s. Lyman and Hannah, Jan. 16, 1840.
Cinda, d. Jonathan and Anna, Dec. 25, 1769.
Deborah, d. Seth and Deborah, bap. Feb. 27, 1763. c.r.
Elisabeth, d. Jesse and Elisabeth, Aug. 17, 1751. In Woburn.
Elisabeth, d. Seth and Deborah, Dec. 3, 1772.
Esther, d. Seth and Deborah, May 22, 1765.
Fanny M., d. Calvin Jr. and Lydia, July 2, 1832.
Francis Evens, s. Lyman and Hannah, Aug. 27, 1825.
Francis Evens, s. Joel and Sall, Jan. 11, 1804.
Francis Henry, s. Lyman and Hannah, Sept. 26, 1826.
George, s. Ozi and Fanny A., Nov. 11, 1835.
George Lucas, s. Lyman and Hannah, June 24, 1836.

ATHOL BIRTHS.   51

KENDALL, Hannah, d. Jesse and Elisabeth, Dec. 18, 1757.
Hannah, d. Jesse and Elizabeth, bap. Jan. 31, 1762. C.R.
Hannah, d. Jonathan and Anna, Dec. 29, 1780.
Helen Frances, d. Ozi and Fanny A., July 10, 1841.
Henry, s. John Jr. and Cynthia, Nov. 6, 1837.
Jane Oliver, d. Jonathan and Anna, Nov. 25, 1766.
Jane Rebecca, d. Joel and Rebecca, Dec. 25, 1829.
Jane Rebecca, d. Joel and Rebecca, March 22, 1837.
Jesse, s. Jesse and Elisabeth, Feb. 11, 1756. In Medford.
Joab, s. John and Susanna, Dec. 22, 1805.
Joel, s. Jesse and Elisabeth, March 11, 1762.
Joel, s. Joel and Sall, July 1, 1801.
Joel Chase, s. Joel and Rebecca, Nov. 9, 1830.
John, s. Jonathan and Anna, July 9, 1772.
John, s. John and Susanna, Oct. 26, 1812.
John L., —— ——, 1814. G.S.2.
Jonathan Jr., s. John and Susanna, Feb. 14. 1797,
Joseph, s. Joel and Rebecca, Jan. 4, 1832.
Lucius, s. Calvin and Abigail, May 20, 1815.
Lucius W., s. Calvin Jr. and Lydia, Dec. 25, 1839.
Lucy, d. Seth and Olive, Oct. 12, 1802.
Lucy, d. Samuel and ——, bap. Aug. 11, 1799. C.R.
Lydia, d. John and Susanna, Aug. 19, 1808.
Lyman, s. Joel and Sall, Sept. 14, 1788.
Maria, d. John and Susanna, July 29, 1816.
Maria Sterling, d. Lyman and Hannah, Nov. 21, 1832.
Mary, d. Jesse and Elisabeth, Nov. 26, 1753. In Woburn.
Mary, d. Joel and Sall, Sept. 19, 1790.
Mary, d. Calvin Jr. and Lydia, March 23, 1835.
Mary Ann, d. Lyman and Hannah, Dec. 3, 1830.
Mary C., —— ——, 1835. G.S.2.
Mary Elizabeth, d. Joel and Rebecca, Jan. 25, 1834.
Meribah, d. Calvin and Abigail, March 25, 1794.
Molle, d. Jonathan and Anna, Dec. 10, 1775.
Molley, d. Jonathan and Anna, Feb. 15, 1779.
Nancy, d. Joel and Sall, Aug. 20, 1807.
Olive, d. Jesse and Elisabeth, March 31, 1760.
Olive Graves, d. Calvin and Abigail, May 29, 1813.
Ozi, s. John and Susanna, Sept. 13, 1810.
Royal, s. Seth and Olive, Nov. 2, 1800.
Salla, d. Jonathan and Anna, Dec. 5, 1782.
Sally, d. Jonathan and ——, bap. March 9, 1783. C.R.
Sally, d. Joel and Sall, March 9, 1797.
Samuel, s. Seth and Deborah, Aug. 27, 1757.

ATHOL BIRTHS.

KENDALL, Samuel, s. Jesse and Elisabeth, Jan. 20, 1764.
Sarah Rebecca, d. Joel and Rebecca, Jan. 22, 1842.
Seth, s. Seth and Deborah, May 1, 1770.
Silas, s. Silos and Eunis, April 18, 1776.
Sophrona, d. Calvin and Abigail, July 7, 1805.
Stephen, s. John and Susanna, Feb. 16, 1799.
Stephen Batchelor, s. Calvin and Abigail, Sept. 13, 1807.
Susan, d. John Jr. and Cynthia, Feb. 24, 1840.
Susanna, d. Seth and Deborah, Sept. 20, 1767.
Thomas, s. Calvin and Abigail, April 29, 1796.
Walter Sherman, s. James B. and Maria, Oct. 27, 1842.
Wiman Smith, s. John and Susanna, Dec. 24, 1800.
———, d. Calvin and Lydia, Jan. 12, 1845.

KETCHUM, Chancy, s. Roger and Wealthy, Aug. 16, 1805.
Harrison, s. Roger and Wealthy, May 25, 1808.
Justus, s. Roger and Wealthy, Jan. 6, 1799.
Silas, s. Roger and Wealthy, Nov. 29, 1800.
Wealthy, d. Roger and Wealthy, March 21, 1803.

KIDDER, Elmer, s. Jonathan and Nancy R., Nov. 23, 1835.
Harriet Jane, d. John and Maria E., Jan. 11, 1843.
Jonathan Frederick, s. Jonathan and Nancy R., Oct. 2, 1829.
Joseph Severance, s. Jonathan and Nancy R., Feb. 6, 1842.
Nancy, d. Jonathan and Nancy R., Oct. 5, 1821.
Rice, s. Jonathan and Nancy R., July 23, 1825.
Sylvia, d. Jonathan and Nancy R., Oct. 24, 1819.
———, d. John and ———, Sept. 30, 1844.

KILTON (see Kelton), Abigail, d. George and Lydia, bap. Nov. 1, 1772. C.R.
Calvin, s. Jonathan and Margaret, Jan. 26, 1774.
Fanny, d. George and Lydia, bap. Aug. 14, 1763. C.R.
George, s. Jonathan and Margaret, April 6, 1772.
George Oliver, s. Jonathan and Dolly, Feb. 28, 1805.
James, s. James and Sally, June 11, 1798.
Jonathan, s. George and Lydia, bap. Nov. 17, 1765. C.R.
Lois, d. Jonathan and Dolly, Aug. 22, 1790.
Lois, d. James and Sally, Sept. 10, 1795.
Lydia, d. George and Lydia, bap. Sept. 13, 1778. C.R.
Mary, d. George and Lydia, bap. June 28, 1761. C.R.
Reuben, s. George and Lydia, bap. June 25, 1775. C.R.
Samuel, s. James and Sally, March 18, 1792.
William, s. Jonathan and Margaret, March 30, 1770.

ATHOL BIRTHS. 53

KIMPLAN (see Kimpland), Jesse, s. William and Jemima, Jan. 22, 1760.
Samuel, s. William and Jemima, May 2, 1761.

KIMPLAND (see above), Elizabeth, d. William and Katarine, bap. Oct. 11, 1767. C.R.
Landsclotte, s. William and Katarine, bap. April 15, 1770. C.R.
Samuel, s. William and Jemima, bap. July 25, 1761. C.R.
William, s. William and Catarine, bap. June 30, 1765. C.R.

KINDALL (see Kendall) [Kendall in C.R.], David, s. Jesse and Elisabeth, March 20, 1768.
Lois, d. Jesse and Elisabeth, Sept. 11, 1772.
Lydia, d. Seth and Deborah, July 11, 1760.

KINSLY, Alonzo Williams, s. Abial and Olive, bap. Oct. 5, 1799. C.R.

KING, Alfred T., —— —, 1830. G.S.2.
Allen E., s. Isaac and Polly, Dec. 3, 1829. At New Salem.
Amos F., s. Isaac and Polly, May 13, 1835. At New Salem.
Asa, s. Jonathan and Ruth, Sept. 9, 1809.
Austin W., s. Isaac and Polly, April 3, 1826. At New Salem.
Baxter H., s. Isaac and Polly, Nov. 17, 1839.
Charlotte W. Knight, w. Jonathan H., —— —, 1827. G.S.2.
Daniel, s. Jonathan and Ruth, Oct. 2, 1811.
Emily S., d. Isaac and Polly, Jan. 26, 1828. At New Salem.
Jonathan H., —— —, 1828. G.S.2.
Loriston I., s. Isaac and Polly, Oct. 2, 1833. At New Salem.
Lucretia E., d. Isaac and Polly, Feb. 10, 1824. At New Salem.
Martha E., w. Alfred T. ?, —— —, 1832. G.S.2.
Mary E., d. Isaac and Polly, Oct. 29, 1822. At New Salem.
Nancy, d. Jonathan and Ruth, Aug. 15, 1807.
Porter, s. Jonathan and Ruth, Dec. 19, 1813.

KINGSLEY, ——, s. Allen R. and Mary, Dec. 26, 1846.

KNAPP, Caroline M., d. Hiram and Elizabeth P., Nov. 26, 1849?.
Elizabeth, w. Hiram, Sept. 1, 1825. G.S.2.
Hiram, April 20, 1820. G.S.2.

KNEELAND, Asa Leonard, s. Leonard and Sylvia, Sept. 19, 1842.
Ellen M., d. Leonard and Sylvia, June 2, 1837.
Jonas Goddard, s. Leonard and Sylvia, April 8, 1849.
Lucy W., d. Leonard and Sylvia, June 4, 1834.

KNIGHT (see Knights, Night), Emily, of Upton, —— —, 1833. G.S.2.

KNIGHT, Hollis, s. Isaac and ———, bap. March 18, 1798. C.R.
Isaac, s. Isaac and ———, bap. Sept. 21, 1783. C.R.
Joanna, w. Rufus, ———, 1790. G.S.2.
Lucena, ———, 1824. G.S.2.
Lucy Thurston, d. Isaac and ———, bap. March 14, 180 C.R.4.
Mandana, d. Isaac ? and ———, bap. March 16, 1800. C.R.
Rufus, ———, 1793. G.S.2.
KNIGHTS (see above), Abraham, s. Isaac and Patty, bap. Nov. 14, 1779. C.R.
Jesse, s. Isaac [?] and ———, bap. Aug. 16, 1789. C.R.
Levi Walker, s. Isaac and Patty, bap. Nov. 14, 1779. C.R.
Lucy, d. Isaac and Patty, bap. Aug. 12, 1781. C.R.
Persis, d. Isaac and ———, bap. Aug. 8, 1790. C.R.
Submit, d. Ebenezer and Mary, bap. Jan. 19, 1772. C.R.
KNOWLTON, Charles Henry, s. Stillman and Lydia, Aug. 7, 1828.
Charles Walter, s. Stilman and Emily, Aug. 12, 1844.
———, s. Stillman and Lydia, Jan. 13, 1831.
LAMB, Abby Maria, d. James and Elizabeth, Jan. 13, 1838.
Charles, s. James and Elizabeth, Dec. 25, 1834.
Martha Elvira, d. James and Elizabeth, Oct. 30, 1842.
Sarah Elizabeth, d. James and Elizabeth, May 26, 1840.
LAMSON, Calvin, s. Daniel and Martha, Aug. 15, 1776.
Charles, s. Daniel and Martha, Aug. 14, 1782.
Daniel, s. Daniel and Martha, Dec. 19, 1773. Dup.
Leonora, d. Daniel and Martha, June 27, 1779.
Lois, d. Daniel and Martha, Feb. 6, 1788. At Castleton, Vt.
LARNARD, Martha, w. Nehemiah, bap. at New Salem, July 10, 1777. C.R.
LARRABEE, Susan S., ———, 1815. G.S.1.
LATHROP, Frederick Otis, s. Chauncey and Relief, Aug. 3, 1840.
George Whipple, s. Chauncey and Relief, Nov. 25, 1837.
LAWRANCE, Levi, s. Joseph and Susannah, bap. Nov. 23, 1766. C.R.
Sarah, d. Joseph and Susannah, bap. Aug. 14, 1768. C.R.
LAWRENCE, John, s. Joseph and Susannah, bap. Sept. 2, 1770. C.R.
Nathan, s. Joseph and Susannah, bap. July 5, 1772. C.R.

ATHOL BIRTHS. 55

LEACH, Mary E. Kendall, w. Valette W., —— —, 1833. G.S.2.
Valette W., —— —, 1833. G.S.2.
LEE, Angeline Maria, d. William D. and Lydia H., Dec. 27, 1820.
Charles Milton, s. William D. and Lydia H., May 23, 1828.
Dennis, s. Henry and Nancy, Sept. 19, 1823.
George Henry, s. William D. and Lydia H., Oct. 23, 1814.
George Henry, s. William D. Jr. and Sarah, Feb. 23, 1842.
Harriet Chastine, d. William D. and Lydia H., May 27, 1830.
Harriet Maria, d. William D. and Lydia H., March 25, 1818.
Henrietta Chastine, d. William D. and Lydia H., Aug. 17, 1839.
Henry, s. Henry and Nancy, May 28, 1825.
Henry, s. Henry and Nancy, Sept. 3, 1828.
James M., s. William D. and Lydia H., March 2, 1822.
John Howard, s. William D. and Lydia H., Aug. 15, 1834.
Joseph, s. Henry and Nancy, June 23, 1822.
Merritt [Merritt L., G.S.], s. William D. and Lydia H., March 22, 1825.
Nancy, d. Henry and Nancy, Aug. 13, 1826.
Samuel, s. Henry and Nancy, Feb. 10, 1834.
Solon Wetherbee, s. William D. and Lydia H., July 11, 1836.
William Dexter, s. William D. and Lydia H., March 8, 1813.
William Dexter, s. William D. and Lydia H., Aug. 7, 1816.

LEWIS, (see Lues, Luis), Anna, d. Thomas and Olive, Feb. 21, 1801.
Cheany, s. Thomas and Olive, Nov. 27, 1798.
Eli, s. William and Sarah, Oct. 12, 1796.
Eunice, d. Hiram and Mary, Dec. 27, 1817.
Harriet, d. Hiram and Mary, July 26, 1824.
Henry A., Aug. 28, 1826. G.S.2.
Hiram, s. Thomas and Olive, Dec. 22, 1790.
Hiram, s. Hiram and Mary, March 11, 1819.
Hiram T., s. Hiram Jr. and Hannah, May 11, 1847.
James Lovel, s. Hiram and Mary, July 22, 1827.
John, s. William and Sarah, July 10, 1784.
Joseph, s. Thomas and Olive, March 20, 1804.
Joseph Aaron, s. Hiram and Mary, Nov. 19, 1829.
Levi, s. William and Sarah, Jan. 1, 1788.
Louisa V., w. John S., Nov. 17, 1817. G.S.2.
Lovil, s. Thomas and Olive, Feb. 25, 1793.
Maria Louisa, d. John S. and Louisa V., Nov. 10, 1845.
Mary, d. Hiram and Mary, Dec. 27, 1815.
Mary Jane, w. Henry A., Aug. 15, 1833. G.S.2.
Nancy, twin d. William and Sarah, July 15, 1799.

LEWIS, Pheby, d. William and Sarah, June —, 1794.
Sally, d. William and Mary, June 12, 1790.
Samuel, twin s. William and Sarah, July 15, 1799.
Thomas, s. Thomas and Olive, June 12, 1795.
Timothy, s. Thomas and Olive, March 13, 1788.
——, s. Hiram Jr. and Hannah, Sept. 6, 1844.
——, d. John S. and Louisa B., Dec. 26, 1846.

LILLEY, Charles A., —— —, 1839. G.S.1.

LINCOLN, Addison Justin [Justus, C.R.], s. Amasa and Zilpha, March 30, 1824.
Algernon Sidney, s. Amasa and Zilpha, Feb. 11, 1812.
Amasa Wales, s. Amasa and Zilpha, March 21, 1818.
Charles Otis, s. Amasa and Zilpha, Jan. 4, 1816.
Estes Milton, s. Amasa and Zilpha, Aug. 21, 1826.
Henry Clay, s. Amasa and Zilpha, Feb. 26, 1828.
Justus [?] Milton, s. Amasa and ——, bap. Nov. 19, 1826. C.R.
Lysander Reed, s. Amasa and Zilpha, March 3, 1820.
Otis Lysander, s. Amasa and Zilpha, Dec. 21, 1813.
William Dwight, s. Amasa and Zilpha, Feb. 4, 1822.

LIPPETT, Palace, d. Nelson and Susan H., Sept. 28, 1847.

LIPPITT, Dwight [Dexter in dup.], s. Nelson and Susan, Nov. 7, 1843.
Job, s. Nelson and Susan, Jan. 16, 1842.
Willie, s. Nelson and Susan, Aug. 10, 1845.

LITCHFIELD, Albee K., —— —, 1827. G.S.2.

LOCKE, Emma Heald, w. Theodore P., —— —, 1796. G.S.2.
Theodore P., —— —; 1799. G.S.2.

LONGLEY (see below), Joseph, s. John and Olive, April 23, 1824.
Susan Maria, d. John and Olive, July 8, 1827.

LONGLY, John Adams, s. John and Olive, July 26, 1821.

LORD, Aaron, s. Thomas and Lenord, Dec. 25, 1766.
Aaron, s. Thomas Jr. and Dezier, June 18, 1801.
Abel, s. Thomas and Leonard, bap. July 9, 1769. C.R.
Abel, s. Thomas and Lenord, March 12, 1774.
Abel, s. Absalom and Clarissa, May 31, 1819.
Abigail, d. Gardner and Sally, Nov. 5, 1816.
Abigal Scot, d. Thomas and Lenord, July 7, 1772.
Absalom, s. Thomas and Lenord, June 30, 1790.

ATHOL BIRTHS. 57

LORD, Asa, s. Thomas and Lenord, Oct. 1, 1761.
Azubah, d. William and Mary, bap. Oct. 18, 1778. C.R.
Benjamin, s. Stephen and Mary, April 14, 1769.
Chester, s. Absalom and Clarissa, Nov. 2, 1817.
Emerson, s. Cyrell C. and Betsey, Aug. 31, 1833.
Emma Carlina, d. Abel and Lucy A., Dec. 7, 1849.
Esther Fatima, d. Abel and Adaline F., Nov. 3, 1844.
Franklin, s. Thomas Jr. and Dezier, March 1, 1808.
Franklin Goddard, s. Gardner and Sally, Oct. 4, 1827.
Gardner, s. Thomas and Lenord, April 3, 1788.
Gardner, s. Gardner and Sally, Feb. 26, 1824.
Hannah, d. William and Mary, bap. Aug. 19, 1765. C.R.
Hannah, d. William and Mary, bap. Dec. 31, 1769. C.R.
Hiram, s. Absalom and Clarissa, Nov. 18, 1829.
Ichabod, s. Stephen and Mary, Nov. 27, 1762.
John, s. Stephen and Mary, April 19, 1771.
Jonathan, s. William and Mary, bap. March 6, 1781. C.R.
Joseph, s. Thomas and Lenord, Oct. 26, 1763.
Joseph, s. Absalom and Clarissa, Dec. 30, 1833.
Joshua, s. Stephen and Mary, bap. June 18, 1775. C.R.
Jotham, s. Thomas and Lenord, June 4, 1783.
Laura L., d. Abel and Adaline, Nov. 19, 1846.
Leonard?, w. Capt. Thomas, —— —, 1744. G.S.I.
Lenord, d?. Thomas and Lenord, —— —, ——. [1785 or 1786?.]
Lucy, d. Absalom and Clarissa, Aug. 18, 1824.
Mariam, d. Doct. Joseph and Sarah, bap. Jan. 21, 1753. C.R.
Mary, d. Absalom and Clarissa, Jan. 29, 1821.
Molle, d. William and Mary, bap. April 14, 1776. C.R.
Naby, d. Thomas Jr. and Dezier, July 9, 1803.
Nancy Young, d. Gardner [Chandler in C.R.] and Nancy, Jan. 14, 1814.
Nathaniel Young, s. Gardner and Sally, Sept. 22, 1819.
Preston, s. William and Mary, bap. May 3, 1767. C.R.
Quincy M., s. Stephen L. and Mary A., Feb. 26, 1848.
Reuben, s. William and Mary, bap. April 4, 1773. C.R.
Rhoda, d. Thomas and Lenord, March 1, 1776.
Sally, d. Absalom and Clarissa, Jan. 3, 1832.
Samuel, s. Stephen and Mary, Feb. 9, 1767.
Sarah, d. William and Mary, bap. June 5, 1763. C.R.
Sarah Smith, d. Gardner and Sally, July 30, 1822.
Stephen, s. Stephen and Mary, June 15, 1760.
Capt. Thomas, —— —, 1736. G.S.I.
Thomas, s. Thomas and Lenord, Jan. 17, 1780.
Thomas Chandler, s. Thomas Jr. and Dezier, Nov. 24, 1805.

LORD, William, s. William and Mary, bap. Aug. 2, 1761. C.R.
———, d. Ethan and Thankful, Feb. 6, 1847.
———, s. Ethan and Thankful, July 11, 1849.

LOTHROP, ———, s. Chauncey and Releif A., April 10, 1847.

LOVERING, Marcy Jinning, d. Levi and Sally, Nov. 16, 1805.
Sarah Jones, d. Levi and Sally, Aug. 1, 1803.

LUCE, Polly G., w. Sargent, ———, 1800. G.S.5.
Sargent, ———, 1797. G.S.5.

LUES (see Lewis, Luis), Abiger, s. William and Sarah, Nov. —, 1777.
Elijah, s. William and Sarah, July 30, 1779.

LUIS (see Lewis, Lues), Marcy, d. William and Sarah, Aug. 30, 1781.

LUMBARD [Lombard in C.R.], James, s. James and Thankfull, March 4, 1773.

LUMBERD [Lumbard in C.R.], Salle, d. James and Thankfull, Sept. 2, 1775.

McCABE, ———, d. Simeon and Bridget, Feb. 27, 1847.

McCLALLEN, Horatio William, s. Horace and Lucy, Dec. 21, 1844.

MACCOLLEY, Rebecca, w. Samuel, ———, 1805. G.S.4.
Samuel, ———, 1802. G.S.4.

McCRILLIS, Julia M., w. Lewis M., ———, 1842. G.S.2.
Lewis M., ———, 1838. G.S.2.

McGINNIS, William Francis, s. John and Sarah, June 30, 1842.

McLANE (see McLean), Emma S. Barton, w. Robert E., ———, 1838. G.S.2.
Robert E., ———, 1834. G.S.2.

McLEAN (see above), Annie, w. Daniel, ———, 1844. G.S.1.
Daniel, ———, 1834. G.S.1.

McREEL, Alexander, ———, 1839. G.S.1.
Helen F., w. Alexander, ———, 1842. G.S.1.

MAN (see Mann), Ensign Junior, s. Ensign and Allice (Petersham), bap. Sept. 19, 1779. C.R.
Hannah, d. Ensign and ———, bap. Sept. 20, 1801. C.R.

ATHOL BIRTHS. 59

MAN, Lucy, d. Ensign and Allice, bap. May 10, 1778. c.r.
Thomas, s. Ensign and Allis, bap. Oct. 15, 1780. c.r.

MANLY, Ann, d. Obed and Betsey, Feb. 9, 1807.
Caroline, d. Obed and Betsey, Feb. 9, 1815.
Fidelia, d. Obed and Betsey, Sept. 28, 1817.
Lucinda, d. Obed and Betsey, July 29, 1804.
Melinda, d. Obed and Betsey, Aug. 19, 1809.
Stillman, s. Obed and Manly, Feb. 2, 1813.

MANN (see Man), Esther E., [sister of Mrs. Austin Ellinwood],
—— —, 1823. g.s.5.

MARBLE, Aaron, Junior, s. Aaron, s. Aaron and Patience, bap. June 4, 1781. c.r.
Abel, s. Silas and Catarine, bap. June 13, 1779. c.r.
Abigail, d. Silas and Katarine, bap. April 9, 1775. c.r.
Abijah, s. Silas and Katarine, bap. April 1, 1770. c.r.
Elizabeth, d. Silas and Katarine, bap. May 17, 1772. c.r.
Hannah, d. Moses and Sarah, bap. Aug. 19, 1781. c.r.
Miriam, d. Silas and Catarine, bap. June 14, 1777. c.r.
Moses, s. Robert and Hannah, Oct. 19, 1796.
Paul, twin s. Silas and Katarin ?, bap. Dec. 9, 1781. c.r.
Salle, d. Moses and Sarah, bap. Oct. 18, 1778. c.r.
Silas, Junior, twin s. Silas and Katarin ?, bap. Dec. 9, 1781. c.r.
Susannah, d. Moses and Sarah, bap. Nov. 10, 1776. c.r.

MARSH, Amos Alfred, s. Peter H. and Sarah N., May 3, 1844.
———, s. Peter H. and Sally, May 3, 1843. [1844 in dup.]
———, s. Peter H. and Sally, Dec. 14, 1845.

MARVEL, Abijah, s. Silas and Catarine, bap. Sept. 7, 1766. c.r.
Patience, d. Silas and Catarine, bap. May 1, 1768. c.r.

MATTHEWS, Emily, d. Nelson and ———, Oct. 3, 1849.

MAY, Sarah A., w. A. W., —— —, 1842. g.s.2.

MAYO, Calvin, s. Benjamin and Doratha, bap. Jan. 6, 1779. c.r.
Lydia Avelena, d. Matthias C. and Lydia, Jan. 10, 1844.
Rachel, d. Simeon, Nov. 21, 1836.

MEACHAM, Charles Francis, s. George W. and Martha, Aug. 14, 1849.
Charles Orason, s. Mason and Abigail, Jan. 1, 1843.
Ozi, s. Mason and Abigail, Jan. 11, 1841.
Wilder, —— —, 1813. g.s.6.
William Wilder, s. William and Polly, Jan. 17, 1812.

MERRIAM, Adaline, d. Freeman and Adaline, Feb. 26, 1848.
Fanny, Dec. —, 1832. G.S.2.
Orren, June —, 1822. G.S.2.

MERRITT, Dorcas Sarah, d. Increase Sumner, Nov. 15, 1828.
Sumner Lincoln, s. Increase Sumner and Susan, Feb. 25, 1827.

MILES, Charles Edward, s. Clough R. and Abb[y?], Jan. 10, 1823.

MILLER, Joseph, s. Thomas and Mary Ann, June 11, 1843.
Joseph Henry, s. Thomas and Mary, Dec. 6, 1840.

MILLS, Submit, d. Eunice, bap. Sept. 6, 1789. C.R.

MOOR (see Moore, More), Asenath, d. Josiah and Mary, June 6, 1790.
Joseph, s. Josiah and Mary, Nov. 29, 1793.
Lecte, d. Josiah and Mary, Sept. 10, 1781.
Lois, d. Josiah and Mary, Dec. 6, 1779.
Phebe, d. Josiah and Mary, Jan. 17, 1777.

MOORE (see above and More), Ansel, Oct. 22, 1840. G.S.1.
Caroline L., d. Joseph P. and Susan T., March 30, 1844. G.S.2. [Probably same as following.]
Caroline L., d. Joseph F. and Susan, March 30, 1845.
Caroline Mario, d. Joseph P. and Susan E., March 30, 1844.
Chandler Wright, —— —, 1819. G.S.1.
Daniel, s. Chandler Wright and Susan, —— —, 1846. G.S.1. [Perhaps same as following.]
Daniel, s. Chandler W. and Susan, Aug. 27, 1847.
Dwight L., s. George W. and Millie ?, —— —, 1833. G.S.2.
Ellen J., w. Norman ?, —— —, 1839. G.S.2.
Frances A., w. R. D., —— —, 1834. G.S.2.
George Frederick, s. George W. and Milla, Sept. 1, [1844 ?].
George W., Sept. 29, 1811. G.S.2.
Joseph P., Dec. 14, 1811. G.S.2.
Millie Shepardson, w. George W., March 25, 1812. G.S.2.
Norman, —— —, 1832. G.S.2.
Octavo M., d. Joseph P. and Susan T., Feb. 21, 1847. G.S.2.
R. D., —— —, 1834. G.S.2.
Richard, s. Richard and Mary, Sept. 13, 1848.
Susan, w. Chandler Wright, —— —, 1819. G.S.1.
Susan T., w. Joseph P., —— —, Dec. 14, 1811. G.S.2.
———, s. Joseph and Susan B., Feb. 21, 1846.

MORE (see above), Arad, s. Joshua and Deborah, March 13, 1802.
Chauncey Lovell, s. Joseph P. and Susan T., April 8, 1834. At Framingham.

ATHOL BIRTHS. 61

More, Eliza, d. Joshua and Deborah, April 27, 1800.
Emmaly, d. Joshua and Deborah, Aug. 26, 1804.
Hiram Cheney, s Joseph P. and Susan T., Sept. 1, 1835. At Framingham.
James Albert, s. Joseph P. and Susan T., June 4, 1840.
Joseph Edwin, s. Joseph P. and Susan T., Aug. 8, 1837. At Petersham.
Josiah Frederick, s. Joseph P. and Susan T., March 29, 1842.

MOREY, Emma Sophia, d. John O. and Emeline, Sept. 22, 1849.
Oscar C., s. John O. and Emeline, Oct. 2, 1848.

MORS, Samuel, s. William and Mary, Oct. 27, 1772.

MORSE (see Moss), Abigail, d. William Jr. and Charlotte, Dec. 26, 1793.
Alvira, d. Samuel and Deborah, Feb. 5, 1808.
Alma Ruggles, d. William and Phila, Dec. 1, 1822.
Ann Riplay, d. Joseph and Jamima, April 8, 1774.
Anna, d. William and ———, bap. July 11, 1784. c.r.
Asa Evans, s. Samuel Jr. and Ruth, April 22, 1828.
Betsy, d. John and Betsey, May 25, 1804. At Ashby.
Catharine, d. William and Phila, Nov. 16, 1818.
Charles, s. William and Phila, Jan. 1, 1828.
Charles, s. William and Sally, ——— ———, ——— [1847 ?].
Charles O., s. James E. and Sarah, May 9, 1847.
Charles Waterman, s. Paul and Sally, July 1, 1825.
Charlotte, d. William Jr. and Charlotte, Jan. 24, 1804.
Clarence Edward, s. Cushing B. and Julia A., Sept. 11, 1849.
Cushing Burr, s. Paul and Sally, Sept. 16, 1820.
Frank Fisk, s. Laban and Esther, Nov. 7, 1848.
Frederick Proctor, s. George and Mary Sophia, Aug. 22, 1842.
George, s. Paul and Sally, Oct. 31, 1813.
George H., s. Levi and Lucy A., ——— ———, 1844. g.s.2.
George Henry, s. Samuel Jr. and Ruth, June 29, 1830. In ———, New York.
George Henry, s. Levi and Lucy, Nov. 22, 1844.
Hannah, d. William and Mary, bap. June 30, 1765. c.r.
Henry Tyrrell, s. Laban and Esther, Jan. 11, 1840.
Jeremiah Morton, d. William Jr. and Charlotte, Jan. 3, 1806.
Jesse, s. Samuel and Deborah, May 3, 1809.
John, s. William and Mary, bap. Apr. 16, 1769. c.r.
John Edwin, s. Paul and Sally, May 12, 1817.
John Hill, s. Samuel and Sally, Sept. 2, 1796.
John Rice, s. George and Mary Sophia, June 26, 1844?.

ATHOL BIRTHS.

MORSE, Josephine M., d. Levi and Lucy A., —— ——, 1846. G.S.2.
Laban, s. Paul and Sally, Jan. 30, 1812.
Leander Brigham, s. Laban and Esther, March 29, 1842.
Levi, s. William Jr. and Charlotte, Sept. 19, 1796.
Levi, s. William and Phila, Oct. 1, 1820.
Lucy A., w. Levi, —— ——, 1825. G.S.2.
Mima, d. Joseph and Jamima, March 28, 1776.
Molle, d. William and Mary, bap. Oct. 21, 1781. C.R.
Olive, d. William and Mary, bap. Oct. 6, 1776. C.R.
Oliver, s. Samuel and Deborah, June 11, 1802.
Ollive, d. John and Betsey, March 30, 1806. At Peckersfield.
Paul, s. William and Mary, bap. May 16, 1779. C.R.
Phila Jane, d. William and Phila, June 24, 1832.
Reuben, s. Samuel and Deborah, Sept. 16, 1800.
Reubin, s. Samuel and Deborah, Oct. 14, 1799.
Richard M., s. Levi and Lucy A., —— ——, 1847. G.S.2.
Sally, d. Paul and Sally, Dec. 18, 1803. At Ashby.
Sally, d. William and Phila, March 25, 1824.
Sally Sheffil, d. William Jr. and Charlotte, Oct. 4, 1801.
Samuel, s. Samuel and Deborah, Jan. 10, 1804.
Sarah, d. Samuel and Deborah, Nov. 10, 1805.
Sarah Bancroft, —— ——, 1826. G.S.1.
Sumner, s. Paul and Sally, Oct. 28, 1806. At Ashby.
Sumner Rice, s. Paul and Sally, Dec. 8, 1808.
William, s. William and Mary, bap. Oct. 26, 1767. C.R.
William 3d, s. William Jr. and Charlotte, April 26, 1799.
William, s. William and Phila, June 1, 1825.
William H. Lafayette, s. William and Sarah E., Feb. 13, 1848.
——, inf. William and Sally, Sept. 14, 1843.
——, d. William Jr. and Sarah E., Jan. 11, 1846.
——, s. Levi and Lucy, Dec. 20, 1846.

MORTON, Abner, s. Abner and Sophia, bap. Oct. 30, 1774. C.R.
Abraham, s. Benjamin and Mary, March 28, 1763.
Alexander, s. Jeremiah and Alice, June 9, 1773.
Alice, d. Joel and Anna, July 28, 1801.
Amanda, d. —— and Roxelana, Aug. 28, 1804.
Asa, s. Martin and Jerusha, May 28, 1782.
Asahel, s. of Joshua Junr. and Melenda, bap. May 25, 1817. C.R.
Austine J., Sept. 8, 1832. G.S.2.
Azuba, d. Benjamin and Mary, April 16, 1761.
Azubah Graves, d. Joshua Jr. and ——, bap. Dec. 5, 1819. C.R.
Balebishop [Baily Bishop in C.R.], s. Martin and Jerusha, Aug. 24, 1771.

ATHOL BIRTHS. 63

Morton, Benjamin Freeman, s. Reubin and Judath, Feb. 15, 1796.
Caroline, d. Martin and Jerusha, March 15, 1775.
Charlotte, d. Jeremiah and Alice, Oct. 2, 1768.
Daniel, s. Jeremiah and Alice, July 26, 1767.
Dolle, d. Martin and Jerusha, Nov. 25, 1756.
Electa, d. Daniel and Electa, March 13, 1797.
Elisibeth, d. Reubin and Judath, Feb. 10, 1785.
Elizabeth, d. Martin, Dec. 18, 1765.
Elizabeth, d. Reuben and ———, bap. Aug. 21, 1785. c.r.
Fanny, d. Joel and Anna, Jan. 26, 1812.
Fanny Almeda [Elmedia in c.r.], d. Daniel and Electa, Jan. 31, 1805.
Gadweight [Gad Wait in c.r.], s. Martin and Jerusha, March 15, 1768.
Gadweight [Gad Wait in c.r.], s. Martin and Jerusha, May 24, 1770.
Hannah, d. Noah and Rhoda, bap. June 3, 1754. c.r.
Hannah, d. Martin and Jerusha, March 13, 1758.
Hannah Graves, d. Daniel and Electa, March 13, 1802.
Jeremiah, s. Jeremiah and Alice, Dec. 14, 1778.
Jerusha, d. Martin and Jerusha, June 12, 1761.
Joel, s. Jeremiah and Alice, Dec. 17, 1770.
John, s. Jeremiah and Alice, March 18, 1775.
John, s. Martin and Jerusha, April 20, 1777.
John Dwight, s. Jeremiah and Olive, Oct. 3, 1831.
Joseph, s. Reubin and Judath, Dec. 10, 1787.
Judith, d. Ruben and ———, bap. Sept. 28, 1777. c.r.
Julius, s. Abner and Sophia, Sept. 8, 1772.
Julius Sidney, s. ——— and Roxelana, Sept. 12, 1809.
Kimball, s. Joshua Jr. and Melinda, bap. May 25, 1817. c.r.
Kinsley, s. Joshua Jr. and Melinda, bap. May 25, 1817. c.r.
Levi, s. Abner and Sophia, Jan. 14, 1770.
Lidea, d. Joshua Jr. and Melinda, bap. May 25, 1817. c.r.
Lucinda, d. Joel and Anna, May 11, 1808.
Lucy, d. Reubin and Judath, March 22, 1790.
Malona, d. Joshua Jr. and Melinda, bap. May 25, 1817. c.r.
Margerett, b. Oct. 1, 1738. The first female born in this Toun. c.r.
Martin, s. Martin and Jerusha, July 14, 1773.
Mary, d. Phinehas and Huldah, April 24, 1801.
Merium, d. Martin and Jerusha, Feb. 21, 1779.
Moses, s. Phinehas and Huldah, April 1, 1806.
Noah, s. Phinehas and Huldah, Aug. 18, 1803.
Olive, March 30, 1806. g.s.2.
Olive Fairbanks, d. Daniel and Electa, Feb. 14, 1794.

ATHOL BIRTHS.

MORTON, Rhoda, d. Hannah Morbon, now w. Samuel, bap. June 27, 1803 [aged 18 y.]. C.R.
Richard, s. Martin and Jerusha, June 16, 1755.
Roxalena, d. Reubin and Judath, June 1, 1782.
Salle, d. Martin and Jerusha, Sept. 25, 1759.
Salmon, s. Abner and Sophia, May 11, 1767.
Salmon, s. Ruben and Judah [Judith, C.R.], Jan. 5, 1778.
Sarah, d. Rhuben and ———, bap. July 7, 1793. C.R.
Seth, s. Martin and Jerusha, March 31, 1754.
Sylva, d. Thomas and Polly, July 15, 1790.
Tarzah [Tirzah in C.R.], d. Ruben and Judah, Oct. 13, 1779.
Thomas, s. Samuel and Lydia, bap. Aug. 24, 1752. C.R.
Thomas, s. Abner and Sophia, April 5, 1765.
Vertue, d. Martin and Jerusha, April 22, 1763.

MOSS (see Morse) [Morse in C.R.], Deneson, twin s. Joseph and Jamima, May 20, 1772.
Eunice [Unice Morse in C.R.], twin d. Joseph and Jamima, May 20, 1772.
[Morse in C.R.], James, s. Joseph and Jamima, May 7, 1769.

MOULTON, Ardelia Agustia, d. Aaron and Elenor, June 25, 1840.
Ellen Elmira, d. Aaron and Elenor, April 22, 1835.
Jane Eliza, d. Aaron and Elenor, Feb. 16, 1837.
Leonard Otis, s. Aaron and Elenor, Jan. 13, 1830. At Wayland.
Roxse, d. Aaron and Elenor, Sept. 28, 1831.
Wesley Asbury, s. Aaron and Elenor, June 7, 1833.

MYRICK, Elvira, d. Joshua and Patty, Nov. 25, 1802.
Joseph Peirce, s. Joshua and Patty, April 25, 1805.
Rhoda, d. Joshua and Rhoda, April 12, 1798.
Thomas Eaton, s. Joshua and Patty, March 23, 1807.

NASH, Celia, d. Terry and Sarah, Feb. 25, 1849.

NEEDHAM, Betsy, d. Isaac and Sarah, bap. Sept. 19, 1781. C.R.
Lucy, d. Isaac and Sarah, bap. Jan. 19, 1776. C.R.

NELSON, Anna M., w. George W., May 11, 1836. G.S.2.
George W., Feb. 22, 1832. G.S.2.

NEWELL (see Newhall), Anna, w. Ezekiel, ——— —, 1806. G.S.1.
Asa, ——— —, 1826. G.S.1.
Ezekiel, ——— —, 1797. G.S.1.
Lucy S., w. Asa, ——— —, 1824. G.S.1.
Solomon, s. Ebenezer and Sarah, April 5, 1786.

ATHOL BIRTHS. 65

NEWHALL (see Newell), Augustine Washington, s. Hiram and Jerusha, Jan. 31, 1795.
Caroline Frances, d. Samuel and Betsy, May 12, 1834.
Chaney? s. Joshua and Polly, June 6, 1794.
Chancey, s. Joshua and Polly, Aug. 25, 1801. At Stratton, Vt.
Cyrenius, gr.-s. Shebna and Mary Dyer, March 2, 1795.
George, s. Joshua and Polly, March 26, 1792.
George Harrison, s. George and Mary, Nov. 15, 1825.
Hannah, d. Hiram and Jerusha, Aug. 29, 1785.
Harriot Atwood, d. Samuel and Betsy, May 1, 1828.
Hiram, s. Hiram and Jerusha, Sept. 16, 1780.
Hiram, s. Joshua and Polly, Jan. 20, 1800.
Jerusha, d. Hiram and Sarah, July 5, 1776.
John Phillips, s. William and ——, bap. May 25, 1817. C.R.
Jonathan, s. Hiram and Sarah, Sept. 12, 1772.
Joshua, s. Hiram and Sarah, July 3, 1770. At Leicester.
Lois, d. Hiram and Jerusha, Sept. 28, 1787.
Lucia, d. Joshua and Polly, June 6, 1797.
Lucinda Graves, d. Jonathan and Susanna, Sept. 29, 1800.
Lucy, d. Hiram and Jerusha, March 3, 1792.
Lucy, d. Joshua and Polly, March 6, 1796.
Lucy Maria, d. Samuel and Betsey, Sept. 15, 1840.
Lusy Flora Kate, d. Samuel and Betsy, April 20, 1846.
Mary, d. Hiram and Mary, June 28, 1768. At Leicester.
Mary, w. George, Feb. 12, 1792. G.S.1.
Mary Jane, d. George and Mary, March 8, 1831.
Nancy, d. Wm. and ——, bap. Aug. 18, 1822. C.R.
Olive, d. Hiram and Jerusha, Nov. 18, 1789.
Olive, d. Hiram and Jerusha, Feb. 16, 1797.
Olive, d. Hyram Sen. and Jerusha, bap. Dec. 20, 1789. C.R.
Samuel, s. Hiram and Jerusha, Nov. 26, 1800.
Sarah, d. Hiram and Sarah, Nov. 13, 1774.
William, s. Hiram and Jerusha, June 10, 1783.

NEWTON, Ann M., w. Charles O., —— —, 1837. G.S.2.
Charles O., —— —, 1829. G.S.2.
Frederick S., s. Stephen and Mary, Oct. 25, 1849.
Susan K., w. Simeon B., —— —, 1840. G.S.2.
Simeon B., —— —, 1835. G.S.2.

NIGHT (see Knight), Patty, d. Isaac and ——, bap. Sept. 11, 1796. C.R.

NORTON, Ann Maria, w. Rev. John Foot, —— —, 1823. G.S.2.
Rev. John Foot, —— —, 1809. G.S.2.

NUTT, Abraham, s. Abraham and Sarah, April 23, 1762.
James, s. Abraham and Grace, June 6, 1744.
Jerusha, d. Abraham Jr. and Jerusha, April 24, 1795.
John, s. Abraham and Grace, Jan. 20, 1742.
Newhall, s. Abraham Jr. and Jerusha, Dec. 12, 1793.
Susanna, d. Abraham and Grace, Sept. 16, 1739.

OAKES (see Oaks), Abraham, s. Abraham and Joanna, June 29, 1806.
Asa, s. Daniel and Hepzibah, May 5, 1801.
Jefferson G., —— —, 1838. G.S.I.
Loisa, d. Daniel and Hepzibah, June 14, 1806.
Luke, s. Daniel and Hepzibah, Oct. 16, 1802.
Mary d. Daniel and Hepzibah, Sept. 13, 1807.
Merric, s. Daniel and Hepzibah, April 9, 1804.

OAKS (see above), Adin, s. Ira and Mary, Feb. 19, 1836.
Almeda, d. Abraham Jr. and Mary Ann, Nov. 4, 1841.
Geraldine Low, d. Abraham and Mary Ann, Oct. 19, 1843.
Harriet A., d. Ira and Harriet, Aug. 15, 1844.
Martha Ann Drury, d. Abraham Jr and Mary Ann, Dec. 13, 1838.
Mary Ann Adelaid, d. Abraham Jr. and Mary Ann, Sept. 13, 1832.
Mary Ann Sophia, d. Abraham Jr. and Mary Ann, Aug. 27, 1830.
Mary Jane, d. Ira and Lucy, Dec. 1, 1840.
Roland Turner, s. Abraham Jr. and Mary Ann, Jan. 22, 1835.
Rosette, d. Abraham Jr. and Mary Ann, Jan. 3, 1837.
————, d. Ira and Harriet, Feb. 23, 1846.
————, s. Abraham and Mary A., Oct. 12, 1846.

OLIVER, Aaron, s. John and Mary, Sept. 15, 1748.
Aaron, s. Capt. John, one of the first settlers of Athol, —— —, 1749. G.S.I. [Probably same as above.]
Aaron, s. James and Hannah, May 2, 1804.
Aaron, s. Thomas and Lois, Aug. 17, 1841.
Andrew, s. Robart and Lydia, Feb. 16, 1771.
Anna, d. William and Anna, Junior, bap. Dec. 20, 1778. C.R.
Anne Durham, d. John and Mary, Aug. 11, 1764.
Asaph, s. Aaron and Lucy, June 1, 1782.
Caleb, s. Aaron and Lucy, April 21, 1780.
Caleb, s. Deborah, —— —, 1825. G.S.I.
Calvin Humphrey, s. Moses and Lois [Wiswell, C.R.], Aug. 17, 1781.
Catharine Penniman, d. Deborah, —— —, 1819. G.S.I.
Charles, s. Moses and Lois, June 8, 1789.
Charles, s. George and Rhoda, Nov. 29, 1812.
Cinda, d. James and Hannah, Nov. 1, 1806.

ATHOL BIRTHS.

Oliver, Cornwell, s. George and Rhoda, Oct. 13, 1802.
Clark, s. Robart and Lydia, June 21, 1773.
Cynthia Goddard, 3d w. George, —— —, 1798. G.S.I.
Cynthia White, d. Deborah, —— —, 1820. G.S.I.
Daniel, s. Robart and Lydia, Oct. 8, 1761.
Daniel, s. Robart and Lydia, Dec. 18, 1775.
Deborah White, 2d w. George, —— —, 1779. G.S.I.
Edna Stone, s. Thomas and Lois, April 1, 1839.
Elizabeth, d. John and Mary, May 25, 1773.
Forbes, s. William and Anna, bap. Dec. 2, 1770. C.R.
Franklin, s. James and Hannah, March 24, 1810.
Franklin, s. Franklin and Emily Eaton, Sept. 13, 1838.
Franklin, s. Franklin and Emily Eaton, May 3, 1843.
Franklin Jr., May 2, 1844. G.S.2. [Probably same as above.]
Lois S., w. Thomas K., —— —, 1820. G.S.4.
George, s. Aaron and Lucy, April 2, 1776.
George, s. George and Rhoda, Sept. 4, 1808. In Stratton, Vt.
George Sidney, s. James and Minerva, —— —, 1843. G.S.2.
Hannah, d. John and Mary, March 2, 1758.
Hannah, d. Thomas and Lois, Feb. —, 1847.
Harriet R., d. James and Minerva, Nov. 27, 1828.
Hepsibah, d. George and Rhoda, Jan. 7, 1801.
Hepzibeth, d. Aaron and Lucy, —— —, ——. G.S.I.
Isable [Izabell in C.R.], d. Robart and Lydia, May 30, 1760.
James, s. William and Anna Oliver Jr., bap. Nov. 21, 1773. C.R.
James, s. Aaron and Lucy, April 9, 1778.
James Jr., s. William and Anna, bap. Dec. 31, 1780. C.R.
James, s. James and Hannah, July 31, 180-. [1802?.]
James, M.D., —— —, 1836. G.S.2. [Perhaps same as next.]
James, s. James and Minerva, June 28, 1836.
James Durham, s. Robart and Lydia, March 13, 1765.
Jane T., d. James and Minerva, Jan. 26, 1834.
Jemima, d. John and Mary, April 7, 1751.
Jenny, d. William and Anna, bap. May 21, 1769. C.R.
John, s. John and Mary, Dec. 2, 1766.
?, Louise, d. Rhoda, —— —, 1815. G.S.I.
Lucinda, d. James and Hannah, Nov. 9, 1813.
Lucy, d. Aaron and Lucy, Nov. 22, 1791.
Lucy Smith, w. Aaron, —— —, 1751. G.S.I.
Mary, d. John and Mary, June 17, 1762.
Mary, d. Aaron and Lucy, Feb. 25, 1787.
Maribah, d. Aaron and Lucy, April 19, 1774.
Minerva, w. James, —— —, 1803. G.S.2.
Minerva, s. James and Minerva, —— —, 1846. G.S.2.

OLIVER, Moses, s. John and Mary, Aug. 9, 1753.
Moses Warren, s. Calvin H. and Dolly, Sept. 21, 1805. In Gardner.
Moses W., s. George and Deborah White, —— —, 1823. G.S.I.
Nancy, d. James and Hannah, Aug. 16, 1817.
Nancy Jane, d. Thomas and Lois, March 14, 1844. [1845 in dup.]
Nathaniel Jennison, s. Moses and Lois, March 14, 1783.
Nathaniel Young, s. George and Rhoda, June 8, 1810. In Stratton, Vt.
Orwell Orson, s. Franklin and Emily E., Jan. 10, 1848.
Otis, s. Franklin and Emily Eaton, July 31, 1836.
Ozi, s. Franklin and Emily Eaton, Dec. 1, 1833.
Rachel, d. John and Mary, Sept. 15, 1755.
Rachel, d. John and Mary, April 13, 1770.
Rhoda Young, 1st w. George, —— —, 1777. G.S.I.
Robart, s. Robart and Lydia, Dec. 28, 1768.
Rosella 2d, d. James and Minerva, Oct. 11, 1839.
Rosella, d. James and Minerva, July 27, 1830.
Rosella A., d. James and Minerva, —— —, 1839. G.S.2.
Royal, s. Moses and Lois, Nov. 11, 1786.
Sally, d. Calvin H. and Dolly, Aug. 28, 1808. In Stratton, Vt.
Sally Elisabeth, d. Franklin and Emily Eaton, Feb. 27, 1841.
Samuel Cornwell, s. George and Rhoda, June 6, 1806. In Stratton, Vt.
Sarah, d. Moses and Lois, May —, 1791.
Sydney, s. James and Minerva, April 14, 1843.
Sylvester Eaton, s. Franklin and Emily, March 20, 1835.
Thomas, s. James and Hannah, Aug. 29, 1815.
Thomas K., —— —, 1816. G.S.4.
Tirzah [Tarzah in c.R.], d. John and Mary, March 29, 1760.
William, s. Robart and Lydia, Nov. 21, 1763.
William, s. Robart and Lydia, Dec. 27, 1766.
William, Tertius, s. William and Anna, Jr., bap. Jan. 18, 1776. C.R.

ORCUTT, Abner Graves 2d, s. Jonathan and Alice, March 5, 1814.
Alice, d. Aug. —, 1812.
Caroline Amelia, d. David and Lucretia, April 18, 1824.
Jonathan, s. Jonathan and Alice, Dec. 26, 1815.

OSGOOD, Adaline, d. David and Molly, Oct. 12, 1811.
Charles, s. David and Molly, Feb. 2, 1809.
Mary Ann, d. David and Molly, May 19, 1807.

PAIGE, John s., —— —, 1832. G.S.2.

ATHOL BIRTHS. 69

PARKER, Joseph R., s. Joseph P. and Eliza H., Dec. 17, 1847.
Mary Jane, d. Joseph P. and Eliza H., Jan. 11, 1843.
Nancy, d. Joseph P. and Lydia, Dec. 2, 1833.

PARKMAN, George Ebenezer, s. Chauncey and Harriet, Oct. 19, 1830.
Lurana, d. Chauncey and Harriet, Oct. 12, 1824.
Lydia Marcena, d. Chauncey and Harriet, June 30, 1828.
Sally, d. Chauncey and Harriet, June 24, 1826.

PARMATOR, Salle, d. Jason and Abagail, bap. June 28, 1761. C.R.

PARMENTER, Frank Sumner, s. Joseph S. and Caroline P. ? B., Oct. 26, 1849.

PARTRIDGE (see Patridge), Alpheus, s. Amos and Salley, Aug. 27, 1787.
Amos, s. Amos and Salley, June 11, 1794.
Arethusa, d. Amos and Salley, Feb. 27, 1800.
Betcy, d. Amos and Salley, July 25, 1796.
Hannah, d. Amos and Salley, Aug. 23, 1784.
James, s. Amos and Salley, March 3, 1786.
Polly, d. Amos and Salley, Aug. 12, 1792.
Rachel, d. Amos and Salley, March 19, 1791.
Salley, d. Amos and Salley, July 26, 1789.
Sophrona, d. Amos and Salley, April 17, 1798.

PATRIDGE (see above), A. Mason, —— —, 1847. G.S.2.
Anna L., w. A. Mason, —— —, 1847. G.S.2.

PATTERSON, Jonathan, s. Andrew and Anna, April 2, 1788.

PEABODY, Hannah Crosby, d. Isaak K. and Sally, bap. June 22, 1821. C.R.
Otis Willard, s. [Isaac?] Kitteridge and Sally, March 16, 1815.
Phila Millar, d. Isaac K. and Sally, bap. June 22, 1821. C.R.

PERRY, Caleb, —— —, 1774. G.S.2.
George Elliot, s. John and Ann H., July 4, 1845.

PHELPS, Annie R., w. Charles C., —— —, 1848. G.S.2.
Charles Carroll, s. Leander and Lucy, July 14, 1838.
George, s. Leander and Lucy, July 24, 1842.
Janette, d. Leander and Lucy, Feb. 24, 1836.

PHILIPS (see Phillips), Jedediah, s. John and Huldah, Nov. 1, 1779.

PHILIPS, Joanna, d. Samuel and Joanna [Jemima, c.r.], March 10, 1781.
Jonas, s. Samuel and Joanna [Jemima, c.r.], Aug. 13, 1776.
Josiah, s. Samuel and Joanna [Jemima, c.r.], Sept. 25, 1778.
Zeokiah, s. Samuel and Joanna, June 29, 1772.
PHILLAPS, Andrew, s. Nathaniel and Mary, Aug. 10, 1784.
PHILLIPS (see above), Abner Smith, s. Seth and Ruth, Oct. 29, 1814.
Angeline Abigail, d. Jonas A. and Abigail B., April 8, 1840.
Asa Wilson, d. Seth and Ruth, June 29, 1809.
Betty, d. John and Huldah, Nov. 25, 1781.
Daniel, s. Nathaniel and Mary, March 6, 1793.
David Abner, s. Abner S. and Lucinda, Oct. 4, 1848.
Jonas Allen, s. Seth and Ruth, Oct. 8, 1811.
Lucy M., d. Abner S. and Lucinda, Nov. 6, 1845.
Lydia, d. Samuel and Joanna, May 27, 1785.
Mary Ann, d. Alonzo D. and Mary A., Feb. 20, 1847.
Sarah, d. Samuel and Joanna [Jemima, c.r.], Aug. 1, 1774.
Soprhonia Idelia, d. Seth and Ruth, Dec. 31, 1805.
———, s. Alonzo D. and Mary Ann, Aug. 11, 1845.

PIERCE, Albert T., s. Josiah G. and Lydia, April 1, 1824.
Arba, s. James and Lois M., Aug. 3, 1833.
Elianor, d. Joseph and Eleanor, May 20, 1797.
Fanny B., d. Josiah G. and Lydia, March 14, 1821.
Franklin, s. Joseph and Eleanor, March 18, 1794.
Joseph, s. Franklin and Eleanor, May 29, 1825.
Leander G., s. Josiah G. and Lydia, Nov. 17, 1822.
Lewis T., s. Josiah G. and Lydia, June 14, 1828.
Lydia E., d. Josiah G. and Lydia, Oct. 31, 1825.
Patty, d. Joseph and Eleanor, April 8, 1783. At Shrewsbury, North Parish.
Polly, d. Joseph and Eleanor, March 11, 1791.
Serephinia, d. Joseph and Eleanor, March 20, 1786.
Watson, s. James and Lois M., Oct. 21, 1835.
William Crawford, s. Franklin and Eleanor, Jan. 28, 1818.
William Crawford, s. Franklin and Eleanor, May 1, 1820.

PIKE, Albert L., ———, 1844. G.S.2.
Edwin Amasa, s. Silas and Clarissa, June 18, 1847.
Martha, a servant child to Edward and Doratha Foster, bap. April 24, 1774. c.r.
Mary L., w. Albert L., ———, 1839. G.S.2.

ATHOL BIRTHS.

PIKE, Sophronia, d. Joseph and Eliza, Jan. 11, 1846.
——, s. Mason and Abigail, May 7, 1845.

PIPER, James M., —— —, 1813. G.S.1.
Sally, w. James M., —— —, 1799. G.S.1.

PITTS, Harriet K., w. Samuel B., Nov. 27, 1828. G.S.2.
Samuel B., Sept. 7, 1824. G.S.2.

POLLARD, Ivers E., —— —, 1842. G.S.2.
Lucy, w. William, —— —, 1801. G.S.6.
Mary, w. Ivers E., —— —, 1840. G.S.2.
William, —— —, 1796. G.S.6.

POND, Esther L., w. Francis L., —— —, 1840. G.S.2.
Francis L., —— —, 1834. G.S.2.
Mary F., w. George S., Jan. 22, 1841. G.S.1.
M. R., —— —, 1833. G.S.2.
M. R., —— —, 1838. G.S.2.

PRATT, Emily, d. Alden and Achsah [Archisa in dup.], Jan. 9, 1844.

PRESON (see Presson) [Preston in C.R.], Mahala, d. Benjamin and Abigail, Feb. 6, 1773.
[Preston in C.R.], Mary, d. Benjamin and Abigail, July 10, 1769.
Persicles, s. Benjamin and Abigail, Jan. 15, 1762.
[Preston in C.R.], Phebe, s. Benjamin and Abigail, May 4, 1764.
Samuel [Samuel Bowen Preston in C.R.], s. Benjamin and Abigail, Oct. 30, 1766.
[Preston in C.R.], Stephen, s. Benjamin and Abigail, Sept. 10, 1775.
[Preston in C.R.], Zaccheus, s. Benjamin and Abigail, Feb. 22, 1779.

PRESSON (see Preson and below), Durham, s. Percicles? and Martha, Jan. 24, 1811.
Emerly Emerson, d. William and Lydia Drury, March 12, 1824.
Letsy, d. Percide? and Martha, March 14, 1803.
Lucinda, d. Percide? and Martha, June 8, 1806.
Mary, d. Percide and Martha, Jan. 11, 1809.
Sarah, d. Percide? and Martha, June 18, 1801.

PRESTON (see above), Abigail, d. Percide? and Martha, March 17, 1799.
Daniel, s. Percide? and Martha, Dec. 10, 1794.
Oliver, s. Percide? and Martha, Jan. 12, 1797.

PRIEST, Angie M., w. H. Alonzo, —— —, 1834. G.S.1.
H. Alonzo, —— —, 1840. G.S.1.

ATHOL BIRTHS.

PROCTOR, Anne Maria, d. Joseph and Mary H., Feb. 16, 1812.
Charles, s. Joseph and Mary H., Dec. 5, 1815.
Frances Jane, d. Joseph and Mary H., April 12, 1820.
Harriet Humphrey, d. Joseph and Mary H., March 31, 1814.
Joseph Henry, s. Joseph and Mary H., Feb. 20, 1822.
Maria Sophia, d. Joseph and Mary, Jan. 17, 1817.
Mary H., —— —, 1840?.

PROUTY, Frances M., d. Adam and Hannah, June 14, 1829.
George C., s. Adam and Hannah, Dec. 14, 1831.
George Henry, s. Adam and Hannah, June 9, 1848.
George P., s. Adam and Hannah, July 2, 1836.
Harriet Maria, d. Adam and Hannah, Nov. 7, 1843.
Maria F., d. Adam and Hannah, April 1, 1834.
Mary F., d. Adam and Hannah, Feb. 22, 1828.
Sarah J., d. Adam and Hannah, May 9, 1838.

PUFFER, Charles N., s. Edward A. and Almira, Oct. 4, 1849.

PUTNAM, Alice, w. Bela W., May —, 1801. G.S.5.
Bela Addison, s. Bela W. and Alice, April 16, 1828.
Joel Morton, s. Bela W. and Alice, Dec. 26, 1829.
Mary A., w. J. M., —— —, 1829. G.S.5.

RAINER (see Rayner), Jacob Stone, s. Jacob and Sobrina, Oct. 28, 1844.

RANDALL, Andrew Jackson, s. Stephen and Lois, April 24, 1815.
Stephen P., s. Stephen and Lois, Oct. 21, 1809. In Orange.

RAYMOND (see Reymond), Abigal, d. Freeborn and Mary, June 11, 1772.
Anne [Anna in C.R.], d. Freeborn and Mary, March 17, 1768.
Anna, d. Freeborn and Sarah, June 13, 1795.
Anna, d. Edward and ——, bap. Oct. 6, 1805. C.R.
Daniel, s. Freeborn and Sarah, Feb. 26, 1787.
Edward, s. Edward and Janney, March 17, 1805.
Elizabeth, d. Freeborn and Sarah, April 20, 1779.
Elizebeth, d. Edward and Jenne Oliver his wife, bap. Aug. 5, 1810. C.R.
Freeborn, s. Freeborn and Mary, June 4, 1765.
Freeborn F., s. Freeborn Jr. and Jain, Dec. 2, 1806.
Freeman C., s. Freeborn Jr. and Jain, Dec. 13, 1801.
Kendal, s. Edward and Janney, Oct. 15, 1799.
Lois K., d. Freeborn Jr. and Jain, Sept. 2, 1803.
Lucy, d. Freeborn and Sarah, May 12, 1785.

ATHOL BIRTHS. 73

RAYMOND, Lydia, d. Freeborn and Sarah, April 27, 1783.
Lydia [Lidea in c.r.], d. Freeborn and Sarah, Oct. 23, 1788.
Molley, d. Freeborn and Mary, April 2, 1764.
Nathan, s. Edward and ———, bap. March 1, 1772. c.r.
Oliver Powers, s. Freeborn and Sarah, Jan. 27, 1793.
Pattey, d. Freeborn and Mary, July 4, 1770.
Paul, s. Freeborn and Sarah, Oct. 29, 1780.
Polly, d. Edward and Janney, March 19, 1808.
Rachel, d. Freeborn and ———, bap. Feb. 24, 1792. c.r.
Sall [Salle in c.r.], d. Freeborn and Mary, Dec. 26, 1766.
Susanna, d. Freeborn and Mary, Dec. 26, 1774.
Susanna, d. Edward and Janney, Aug. 12, 1803.
Thatcher R., s. Freeborn Jr. and Jain, March 9, 1808.
Wymon Graves, s. Freborn and Lucinda, Jan. 31, 1788.
Wyman Graves, an adopted s. Abner Graves and his wife, bap. July 20, 1789. c.r. [Probably same as above.]

RAYNER (see Rainer), Abby Stone, d. Jacob S. and Sabrina, Aug. 26, 1837. At South Reading.
Adelaid Agusta, d. Jacob S. and Sabrina, June 27, 1842.
Alphonso Benton, s. Jacob S. and Sabrina, July 10, 1840. At South Reading.
Ann Maria, d. Jacob S. and Sabrina, May 11, 1836. At South Reading.

REED, Charles Badger, s. Charles and Harriot M., July 20, 1823.
George Armstrong, s. Charles and Harriot M., Aug. 4, 1825.
Joseph Alonzo, s. Charles and Harriot M., Oct. 20, 1827.

REYMOND (see Raymond), Abigail, d. Edward and Janney, Aug. 6, 1785.
Anna, d. Edward and Janney, Feb. 19, 1784.
Betcy, d. Edward and Janney, Aug. 1, 1788.
Cinda, d. Edward and Janney, Sept. 30, 1790.
Lois, d. Edward and Janney, April 19, 1797.
Patty, d. Edward and Janney, Sept. 1, 1792.
Salley, d. Edward and Janney, July 17, 1795.

RICE, Abner Stimpson, s. Jonas and Olive, Nov. 10, 1842.
Benjamin, s. Uriah and Rachel, bap. July 5, 1767. c.r.
Eliza Melvina, d. Jonas and Olive, April 29, 1834.
Elvira Jeanett, d. Jonas and Olive, Nov. 27, 1825.
Ephraim, ——— —, 1833. g.s.4.
Henary [Henry, c.r.], s. Luke and Prudence, Nov. 18, 1773.
James Madison, s. Jonas and Olive, Sept. 10, 1827.

ATHOL BIRTHS.

RICE, Jane, d. Aaron and Lydia, Dec. 7, 1843. In Petersham. Dup.
John Emory, s. Jonas R. and Olive, March 31, 1845.
Lucinda Faustina, d. Jonas and Olive, Sept. 13, 1838. Dup.
Mary, d. Luke and Prudence, Jan. 18, 1771.
Nancy, d. Samuel and Nancy, Jan. 24, 1794.
Prudence, d. Luke and Prudence, bap. June 30, 1776. C.R.
Tyla Ann, d. Jonas and Olive, Jan. 26, 1830.
Violaty, d. Luke and Prudence, Jan. 24, 1773.
William, s. Luke and Prudence, Aug. 27, 1772.
William, s. Luke and Prudence, bap. May 10, 1778. C.R.

RICH, Augustine A., s. Robert and Almira, Dec. 25, 1844.
Bette, d. Zacheus and ———, bap. July 20, 1777. C.R.
Cratus ?, s. Robert T. and Almira, March 1, 1847.
David, s. David and Hannah, April 7, 1795.
Elcy, d. David and Hannah, Oct. 1, 1785.
Hannah, d. David and Hannah, March 9, 1799.
Harrison, ———, 1835. G.S.2.
Isaac, s. David and Hannah, April 28, 1790.
Joshua, s. David and Hannah, March 28, 1797.
[Rice ?], Liza, d. Jonathan and Thankfull, bap. June 30, 1776. C.R.
Mehitable, d. David and Hannah, April 28, 1788.
[Rice ?] Nehemiah, s. Jonathan and Thankfull, bap. June 5, 1774. C.R.
Obidiah, s. David, bap. May 24, 1801. C.R.
Polly, d. David and Hannah, Nov. 14, 1792.
Rachel, d. Zaccheus and Jemima, bap. Aug. 15, 1778. C.R.
Rebeckah, d. David and Hannah, Feb. 26, 1786.
Ruth, d. Zecehaus and Jemima, June 4, 1775. C.R.
Sally, d. David and Hannah, June 22, 1781.
Sally, d. Capt. and wife of Gerry, bap. April 13, 1788. C.R.
———, d. Robert T. and Almira, April 1, 1849.

RICHARDS, Caroline A., d. William B. and Laura A., Dec. 28, 1847.
George N., ———, 1830. G.S.2.
Jeremiah M., Aug. 31, 1806. G.S.2.
Judith C., w. Jeremiah M., July 11, 1814. G.S.2.
Mary Greenleaf, w. George N., ———, 1831. G.S.2.

RICHARDSON, Abbie J. C., w. Lysander, ———, 1838. G.S.1.
Almera, d. Isaiah and ———, bap. Aug. 3, 1794. C.R.
Ann H., ———, 1825. G.S.6.
Betcy, d. Amos and Martha, April 16, 1796.
Charles Frederick, s. Nathaniel and Emerline, Sept. 28, 1839.

ATHOL BIRTHS. 75

RICHARDSON, Charles Orwell, s. Wyman and Arethusa, Nov. 13, 1839.
Delavan, s. Luna B. and Mary, Sept. 8, 1840.
Eastor [Esther in C.R.], d. Parson and Hannah, Aug. 30, 1777.
Emily Ann, d. Lysander and Amanda, July 5, 1833.
Esther, d. Isaiah and ———, bap. Aug. 10, 1788. C.R.
Frederick Douglas, s. Lysander and Amanda, Feb. 2, 1846.
George Henry, s. Nathaniel and Emerline, Dec. 30, 1831. At Peterborough, N.H.
Hamilton, twin s. Lysander and Amanda, May 9, 1839.
Hannibal, twin s. Lysander and Amanda, May 9, 1839.
Homer, s. Lysander and Amanda, April 28, 1837.
Hosea, s. Lysander and Amanda, Nov. 7, 1834.
Isaiah, s. Isaiah and ———, bap. Aug. 29, 1790. C.R.
Isaiah, s. Isaih and ———, bap. April 1, 1792. C.R.
Jesse, s. Amos and Martha, March 4, 1779. In Petersham.
Joseph, s. Amos and Martha, Aug. 30, 1784. In Petersham.
Lyman Collins, s. Wyman and Arethusa, Nov. 26, 1831. At Corinth, Orange Co., N.Y.
Senaca Merrill, s. Wyman and Arethusa, Dec. 5, 1829. At Corinth, Orange Co., N.Y.
Margaret, d. Isaiah and ———, bap. March 17, 1788. C.R.
Matilda, d. Isaiah and ———, bap. March 17, 1788. C.R.
Martin, —— —, 1818. G.S.6.
Mary, d. Isaiah and Ester, bap. Dec. 22, [1799]. C.R.
Olive, d. Amos and Martha, May 8, 1792.
Patty, d. Amos and Martha, March 4, 1788. In Petersham.
Perrson, s. Parson and Hannah, May 16, 1779.
Polly, d. Amos and Martha, Sept. 27, 1777. At Barre.
Solon Oscar, s. Wyman and Arethusa, July 3, 1828. At Corinth, Orange Co., N.Y.
Willard, s. Isaiah and ———, bap. Aug. 20, 1797. C.R.
William Augustus, s. Wyman and Arethusa, Dec. 20, 1833.
———, s. Lysanda and Amanda, June 14, 1844.

ROBBINS, Abigail, d. Luke and Mary, Feb. 19, 1785.
Chloe, d. Luke and Mary, bap. May 20, 1790. C.R.
Joshua, s. Luke and Mary, Oct. 10, 1777.
Levi, s. Luke and Mary, Aug. 26, 1775.
Lucy, d. Luke and Mary, bap. March 2, 1788. C.R.
Martha, d. Luke and Mary, May 21, 1780.
Mary, d. Luke and Mary, June 30, 1782.

ROBINS, Daniel, s. Luke and ———, bap. Aug. 26, 1792. C.R.
Martha, d. Luke and ———, bap. Dec. 6, 1795. C.R.

ROGAN, Rev. Daniel H., —— —, 1830. G.S.2.
Harriet E. Hunt, w. Rev. Daniel H., —— —, 1832. G.S.2.

ROGERS, Abel, s. Abel and Sarah, bap. July 1, 1770. C.R.
Abel, —— —, 1771. G.S.6. [Probably same as above.]
Anner, w. Abel, —— —, 1764. G.S.6.
John, —— —, 1800. G.S.6.
Lucy A. Draper, w. William C., —— —, 1832. G.S.2.
William, s. Abel and Sarah, bap. June 6, 1779. C.R.
William C., —— —, 1828. G.S.2.
See Brock, Cordelia Celia.

ROWE, Charles H., —— —, 1846. G.S.2.
Leonora Washburn, w. Charles H., —— —, 1849. G.S.2.

RUMBLE, Lois, was bap. (upon the account of Thomas and Lenard Lord her master and mistress), June 10, 1766. C.R.

SANDERS, Abiah, d. John and Elizabeth, bap. Dec. 29, 1765. C.R.
Asah, s. Benjamin and Hannah, bap. Nov. 13, 1763. C.R.
Cloe, d. John and Elizabeth, bap. June 12, 1768. C.R.
Elizabeth, d. John and Elizabeth, bap. Jan. 26, 1774. C.R.
Elizabeth Ward, d. John and Elizabeth, bap. May 14, 1775. C.R.
Joel, s. John and Elizabeth, bap. June 23, 1771. C.R.
John Jr., s. John and Elizabeth, bap. May 10, 1778. C.R.
Samuel Grove, s. Benjamin and Hannah, bap. Jan. 29, 1769. C.R.

SANDERSON, Almira, d. James J. and Lydia, Oct. 27, 1821.
Coleman, s. Coleman and Hannah, Oct. 8, 1785. At New Marlborough, [N.H.?].
Louisa, d. James J. and Lydia, April 14, 1816.
Nabbe, d. John and Elizabeth, bap. Sept. 4, 1763. C.R.
Susan, d. James J. and Lydia, July 4, 1820.
Zebina, s. Benjamin and Hannah, bap. April 6, 1766. C.R.

SARTLE (see Sattel, Sawtel, etc.), Henry, Tertius, s. Henry and Jerusha Jr., bap. July 23, 1769. C.R.
Jerusha, d. Henry Jr. and Jerusha, bap. April 18, 1773. C.R.
Levi, s. Henry and Jerusha, bap. Nov. 25, 1770. C.R.

SATTEL (see Sawtel, etc.), Elijah, s. Richard and Sarah, Feb. 19, 1779.

SAUL, Eliza Hamlet, d. Thomas Jr. and Lucy, Sept. 11, 1840.

SAWIN, ——, s. Emory, —— —, ——. [1849.]

ATHOL BIRTHS.

SAWTEL (see Sartle, Sattel, Sawtell, Sawtle), Jerusha, d. Richard and Sarah, July 1, 1783.
Joseph, s. Richard and Sarah, April 13, 1777.
Richard, s. Richard and Sarah, Jan. 2, 1781.

SAWTELL, Frances J., w. J. Franklin, —— ——, 1820. G.S.5.
J. Franklin, —— ——, 1821. G.S.5.
Miriam C., w. J. Franklin, —— ——, 1839. G.S.5.
Rebecca, —— ——, 1790. G.S.5.

SAWTLE (see above), Rufus, s. Henry and Jerusha, bap. Nov. 13, 1774. C.R.

SAWYER, Charles W., —— ——, 1839. G.S.2.
Ellen Sylvia, d. William and Betsey, June 11, 1848.
Lucy M., w. Charles W., —— ——, 1841. G.S.2.
Martha Maria, d. Milton and Thankful, July 16, 1839.

SCOT, Irena, w. Oscar A., —— ——, 1830. G.S.1.
Oscar A., —— ——, 1830. G.S.1.

SEDGER, Sarah Green, d. William D. and Arethhusa, April 12, 1838.

SHEARER, Susan A., w. Thomas D., Aug. 12, 1826. G.S.1.
Thomas D., Oct. 22, 1816. G.S.1.

SHERWIN, Asa, s. Sylvenus and Ellinor, Jan. 14, 1791.
Lemuell, s. Sylvenus and Ellinor, March 14, 1789. At Winchendon.
Theodosius, d. Sylvenus and Ellinor, Jan. 4, 1788. At Winchendon.
Thomas, s. Sylvenus and Ellinor, Aug. 20, 1792.

SIBLEY, A. F., —— ——, 1847. G.S.2.
Charles W., s. Willard and Luthera, Nov. 9, 1849.
Clarissa Jane, d. Sumner and Clarissa B., April 28, 1839.
Eliza, d. Pearley and Polly, Aug. 25, 1820.
Emaly, d. Pearley and Polly, Feb. 23, 1813.
Emily, d. Sumner and Clarissa B., March 28, 1832.
George P., s. Willard and Luthera, Aug. 25, 1846.
George Pearley, s. Gideon and Elvira, Jan. 16, 1830.
Gideon, s. Pearley and Polly, July 2, 1799. At Sutton.
Luthera, w. Willard, —— ——, 1825. G.S.1.
Maria, d. Gideon and Elvira, Oct. 16, 1826.
Mary, d. Pearley and Polly, Sept. 9, 1810.
Mary, d. Sumner and Clarissa B., March 14, 1834.
Nancy, d. Pearley and Polly, Oct. 20, 1818.
Paul, s. Pearley and Polly, Aug. 21, 1808.

SIBLEY, Pearley, s. Pearley and Polly, June 23, 1802.
Pearley, s. Pearley and Polly, Oct. 14, 1803.
Sumner, s. Pearley and Polly, April 21, 1806.
Sumner, s. Sumner and Clarissa B., May 28, 1836.
Willard, s. Amos and Prudence, Sept. 29, 1810.
Willard, s. Pearley and Polly, Jan. 15, 1816.

SIMONDS (see Simons), Charles Albert, s. Albert F. and Sarah W., Oct. 13, 1842.
Julia Annett, d. Lucius B. and Ann, Aug. 14, 1845.
Laura Isabella, d. Lucius B. and Anna, Nov. 2, 1847.
Sarah Janet, d. Albert and Sarah, April 2, 1848.
———, s. Albert and Sarah, Feb. 9, 1846.

SIMONS (see above) [Simonds in dup.], Joseph Henry, s. Lucius B. and Ann E., Sept. 3, 1843. Dup.

SKINNER, Osrow, s. Benjamin C. and Mary R., Oct. 5, 1843.
———, s. Benjamin C. and Mary, June 16, 1846.

SLOAN, G. P., ——— ——, 1843. G.S.I.
J. W., ——— ——, 1817. G.S.I.

SMITH, Aaron, s. Aaron and Abigail, bap. May 11, 1755. C.R.
Aaron, s. Aaron and Tirzah, Dec. 24, 1794.
Abigail, d. Aaron and Tirzah, Sept. 28, 1779.
Abigail, w. Luther, bap. Aug. 6, 1809. C.R.
Abijah, s. Caleb and Submit, Nov. 3, 1764.
Achsah, d. Aaron and Tirzah, Sept. 2, 1781.
Adelaide S., d. Lynds and Fanny M., July 20, 1836.
Adin Holbrook, s. Joshua and Hannah, June 19, 1815.
Ann Eliza, w. Warren E., ——— ——, 1837. G.S.I.
Anna, d. Luther and Abigail, Nov. 26, 1817.
Anna Maynard, d. Nathaniel and Arathusa, Aug. 22, 1805.
Altemirah A., ch. Lynds and Fanny M., April 28, 1835.
Asa, s. Luther and Abigail, June 23, 1830.
Betcy, d. Asa and Lydia, Oct. 29, 1780.
Caleb, s. Ephraim and Martha, April 6, 1739.
Caleb Jr., s. Caleb and Submit, bap. Dec. 24, 1780. C.R.
Carilener, w. Francis B., ——— ——, 1824. G.S.2.
Charles, s. Luther and Abigail, July 10, 1808.
Charles, s. Luther and Abigail, Nov. 25, 1826.
Charles Webster, s. Charles S. and Abigail, Nov. 9, 1848.
Clarrisa [Clara in C.R.], d. Aaron and Tirzah, Dec. 6, 1792.
Collins, s. Ebenezer and Ruth, Aug. 19, 1834.
Dolly, d. Asa and Lydia, April 3, 1778.

ATHOL BIRTHS. 79

Smith, Dolly, d. Luther and Abigail, July 10, 1820.
Ebenezer, —— —, 1798. G.S.6.
Eliel, s. Moses and Elizabeth, Nov. 19, 1776.
Elihu, s. Caleb and Submit, Jan. 18, 1772.
Elisha, s. Deacon Aaron and Mary, bap. Aug. 6, 1777. C.R.
Elisha Lord [Loud in C.R.], s. Aaron and Tirzah, March 5, 1799.
Ellen Elizabeth, d. Adin H. and Mary C., Sept. 15, 1840.
Emaretta, d. Lynds and Fanny, Aug. 27, 1844.
Ephram, s. Caleb and Submit, Nov. 30, 1770.
Erastus, Oct. 4, 1828. G.S.2.
Fayette, s. Ebenezer and Ruth, June 19, 1825.
Francis B., —— —, 1819. G.S.2.
Gardner, s. Nathaniel and Arathusa, April 3, 1809.
George, s. Luther and Abigail, April 15, 1810.
George Waldo, s. George and Betsey H., May 1, 1842.
Giels [Giles in C.R.], s. Caleb and Submit, March 16, 1770.
Hannah, w. Joshua, May 15, 1779. G.S.1.
Harriet Angaline, d. Gand ? and Charlotte, Nov. 9, 1846.
Hepzibah, d. Epheraim and Martha, Feb. 9, 1749.
Horace S., s. Horace S. and Louisa M., Feb. 25, 1849.
Jane, —— —, 1830. G.S.2.
Joel, s. Caleb and Submit, May 21, 1766.
Jonathan, s. Dea. Aaron and Mary, bap. June 21, 1772. C.R.
Joshua, s. Caleb and Submit, May 16, 1768.
Julia Elthea [Esther ? in dup.], d. George and Betsey H., Jan. 19, 1838.
Justus [Justice in C.R.], s. Caleb and Submit, Feb. 10, 1774.
Laura Elisabeth, d. George and Betsey H., March 29, 1840.
Lemira, d. Joshua and Hannah [Hannah F., G.S.1.], April 19, 1804.
Lois, d. Aaron and Tirzah, April 5, 1797.
Lucretia, —— —, 1844. G.S.1.
Lucy, d. Joshua and Hannah [Hannah F., G.S.1.], March 11, 1806.
Luse [Lucy in C.R.], d. Ephraim and Martha, July 22, 1751.
Luther, s. Asa and Lydia, June 14, 1783.
Luthera, d. Ebenezer and Ruth, Sept. 20, 1828.
Lydia, d. Ephraim and Martha, March 7, 1746.
Lydia, d. Asa and Lydia, Nov. 13, 1787.
Lydia Haven, d. Stephen and Susanna, Dec. 21, 1767.
Lynds, s. Asa and Lydia, June 9, 1771.
Lynds, s. Luther and Abigail, Oct. 12, 1806.
Maria, d. Joshua and Hannah [F. ?], June 4, 1800.
Maria L., d. Russell and Maria, Sept. 13, 1846.
Martha, d. Ephraim and Martha, April 17, 1737.
Martha Jane, d. Adin H. and Mary C., May 10, 1839.

SMITH, Martin Hamilton, s. Russell and Maria, Dec. 9, 1841.
Mary, d. Caleb and Submit, Oct. 28, 1783.
Mary, d. Ebenezer and Ruth, April 16, 1836.
Mary [Jones ?, Gaine in c.r.], d. Aaron and Tirzah, Feb. 8, 1784.
Mary Maynard, d. Gardner M. and Mary A., June 1, 1849.
Moses, s. Aaron and Abigail, bap. July 14, 1751. c.r.
Moses, s. Moses and Elizabeth, Dec. 2, 1774.
Nancy, d. Aaron and Tirzah, April 12, 1788.
Nathaniel, s. Nathaniel and Arathusa, Jan. 1, 1812.
Pamelia, d. Asa and Lydia, bap. July 18, 1773. c.r.
Persis, d. Asa and Lydia, April 18, 1785.
Polly, d. Joshua and Hannah, Feb. 6, 1802.
Polly B., d. Joshua and Hannah F., Feb. 6, 1802. g.s.1.
Rhoda, s. Ephraim and Martha, March 31, 1741.
Rosella [Rosellah in dup.] Maria, d. George and Betsey H., Aug. 31, 1834.
Royal, s. Ebenezer and Ruth, Dec. 1, 1827.
Rubin [Reuben in c.r.], s. Caleb and Submit, April 21, 1763.
Russell, s. Luther and Abigail, Sept. 11, 1812.
Sally, d. Aaron and Tirzah, Oct. 17, 1790.
Sally Freeman, d. Nathaniel and Arathusa, Nov. 29, 1806.
Sally Freeman, d. Nathaniel and Arathusa, Dec. 1, 1813.
Samuel Earl, s. Lafayette and Amelia E., March 2, 1848.
Sarah A. C., w. Erastus ?, Sept. 20, 1831. g.s.2.
Sarah E., d. Lafayette and Amelia E., Sept. 30, 1846.
Solomon, s. Ephraim and Martha, Dec. 25, 1753.
Stephen, s. Ephraim and Martha, Sept. 17, 1743.
Stilman, s. Luther and Abigail, March 27, 1815.
Stilman, s. Luther and Abigail, June 29, 1823.
Submit, d. Caleb and Submit, July 8, 1779.
Sumner, s. Ebenezer and Ruth, May 8, 1832.
Theodore H., s. Lynds and Fanny M., June 15, 1841.
Tirzah, d. Aaron and Tirzah, April 26, 1786.
Warren E., —— ——, 1835. g.s.1.
William A., s. Ebenezer and Ruth, Oct. 17, 1843.
Wilson, s. Ebenezer and Ruth, Oct. 24, 1830.
——, d. Adin H. and Louisa, April 11, 1847.
——, d. Russell and Maria, April 27, 1849.

SNOW, Henry Everett, s. John H. and Louisa, Nov. 2, 1837.
——, s. John H. and Louisa, Jan. 24, 1849.

SOUTHARD, Emma Jane [Emmagene L. on g.s.], d. Gilbert and Lucy A., April 12, 1849.
Gilbert, —— ——, 1820. g.s.2.

SOUTHARD, Lucy A., w. Gilbert, —— —, 1825. G.S.2.
O. Clarence, —— —, 1845. G.S.2.

SPAULDING, Ellen Taylor, —— —, 1834. G.S.2.

SPOONER, Abby, d. Alexander K. and Jane, June 17, 1843. In Deerfield. Dup.
Abigail, d. Asa and Dolly, Sept. 10, 1809.
Abigail, Sept. —, 1810. G.S.2. [Perhaps same as above.]
Albert Josiah, s. Alden and Dolly, June 21, 1824.
Alexexander Kutousoff, s. Asa and Dolly, Jan. 14, 1815.
Byron Flagg, s. Alden and Dolly, Dec. 28, 1838.
Cathârine, d. Asa and Dolly, Jan. 11, 1821.
Charles Milton, s. Asa and Dolly, May 1, 1827.
Edwin Church, s. Alden and Dolly, April 6, 1834.
George Alden, s. Alden and Dolly, Aug. 21, 1821.
Henry Augustus, s. Alden and Dolly, Dec. 14, 1829.
Jane Greene, d. Alden and Dolly, Feb. 1, 1823.
Lucy, d. Asa and Dolly, Nov. 4, 1816.
Samuel Clapp, s. Alden and Dolly, April 10, 1831.
Samuel Wing, s. Asa and Dolly, Feb. 23, 1812.
Solon Webster, s. Alden and Dolly, Aug. 14, 1826.
William Andrew, s. Alden and Dolly, April 2, 1828.

SPRAGUE, Asa Flood, s. Isaael and Phebe, bap. Nov. 3, 1765. C.R.
Caleb, s. Joshua and Lois, Sept. 27, 1809.
Charles Wright, s. Ephraim S. and Sarah T., June 18, 1831.
Dorathy, d. Israel and Phebe, Dec. 16, 1762.
Edwin Loring, s. George and Nancy, July 6, 1838.
Ephraim Stockwell, s. Joshua and Lois, Dec. 14, 1801.
Esther, d. Israel and Phebe, Oct. 28, 1768.
Francis Henry, s. Ephraim S. and Sarah T., June 18, 1834.
Francis James, s. Ephraim S. and Sarah Ann, June 18, 1843.
George, s. Joshua and Lois, Sept. 5, 1796.
George Lorenzo, s. George and Nancy, April 6, 1828.
Harriet Eliza, d. Joseph O. and Hannah S., Jan. 14, 1849.
Hasey Floyd, s. Israel and Phebe, Nov. 1, 1765.
Henry Harrison, s. George and Nancy, Aug. 1, 1841.
Israel, s. Israel and Ruth, Sept. 21, 1784
James Thompson, s. Ephraim S. and Sarah T., Dec. 14, 1837.
Joseph, s. Joshua and Lois, Oct. 2, 1794.
Joshua, Sept. 2, 1767. G.S.2.
Joshua, s. Joshua and Lois, Nov. 2, 1804.
Leander Milton, s. George and Nancy, Oct. 19, 1832.

SPRAGUE, Lois Stockwell, w. Joshua, Aug. 19, 1767. G.S.2.
Loisa, d. Joshua and Lois, March 2, 1803.
Loring, s. Joshua and Lois, March 23, 1792.
Louisa, d. Joshua and Lois, —— ——, 1803. G.S.2.
Lucius Knight, s. George and Nancy, Aug. 7, 1836.
Lucy, d. Hasey Flaud and Mary, Nov. 5, 1795.
Malinda, d. Joshua and Lois, June 1, 1807.
Martha Angeline, d. George and Nancy, Oct. 12, 1829.
Sally, d. Joshua and Lois, Oct. 15, 1798.

STACY, Rebeccah, d. Samuel and Patience, bap. April 19, 1772. C.R.
Rhoda, d. Samuel and Patience, bap. June 19, 1774. C.R.

STAPLES, Nancy, w. Nelson L., —— ——, 1809. G.S.5.

STEARNS, Adison [Addison Wilder in C.R.], s. Samuel and Lydia, March 31, 1815.
Ephraim, s. Samuel and Lydia, July 19, 1799.
George Mason, s. Samuel and Lydia, Nov. 20, 1812.
J. Henry, —— ——, 1844. G.S.2.
James Clements, s. Samuel and Lydia, July 10, 1817.
Lydia Amanda, d. Samuel and Lydia, Jan. 20, 1810.
Mary, d. Samuel and Lydia, Oct. 18, 1807.
Prosper, s. Samuel and Lydia, Nov. 11, 1804.
Samuel, s. Samuel and Lydia, July 6, 1801.

STEPHENS, Susanna, d. Jesse and ——, bap. Oct. 11, 1789. C.R.

STEVENS, Anna Judson, d. Isaac and Eunice Backus, March 11, 1834. G.S.2.
Eunice, d. Jacob and ——, bap. July 11, 1784. C.R.
Eunice Backus, w. Isaac, Feb. 27, 1796. G.S.2.
Isaac, April 12, 1792. G.S.2.
Marcia, d. Isaac and Eunice Backus, March 6, 1826. G.S.2.
Timothy, s. Jacob and Dorcas, Oct. 19, 1780. [Bap. March 11, 1781. C.R.]
Timothy, s. Jacob and ——, bap. Nov. 17, 1782. C.R.

STIMPSON, Abner Twichell, s. John and Tyla, April 16, 1819.
James Humphreys, s. John and Tyla, Feb. 23, 1824.
Mary Ann, d. John and Tyla, Jan. 4, 1815.
Stephen, s. Elias and ——, bap. Oct. 25, 1795. C.R.

STOCKWALL, Lois, d. Ephraim and Sarah, bap. Sept. 27, 1767. C.R.

ATHOL BIRTHS.

STOCKWELL, Adalaide, d. Elisha and Melissa S., Dec. 24, 1841.
Aziba, d. Ephraim and Sarah, bap. Oct. 17, 1762. C.R.
Charles Harvey, s. Ammi and Susan, June 30, 1838.
Cyrus, s. Noah Jr. and Polly, April 29, 1809.
Diantha P., w. George, —— ——, 1842. G.S.2.
Elijah, s. James and Elizabeth, bap. Nov. 22, 1772. C.R.
Elijah, s. Ephraim and Sarah, bap. June 8, 1774. C.R.
Elishar, s. John and Betsy, Oct. 20, 1816
Elizabeth, d. John and Betsy, Sept. 14, 1827.
Elvira Idelia, d. Sylvester and Polly, March 6, 1841.
Ephraim, s. Ephraim and Sarah, bap. June 24, 1764. C.R.
Frances Adaline, d. Sylvester and Polly, July 20, 1835.
Francis Judson, s. Noah and Polly, July 25, 1830.
Freeland, s. Noah Jr. and Polly, March 19, 1808.
Freeman, s. Simon and Dolley, Dec. 31, 1801.
George, s. Cyrus and Ruth [B.?], Dec. 27, 1836.
Harriet, w. Harrison, —— ——, 1844. G.S.2.
Harrison, s. Freeland and Minerva P., Dec. 26, 1839.
Isabella, d. Josiah and ——————, June 3, 1823.
Jane Seaver, w. Stillman, —— ——, 1808. G.S.2.
John, s. John and Betsy, Oct. 4, 1836.
Joseph, s. John and Betsy, Sept. 5, 1823.
Joseph E., s. Sylvester and Polly, Sept. 1, 1847.
Josiah, s. Ephraim and Sarah, bap. Dec. 30, 1775. C.R.
Josiah Bradford, s. Josiah and ——————, Feb. 14, 1825.
Lawson, s. Simon and Dolley, Feb. 24, 1800.
Lucy Ann, d. Joseph and Dorothy, June 19, 1830.
Lydia, d. Ephraim and Sarah, bap. Feb. 23, 1772. C.R.
Marcy, d. Simon and Dolley, Dec. 2, 1803.
Mariah Philena, d. Freeland and Minerva P., June 5, 1836.
Mary, d. Noah and Polly, April 5, 1819.
Mary Elizabeth, d. Sylvester and Polly, July 30, 1833. At Lincoln.
Mary Elizabeth, d. Joseph and Dorothy, April 29, 1834.
Mercy Taft, w. Freeland, June 2, 1812. G.S.2.
Nancy, d. Noah and Polly, July 22, 1825.
Orlando, s. Josiah and ——————, Dec. 23, 1826.
Otis, s. John and Betsy, Dec. 8, 1817.
Otis Jones, s. Sylvester and Polly, Sept. 26, 1844.
Phebe, d. Ephraim and Sarah, bap. Feb. 23, 1772. C.R.
Phebe, d. James and Elizabeth, bap. Nov. 22, 1772. C.R.
Rhoda, d. John and Betsy, June 17, 1833.
Rosella, d. Elisha and Melissa S., June 3, 1844.
Ruth B., w. Cyrus, —— ——, 1812. G.S.2.
Sarah, d. Ephraim and Sarah, bap. Sept. 22, 1765. C.R.

STOCKWELL, Sarah, d. Noah and Polly, Jan. 4, 1821.
Stillman, s. Noah Jr. and Polly, March 31, 1812.
Susan Almanda, d. Ammi and Susan, July 18, 1840.
Sylvester, s. Sylvester and Polly, Sept. 3, 1838.
Wealthy Jane, d. Stilman and Jane [Seaver], Dec. 25, 1844.
———, s. Elisha and Melissa S., June 28, 1846.
———, s. Elisha and M. S., Dec. 10, 1849.

STONE, Edwin, s. Nathan and Nancy, April 9, 1817.
John, s. John and Susannah, bap. Feb. 6, 1774. c.r.
Mary, d. Nathan and Nancy, July 18, 1829.
Nancy, d. Nathan and Nancy, Jan. 24, 1814.
Nathan, s. John and Susannah, bap. April 14, 1776. c.r.
Paul, s. John and Susannah, bap. April 22, 1770. c.r.
Paul Mendall, s. John and Susannah, bap. Nov. 1, 1778. c.r.
Seneca, s. Nathan and Nancy, Jan. 12, 1813.
Timothy, s. John and Susannah, bap. Dec. 15, 1771. c.r.
Timothy, s. John and Susannah, bap. Feb. 11, 1781. c.r.
Willard, s. Nathan and Nancy, Dec. 29, 1825.
———, s. Clark L. and Amy, Aug. 21, 1846.

STOW, Anna, d. John and Hannah, bap. Aug. 4, 1773. c.r.
Hannah, d. Patty Ward now Patty Dike, bap. June 6, 1802. c.r.
Jonathan, s. John and Hannah, bap. Aug. 2, 1775. c.r.

STOWELL, Francis C., ——— —, 1813. g.s.5.
Nancy, w. Francis C., ——— —, 1824. g.s.5.

STRATEN (see Stratton), Asa, s. James and Abigail, bap. July 13, 1760. c.r.
Henry, s. Stephen and Martha, bap. July 2, 1781. c.r.
James, s. James and Abigail, bap. Jan. 13, 1765. c.r.
Meribah, d. James and Abigail, bap. Jan. 12, 1755. c.r.
Stephen Jr., s. Stephen and Martha, bap. Sept. 20, 1778. c.r.
Zebulon, s. James Jr. and Abigail, bap. May 27, 1753. c.r.

STRATTON (see above), A. S., ——— —, ———. g.s.1.
Aaron Smith, s. Ezra and Abigail, March 25, 1809. [Perhaps same as above.]
Abel, s. Peleg and Elizabeth, April 16, 1775.
Abigail [Nabby in c.r.], d. Ebenezer and Abigail, Oct. 23, 1794.
Abigail, d. Abner and Abigail, May 9, 1814.
Abijah, s. Ebenezer and Abigail, May 20, 1797.
Abner, s. Stephen and Martha, May 3, 1776.
Abner G., s. Abner and Abigail, Feb. 8, 1820.
Addisson Dwight, s. Peleg Jr. and Lois, June 30, 1823.

ATHOL BIRTHS.

STRATTON, Alexander A., —— ——, 1811. G.S.1.
Alfred Osman, s. Ebenezer and Harriet L., Aug. 12, 1840.
Alice W., w. Joseph, —— ——, 1813. G.S.6.
Alvin F., s. Walter and Lucy, Nov. 28, 1831.
Amos T., s. Abner and Abigail, July 31, 1818.
Andrew, s. Peleg and Elizabeth, Nov. 15, 1791.
Anna, d. Ebenezer and Hannah, Jan. 10, 1808.
Anstis, d. Thomas and Thankful, Dec. 14, 1784.
Asa, s. William and Elisabeth, Nov. 25, 1785.
Asa, —— ——, 1786. G.S.1. [Perhaps same as above.]
Asa, s. Elias Jr. and Carolina, Oct. 29, 1792.
Asa Alexander, s. Asa and Susanna, Dec. 21, 1811.
Asa Evans, s. Peleg and Elizabeth, June 13, 1798.
Austin C., s. Walter and Lucy, May 6, 1818.
Benjamin Franklin, s. Peleg Jr. and ——, bap. Oct. 18, 1819. C.R.
Betsy, d. Jabez and Mari, Dec. 25, 1801.
Caroline Hill, w. James, April 14, 1821. G.S.2.
Charles, s. Jabez and Mari, Aug. 14, 1808.
Charles T., s. Walter and Lucy, Sept. 14, 1829.
Charles W., s. Joseph and Martha, Dec. 3, 1833.
Clarisa, d. Ebenezer and Abigail, Aug. 4, 1790.
Clarissa, d. Ezra and Abigail, April 4, 1817.
Clark N., s. Joseph, Dec. 2, 1845.
Cyrus Wadsworth, s. David and ——, bap. Nov. 23, 1817. C.R.
Daniel, s. Elias Jr. and Carolina, Jan. 10, 1799.
David, s. Peleg and Elizabeth, June 26, 1786.
David Parks, s. Peleg Jr. and ——, bap. Oct. 18, 1819. C.R.
Deborah, d. Peleg and Elizabeth, July 21, 1770.
Dolly, d. Joseph and Dolly, Nov. 16, 1809.
Eben, s. Ebenezer and Hannah, Jan. 6, 1806.
Ebenezer, —— ——, 1806. G.S.6.
Edward Page, s. Abel and Susan, March 13, 1839.
Eleanor, d. Jonathan and Esther, Dec. 5, 1822.
Elisabeth S., d. Walter and Lucy, April 7, 1835.
Elisha, s. Elias Jr. and Carolina, Aug. 3, 1788.
Eliza Agusta, d. Abel and Susan, March 30, 1842.
Elizabeth, d. Peleg and Elizabeth, Sept. 13, 1778.
Elizebeth, d. Wm. and ——, bap. May 12, 1793. C.R.
Emory F., s. Walter and Lucy, Oct. 18, 1823.
Esther, d. Widow, bap. Dec. 5, 1819. C.R.
Ezra, s. Stephen and Martha, April 26, 1781.
Fannie M., w. Henry W.?, —— ——, 1832. G.S.2.
Francis Albert, s. Joseph and Alace, June 4, 1849.

ATHOL BIRTHS.

STRATTON, Frederick, s. Abner G. and ———, Aug. 1, 1845.
Frederick Eugene, s. Joseph and Alace W., July 5, 1847.
Frederick Alonzo, s. Peleg Jr. and Lois, Sept. 1, 1821.
George Lewis, s. Ebenezer and Harriet L., June 10, 1839.
Hannah, d. Stephen and Martha, Nov. 26, 1767.
Hannah, d. Ebenezer and ———, bap. July 11, 1813. c.r.
Hannah, d. Ebenezer and Hannah, April 21, 1813.
Harriet, w. Ebenezer, ——— —, 1771. g.s.6.
Harriet, d. James and Susannah, June 30, 1822.
Harriet Angeline, d. Ebenezer and Harriet L., Aug. 29, 1837.
Harriet L., w. Ebenezer, June 18, 1804. g.s.6.
Henry H., s. Joseph and Martha, March 16, 1840.
Henry Wisner, s. Ruben and Hannah, March 10, 1836.
Hiram W., s. Walter and Lucy, June 24, 1825.
Horace Mann, s. Joseph and Alice W., May 12, 1843. [Probably same as next.]
Horace Minott, s. Joseph and Alice W., May 12, 1843.
Horris, s. Elias Jr. and Carolina, May 25, 1795.
Ira, s. William and Elisabeth, Feb. 20, 1788.
Jabez, s. Jabez and Mari, April 7, 1806.
Jacob, s. Joseph and Dolly, July 28, 1804.
James, s. William and Elisabeth, Dec. 11, 1780.
James, s. Peleg and Elizabeth, March 13, 1795.
James, s. Walter and Lucy, Dec. 16, 1821.
James Edward, s. James and Susannah, July 23, 1819.
Jesse, s. Peleg and Elizabeth, Aug. 27, 1783.
Jesse, s. Peleg and Elizabeth, Jan. 1, 1789.
Joel, s. Joseph and Dolly, July 14, 1794.
Joel Augustus, s. Joel and Sally, Aug. 26, 1824.
Joel D., s. Walter and Lucy, Aug. 11, 1816.
Joel W., s. Joseph and Martha, Jan. 8, 1838.
John H., s. Joseph and Martha, July 15, 1835.
Jonathan, s. Joseph and Dolly, Oct. 5, 1795.
Jonathan, ——— —, 1796. g.s.6.
Jonathan Windsor, s. Jonathan and Esther, May 18, 1827.
Joseph, s. Joseph and Dolly, May 3, 1798.
Joseph A., s. Joseph and Martha, Oct. 16, 1831.
Joseph Lincoln, s. Joel and Sally, Sept. 15, 1835.
Joshua, s. William and Elisabeth, March 4, 1783.
Joshua Sumner, s. Joel and Sally, June 30, 1827.
Josiah Henry, s. Jonathan and Esther, May 18, 1829.
Laura Maria, d. Ruben and Hannah, March 30, 1838.
Leander Graves, s. Ezra and Abigail, July 28, 1812.
Lemira Diana, d. Asa and Susanna, Nov. 12, 1807.

ATHOL BIRTHS. 87

STRATTON, Levi, s. Stephen and Martha, May 19, 1772.
Levira, d. Levi and Lois, Oct. 30, 1806.
Lois Humphreys, d. Levi and Lois, March 7, 1812.
Lucena, d. Jonathan and Esther, May 11, 1825.
Lucy, d. Levi and Lois, Nov. 12, 1801.
Lucy A., d. Walter and Lucy, Oct. 25, 1827.
Lucy Brooks, d. David and ———, bap. June 25, [1815]. C.R.
Lurinda, d. Walter and Lucy, Jan. 30, 1820.
Lydia, d. Levi and Lois, April 18, 1796.
Lyman, s. Jabez and Mari, Nov. 8, 1812.
Marietta, d. David and ———, bap. April 13, 1825. C.R.
Martha, d. Stephen and Martha, Nov. 20, 1785.
Martha, d. Joseph and Martha, June 2, 1829.
Mary, d. Abner and Abigail, Sept. 3, 1807.
Mary, d. Joseph and Martha, Sept. 2, 1827.
Miranda, d. Ezra and Abigail, Oct. 17, 1807.
Nancy, d. Stephen and Martha, July 3, 1774.
Nancy, d. Abner and Abigail, Aug. 16, 1810.
Nancy, d. Asa and Susanna, April 7, 1817.
Nathanel, s. Stephen and Martha, Jan. 30, 1770.
Peleg, s. Peleg and Elizabeth, Feb. 10, 1781.
Phinehas Wilder, s. Ebenezer and Hannah, June 17, 1815.
Polly, d. Ebenezer and Abigail, June 27, 1792.
Polly, d. Jabez and Mari, Dec. 9, 1803.
Sally, d. William and Elisabeth, Aug. 17, 1790.
Sally, d. Joseph and Dolly, Nov. 14, 1799.
Sally Ward, d. James and Sally, bap. March 4, 1829. C.R.
Samuel, s. Elias Jr. and Carolina, Aug. 30, 1790.
Sarah Maria, d. Joel and Sally, Dec. 5, 1830.
Sarah Rebecca, d. Ruben and Hannah, Aug. 7, 1843. Dup.
Solon Hubbard, s. Abner G. and Ophelia, Sept. 6, 1849.
Sophia, ——— —, 1844. G.S.1.
Stephen, s. Stephen and Martha, July 28, 1778.
Stephen, s. Stephen and Martha, Dec. 24, 1783.
Stephen Austin, s. Ezra and Abigail, Jan. 22, 1815.
Susan, d. Abel and Susan, Dec. 8, 1843. Dup.
Susanna, w. Asa, ——— —, 1786. G.S.1.
Susanna Giles, d. Asa and Susanna, April 15, 1815.
Thomas, s. James and Abigail, Oct. 30, 1758.
Thomas, s. Peleg Jr. and Lois, Sept. 15, 1818.
Walter, s. Ebenezer and Abigail, Oct. 20, 1788.
Wilder, s. Ebenezer and Hannah, April 13, 1803.
William, s. Peleg and Elizabeth, March 14, 1773.
William Masbury, s. Asa and Susanna, June 21, 1809.

ATHOL BIRTHS.

SWEETSER, Abel, s. Samuel and Hannah, July 23, 1802.
Ann Elizabeth, d. Samuel Jr. and Nancy Maria, Sept. 8, 1837.
Artenatus, s. Samuel and Hannah, Feb. 1, 1809.
Caroline, d. Samuel and Hannah, Jan. 24, 181-. [Bap. Feb. 13, 1814, C.R.]
Charles Humphreys, s. Samuel Jr. and Ann R., Jan. 31, 1829.
Charles Humphreys, s. Samuel Jr. and Nancy Maria, Aug. 25, 1841.
George Dwight, s. Samuel Jr. and Ann R., Oct. 12, 1826.
Hannah Augusta, d. Samuel Jr. and Ann R., Sept. 12, 1824.
Luke, s. Samuel and Hannah, Oct. 28, 1800.
Maria, d. Samuel and Hannah, Aug. 3, 1806.
Maria Anna, d. Samuel and Nancy M., Dec. 19, 1845.
Miranda d. Samuel and Hannah, Aug. 2, 1804.
Nabby [Nabby Moor in C.R.], d. Samuel and Hannah, Sept. 14, 1795.
Polly, d. Samuel and Hannah, Feb. 24, 179-. [Bap. Sept. 20, 1795, C.R.]
Samuel, s. Samuel and Hannah, Oct. 18, 1798.
William, s. Samuel Jr. and Ann R., Aug. 8, 1831.

TALBOT (see Talbut, Tolbert), Dean Ward, s. George and Betty, May 7, 1806.
Eliza, d. George and Betty, Jan. 7, 1804.
Mehetabel, d. George and Betty, March 6, 1794.
Sally, d. George and Betty, March 19, 1792.
Samuel Ward, s. George and Betty, Aug. 20, 1817.
William Kendall, s. George and Betty, June 17, 1799.

TALBUT (see above and Tolbert), Josiah, s. George and Betty, Sept. 10, 1790.

TAYLAR [Taylor in C.R.], Mary, d. Rufus and Mary, March 24, 1766.
[Taylor in C.R.], Susanna, d. Rufus and Mary, Feb. 6, 1768.

TAYLOR, David, s. Rufus and Mary, March 25, 1770.
David, s. Rufus and Susanna, April 15, 1779.
Easter [Esther in C.R.], d. Rufus and Mary, March 3, 1772.
Edwin, s. Lucius and Mercy, July 5, 1836.
Ellen, d. Lucius and Mercy, Dec. 18, 1834.
Hannah, d. Rufus and Susanna, Feb. 11, 1777.
Marcy [Mercy, C.R.], d. Rufus and Susanna, April 7, 1781.
Mercy Bryant, —— —, 1811. G.S.2.
Submitt, d. Rufus and Mary, Oct. 27, 1764.
Susanna, d. Rufus and Susanna, April 2, 1775.

TENNEY, Adaline L., d. Charles R. and Silence L., July 18, 1848.

THAYER, Alpheus, s. Moses and Lucinda, Oct. 8, 1849.
Myron Raucious ?, s. Moses and Lucinda, Aug. 28, 1847.

THOMPSON, Eliza Antoinette, d. Clark and Nancy, April 16, 1843.
James Ervin, s. James and Jane B., June 3, 1848.

THORP, Albert, twin s. Eliphalet and Ruthy, Feb. 15, 1810.
Albert Lauriston, s. Albert and Mary Alzina, Nov. 3, 1841.
Ann, d. Eliphalet and Ruthy, March 30, 1826.
Catharine, d. Albert and Mary Alzina, Jan. 5, 1844.
Charles Munroe, s. Ira and Catharine, March 25, 1809. At Dorchester.
Clara, d. Eliphalet and Ruthy, May 13, 1831.
Elbridge, s. Ira and Catharine, Jan. 18, 1811. At Dorchester.
Eli, s. Eliphalet and Ruthy, June 28, 1816.
Ellen Maria, d. Ira and Catharine, Aug. 8, 1830.
Emerline, d. Ira and Catharine, Aug. 7, 1813.
Emily, twin d. Eliphalet and Ruthy, Feb. 15, 1810.
Fenno, s. Eliphalet and Ruthy, Feb. 13, 1814.
Frederick Fenno, s. Fenno and Lucy Brigham, June 6, 1843. Dup.
Frederick Fenno, s. Fenno and Lucy B., Sept. 12, 1849.
Hannah, d. Ira and Catharine, July 10, 1815.
Harriet Sumner, d. Ira and Catharine, Dec. 11, 1823.
Henry Eli, s. Fenno and Lucy B., Nov. 19, 1840.
Henry Gilbert, s. Ira and Catharine, July 24, 1828.
Jane, d. Eliphalet and Ruthy, Feb. 15, 1823.
Janette, d. Albert and Mary Alzina, Dec. 15, 1839.
Jerome, s. Ira and Catharine, March 30, 1819.
Lewis, s. Eliphalet and Ruthy, May 5, 1812.
Lydia, d. Eliphalet and Ruthy, Jan. 7, 1819.
Maria, d. Eliphalet and Ruthy, June 4, 1828.
Martha Mead, d. Ira and Catharine, Jan. 31, 1826.
Mary Earl, d. Albert and Mary Alzina, April 2, 1833.
Oscar, s. Albert and Mary Alzina, Dec. 2, 1834.
Parnell Munroe, d. Ira and Catharine, Sept. 24, 1821.
Phebe Moore Snell, 2d w. Lewis, Dec. 5, 1827. G.S.2.
Walter, s. Eliphalet and Ruthy [Ruth Fenno, G.S.1.], Jan. 5, 1821.
Wiswell H., s. Ferno and Lucy B., Aug. 11, 1846
———, d. Albert and Mary Alzina, Jan. 5, 1844.

THROWER, Ann Maria Ling, s. Abram Ling and Betsy, July 10, 1838. In Suton, N. H.
Francis, s. Abraham and Elizabeth, March 26, 1847.

THROWER, Francis Winditt, s. Abram Ling and Betsy, March 26, 1847.
John A., s. Abraham and Elizabeth, June 1, 1845.
John Winditt, s. Abram Wing and Betsy, June 1, 1845.
Mary Elizabeth, d. Abraham and Elizabeth, March 13, 1849.
Robert Whindard, s. Abram Ling and Betsy, Oct. 26, 1841.
Sally, d. Abram Ling and Betsy, Sept. 1, 1843.
Sarah Ann, d. Abram and Elisabeth, Sept. 1, 1843.
Sarah Ann, d. Abram Ling and Betsy, —— —, 1844. [Perhaps same as above.]
Sarah P., w. William L.?, —— —, 1844. G.S.2.
William, s. Abram Ling and Betsy, Nov. 25, 1839. In Lancaster.
William L., —— —, 1839. G.S.2. [Probably same as above.]

TOLBERT (see Talbot, Talbut), George, s. George and Betty, Aug. 25, 1796.

TOTMAN, Eunice, d. Levi and Elizabeth, Feb. 20, 1809.
Lucy, d. Levi and Elizabeth, Jan. 30, 1811.

TOWNSEND, Abigail Dana, d. Thomas and Abigail, Feb. 18, 1806.
Abigail Raymond, d. Lysander F. and Clarissa, Sept. 22, 1830.
Abigal, d. Thomas and Abigail, Feb. 5, 1801.
Almina, d. Thomas and Abigail, July 28, 1809.
Benjamin, s. Benjamin and Elisabeth, Aug. 5, 1776.
Benjamin, s. Thomas and Abigail, June 22, 1795.
Benjamin, s. William and Elizabeth, April 15, 1818.
Charles Augustus, s. Col. Thomas and Ann, July 1, 1828.
Dana, s. Thomas and Abigail, Feb. 16, 1799.
David, s. William and Elizabeth, June 18, 1809.
Deborah, d. Benjamin and Elisabeth, Sept. 15, 1778.
Elisabeth, d. Benjamin and Elisabeth, May 28, 1774.
Elizabeth, d. William and Elizabeth, Feb. 9, 1807.
George Danvers, s. Lysander F. and Lucy, Feb. 27, 1840.
H. Page, s. James and Lydia, May 26, 1845?.
Harriet [Hariot in c.r.], d. William and Elizabeth, Feb. 13, 1816.
Henry Dexter, s. Thomas and Harriet, Oct. 22, 1842.
Ira, s. William and Elizabeth, Aug. 16, 1811.
James, s. Benjamin and Elisabeth, Oct. 8, 1780.
James, s. William and Elizabeth, Nov. 25, 1813.
John H., s. Lysander F. and Lavinia, Nov. 5, 1846.
Lucy Ann, d. Col. Thomas and Ann, July 25, 1830.
Lysander Edward, s. Lysander F. and Clarissa, Oct. 15, 1837.
Lysander Fairfield, s. Thomas and Abigail, Aug. 30, 1803.

ATHOL BIRTHS. 91

TOWNSEND, Martha Ann, d. Augustus and Meriam, Nov. 27, 1837.
Martin, s. Jonathan and Huldah, bap. April 20, 1777. C.R.
Mary, d. William and Elizabeth, March 29, 1822. [The mother was dead. C.R.]
Royal Augusta [Augustus, C.R.], s. Thomas and Abigail, Aug. 1, 1808.
Royal Fairfield, s. Col. Thomas and Ann, Nov. 27, 1832.
Sylvia Elizabeth, d. Lysander F. and Clarissa, May 2, 1833.
Thomas, s. Benjamin and Elisabeth, July 22, 1770.
Thomas, s. Thomas and Abigail, April 25, 1797.
Thomas, s. William and Elizabeth, Feb. 22, 1820.
Ursula Almina, d. Thomas and Abigail, May 11, 1813.
William, s. Benjamin and Elisabeth, March 15, 1772.
William, s. William and Elizabeth, Jan. 27, 1806.

TRAIN (see Traine), Alexander, s. Jonathan and Marcy, bap. June 11, 1781. C.R.
Hannah, d. David and Hannah, Dec. 30, 1783.
John Hancock, s. Jonathan and Mercy, April 5, 1775.
Jonathan, s. Jonathan and Mercy, July 14, 1777.
Lydia, d. David and Hannah, bap. Aug. 19, 1781. C.R.
Mercy, d. Jonathan and Mercy, April 7, 1779.
Moley [Molle in C.R.], d. Jonathan and Mercy, July 12, 1772.
Moly, d. David and Hannah, April 30, 1786.
Vyney [Vina in C.R.], d. Jonathan and Mercy, April 7, 1774.

TRAINE (see above), David, s. David and Hannah, May 19, 1777.
Oliver, s. David and Hannah, June 21, 1779.

TUPPER, George William [Willard in dup.], s. Erastus and Lois Haven, May 14, 1843. In New Salem.

TWICHEL (see Twichell, Twitchel, Twitchell), Azubah, d. Enos Jr. and Azubah, April 10, 1802.
Calvin, s. Seth and Phebe, Aug. 20, 1794.
Chester, s. Seth and Phebe, June 21, 1800.
David, s. David and Sarah, May 1, 1765.
Dorothy, d. Benony and Zilpah, May 2, 1800.
Elisabeth, twin d. David and Sarah, —— 5, [bap. April 25, C.R.], 1756.
Eliza, d. Samuel and ———, bap. March 16, 1806. C.R.
Elvera, d. Seth and Phebe, Oct. 30, 1802.
Enos, s. Enos Jr. and Azubah, Feb. 14, 1799.
Eri?, s. Enos Jr. and Azubah, Feb. 26, 1797.
Esther, d. David and Sarah, Sept. 29, 1748.

TWICHEL, Franklin, s. Samuel, bap. March 16, 1806. C.R.
Gardner, s. Bala and Sally, May 15, 1800.
Hannah, d. Josiah and Hannah, June 9, 1798.
Hazeltine, s. Bala and Sally, March 30, 1803.
James Pierce, s. Enos Jr. and Azubah, Feb. 3, 1811.
Jane, d. John and Martha [Patey?], bap. Dec. 25, 1781. C.R.
Jeremiah, s. Josiah and Hannah, Aug. 15, 1791.
John, s. David and Sarah, March 14, 1754.
John, bap. (at the house of Deacon Twichel by reason of sickness), April 23, [1789]. C.R.
Joseph, s. David and Sarah, Sept. 10, 1750.
Lemuel Houghton, s. Lemuel and ———, bap. May 29, 1803. C.R.
Lemuel Houghten, s. Lemuel and ———, bap. April 11, 1805. C.R.
Lucetta Orina, d. Enos Jr. and Azubah, Sept. 12, 1818.
Lucinda, d. Bala and Sally, Jan. 13, 1797.
Marian, d. Lemuel and ———, bap. June 13, 1813. C.R.
Mary Bennit, d. David and Sarah, Aug. 30, 1762.
Meriam, d. John and Martha, bap. Feb. 6, 1780. C.R.
Phila, d. Josiah and Hannah, May 23, 1800.
Pliny, s. Enos Jr. and Azubah, Jan. 25, 1805.
Releef, d. Enos Jr. and Azubah, April 26, 1795.
Rhoda, d. Josiah and Hannah, April 6, 1796.
Royal, s. Samuel and ———, bap. Feb. 14, 1802. C.R.
Sally, d. Josiah and Hannah, Aug. 5, 1793.
Sally, d. Seth and Phebe, March 3, 1796.
Sarah, twin d. David and Sarah, ——— 5 [bap. April 25], 1756.
Sarah, the 2, d. David and Sarah, Oct. 22, 1758.
Sena, d. Alfred and Olive, March 22, 1807.
Seth, s. Seth and Phebe, Oct. 31, 1792.
Seth, s. Seth and Phebe, March 5, 1798.
Simeon Fish, s. Franses and Sally, bap. Aug. 3, 1827. C.R.
Stilman, s. Enos Jr. and Azubah, Jan. 7, 1807.
Sylvia, d. Bala and Sally, July 20, 1793.
Willard, s. Josiah and Hannah, Feb. 12, 1803.
William, s. Enos Jr. and Azubah, March 3, 1813.

TWICHELL (see above and Twitchel, Twitchell), Benjamin Marshall, s. Benjamin M. and Asenath, July 21, 1831.
Benoni, s. Enos and Releef, Nov. 25, 1780.
Caroline, d. David G. and Lucy, Nov. 19, 1832.
Catharine Philena, d. David G. and Lucy, Dec. 13, 1836
Charles Brown, s. Chester and Eunice D., April 10, 1846.
David Goddard, s. Seth and Phebe, Oct. 15, 1790.

ATHOL BIRTHS. 93

TWICHELL, Edward, s. Seth and Hulday, Sept. 14, 1785.
Elbridge Chester, s. Chester and Sally, April 4, 1832.
Emma J., d. Uri and Samantha, Oct. 5, 1846.
Enos, s. Enos and Releef, Nov. 13, 1773.
Eunice E., d. Chester and Eunice, Jan. 9, 1848.
Frances, s. Seth and Hulday, Sept. 9, 1783.
Francis, s. Francis and Sally, May 11, 1814.
Freeman, s. Samuel and ———, bap. Oct. 27, 1808. C.R.
Ginery Bachelor, s. Francis and Sally, Aug. 26, 1811.
Hannah, d. Alfred 2d and Hannah, May 4, 1829.
Harriet Asenath, d. Benjamin M. and Asenath, April 2, 1825.
John M., Nov. 14, 1815. G.S.2.
Joseph Seaver, s. Lemuel and Esther, Oct. 8, 1806.
Lemuel, s. Enos and Releef, Dec. 12, 1774.
Lucinda, d. Uri and Lydia, March 31, 1845.
Lucy, d. Leml. and ———, bap. April 7, 1811. C.R.
Lydia, d. Uri and Lydia S., Dec. 30, 1848 [1849 ?].
Lydia S., ———, 1821. G.S.6.
Marian, s. Francis and Sally, Sept. 15, 1817.
Martha Ann, d. Benjamin M. and Asenath, April 22, 1838.
Mary Jane, d. Benjamin M. and Asenath, Oct. 17, 1833.
Miriam, d. Enos and Releef, March 29, 1777.
Miranda Sophia, d. Jeremiah and Preserved, Feb. 28, 1819.
Permelia E., d. Abner W. and Hannah, Aug. 20, 1847.
Phebe Goddard, d. David G. and Lucy, Nov. 24, 1827.
Samuel, s. Enos and Releef, April 12, 1779.
Sarah Ann, d. David G. and Lucy, Aug. 17, 1830.
Sarah Elizabeth, d. Chester and Sally, May 17, 1835.
Silvanus Eaton, s. Francis and Sally, March 15, 1810.
Susan, d. Alfred 2d and Hannah, Oct. 8, 1831.
Uri, s. Francis and Sally, Nov. 19, 1812.
William, s. Seth and Hulday, May 16, 1781.

TWITCHEL, Adaline, d. Lemuel and ———, bap. Feb. 26, 1809. C.R.
David, s. John and Martha, bap. Feb. 22, 1778. C.R.
Georg, s. John and ———, bap. June 15, 1794. C.R.
Samuel, s. John and ———, bap. Aug. 21, 1785. C.R.
Sarah, d. John and ———, bap. Dec. 25, 1791. C.R.
Sibel, d. John and ———, bap. Sept. 8, 1799. C.R.

TWITCHELL (see Twichel, etc.), Alfred, ———, 1793. G.S.4.
Hannah, w. Alfred, ———, 1798. G.S.4.
Sally, w. Francis, ———, 1787. G.S.6.
———, s. Chester and Eunice, April 1, 1845 ?

UNDERWOOD, Charles, s. Nathan and Hanner, Oct. 28, 1822.
Harriet Angelia, d. Nathan and Hanner, June 23, 1820.
James Stone, s. Joshua and Lucy, bap. Nov. 8, 1818. c.r.
Nancy, d. Joshua and ———, bap. Aug. 31, 1817. c.r.
Susan I., d. John and Eliza, June 26, 1847.
Sylvester Thomas, s. Nathan and Hanner, Dec. 8, 1824.

UPTON, Charles S., s. Luther and Phebe E., Feb. 26, 1847.

WADSWORTH, Josephine A., ——— ———, 1838. g.s.2.

WAIT, Eunice, d. Josiah and Sarah, Oct. 29, 1776.
Rhoda, d. Josiah and Sarah, Jan. 28, 1780.

WALKER, Cornelia L., w. Moses, ——— ———, 1831. g.s.2.
Emerline, d. Lyman and Emerline, June 29, 1837.
Freeman Hastings, s. Ebenezer and Sukey, Aug. 13, 1835.
Hannah A., d. Calvin and Lois, ——— ———, 1833. g.s.6.
Moses, ——— ———, 1821. g.s.2.

WARD, Alfred, s. Walter and Susanna, bap. Oct. 12, 1819. c.r.
Ambrose, s. Walter and Susanna, bap. Oct. 12, 1819. c.r.
Anna [Anne Raymond in c.r.], d. Alpheus and Molley, April 29, 1793.
Austin, s. Walter and Susanna, bap. Oct. 12, 1819. c.r.
Beriah, d. Alpheus and Molley, June 2, 1801.
Daniel, s. Nemiah and Sarah, July 11, 1774.
Daniel, s. Alpheus and Molley, June 2, 1785.
Desiah [Desire in c.r.], d. Nemiah and Sarah, July 13, 1779.
Easther, d. Jonathan and Mary, May 8, 1775.
Elisabeth, d. Abner and Elisabeth, Nov. 8, 1774.
Ephraim, s. Abner and Elisabeth, May 5, 1779.
Esther Althine, d. William H. and Lucy, Aug. 25, 1821.
Esther Humphrey, d. Jabez and Esther, Nov. 4, 1803.
Euseba, d. Jabez and Esther, Feb. 22, 1796.
Fanny, d. Jabez and Esther, Nov. 13, 1793.
Francis Sheldon, s. Daniel and Lydia, Nov. 18, 1818.
Hannah, d. Nemiah and Sarah, July 15, 1776.
Harrison, ——— ———, 1815. g.s.2.
Henry, s. Elisah and Mary, bap. Sept. 2, 1770. c.r.
Henry, s. Jabez and Esther, June 16, 1791.
Henry Merritt, s. Jabez and Mary, Sept. 9, 1821.
James, s. Ruggles and ———, bap. Aug. 21, 1785. c.r.
Jane, d. Abner and Elisabeth, Sept. 20, 1776.
Lois, d. Nahum and Patty, bap. Sept. 20, 1801. c.r.
Luana Thompson, w. Harrison, ——— ———, 1819. g.s.2.
Lucretia, d. Jabez and Esther, Jan. 13, 1799.

ATHOL BIRTHS. 95

WARD, Lucretia Richardson, d. William H. and Lucy, Dec. 23, 1828.
Lucy, d. William H. and Lucy, March 25, 1823.
Lydia, d. Alpheus and Molley, Dec. 14, 1782.
Lydia Smith, d. Daniel and Lydia, April 3, 1821.
Lyman, s. Jabez and Esther, Feb. 3, 1807.
Lyman, s. Jabez and Esther, April 18, 1810.
Margit [Margaret in C.R.], d. Jonathan and Sarah, Aug. 16, 1780.
Mary, d. William H. and Lucy, Aug. 27, 1818.
Nahum, s. Elishah and Mary, bap. June 18, 1769. C.R.
Nahum, s. Beriah and Hannah, bap. May 30, 1773. C.R.
Nahum, s. Jabez and Esther, Oct. 10, 1801.
Nancy Maria, d. Daniel and Lydia, July 24, 1824.
Nancy Stratton, w. George, —— —, 1817. G.S.1.
Nathan, s. Alpheus and Molley, May 5, 1788.
Persis Diana, d. Daniel and Lydia, Oct. 30, 1826.
Polly, d. Alpheus and Molley, Oct. 27, 1790.
[Mrs.?] Rossie M., Sept. 28, 1832. G.S.2.
Sally Nutt, d. Ruggles and ———, bap. Sept. 21, 1783. C.R.
Samuel, s. Jonathan and Mary, March 2, 1777.
Sarah, d. James and Sally, Dec. 21, 1828.
Susan Stratton, d. Walter and Susanna, bap. Oct. 12, 1819. C.R.
Susanna, d. Nahum and Patty his widow, bap. Sept. 20, 1801. C.R.
Sylvester Lee, s. Jabez and Mary, March 6, 1823.
Willard, s. William H. and Lucy, July 1, 1827.
William, s. Elishah and Mary, bap. June 18, 1769. C.R.
William Humphrey, s. Jabez and Esther, July 22, 1788.
William Humphrey, s. William H. and Lucy, Nov. 23, 1824.
William Leonard, s. Daniel and Lydia, June 24, 1816.

WARREN, Benjamin, s. Benjamin and Margery, bap. June 7, 1772. C.R.

WASHBURN, Mary A., w. Henry, —— —, 1833. G.S.2.
Theodore Wales, s. Dexter and Nancy, Nov. 4, 1844.

WELLMAN, L. Merrill W., —— —, 1848. G.S.2.

WETHERBY, Helen M., w. Maxon R., —— —, 1840. G.S.2.
Hipzibah, d. John and Mary, bap. Sept. 13, 1780. C.R.
John Jr., s. John and Mary, bap. Sept. 13, 1780. C.R.
Levina, d. John and Mary, bap. Sept. 13, 1780. C.R.
Maxon R., —— —, 1832. G.S.2.

WHEATON, Christopher C., M.D., July 8, 1802, at Leicester. G.S.1.

ATHOL BIRTHS.

WHEELER, Cynthia S. Cook, w. Oren S., —— —, 1839. G.S.2.
Everett Oliver, s. Jonathan and Hannah, Oct. 12, 1839.
Franklin, s. Jonathan and Hannah, Oct. 14, 1845.
Hannah Augusta, twin d. Jonathan and Hannah, March 12, 1838.
Jonathan, s. Jonathan and Hannah, July 11, 1836.
Jonathan Augustine, twin s. Jonathan and Hannah, March 12, 1838.
Josiah, s. Paul and Eunice, Feb. 14, 1795.
Lucinda, d. Paul and Eunice, Jan. 29, 1801.
Margaret, d. Jonathan and Hannah, July 12, 1841.
Mary, d. Jonathan and Hannah, May 21, 1832.
Miranda Fisher, d. Jonathan and Hannah, Nov. 23, 1833.
Oren S., —— —, 1835. G.S.2.
Rhoda, d. Paul and Eunice, June 25, 1797.

WHIT [White?], Sarah Breck, d. Thomas and Rebeccah, bap. Aug. 18, 1771. C.R.
Thomas, s. Thomas and Rebeccah, bap. April 29, 1770. C.R.

WHITE, Lucy, 2d d. William and Lucy, Sept. 25, 1806.
———, d. Isadore and Laura, April 17, 1847.

WHITMAN, Hannah G., w. Dr. W. F., —— —, 1834. G.S.2.
Julia M., w. Dr. W. F., —— —, 1837. G.S.2.
Dr. W. F., —— —, 1823. G.S.2.

WHITNEY, Abby M., d. Lemuel and Almira, —— —, 1847. G.S.6.
Almeda, d. Edward and Rhoda, April 15, 1821.
Alva, d. Nathan and Sina, March 6, 1806.
Ammi, s. Lemuel and Anna, June 1, 1817.
Anna, d. Nathan and Sina, March 30, 1809.
Bartholomew W., s. William K. and Deborah, July 19, 1825.
Barzillia J., s. William K. and Deborah, April 21, 1822.
Betcy Bowker, twin d. Moses and Tabitha, Dec. 22, 1804.
Charles, s. Edward and Rhoda, July 21, 1823.
Deborah W., d. William K. and Deborah, Oct. 30, 1823.
Elbridge W., s. William K. and Deborah, May 26, 1819. At Dana.
Esther Desire Fuller, d. Jacob and Sally, Oct. 20, 1844.
Esther Maria, d. Lemuel and Anna, Nov. 21, 1818.
Frances Adeliza, d. Elbridge W. and Sopha, Jan. 5, 1846.
Freeman Bowker, twin s. Moses and Tabitha, Dec. 22, 1804.
Gilbert H., —— —, 1824. G.S.1.
Helen M., w. Gilbert H., —— —, 1827. G.S.1.
Ira, s. Nathan and Sina, July 30, 1807.

ATHOL BIRTHS.

WHITNEY, John F., s. William K. and Deborah, March 29, 1828.
John P., July 14, 1831. G.S.2.
Josiah C., s. William B. and Marilla L., July 14, 1843.
Lewis J., —— —, 1802. G.S.1.
Mary W., d. William K. and Deborah, March 16, 1830.
Melinda L., w. Gilbert H., —— —, 1826. G.S.1.
Nancy, d. Edward and Rhoda, March 25, 1818.
Ruth, w. Lewis J., —— —, 1803. G.S.1.
Sophia A., w. E. W., —— —, 1823. G.S.2.
Susannah K., d. William K. and Deborah, Nov. 1, 1820.
Washburn Whiting, s. Lemuel and Anna, Nov. 11, 1820.
William Wheeler, s. Nathan and Sina, March 12, 1811.
——, d. William K. and Mary Ann, —— —, ——. [1844 or 1845.]

WIGGINS, Jane S., w. William S.?, —— —, 1819. G.S.2.
Sarah Jane, d. William F. [or S.?] and Jane, May 17, 1847.
William S., —— —, 1823. G.S.2.

WILDER, Nancy, d. widow Lidea, bap. April 6, 1817. C.R.

WILEY, Amos Drury, s. Samuel and Nancy, Oct. 18, 1828.
Hannah, d. Samuel and Nancy, June 8, 1833.
Ira Lyman, s. Samuel and Nancy, April 20, 1841.
Susan, d. Samuel and Nancy, July 1, 1830.

WILKINSON, John W., —— —, 1831. G.S.2.
Melissa M., w. John W., —— —, 1835. G.S.2.

WILLARD, Elvira, d. Ephraim and Lucy, Jan. 20, 1802.
Julia, —— —, 1825. G.S.2.
Lucy Ann, d. Josiah and Parnea, Jan. 25, 1830.
Sarah Jane, d. Josiah and Parnea, Jan. 25, 1826.

WILLIAMS, John Humphreys, s. William H. and Frances W., Aug. 24, 1824.
Mary Hoyt, d. William [H.] and Frances W., Aug. 13, 182[6?].

WINCHESTER, Mary Ann, d. Harriss and Ann S., Jan. 2, 1849.

WINTERS, James, s. Patrick and Margaret, Oct. 24, 1845.

WOOD (see Woods), Mrs. Abby M., Sept. 14, 1795. G.S.2.
Miss Abigail A., —— —, 1795. G.S.5.
Abigail Farrar, d. Elijah and Sally, Dec. 9, 1800.
Anna, d. Jonathan and Anna, Dec. 23, 1778.
Arthur G., s. Elbridge G. and Sally T., Feb. 22, 1845.

ATHOL BIRTHS.

Wood, Caroline R., w. John C., ———, 1830. G.S.2.
Catherine, d. Jona. and ———, bap. July 18, 1790. C.R.
Cyrus K., ———, 1825. G.S.2.
Elisabeth, d. Jonathan Anna, Jan. 24, 1771.
Elvira, d. Elijah and Sally, Feb. 2, 1803.
Eunice, d. Jonathan and Anna, March 17, 1784.
Isabel [Isabella Woods in C.R.], d. Jonathan and Anna, Sept. 5, 1768.
[Woods in C.R.], Jeremiah,.s. Jonathan and Anna, July 6, 1773.
John C., ———, 1828. G.S.2.
Jonathan, s. Jonathan and Anna, Oct. 25, 1781.
Joseph, s. Joseph and Marcy [Mary ?], May 26, 1786.
Josephus, s. twin [with Augustus] Joel and Abby M., Aug. 19, 1832. G.S.2.
[Woods in C.R.], Mary, d. Kimbal and Mary, July 23, 1766.
[Woods in C.R.], Oliver, s. Kimbal and Mary, Aug. 15, 1778.
Sarah, d. Jonathan and ———, bap. July 11, 1784. C.R.
Silas, s. Jonathan and Anna, March 4, 1776.
Susanna [Susannah Woods in C.R.], d. Kimbal and Mary, March 29, 1772.
Susanna [Susannah Woods in C.R.], d. Kimbal and Mary, Sept. 3, 1781.
Thomas, s. William and Zerviah, May 3, 1770.
[Woods in C.R.], William, s. William and Zerviah, Dec. 20, 1759.

WOODARD (see Woodward), Anna, d. Jonathan and Hipzibah, bap. Dec. 1, 1779. C.R.

WOODS (see Wood), Abigail, d. Benjamin and Sarah, April 18' 1773.
Anna, d. Benjamin and Sarah, bap. Nov. 6, 1781. C.R.
Benjamin Jr., s. Benjamin and Sarah, bap. May 10, 1778. C.R.
Elizabeth, d. Jonathan and Anna, bap. March 17, 1771. C.R.
Hannah, d. William and Zerviah, bap. June 10, 1766. C.R.
Hannah, d. Jonathan and Anna, bap. Feb. 20, 1779. C.R.
Lois, d. Benjamin and Sarah, May 7, 1767.
Lucinda, d. Benjamin and Sarah, Feb. 12, 1769.
Lucy, d. Benjamin and Sarah, bap. Nov. 1, 1775. C.R.
Mary, d. Benjamin and Sarah, Feb. 5, 1771.
Rhoda, d. William and Zerviah, bap. June 10, 1766. C.R.
Sarah, d. William and Zerviah, bap. June 10, 1766. C.R.
Sarah, d. Benjamin and Sarah, bap. Aug. 22, 1779. C.R.

WOODWARD (see Woodard), Abijah, s. Abijah and Elizabeth, May 3, 1813
Anna, d. Jonathan and Hepsabe, Oct. 13, 1779.

WOODWARD, Beriah, s. Abijah and Elizabeth, Oct. 12, 1806.
Dorothy, d. Jonathan and Hepsabe, Nov. 11, 1772.
Emiline, d. George W. and Eluta M., Sept. 1, 1842. G.S.2.
Emily Eaton, d. Bartholomew and Sally, Feb. 14, 1817.
Fanny, d. Jonathan and Hepsabe, Jan. 2, 1771.
George Clarence, s. George W. and Lecta M., May 9, 1849.
George W., July 5, 1825. G.S.2.
Hepsith [Hepzibah, C.R.], d. Jonathan and Hepsabe, April 11, 1777.
James Manson, s. Manson J. and Nancy, Aug. 11, 1842.
Lois, d. Jonathan and Hepsabe, Oct. 27, 1774.
Lucy, d. Jonathan and Hepsabe, born in Orange Jan. 4, 1787.
Rhoda, d. Abijah and Elizabeth, Feb. 15, 1810.
Sally Lincoln, d. Bartholomew and Sally, Nov. 5, 1818.
Wallis Watson, s. Manson J. and Nancy, Feb. 6, 1840.
———, d. Manson J. and Nancy, Aug. 27, 1844.

WORRICK, A. A., ———, 1834. G.S.2.

WYGANT, John Anning, s. Anning S. and Harriet Lucinda, Dec. 22, 1841.

YOUNG, Abner, s. William and Kezia, Dec. 18, 1790.
Amasa, s. William and Kezia, July 26, 1784.
Anna, dau. Robert and Sarah, bap. March 5, 1758. C.R.
Anna, d. Robert and Elizabeth, bap. June 26, 1768. C.R.
Anna, d. David and Hannah, Jan. 20, 1800.
Arathusa, d. David and Hannah, Feb. 7, 1796.
Caroline, d. Abner and Lucy, Nov. 2, 1822.
Charles, s. James and Patty, Oct. 4, 1815.
David, s. David and Hannah, Jan. 7, 1789.
David, s. Robert and Sarah, bap. Sept. 14, 1755. C.R.
David 3d, s. David Jr. and Philinda, Dec. 25, 1824.
Delia Maria, d. Abner and Lucy, Feb. 1, 182[8?].
Eunice, d. William and Kezia, Dec. 18, 1789.
George Henry Clark, s. ——— and Polly, Nov. 23, 1845.
Hannah, d. William and Kezia, Oct. 11, 1782.
Hannah, d. David and Hannah, Jan. 7, 1798.
Hannah, d. Wm. and ———, bap. Oct. 6, 1805. C.R.
Harriot, d. James and Patty, Oct. 14, 1812.
Hiram B., s. Hiram and Catharine, Nov. 24, 1849.
Isabella, d. Hyram and Catharine, July 4, 1838.
James, s. David and Hannah, April 17, 1785.
James, s. James and Patty, Jan. 20, 1825.
Jarvis, s. Joseph and Sophia, July 4, 1835.
Joab, s. Samuel and Lois, Nov. 21, 1790.

YOUNG, Joel, s. Robert and Elizabeth, bap. Aug. 5, 1770. C.R.
Joel, s. Joel and Sarah, April 10, 1801.
John, s. Robert and Elizabeth, Aug. 10, 1766. C.R.
John, s. Samuel and Rhoda, Sept. 16, 1774.
John, s. Joel and Sarah, March 28, 1799.
John Stilman, s. David Jr. and Polly, Oct.? or Nov. 10, 1816.
Jonathan, s. Joel and Sarah, Sept. 22, 1802.
Joseph, s. David and Hannah, June 12, 1791.
Joseph, s. Joseph and Sophia, April 19, 1832.
Joseph Estabrook, s. Abner and Lucy, Aug. 14, 1830.
Josephine, d. Abner and Lucy, July 5, 1837.
Joshua, s. David and Hannah, March 12, 1802.
Lemuel, s. Robert and Mary, bap. Aug. 27, 1780. C.R.
Levi, s. Samuel and Rhoda, Dec. 4, 1772.
Levi, s. Samuel and Lois, Dec. 27, 1783.
Lois, d. Samuel and Lois, Nov. 7, 1779.
Lucy, d. David and Hannah, April 10, 1804.
Lucy Cushing, d. Abner and Lucy, Oct. 31, 181– [1818 ?].
Lydia, d. Samuel and Rhoda, Feb. 7, 1777.
  "The above Lydia Young after the death of her mother, by her father is named Rhoda."
Lydia, d. Robert and Mary, bap. Aug. 27, 1780. C.R.
Maria, d. Joseph and Sophia, Feb. 5, 1825.
Mary Eugenia, d. Abner and Lucy, July 23, 1835.
Mercy, d. Robert and Mary, bap. Aug. 27, 1780. C.R.
Merrill Cheney, s. David Jr. and Philinda, May 4, 1823.
Moses, s. David and Hannah, Sept. 14, 1793.
Nancy, d. Samuel and Lois, July 17, 1788.
Nathaniel, s. Samuel and Lois, April 12, 1786.
Philinda, d. David Jr. and Philinda, April 26, 1827.
Polly, d. William and Kezia, March 14, 1781.
Polly, d. Joel and Sarah, Sept. 10, 1806.
Polly, d. David and Hannah, Sept. 5, 1807.
Reuben, s. David and Hannah, Sept. 24, 1786.
Rhoda, see Young, Lydia.
Robert, s. Robert and Sarah, bap. May 6, 1753. C.R.
Royal, s. William and Kezia, Dec. 29, 1787.
Sally, d. Joel and Sarah, July 16, 1804.
Sally Cowen ?, d. Samuel and Lois, May 4, 1793.
Samuel, s. Samuel and Lois, Aug. 12, 1791 [1781 ?].
Sarah, d. Robert and Sarah, bap. Nov. 4, 1750. C.R.
Sarah Jane, d. Hyram and Catharine, June 16, 1843.
Simeon, s. Robert and Sarah, bap. Aug. 8, 1760. C.R.
Sophia, d. Joseph and Sophia, June 24, 1829.

YOUNG, William, s. William and Kezia, Jan. 22, 1786.
William, s. Abner and Lucy, Aug. 11, 182– [1820 ?].
Zachariah Field, s. Joseph and Sophia, March 10, 1821.

UNIDENTIFIED

——, Roger, a negro boy, servant child to James and Hannah Oliver, bap. July 16, 1769. C.R.

——, Sally, d. William Bigelow's wife [Betsey], bap. April 15, 1817. C.R.

——, Sophia, a negro girl, servant child to James and Hannah Oliver, bap. July 16, 1769. C.R.

——, Stephen, a negro boy, servant to the Rev. James Humphrey, bap. Jan. 15, 1793. C.R.

——, Titus, a negro boy, was born May 9, 1770. Given to James and Esther Humfrey by the Rev. Mr. Aaron Whitney of Petersham. C.R.

——Violet, a negro woman belonging to James and Esther Humphrey, bap. April 24, 1774. C.R.

——, Zerah, a negro child belonging to John and Mary Oliver, bap. May 21, 1775. C.R.

ATHOL MARRIAGES.

ATHOL MARRIAGES.

To the year 1850.

ADAMS, Franklin and Somantha Rice, of New Salem, Jan. 3, 1842. In New Salem.
John J., of Taunton and Phebe Ann Allen, June 19, 1833.
Laura and Daniel Crawford, Nov. 4, 1841. In New Salem.
Louisa M. of Orange and Adin H. Smith, March 2, 1843.
Lucy of New Salem and Seth Fay, int. April 10, 1819.
Melvin and Mary Marble of Orange, int. Nov. 21, 1825.
Milley and Gilbert Capron of Barre, int. Feb. 7, 1818.
Olive of Winchendon and John Longley, June 15, 1820.
Polly and Paul Marble of Orange, April 26, 1823.
Sybil of New Salem and John Oldham, int. Dec. 2, 1818.

ADDISON, Abigail and Stephen Beal of Royalston, May 18, 1824.
Sarah of Greenfield, N. H., and Thomas Lewis, int. Jan. 16, 1816.

AINSWORTH, Mason of Barre and Ann Stratton, April —, 1836.
Merrick E. and Susan H. Partridge, April 28, 1842. Dup.

ALDEN [Allen in int.], Phinehas of Jameca, Vt., and Elizabeth Oliver, Feb. 18, 1796.

ALDRICH, Dexter (s. Moses and Priscilla, a. 25) and Ursula Stone of Dana, April 12, 1849.

ALGER, Salma of Northfield and Rebecka Peck of Royalston, Dec. 1, 1808.*

ALLEN, Elijah of Halifax, Vt., and Susanna Brown, Sept. 7, 1813.
Hiram H. of Amherst and Esther Humphreys, July 14, 1841.
John and Dolly Dalrymple, both of Northbredge, July 5, 1781.*
Julia of Orange and Jotham Lord, int. March 18, 1806.
Mary W. and B. Ellsworth Smith of Amherst, May 5, 1841.
Phebe Ann and John J. Adams of Taunton, June 19, 1833.
[Alden in marriage] Phineus of Jemecha, Vt., and Elisebeth Oliver, int. July 3, 1795.
Sarah P. and Levi Willard of Decatur, Ga., May —, 1835.

ALLIS, Luscius of Conway and Lois Graves, May 25, 1801.

* Intention not recorded.

AMSDEN, David and Rebeccah Peckham, both of Petersham, Dec. 8, 1818.*

ANDREWS, Collins and Hannah Twitchell, Oct. 1, 1827.
Thurston and Aminta Holmes of Winchester, N. H., int. Nov. 25, 1821.

ANGER, Polly and William Pierse [Rice in Royalston V.R.] of Royalston, Sept. 13, 1784. In Royalston.

ATKINS, Thomas and Anna Kindall, both of Gerry, Oct. 24, 1799.*

AUGUSTUS, Anne of Sutton and Prince Tuzadrick [Fradrick?], Nov. 16, 1780. In Sutton.

AVERELL, Sarah L. of Milford, N. H., and Joseph P. Myrick, int. Aug. 30, 1834.

AXDAIL, Tabatha and Elisha Whitmore of Royalston, Aug. 13, 1782. In Royalston.

BABBET (see below), George W. and Susan A. Cutting, March —, 1837.

BABBIT, Mary L. of Petersham and Jonathan W. Fay, int. July 31, 1828.
Nathaniel and Mary Mandell of Barre, March 3, 1778. In Barre.

BABBITT (see above), Emeline of Petersham and Simeon W. Hodges of Norton, June 27, 1841.*
George Willard (s. Levi and Polly, a. 32, married) and Elvira Brigham Witt, Oct. 22, 1844.

BABCOCK, Samuel of Milton (s. Josiah and Nancy, a. 32) and Lydia Thorp, Dec. 4, 1844.

BACHELER (see Batchelder, etc.), Abigal of Royalston and Calvin Kendall, June 27, 1793. In Royalston.

BADGER, James and Hannah Sawyer of Templeton, int. Jan. 13, 1800.

BAITS (see Bates), Marcy and Jonathan Train, Sept. 12, 1770.

BAKER, Abigail of Northampton and Caleb Smith, int. Feb. 1, 1789.
Amanda of Orange and Lysander Richardson, int. July 26, 1831.

* Intention not recorded.

ATHOL MARRIAGES. 107

BAKER, Charles Jr. [of Templeton c.r.] and Anna Jackson [of Petersham, c.r.], Nov. 25, 1779.*
David Daniels and Lydia Jacobs, Sept. 15, 1802.
Delia (d. Sher. and Hannah, a. 36) and George O. Kelton, Sept. 3, 1846.
Ira of Orange and Mary Young, Dec. 1, 1831.
Lucretia and Benjamin Bowen, both of Grafton, May 27, 1807.*

BALDWIN, Lucretia of Phillipston and David Orcutt, int. Nov. 15, 1823.

BALEY [Bailey in int.] Hannah and Ebeneser Dunton, Feb. 24, 177[8].
Mary of Stow and Ebenezer Nights, int. Sept. 2, 1772.
Mary and Nathaniel Phillips, April 29, 1784.
Neomi and John Barrett, Nov. 13, 1792.

BALL, Abraham and Betty Lampson of Unity, N.H., int. May 26, 1793.
Absolem and Eunice Fish, Dec. 5, 1803.
Adinijah and Mary Phillips of Gerry, Feb. 28, 1788.
Capt. Adonijah and Anna Taft of Royalston, int. Dec. 26, 1818.
Grace Cachran and Nathan Cutting Jr. of Royalston, Nov. 12, 1799.
Wid. Hannah and Joseph Godard, May 3, 1819.
Hannah Ann and Alfred Peckam of Templeton, Jan. 12, 1841.
Isaac Jr. and Hannah Commins [of Templeton, in int.], May 3, 1778.
Jacob and [wid. c.r.] Hannah Lamb of Gerry, Jan. 16, 1806.
James and Maria Tuttle, Dec. 2, 1819.
Minerva P. and Freeland Stockwell, in year ending April 1, 1834.
Moses and Susannah Nutt, Feb. 18, 1762.
Moses and Releaf Twichell, Sept. 4, 1816.
Persis F. and Thomas Ellenwood, Nov. 13, 1825.
Moses P. and Susan H. Peirce of Petersham, int. March 11, 1825.
Rachel and Asa Lampson, Dec. 1, 1762.
Sarah and Joel Young, Feb. 23, 1797.
Susanna and Joel Buckman of Unity, Vt., Jan. 17, 1803.

BALLARD (examine Bullard), Anna and Asa Hill, June 20, 1820.
Edward and Hepzibah Dexter of Orange, Dec. 21, 1841.
Elijah and Elisabeth Crosby, July 21, 1814.
Dea. Elijah and Polly Cutting of Templeton, int. Oct. 30, 1819.
Hepzibath and Benjamin Dexter Jr., April 15, 1798.
Molly and Elijah Towne, Jan. 26, 1786. In Royalston.
Polly and Amos Bullard, Oct. 30, 1806.

* Intention not recorded.

ATHOL MARRIAGES.

BANCROFT, Benjamin of Petersham and Susanna Fay, Feb. 9, 1819.
Charles and Nancy Dike, Feb. 3, 1825.
Eliza and Enoch Lang[?] of Eaton, N. H., Feb. 24, 1833.
Elvira of Wendel and Alexander Gray, int. Dec. 3, 1825.
Harrisson and Sally Bosworth, both of Petersham, June 29, 1818.*
Jacob and Sally Turner of Royalston, Aug. 28, 1833.
Mary and Samuel Stevens of Thetford, Vt., Jan. 31, 1836.
Nancy and Samuel Clapp Jr., both of Petersham, May 6, 1819.*
Ruth of Ewings Grant and Cyrus Stockwell, Dec. 3, 1835.
Samuel and Harriet S. Chase of Gill, int. Feb. 26, 1830.
Samuel and Esther Briggs, Oct. 5, 1835.
Sarah B. (d. Charles and Nancy, a. 19) and James E. Morse, Nov. 15, 1844.

BANKS, John S. and Emily E. Piper, both of Ewings Grant, April 18, 1838.*

BARBER, Addison P. of Amherst (s. Ira and Lovina, a. 36, widr.) and L. Maria Totman of Hardwick, Sept. 21, 1848.*.
Sarah G. (d. John P. and Ellen) and Albert F. Young, Aug. 27, 1843.

BARDWELL, Josephus of Williamston and Abigail Stratton, Feb. 25, 1816.

BARLOW, Wyatt of Hardwick (s. Joshua and Roxana, a. 28) and Mary G. Flint, Jan. 19, 1848.

BARNARD, Gen. Ebenezer L. of Worcester and Caroline Sweetser, May 23, 1838.

BARNS, Clarissa of Gill and Sumner Sibley, int. Nov. 6, 1830.

BARR, James P. of Ware and Lydia E. Tenney of Royalston, May 19, 1842*.

BARRET (see Barrett), Lydia and David Lamb of Framingham, Nov. 13, 1795.
Lydia of Berre and Moses Marble, June 7, 1788.
Lydia of Ashby and Charles Richardson, int. Aug. 25, 1814.

BARRETT (see above), Alice and Franklin Saunders of Westminster, Oct. 30, 1831.
Anna of Ashby and Benjamin Dexter Jr., int. Aug. 19, 1800.
John and Neomi Baley, Nov. 13, 1792.

* Intention not recorded.

BARROUS, Simon of New Bedford (s. William and Asenath, a. 34) and Caroline Twichell, Dec. 25, 1845.

BARRY, Elizabeth L. (d. Thomas, a. 18) and Charles A. Corey of Ashburnham, July 13, 1848.
Luthera and Willard Sibley, Oct. 19, 1842.
Thomas and Lucinda Dike, Sept. 8, 1822.

BARTLETT, Joseph (s. David and Abigail, a. 23) and Harriot N. Wiggins, Nov. 3, 1845.

BARTON, Ophelia and Abner G. Stratton, July 7, 1842.

BASSETT, Rowena S. (d. Elias and Amy, a. 20) and Charles S. Root of Greenwich, Feb. 3, 1847.

BATCHELDER (see Bacheler), Joseph Jr. of Greenfield, N. H. and Mary T. Humphreys, May 20, 1819.

BATCHELOR, Betcy of Fitchburg and Abel Stratton, int. Aug. 22, 1801.
Hannah and Abel Bigelow, April 11, 1816.
Nabby of Fitchburg and Josiah Wesson, int. Sept. 20, 1803.
Stephen and Marabah Stratton, April 28, 1774.

BATES (see Baits), Achsah of Phillipston and Darius Buckman, int. Feb. 11, 1832.
Hannah and David Train, int. April 22, 1774.
Sarah and James Whealler, int. Feb. 13, 1779.
Theadore and Polley Shattuck, both of Templeton, Sept. 1, 1785.*
William and Sarah Stockwell of Chesterfield, int. April 26, 1777.

BATTLE, Clarissa and Amos P. Holden, May 20, 1838.
Laurinda of Orange and Samuel F. Cheney, int. Dec. 30, 1824.

BEAL (see Beul), Joseph and Sally Haven, Aug. 31, 1807.
Stephen of Royalston and Abigail Addison, May 18, 1824.

BELLOWS, Lydia of Western and Jonathan Fairbank, int. March 6, 1807 [1817].

BEMIS, Elvira S. and Eli [Eri ?] Shepardson, both of Royalston, Jan. 5, 1843.*

BENJAMIN, Daniel [of Ashburnham in int.] and Tomasan Fulton [Felton ?], Nov. 10, 1779.

BEUL (see Beal) [Beal in Royalston v.r.], John of Royalston and Lydia Holman, May 10, 1789. In Royalston.

* Intention not recorded.

ATHOL MARRIAGES.

BIGELOW, Abel and Hannah Batchelor, April 11, 1816.
Abel and Eunice Sawtell of Phillipston, int. Oct. 13, 1828.
Daniel and Hannah Stockwell, April 29, 1827.
David and Lois Taylor, June 3, 1779.
Esther and Josiah [Isaiah in int. and Petersham v.r.] Richardson of Petersham, July 3, 1783. In Petersham.
Esther (d. Abel and Hannah) and Sylvester Sawyer of Royalston, June 27, 1843.
Frances and Leonard C. Fuller, April 13, 1842. Dup.
Jotham and Mary Powers of Petersham, int. July 9, 1771.
Patty and Joel Devenport of Petersham, April 9 [7 ?], 1807.
Rebecca of Royalston and Elisha [Elihu in int.] Smith, Nov. 29, [17—] [1798]. In Royalston.
William and Betsy Maynard of Stow, int. Jan. 13, 1809.

BILLINGS, Mary Ann and William K. Whitney, April 2, 1843.
Sophia Ann and Elbridge W. Whitney of Petersham, Oct. 20, 1841.

BINGHAM [Brigham ?], Chester of Chesterfield and Deborah Rich, int. May 31, 1786.

BISHUP, Sally and Bala Twichel, Sept. 2, 1792. In Richmond.

BLAKE, Martha S. of Warwick (d. James and Susan, a. 26) and Windsor Drury of Wendell, Jan. 1, 1849.
Mary and Joshua Davis of Newfane, Vt., Jan. 26, 1804.

BLANCHARD (see Blanshard), Betsey and John Flagg, June 2, 1790. In Winchendon.
Moses and Azubah Blogget of Westford, int. Aug. 17, 1779.
Stephen of Winchendon and Molly Dyer, int. July 11, 1801.

BLANDEN, Olive of Royalston and Seth Kendall, int. Dec, 21, 1799.
Polly of Royalston and Seth Kendall, int. Oct. 20, 1804.

BLANSHARD (see Blanchard), Aaron and Dorcas Pike, int. July 23, 1784.

BLISS, Elisabeth of Royalston and Asa W. Burnap of Bennington, June 20, 1799.*
Perrin and Persis Ann Bullard of Worcester, int. Dec. 5, 1835.
Stephen W. and Persis Boyden of Orange, int. July 6, 1833.
William and Mary Boutwell, Sept. 27, 1838.

BLODGET, Amos and Phebe Harwood, Jan. 13, 1814.

* Intention not recorded.

BLODGETT, Levi and Ardilisa Hodges, Aug. 16, 1816.

BLOGGET, Azubah of Westford and Moses Blanchard, int. Aug. 17, 1779.

BLUNT, Andrew and Unice Davice, March 25, 1760. [Belonged to Sturbride, c.r.]

BOSWORTH, Sally and Harrisson Bancroft, both of Petersham, June 29, 1818.*

BOUKER, Lydia and Timothy Hoar, Jan. 21, 1819.
Susanna of Gerry and Eleaser Graves, int. Dec. 14, 1811.

BOUTELL, James (s. Loami and Hannah, a. 25) and Martha Burleck, April 3, 1845.
John and Ann M. Wilder, int. Oct. 24, 1834 [1835 ?].

BOUTWELL, Mary and William Bliss, Sept. 27, 1838.

BOWEN, Benjamin and Lucretia Baker, both of Grafton, May 27, 1807.*
John (a. 24) and Sabrina W. Hinds, July 8, 1849?.

BOYDEN, Elbridge and Louisa Davis of Royalston, int. Dec. 27, 1833.
Persis of Orange and Stephen W. Bliss, int. July 6, 1833.

BRADBURY, Hannah and Abel How, both of Petersham, Dec. 3, 1778.*

BRADISH, Jerusha of Winchendon and Zebulan Stratton, June 9, 1780. In Winchendon.
Jonas and Jerusha Morton, Nov. 29, 1757.
Robart and Lydia Mortin, Oct. 29, 1754.
Robert and Nabby Jackson of Petersham, Sept. 23, 1793. Petersham.

BRAGG, Harriet and Calvin A. Drury, Dec. 25, 1843. In Royalston.
Lucy of Royalston and Joseph Godard, int. Feb. 22, 1804.
Polly of Royalston and Daniel Bullard, int. Nov. 10, 1833.
Sarah of Royalston and Joseph Jacobs, May 17, 1792. In Royalston.

BRIDE, Hannah of Westminster and Joseph Commings, int. June 25, 1775.

BRIDGES, Benjamin and Rachel Oliver, Oct. 10, 1790.

* Intention not recorded.

BRIGGS, Betsy and John Stockwell, Nov. 30, 1815.
Esther and Samuel Bancroft, Oct. 5, 1835.
John and Hannah Mann, int. May 24, 1823.
John Jr. and Mary F. Hemmingway, both of Orange, Nov. 25, 1841.*
Moses and Adeline Grey, int. May 3, 1831.
Nancy and Stephen Fairbank, Sept. 2, 1812.
Nathan G. of Orange and Betsey Cummings, Dec. 11, 1838.
Polly and Noah Stockwell, Sept. 29, 1807.
Sophronia and Daniel L. Holt of Hardwick, June 30, 1840.
Tabetha and Solomon Smith, Dec. 27, 1780.

BRIGHAM [Bingham?], Chester of Chesterfie[ld] and Deborah Rich, Sept. 23, 1786.
Lucy of Fitzwilliam, N. H. and James Humphrey Jr., int. Oct. 13, 1793.
Lydia of New Brantree and Lemuel Ruggles, int. Dec. 25, 1779.

BROCK, David Southwick (s. David and Lucy, a. 33, married) and Fidelia Hill, Nov. 19, 1844.
Ebeneser and Caroline Humphreys, Sept. 15, 1841.
Isaac and Louisa Hair, Aug. 20, 1837.
Isaac Z. and Esther Cook, Sept. 29, 1841.
John A. of Worcester (s. Robert and Sabra, a. 27) and Martha A. Mayo, April 4, 1848.

BRONSDEN, William of Phillipston and Phebe Lewis, March 2, 1829.

BRONSDON, William and Martha S. Holt, April 22, 1840.

BROOKS, George E. (s. John and Puah, a. 22) and Juliaet Brown, Aug. 6, 1846.
Wid. Joanna and Elias Stratton, March 25, 1796.
Joanna and John Collins of Malden, May 1, 1797.
Phebe and Oliver Greenwood of Winchendon, Jan. 15, 1807.
Polly and Jerome Devenport of Petersham, Sept. 20, 180[7].
Susanna and John Death of Gerry, Jan. 29, 1798.

BROWN, Hannah of New Salem and Abner Twitchell, Aug. 16, 1785. In Orange.
Hannah of Chesterfield, N. H., and Abraham Nutt Jr., int. Jan. 10, 1796.
Hannah and William Peirce Jr., both of Royalston, June 9, 1819.*
Huldah of Petersham and Phinehas Morton, int. March 18, 1800.
John G. and Lydia S. Ward, April 4, 1838.

* Intention not recorded.

BROWN, Joseph of Orange, alias Ewinshire, and Anna Wesson, int. June 18, 1802.
Juliaet (d. E., a. 21) and George E. Brooks, Aug. 6, 1846.
Lydia and Zaccheus Rich Jr., Nov. 7, 1781. [Int. Oct. 13, 1782?.]
Lyman of Hubbardston and Salome Rich, int. April 27, 1836. [Married May 31, C.R.]
Russell of Ashburnham and Julia Goddard, July 3, 1836.
Susannah of Royalston and David Dike, April 22, 1795. In Royalston.
Susanna and Elijah Allen of Halifax, Vt., Sept. 7, 1813.
William of Gerry and Meriam Newell, int. Aug. 10, 1794.

BRUCE, Charles and Cynthia Rich of Phillipston, int. Aug. 23, 1829.
Charles S. (s. Isaac and Fanny, a. 34, widr.) and Lucretia E. King, April 9, 1846.

BRYANT, Albigence P. of Templeton (s. Nathan and Tabitha, a. 22) and Diana Willmarth, June 4, 1846.
Betsey L. and Cyroll C. Lord, March 19, 1833.
Clemant and Rachel Wheeler, Nov. 27, 1806.
George and Louisa Ann Roby, Oct. 24, 1841.
Joel of Petersham and Hannah Lord, Feb. 3, 1801.
John and Betsy Lewis, May 2, 1821.
Mary Ann and Thomas Miller, Dec. 4, 1837.
Mercy and Lucius Taylor, Nov. 28, 1833.
Silence L. (d. Clement) and Charles R. Tenny, Dec. 3, 1843.

BUCKLEY, Robert B. of Templeton and Sophronia J. Gould, int. May 3, 1836. [Married July 3, C.R.]

BUCKMAN (see Bucknam, Bucknum), Joel of Unity, Vt., and Susanna Ball, Jan. 17, 1803.
Darius and Achsah Bates of Phillipston, int. Feb. 11, 1832.

BUCKNAM, Amos and Marcy Poor, May 20, 1767.

BUCKNUM (see above), Joseph Jr. and Hannah Marble, Nov. 23, 1758.

BULLARD (examine Ballard), Amos and Polly Ballard, Oct. 30, 1806.
Amos and Martha Twichel, March 12, 1812.
Daniel and Polly Bragg of Royalston, int. Nov. 10, 1833.
[Ballard in int], Joshua and Anna Raymond, June 15, 1775.
Martha and Stephen Harwood, May 16, 1827.

BULLARD, Mary and Charles O. Lincoln of Wendell, Sept. 13, 1838.
Nathan and Elizabeth Fay, Aug. 20, 1800.
Persis Ann of Worcester and Perrin Bliss, int. Dec. 5, 1835.

BULLOCK, Charles A. of Fitchburg (s. Rufus and Sarah, a. 29) and Maria A. Humphreys, June 3, 1847.
Welcome and Grace Fay, Nov. 28, 1799.

BURBANK, Abigail and Paul West of New Braintree, Nov. 5, 1795.
Eleasor and Elisabeth Copland, int. Nov. 28, 1786.
John and Elizabeth Woodbury of Royalston, June 15, 1788.

BURLECK, Martha (d. John and Hepzibah, a. 20) and James Boutell, April 3, 1845.

BURNAP, Asa W. of Bennington and Elizabeth Bliss of Royalston, June 20, 1799.*

BURROUGS, Maria of Alstead, N. H., and Loring Willson, int. Oct. 5, 1834.

BURT, Asahel of Westmoreland, N. H., and Charlotte MacBride, Nov. 14, 1802.

CADY, Ephraim Jr. and Sarah Parker, March 4, 1776.

CADEY, Ephraim Jr. and Marcy Ford, Jan. 10, 1770.
Ephraim Jr. and Lydia Moor, March 31, 1774.

CALDWELL, James and Isabella Oliver, Jan. 15, 1751.

CALHOON, Anna of Petersham and Phinehas Robbins, April 18, 1793. In Petersham.

CAMPBELL, Dolly F. (d. Joseph and Lydia Farnum [Farmer ?], a. 35, wid.) and Charles H. Stevens of Manchester, N. H., Sept. 7, 1846.

CAPRON, Ephraim and Sarah Fairban[k], May 18, 1784.
Ephraim and Lucy Garfield, Nov. 22, 1792.
Gilbert of Barre and Milley Adams, int. Feb. 7, 1818.
Sally and James Kelton, April 27, 1788.

CARCLESS, Thomas and Abigail Sawtell, both of Templeton, Aug. 16, 1783.*

CARPENTER, Thankfull B. of Swansey, N. H., and Elbridge Foskett, int. May 12, 1836.

* Intention not recorded.

ATHOL MARRIAGES. 115

CARRIEL, Mary and Thaddeus Marsh, May 5, 1819.

CARROLL, Sally and Thomas Lewis Jr. of Harvard, Oct. 14, 1823.

CARTER, Jacob and Arathusa Young, Nov. 28, 1816.

CARUTH, Amos and Anna Raymond, Dec. 17, 18[07].
Jemima of Gerry and Jabez Sawyer of Wendell, Feb. 23, 1798.*

CHAMBERLAIN (see Chamberlin), Mehitable of Dana and Joseph Sprague, int. Aug. 20, 1819.
Ruth of Dana and Barnabas Wendell, int. June 26, 1819.
Sophia and Alanson Rice of Greenwich, Jan. 7, 1817.

CHAMBERLIN (see above), Priscilla E. of New Salem and Lysander Fay, int. May 8, 1830.

CHANY (see Cheney), Joanna and David Pike, Oct. 26, 1786.

CHAPLIN, Dr. Ebeneser and Abigail Ellenwood, May 2, 1820.

CHASE, Abba of Cornish, N. H., and Meriam Chase of Keene, N.H., Nov. 13, 1838.*
Betsey P. and William Sawyer of Stoneham, Oct. 27, 1841. In Royalston.
Charles of Keene, N. H., and Hannah Chase, June 7, 1832.
Clarissa and Lysander F. Townsend, int. Oct. 24, 1829.
David of Royalston and Sarah Raymond, Nov. 29, 1786. In Royalston.
Deborah of Petersham and Seth Rider, int. March 22, 1776.
Dulcenia and Daniel Ellenwood, Oct. 6, 1835.
Freeman and Adaline Pierce of Chesterfield, N. H., int. May 9, 1833.
Hannah and Charles Chase of Keene, N. H., June 7, 1832.
Harriet S. of Gill and Samuel Bancroft, int. Feb. 26, 1830.
Henry of Nichewaug and Abigail Stratton of Pequioge, Dec. 29, 1746. In Petersham.
Meriam of Keene, N.H., and Abba Chase of Cornish, N.H., Nov. 13, 1838.*
Moses and Meriam Twichel, June 6, 1797.
Rebecca of Keene, N. H., and Joel Kendell Jr., int. Oct. 11, 1828.
Sylvia and David Cole of Mt. Holly, Vt., April 8, 1840.

CHENEY (see Chany), Amos and Elvira Mallard of Gill, int. Nov. 13, 1825.
Amos L. and Lucy Fish, Oct. 31, 1843.

* Intention not recorded.

CHENEY, Betsey (d. Phillip and Lorinda a. 21) and Josiah Holden, both of Orange, March 31, 1846.
Matthew (s. Mark and Sally, a. 24) and Susan G. Horr, May 24, 1846.
Nathan Jr. and Rhoda Holbrook of Swansey, N. H., int. Oct. 28, 1826.
Samuel F. and Laurinda Battle of Orange, int. Dec. 30, 1824.

CHILDS, Sabrina and Welcome Mason, Dec. 14, 1809.

CHIPMAN, Ebenezer M. of Salem (s. R. M. and Elizabeth, a. 34) and Abigail M. Mansfield of Bath, Me., Feb. 24, 1846.

CHOAT, Patience and Samuel Duncan, both of Warwick, April 13, 1779.*

CHUB, Silance and Samuel Hasay, Oct. 12, 1775.

CHUBB, Andrew S. of Phillipston and Harriet Hoar of Westminster, Aug. 29, 1843.

CHURCH, Artemas of Templeton and Wid. Mehitable Young, int. April 5, 1832. [Married May 2, c.r.]
Mercy and Roswell Davis of Waterford, Vt., Feb. 17, 1812.
Paul and Esther Hasy, June 16, 1774.
Paul and Mehitable Marsh of Barre, Jan. 18, 1797.
Phebe and Oliver Cutting of Concord, Vt., Jan. 18, 1801.
Sally and Elijah Nichols, Nov. 29, 1797.
Unice and Uriah Rice, Sept. 7, 1780.*

CLAPP, Elvira P. and James I. Goulding, Feb. 10, 1841.
Nancy Angelia (d. Samuel and Nancy, a. 20) and Sumner J. Lincoln, of Brookfield, Aug. 4, 1846.
Samuel Jr. and Nancy Bancroft, both of Petersham, May 6, 1819.*

CLARK, Aurelia of Wendell and John Dike, int. April 2, 1828.
Edson and Lepha Fuller, both of Royalston, May 31, 1805.*
Elon of New Salem and Calista Giles, int. May 14, 1821.
Florella of Wendell and Job Fry Jr., int. May 23, 1830.
Levi B. of Boston and Eleanor Peirce, Nov. 24, 1822.
Mary of Medfield and Jacob Hutchson, int. Nov. 7, 1778.
Samuel and Luseba Ward, May 2, 1821.
Samuel (s. Samuel and Huldah, a. 55, married) and Polly Young, April 23, 1846.

CLEAVELAND (see Cleveland), Delight of Walpole and Artemas Fay, Feb. 20, 1797. In Walpole.

* Intention not recorded.

ATHOL MARRIAGES. 117

CLEMENCE [Clemmon in int.], James Jr. of Petersham and Mary Moore, May 27, 1772. In Petersham.

CLEMENT, Jonathan of Richfield, N.Y. and Betsy Smith, Aug. 7, 1806.

CLEMONTS, Lydia and Samuel Stearns, Sept. 7, 1796.

CLEVELAND (see Cleaveland), Charles R. of Hardwick and Eunice S. Thayer, Sept. 21, 1842.
Persis of Hardwick and Aaron Cooley, int. July 28, 1783.

COALMAN [Colman in int.], John Jr. and Susa Shute of Templeton, March 18, 1784.

COBB, Miles of Hardwick and Lucretia Totman of Petersham, Jan. 31, 1827.*
Rodolphus and Caroline Thompson, int. Jan. 4, 1836.
Samuell and Dolly Stratton, Sept. 9, 1835.

COCHRAN, Susannah of Blanford and James Nutt, —— —, 1770. In Blandford.

COLE (see Coles), David of Mt. Holly, Vt. and Sylvia Chase, April 8, 1840.
Kimball of New Market, N.H. and Mary Stockwell, March 17, 1842.

COLES [Coats in int.], Judith and Reuben Morton, March 27, 1777.

COLLAR, Lucy of Orange and Lysander F. Townsend, June 23, 1839.

COLLINS, John of Malden and Joanna Brooks, May 1, 1797.

COLONY, Dr. George D. (s. Josiah, a. 27) and Harriet N. Stevens, May 23, 1849.

COMMING, Elizebeth and Isaac Train, Sept. 17, 1779.
Elizebeth and Elijah Flagg, [b]oth of Templeton, April 26, 1781.*

COMMINGS, Joseph Jr. and Hannah Bride of Westminster, int. June 25, 1775.

COMMINS [Comings in int], Hannah and Isaac Ball Jr., May 3, 1778.

CONANT, Sally and Edward Loud of Fitzwilliam, N. H., Feb. 15, 1825.

* Intention not recorded.

COOK, Abigail and William Mann of New Salem, in year ending, April 1, 1834.
Benjamin Jr. and Betsey Stratton, May 29, 1828. Dup.
Esther and Isaac Z. Brock, Sept. 29, 1841.
Ruth and Joshua Wyatt, both of Petersham, June 13, 1833.*
Salina and Frederick Rich, Nov. 13, 1839.
Somantha and David Marshall Twichell of Warwick, March 9, 1842.

COOLEDGE, Mary and Eli B. Davis, both of Orange, Feb. 8, 1838.*

COOLEY, Aaron and Persis Cleveland of Hardwick, int. July 28, 1783.

COPLAND, Elisabeth and Eleazor Burbank, int. Nov. 28, 1786.

COREY, Charles A. of Ashburnham (s. Asahel and Polly, a. 22) and Elizabeth L. Barry, July 13, 1848.

COTTING [Cutting in Petersham v.r.], Lois and Samuel Young, int. Nov. 21, 1778.

CRAWFORD, Chester and Hannah Stratton, April —, 1837.
Daniel and Laura Adams, Nov. 4, 1841. In New Salem.

CROSBEY (see Crosby), Hannah and Josiah Twichel, June 9, 1789.
Josey and Rhody Fairbank, Oct. 2, 1788.

CROSBY (see above), Wid. Anna and Joel Kendall, Dec. 31, 1822.
Charles and Hannah L. Young, April 21, 1819.
Elizabeth and Elijah Ballard, July 21, 1814.
John and Sinda Kendall, Oct. 1, 1794.
John and Betsy Morse of Ashby, int. Aug. 27, 1808.
Nancy and George Fitts, Jan. 5, 1815.
Nancy of Putney, Vt. and Joseph Fish, int. Oct. 8, 1818.
Reliance Crocker and Josiah Richardson of Leominster, int. March 1, 1808.

CROSSMAN, Huldah and Clark Fisk of Orange, March 19, 1839.
Lydia H. (d. Daniel and Amy) and Joseph O. Spear, March 21, 1844

CROWL, Mrs. Almira and Daniel E. Morrison of Orange, Nov. 2, 1840

CUMMINGS, Betsey and Nathan G. Briggs of Orange, Dec. 11, 1838.

* Intention not recorded.

ATHOL MARRIAGES. 119

CUMMINGS, Laura A. (d. Jonathan B. and Polly, a. 18) and William Richards, Oct. 27, 1846.
Lucy A. and Levi Morse, May 31, 1843.

CURTICE, Betsy and Stephen Gleason, both of Petersham, Jan. 20, 1808.*

CUSHING, Lucy of Pembroke and Rev. Joseph Estrebrooks, Sept. 3, 1788. In Pembroke.
Mehitable of Hanson and Gen. Nathaniel C. Estabrook, int. Jan. 25, 1823

CUSHMAN, Dr. Earl of Orwell, Vt. and Lucy R. Young, Sept. 11, 1834.

CUTING, Dolly and Jonathan Kelton, Sept. 10, 1789.

CUTTING, Earll and Lydia Kindall, Dec. 10, 1784.
Judith and Eleazer Graves, Oct. 29, 1767.
Mary and Robart Love, May 20, 1778.
Nathan Jr. of Royalston and Grace Cachran Ball, Nov. 12, 1799.
Oliver of Concord, Vt., and Phebe Church, Jan. 18, 1801.
Polly and Joshua Newhall, April 24, 1791.
Polly of Templeton and Dea. Elijah Ballard, int. Oct. 30, 1819.
Susan A. and George W. Babbet, March —, 1837.

DAKIN, Hannah of West Sudbury and Walter Godard, int. Aug. 28, 1805.

DALRYMPLE, Dolly and John Allen, both of Northbredge, July 5, 1781*

DANFORTH, Erastus and Hannah Newhall, April 6, 1815.

DAVENPORT (see Devenport), Jesse C. of Petersham and Hannah M. Russell, April 5, 1841.

DAVICE [?], Olive and Rubin Hale, int. Dec. 31, 1785.
Unice and Andrew Blunt, March 25, 1760.

DAVIS (see above), Benjamin of Holden and Mary Peirce, Jan. 18, 1816.
Daniel and Laura W. Stratton, July 6, 1842.
Dolly of Concord and Jacob Stevans, March 28, 1797. In Concord.
Eli B. and Mary Cooledge, both of Orange, Feb. 8, 1838.*
Eunice of Orange and Henry Smith of Swansey, N. H., Dec. 17, 1840.*
Ezekiel G. of Grafton and Lydia S. Kendell, Oct. 4, 1827.

* Intention not recorded.

ATHOL MARRIAGES.

DAVIS, Joshua of Newfane, Vt., and Mary Blake, Jan. 26, 1804.
Louisa of Royalston and Elbridge Boyden, int. Dec. 27, 1833.
Lydia H. of South Orange and James Townsend, Sept. 25, 1839.
Narcissa of Orange and John Warden of Worcester, June 14, 1837.*
Norris of Orange and Lucy Ann Howard, Oct. 30, 1831.
Roswell of Waterford, Vt., and Mercy Church, Feb. 17, 1812.

DAY, John and Lois Walker, Aug. 26, 1795.
Lucy of Winchendon and Benjamin Fuller, int. Aug. 3, 1797.
Mrs. Mary L. of Gardner and Joseph Rich Jr., May 4, 1842. In Gardner.
Nabby and Benjamin Rich, both of Phillipston, Oct. 4, 1821.*
Susan and Ammi Stockwell, April 14, 1837. In Winchendon.

DEANE, Joshua [of Warwick in int.] and Marcy Goddard, Dec. 18, 1777.

DEATH, An— [Ann in int.] and Edward Goddard, Nov. 11, 1784.
Benjamin and Huldah Edson, Oct. 26, 1778.
Hannah and Ebenezer Goddard, July 6, 1775.
John of Gerry and Susanna Brooks, Jan. 29, 1798.
Martha and John Haven Jr., Sept. 8, 1777.

DERBY, Abraham and Damarious Derby of Leominster, int. March 17, 1804.
Damarious of Leominster and Abraham Derby, int. March 17, 1804.
Levi and Sally Stratton, Jan. 14, 1810.
Mary and Asa Nichols, both of Westminster, Jan. 16, 1806.*

DEVENPORT (see Davenport), Jerome of Petersham and Polly Brooks, Sept. 20, 180[7].
Joel of Petersham and Patty Bigelow, April 9[7 ?], 1807.
Stephen (married) and Rowena L. Stebbins, Feb. 8, 1844.

DEWING, Miriam of North Brookfield and Aden Manley, int. Dec. 18, 1816.
Mary and Leonard Howard, both of Orange, April 16, 1836.*

DEXTER, Anna and Job Fry Jr., June 24, 1834.
Benjamin and Hannah Stone of Rutland, int. Oct. 10, 1769.
Benjamin Jr. and Hepsibath Ballard, April 15, 1798.
Benjamin Jr. and Anna Barrett of Ashby, int. Aug. 19, 1800.
Betsey of Orange and Zacheus Wheeler Jr., int. Oct. 31, 1803.
David and Maria Hubbard of Royalston, int. Oct. 18, 1835.
Hepzibah of Orange and Edward Ballard, Dec. 21, 1841.

* Intention not recorded.

DEXTER, Ichabod and Abigail Smith, Aug. 2, 1759.
Joseph and Martha Smith, Dec. 9, 1756.
Mary and Benjamin Mortin, Sept. 28, 1760.
Moses and Persis Lord, both of Orange, April 13, 1837.*

DICKERSON, John of Orwell, Vt., and Submit Smith, Feb. 8, 1800.

DIKE, David and Susannah Brown of Royalston, April 22, 1795. In Royalston.
David and Patty Ward, June 17, 1801.
Edward and Susanna Wood, Feb. 22, 1803.
George L. and Laura Stratton, Sept. 29, 1833.
John and Aurelia Clark of Wendell, int. April 2, 1828.
Lucinda and Thomas Barry, Sept. 8, 1822.
Nancy and Charles Bancroft, Feb. 3, 1825.
Rachel and David Stratton, Sept. 25, 1825.
Sally and Joab Young, Sept. 5, 1833.
Samuel and Hannah Young, Aug. 14, 1803.

DOANE, Ebenezer of Petersham and Relief Twichel, Jan. 11, 1815.
Harden and Aurelia D. Witt, Aug. 30, 1819.
Henry of Boston (s. Jesse and Ruth, a. 33, widr.) and Sophronia Doane, Dec. 28, 1847.
Joshua and Ruth Parker, of Gerry, Oct. 5, 1801.
Sophronia (d. Isaac Y. and Priscilla, a. 28) and Henry Doane of Boston, Dec. 28, 1847.

DODGE, Susan of Templeton and Lewis Liverboo, int. June 3, 1825.

DRAKE, Bradey (s. Cyrus and Eunice, a. 23) and Harriet Lewis, April 2, 1846.
Caroline and Seth K. Harwood, Oct. 23, 1831.
Harriet and Benjamin M. Harwood, Oct. 4, 1841.

DREWRY, Joel and Ruth Hill, June 12, 1793.

DRURY, Amos and Lucy A. Hemenway of Bredport, Vt., int. Jan. 23, 1822.
Amos of Wendell (s. Joel and Mary, a. 37) and Sarah Stockwell, May 5, 1847.
Asenath and Isaac Miller Jr. of Keene, N. H., April 22, 1832.
Calvin A. (s. Jonathan) and Harriet Bragg, Dec. 25, 1843. In Royalston.

* Intention not recorded.

ATHOL MARRIAGES.

DRURY, Damarias and Samuel Haile, Nov. 29, 1792.
David and Lois Young, March 5, 1805.
Dorothy and Joseph Stockwell of Royalston, April 26, 1821.
Edward and Elizabeth Townsend, March 17, 1835.
Eliza and John R. Goodnough, Aug. 1, 1822.
George W. and Sally Stockwell of Royalston, int. Feb. 24, 1827.
Horace and Sally Thompson of Swansey, N. H., int. Dec. 29, 1827.
Joel Jr. and Louise Whitcomb of Phillipston, int. April 6, 1835.
Joel E. of Wendell and Sally Young, Nov. 16, 1831.
John and Lydia Smith, July 3, 1765.
John S. and Harriet Townsend, Aug. 16, 1836.
Jonathan Jr. and Martha Ann Garfield, March 14, 1837.
Lois Y. and Ruben Garfield, June 1, 1842.
Lucy and Joseph Goddard, May 17, 1798.
Wid. Molly and Levi. Norcross of Templeton, int. June 28, 1823.
Rhoda and Elias Walker of Royalston, Jan. —, 1835.
Ruth and Samuel Morse Jr., April 12, 1827.
Sally and William Morse, Nov. 23, 1839.
Silas of Wendell (s. Joel and Mary, a. 32, widr.) and Susan Jennings of Ewing, Sept. 7, 1847.
Susanna and Joseph Wiley of Hubbardston, March 24, 1803.
Windsor, of Wendell, [s. Joel and Mary, a. 27] and Martha S. Blake of Warwick, Jan. 1, 1849.*

DUDLEY, Lucy of Petersham and Walter Stratton, int. Aug. 26, 1815.
Mari of Sutton and Jabez Stratton, int. March 8, 1800.

DUNCAN, Samuel and Patience Choat, both of Warwick, April 13, 1779.*

DUNBAR, Polly of Orange and William More, int. April 10, 1811.

DUNTON [Donton in int.], Ebeneser and Hannah Baley, Feb. 24, 177[8].
Samuel and Mary Martin of Templeton, int. Oct. 21, 1780.

DYER, Abigail and Benjamin Goodridge Spaulding, int. Nov. 18, 1802.
Emeline (d. James and Polly, a. 24) and Frederick L. Heyward of Royalston, Nov. 29, 1849. In Royalston.
Mary (d. James and ———, a. 18) and Stephen Newton, March 14, 1848.
Molly and Stephen Blanchard of Winchendon, int. July 11, 1801.
Nancy and Jonathan J. Hill, Jan. 31, 1838.

* Intention not recorded.

ATHOL MARRIAGES. 123

EAMES, Sally of Holliston and Levi Lovering, Jan. 29, 1802.

EARL, Fanny and Jonas Pierce of Royalston, April 20, 1826.
Shade [?] A. and Fanny R. Mathews, both of North Brookfield, May 24, 1835. In North Brookfield.*

EASTY, Isaac and Lydia Forbes, both of Royalston, Nov. 26, 1801.*
Sarah and Timothy Richardson, Dec. 31, 1767. In Royalston.

EATON, Hulday of New Salem and Seth Twichel Jr., int. June 9, 1780.
Maltire and Huldah Haynes of Sudbury, Dec. 31, 1778. In Sudbury.
Mary of Framingham and Simon Goddard, int. Aug. 29, 1771.
Thankful of New Salem and Richard Morton, int. Jan. 12, 1782.

EBIT, Esther of Petersham and John K. Williams, int. July 1, 1822.

EDSON, Huldah and Benjamin Death, Oct. 26, 1778.

ELLENWOOD (see Ellinwood), Abigail and Dr. Ebenezer Chaplin, May 2, 1820.
Daniel and Dulcenia Chase, Oct. 6, 1835.
Lucy and Artemas Wilder of Petersham, March 13, 18[08].
Maria and Ezra Sargent of Putnam Co., Ga., Dec. 12, 1824.
Senaca and Metilda Fay, Jan. 18, 1807.
Thomas and Persis F. Ball, Nov. 13, 1825.

ELLINWOOD (see above), Belinda and Calvin Kelton Jr., int. April 10, 1829.
Daniel and Dorothy Fay, Feb. 7, 1799.
David A. (s. Daniel and Dorothy, a. 30, widr.) and Priscilla A. Mann of Petersham, Dec. 9, 1846.

ELLIOT, Stephen and Polly Fairbank, Dec. 29, 1799.

ELLIS (see Elliss), Abijah of Orange and Abigail Scot Lord, May 28, 1788.
Clark and Mary Ann Twichell, March 29, 1840.
Ira and Mercy F. Jenkins of Barre, int. Oct. 1, 1823 [1825 ?].
John L. and Lovicy Hemenway of Barre, int. Feb. 23, 1811.

ELLISS (see above), Mary of Royalston and Thomas Stow [How ?], June 22, 1779. In Royalston.

ELLSWORTH, Samuel of Greenwich and Harriet H. Proctor, Sept. 15, 1840.

* Intention not recorded.

EMERSON, Dea. Joseph of Wendell and Mary Kelton, Sept. 11, 1817.

EMORY, Almira K. and John Turner, both of South Orange, Nov. 21, 1839.*

ESTABROOK (see Estrebrooks), Benjamin and Candace Holbrook, May 23, 1831.
Lephe of Holden and Amos Jones Jr., int. April 12, 1800.
Lucy and Abner Young, Jan. 15, 1818.
Luisa and John Jones of Hope, Me., Feb. 4, 1826. At Vernon, Vt. c.r.
Marcia and Theodore Jones, Aug. 29, 1819.
Gen. Nathaniel C. and Mehitable Cushing of Hanson, int. Jan. 25, 1823.

ESTREBROOKS [Estabrook in int.], Rev. Joseph and Lucy Cushing of Pembroke, Sept. 3, 1788. In Pembroke.

FAIRBANK (see Fairbanks), Benjamin and Hannah Stratton, Nov. 25, 1787.
Ephraim and Metilda Twichel, May 26, 1802.
John Jr. and Fanny Kilton, July 16, 1780.
Johathan and Lydia Bellows of Western, int. March 6, 1807 [1817 ?].
Lecte and Daniel Morton, June 14, 1792.
Mehitable and Giles Smith, April 3, 1794.
Olive and Abiel Kinsley of Orange, Aug. 27, 1797.
Perny and Benjamin Warren, Feb. 2, 1792.
Polly and Stephen Elliot, Dec. 29, 1799.
Relief and Enos Twichel, Dec. 1, 1772.
Reuben and Lucinda Fish, Oct. 5, 1806.
Rhody and Josey Crosbey, Oct. 2, 1788.
Fairban[k], Sarah and Ephraim Capron, May 18, 1784.
Stephen and Nancy Briggs, Sept. 2, 1812.
Thomas and Hannah Graves, May 9, 1766.
Thomas and Rane Haskins of N. Salem, int. April 13, 1804.
Thomas and Susanna Welmarth, [Wid. Susanna Wilmarth in c.r.] Aug. 17, 1808.

FAIRBANKS (see above), John and Wid. Tabitha White of ———, Dec. 15, 1796. In Leominster.
Philemon and Sally Smith, both of Athol, June 19, 1779. In Bolton.

FALES, Lemuel Jr. of Claremont, N. H. (s. Lemuel, a. 26) and Letsey P. Twichell, May 13, 1847.

* Intention not recorded.

FANTON, Aseph and Rachel Wild of Brantree, int. Oct. 13, 1780. 1849.

FARR, Albert (s. Amariah and Clarrissa) and Almeda Rich, Jan. 15, 1849.
Charles and Cynthia P. Howard, March 27, 1838.
George (s. Amariah and Clarisa, a. 24) and Emily M. Howard, April 30, 1846.
Hollon (s. Amariah and Clarissa) and Mary Wheeler, Oct. 17, 1849.

FARRAR, Sally and Elijah Wood, May 29, 1800.

FAUNCE, Polly and Daniel Foster, March 17, 1791.

FAY, Adaline and Abel Lord, May 25, 1842.
Anna and John Haven, March 5, 1823.
Artimas and Delight Cleaveland of Walpole, Feb. 20, 1797. In Walpole.
Betsey and John Gates Jr., May 26, 1839.
Dorothy and Daniel Ellinwood, Feb. 7, 1799.
Elizabeth and Nathan Bullard, Aug. 20, 1800.
Emerson and Nancy A. Foster of New Salem, int. May 8, 1830.
Esther and Jonathan Stratton, March 8, 1821.
Freeborn R. (s. Jonas and Anna, a. 22) and Lucy Augusta Foster, June 4, 1849.
Grace and Welcome Bullock, Nov. 28, 1799.
Hannah and George Mason of Warwick, May 12, 1814.
James S. (s. Josiah and Molly, a. 40, widr.) and Harriet A. Twichell, May 31, 1848.
Jonas and Anna Ward, Jan. 19, 1815.
Jonathan W. and Mary L. Babbit of Petersham, int. July 31, 1828.
Joseph and Abagail Twichel, June 3, 1773.
Josiah and Molly Ward of Orange, Sept. 18, 1798.
Mrs. Lucy and Ira Oak, Sept. 3, 1839.
Lysander and Priscilla E. Chamberlin of New Salem, int. May 8, 1830.
Maryann A. and Moses Morton, both of Orange, Aug. 30, 1829. c.r.
Metilda and Senaca Ellenwood, Jan. 18, 1807.
Minerva and James Oliver Jr., Sept. 20, 1827.
Nabbie and John Haven, Feb. 10, 1784.
Nahum and Sarah White, Oct. 18, 1804.
Polly and Sylvestre Stockwell, int. Aug. 12, 1832.
Seth and Lucy Adams of New Salem, int. April 10, 1819.
Solomon and Mary Pratt, Sept. 3, 1761.

ATHOL MARRIAGES.

FAY, Susanna and Benjamin Bancroft of Petersham, Feb. 9, 1819.
Vina and Oliver Perminter of Molberough, N. H., April 4, 1793.
William G. (s. Jonas and Anna, a. 23) and Emily King, Oct. 21, 1846.

FELTON (see Fulton), David H. and Nancy Fish, Jan. 31, 1819.
George Web— of Petersham and Hannah Oliver, Sept. 12, 1785.
Wid. Nancy and Henry Lee, June 21, 1821.

FERNALD, William of Milton, N. H. and Nancy Mason, June 16, 1842

FESSENDEN, Levi G. of Fitchburg (s. Nathan and Jane, a. 33) and Sarah M. Stratton, Oct. 22, 1849.

FESSENDON, Stephen of Rutland and Sally Newhall, April 16, 1801.

FESSONDON, Martha and Perciulls Preson, int. Sept. 8, 1793.

FIELD, Christianna H. and James Jones of Wensor, Vt., Feb. 16, 1819.
Elisha of New Salem and Betsey Stratton, Oct. 6, 1812 [1811 ?].
Lucius and Lucia Hubbard of Chester, Vt., int. Aug. 27, 1813.
Salla and John Holman, Oct. 23, 1788.
Sophia and Joseph Young, Sept. 29, 1817.
Spencer of Boston and Clarissa Humphreys, April 28, 1829.

FISH, Benjamin and Mary Lealand of New Salem, int. Nov. 4, 1813
Betsy and Samuel Newhall, May 28, 1826.
Esther and Laban Morse, April 16, 1838.
Eunice and Absolem Ball, Dec. 5, 1803.
Ezra and Chloe Johnson of Mendon, June 27, 1798.   In Mendon.
Hannah and Joshua Smith, Jan. 8, 1799.
Harriet Y. (d. Moses and Anna, a. 19) and Henry B. Underhill of Warren, Feb. 18, 1847.
Henry and Sally Fish, June 16, 1835.
Joseph and Nancy Crosby of Putney, Vt., int. Oct. 8, 1818.
Lucinda and Reuben Fairbank, Oct. 5, 1806.
Lucinda and Eber Goddard, June 12, 1823.
Lucy (d. Ezra and Chloe) and Amos L. Cheney, Oct. 31, 1843.
Moses and Anna Young, May 8, 1823.
Nancy and David H. Felton, Jan. 31, 1819.
Sally and Francis Twichel, Feb. 12, 1809.
Sally and Henry Fish, June 16, 1835.

FISHER, Betsey and Moses W. Oliver, int. Sept. 19, 1829.
Wid. Hannah and Jonathan Wheeler, int. Oct. 15, 1830.

FISK, Betsey [Waters] of Wendell and Amos Mansfield, between April 30, 1795, and April 30, 1796. In Wendell.
Clark of Orange and Huldah Crossman, March 19, 1839.
Jonathan and Mary Smith of Weston, Feb. 23, 1774. In Weston.
Ruth of Templeton and Irael Sprague, Oct. 16, 1783. In Templeton.

FISSINGTON, Peter and Mary Oliver, Nov. 16, 1761.

FITTS, George and Sally Holmes of Templeton, int. May 3, 1809.
George and Nancy Crosby, Jan. 5, 1815.

FLAGG, Dolly of Lancaster and Alden Spooner, int. Oct. 1, 1820.
Elijah and Elisebeth Comming both of Templeton, April 26, 1781.*
John and Betsey Blanchard, June 2, 1790. In Winchendon.

FLETCHER, Levi [of Westford in int], and Gerusha Morton, March 13, 1783.
William and Betsey Harrington of Orange, int. April 7, 18[33].

FLINT, Josiah of Royalston and Elizabeth Hill, April 10, 1827.
Mary G. (d. Josiah and Elizabeth, a. 20) and Wyatt Barlow of Hardwick, Jan. 19, 1848.

FORBES, Anna of Rutland District and William Oliver, Dec. 7, 1767. In Barre.

FORBS, Lydia and Isaac Easty, both of Royalston, Nov. 26, 1801.*

FORBUSH (see Furbus), Polly of Royalston and Luther Godard, int. May 30, 1811.

FORD, Alice and Jeremah Morton, Nov. 30, 1766.
Josiah and Jemima Oliver, May 27, 1773.
Marcy and Ephraim Cadey Jr., Jan. 10, 1770.

FORRESTALL, Mary of Holliston and Jonathan Goddard, int. March 3, 1783.

FORRESTER, Moses and Patty Johnson of Orange, int. Aug. 2, 1808.

FOSKETT, Elbridge and Thankfull B. Carpenter, of Swansey, N. H., int. May 12, 1836.

* Intention not recorded.

FOSKETT, Harriet of Orange and Jesse G. Wheeler, int. Oct. 8, 1829.
Prescott of Orange and Martha Orcutt of Ewings Grant, April 20, 1836.*

FOSTER, Daniel and Polly Faunce, March 17, 1791.
Elizabeth of Royalston and Daniel Warren, Sept. 20, 1789. In Royalston.
Hugh and Rutina Peck of Royalston, int. Feb. 14, 1818.
John M. of Royalston and Dorinda Godard, April 18, 1826.
Lucy Augusta (d. John W. and Dorinda, a. 22) and Freeborn R. Fay, June 4, 1849.
Lurana [Susanna in int.] of Orange and Levi Witt, Nov. 29, 1795. In Orange.
Nancy A. of New Salem and Emerson Fay, int. May 8, 1830.
Ruth of No. Salem and Jonathan Stratton, Nov. 10, 1788.
Stephen of Sullivan, N. H., and Lois Stratton, May 14, 1834.
Susanna of Orange and Levy Witt, int. Oct. 12, 1794.

FOWLER, William and Martha Houghton of Bolton, int. April 12, 1817.

FOX, Lyman and Deborah Whitney, Aug. 20, 1848.

FRADRICK, see Tuzadrick.

FREDERICK, Anne and Francis Mazro of Petersham, April 12, 1784.

FRENSH [French in int.], Bartholomew and Susannah Gale of Royalston, Oct. 16, 1777. In Royalston.

FRY (see Frye), Job Jr. and Florella Clark of Wendell, int. May 23, 1830.
Job Jr. and Anna Dexter, June 24, 1834.
Mary of Royalstone and Hiram Lewis, int. Sept. 8, 1814.
Silas and Susanna K. Whitney, May 16, 1840.

FRYE (see above), Phebe and Hiram Lewis, May 23, 1822.

FULLER, Benjamin and Lucy Day of Winchendon, int. Aug. 3, 1797.
Hannah and Stephen Holman, Sept. 5, 1799.
Leonard C. and Frances Bigelow, April 13, 1842. Dup.
Merrill D. of Phillipston (s. Rufus P. and Mary, a. 23) and Lucy A. Stratton, May 31, 1848.
Persis of Keene, N. H., and Eleaser Graves, int. Dec. 18, 1810.
Lepha and Edson Clark, both of Royalston, May 31, 1805.*

* Intention not recorded.

ATHOL MARRIAGES. 129

FULTON [Felton in int], Tomasan and Daniel Benjamin, Nov. 10, 1779.

GABYER, George and Esther Twichel, Jan. 16, 1777.

GAIL, Huldah and Ephraim Town, both of Warwick, Dec. 18, 1777.

GALE, Susannah of Royalston and Bartholomew Frensh, Oct. 16 1777. In Royalston.

GARFIELD, Cynthia and John Kendall Jr., Nov. 30, 1837.
Lucy and Ephraim Capron, Nov. 22, 1792.
Martha Ann and Jonathan Drury Jr., March 14, 1837.
Ruben and Lois Y. Drury, June 1, 1842.

GATES, John Jr. and Betsey Fay, May 26, 1839.

GAY, Clarissa and Isaac K. Peabody, Jan. 1, 1822.

GENING, Lydia of Brookfield and Eli Gould, int. Nov. 2, 1769.

GENNISON, Caroline of Orange and Jonas B. Nason of Boston, Dec. 19, 1839.*

GILES, Calista and Elon Clark of New Salem, int. May 14, 1821.
Nancy and Zebodee Simonds of Concord, N.Y., Aug. 26, 1821.
Prescott of New Salem and Lemira D. Stratton, int. Oct. 17, 1829.
Susanna of N. Salem and Asa Stratton, int. Aug. 15, 1807.

GILBART, Sally of Brookfield and Daniel Haven, int. March 7, 1805.

GILMORE, Evelina S. and Senaca W. Linoln of Deerfield, May 28, 1843.
Phelps P. (s. William and Zilpha, a. 22) and Mariann A. Oaks, July 4, 1847.

GLEASON, Berzaleel of Hubbardston and Molly Stratton, March 17, 1795.
Stephen and Betsy Curtice, both of Petersham, Jan. 20, 1808.*

GODARD (see Goddard), Ann of Petersham and Col. Thomas Townsend, int. Aug. 31, 1827.
Betsy and Nathaniel Smith Jr. of Phillipston, May 11, 1819.
Dorinda and John M. Foster of Royalston, April 18, 1826.
Dorothy and Samuel Haven, Dec. 23, 18[07].
Goodell and Hannah Paine of Greenwich, int. Dec. 10, 1818.

* Intention not recorded.

ATHOL MARRIAGES.

GODARD, Hannah and Aaron Hill of Sterling, Oct. 28, 1801.
Joseph and Lucy Bragg of Royalston, int. Feb. 22, 1804.
Joseph and Susanna Jones of Royalston, int. Nov. 29, 1810.
Joseph and Wid. Hannah Ball, May 3, 1819.
Luther and Polly Forbush of Royalston, int. May 30, 1811.
Maria of Orange and Nathan Ward, int. April 20, 1816.
Nathan and Nancy Parker of Royalston, May 24, 1803.
Sally and John Jacobs Jr. of Royalston, Oct. 10, 1804.
Walter and Hannah Dakin of West Sudbury, int. Aug. 28, 1805.

GODDARD (see Godard), Amelia E. (d. Martin and Sylvia T., a. 24) and Lafayette Smith, Nov. 27, 1845.
Asa [of Royalston in int.] and Lucy Goddard, Nov. 2, 1779.
Betty of Shrewsbury and James Goddard, June 24, 1767. In Shrewsbury.
Caty and Amos Woodward of Royalston, int. July 17, 1783.
Clarry and Levi Spaulding of Lyndsborough, N. H., March 3, 1796.
David and Sarah Shaw of Lecester, int. Nov. 10, 1769.
David of Orange and Clarissa Perry, March 29, 1829.
David and Sally Goddard of Orange, int., Dec. 11, 1829. [Married Jan. 1, 1830. C.R.]
Ebenezer and Hannah Death, July 6, 1775.
Eber and Lucinda Fish, June 12, 1823.
Edward and An— [Ann in int.] Death, Nov. 11, 1784.
Elijah and Mehitable Goodel, March 27, 1794.
Ephraim and Huldah Goodell of Charlton, int. Sept. 2, 1797.
Esther and Samuel Morton Jr., Aug. 23, 1773.
Eunus of Royalston and Moses Goddard, Jan. 8, 1778. In Royalston.
Hannah of Petersham and Silvanus Ward, int. Nov. 22, 1775.
Hannah and Ruben Roberts of Amherst, Aug. 4, 1841.
Hezekiah of Orange and Ann L. Oliver [Anne Durham Oliver in int.], Aug. 15, 1784. In Orange.
James and Betty Goddard of Shrewsbury, June 24, 1767. In Shrewsbury.
Jonathan and Mary Forrestall of Holliston, int. March 3, 1783.
Joseph and Lucy Drury, May 17, 1798.
Joseph W. of Royalston and Abigail D. Townsend, April 9, 1833.
Josiah and Ruth Raymond, Nov. 8, 1774.
Julia and Russell Brown of Ashburnham, July 3, 1836.
Lucy and Asa Goddard, Nov. 2, 1779.
Marcy and Joshua Deane of Warwick ?, Dec. 18, 1777.
Mary and Rufus Tayler, Dec. 8, 1763.

GODDARD, Moses and Eunus Goddard of Royalston, Jan. 8, 1778. In Royalston.
Nabby and Samuel Goddard Jr. of Royalston, May 4, 1796.
Phebe and Seth Twichel Jr., May 13, 1790.
Polly and Benjamin Townsend, May 12, 1802.
Ruth and Ebenezer Smith of Newsalem, March 22, 1825.
Sally of Orange and David Goddard, int. Dec. 11, 1829.
Samuel of Royalston and Catharine Parks of Gerry, June 29, 1790.*
Samuel Jr. of Royalston and Nabby Goddard, May 4, 1796.
Sibbel and Joseph Woodward, July 3, 1765.
Simon and Mary Eaton of Framingham, int. Aug. 29, 1771.
Sopha (Sophia in int.) and Abner Morton, May 14, 1764.
Susanna and Rufus Tayler, int. March 10, 1774.
Susanna and James Woodbury of Royalston, Jan. 28, 1802.
Sylvia of Orange and Leonard Kneeland, int. Nov. 2, 1833.
William I. (s. Joseph and Hannah, a. 25) and Mary Townsend, Nov. 9, 1845.

GOLDSBURY, James of Warwick and Maranda Sweetser, Jan. 3, 1827.

GOODALE (see Goodel, Goodell), Ephraim and Margaret Wheeler, Nov. 25, 1802.
Lydia of Templeton and Josiah Talbert, int. July 1, 1815.
Unice and Rufus Little of Sudbury, Vt., Feb. 14, 1797.

GOODEL, Mehitable and Elijah Goddard, March 27, 1794.

GOODELL (see above), Huldah of Charlton and Ephraim Goddard, int. Sept. 2, 1797.

GOODNOUGH, John R. and Eliza Drury, Aug. 1, 1822.

GOODNOW, Augustus (*sic*) A. of New Salem (d. Elmer and Fanny, a. 25) and Proctor Moulton, of Prescott, Nov. 8, 1848.*

GOSS, Calvin and Ruth Sawtell, both of Gerry, June 3, 1790.*
Jonas and Elizabeth Pike, Nov. 11, 1766.*

GOULD, Curtiss and Sally Stratton, March 9, 1825.
Eli and Lydia Gening of Brookfield, int. Nov. 2, 1769.
Sophronia J. and Robert B. Buckley of Templeton, int. May 3, 1836.

GOULDING, James I. and Elvira P. Clapp, Feb. 10, 1841.

GRANT, Joshua of Partridgefield and Mary Kilton, int. May 7, 1785.
"Mary Kilton appeared May 11 and forbid band,"

* Intention not recorded.

ATHOL MARRIAGES.

GRAVES, Abner and Alice Richardson, Feb. 12, 1768.
Abner Jr. and Dolly Smith, June 12, 1806.
Allice and Jonathan Orcutt of Templeton, Nov. 9, 1806.
Azubah and Joshua Morton, Feb. 1, 1774.
Azubah and Rev. William B. Wesson of Hardwick, Nov. 5, 180[7].
Eleazer and Judith Cutting, Oct. 29, 1767.
Eleazer Jr. and Olive Kendall, March 13, 1787. In Royalston.
Eleazer and Persis Fuller of Keen, N. H., int. Dec. 18, 1810.
Eleazer and Susanna Bouker of Gerry, int. Dec. 14, 1811.
Hannah and Thomas Fairbank, May 9, 1766.
Hannah and Aaron Lord, Oct. 3, 1793.
Laura and Alanson Lincoln of Petersham, Sept. 9, 1818.
Lois and Lucius Allis of Conway, May 25, 1801.
Lucinda and Freeborn Raymond Jr., Nov. 5, 1787. In Royalston.
Lydia and George Kelton, Aug. 28, 1760.
Martha and Stephen Stratten, Sept. 24, 1767.
Nathaniel Jr. and Hannah Richardson, June 16, 1774.
Nathaniel and Mercy Page of Hardwick, int. April 12, 1777.
Rebekah and Timothy Kendal, July 15, 1775.
Reuben [of Chesterfield in int.] and Hannah Kindall, July 8, 1778.
Susanna and Jonathan Newhall, Oct. 24, 1799.

GRAY (see Grey), Alexander and Elvira Bancroft of Wendel, int. Dec. 3, 1825.
Elisabeth of Pelham and Robert Young, int. Nov. 24, 1764.
Eliza and Pliney Putnam of Sutton, Nov. 29, 1827.

GREEN, Mary of Stoddard, N. H., and John P. Henshaw, int. April 5, 1823.

GREENLEAF, Zerah and Presella Lowis of Barry, Aug. 30, 1801.

GREENWOOD, Oliver of Winchendon and Phebe Brooks, Jan. 15, 1807.

GREGORY, David H. of Princeton and Mary A. Howe of South Orange, Dec. 15, 1841.*

GREY (see Gray), Adeline and Moses Briggs, int. May 3, 1831.

GRO ?, Mrs. ? Rebeca of Abington, Conn., and Whitman Jacobs, int. May 8, 1773.

GROUT, Annis of Templeton and Jesse Stockwill, April 3, 1782.

GUILD, William of Dedham and Anna Lewis, Nov. 9, 1819.

* Intention not recorded.

ATHOL MARRIAGES. 133

HADLEY, John and Abigail Jones of Weston, June 16, 1785. In Weston.

Phebe of Hardwick and Simeon Howard, int. Sept. 6, 1828.

HAGAR, James L. (s. Jesse and Cynthia, a. 22) and Luthera A. Smith, Jan. 1, 1849.

HAIR, Louisa and Isaac Brock, Aug. 20, 1837.

HALE, David A. of New York (s. David and Laura, a. 27) and Mary Isabella Simonds, Sept. 3, 1849.

Joel S. and Cinthia Oak, Dec. 23, 1819.

Nancy of Winchester, N. H., and James C. Meacham, int. Feb. 6, 1836.

Rubin and Olive Davice [?], int. Dec. 31, 1785.

HAILE, Samuel and Damarais Drury, Nov. 29, 1792.

Samuel and Mary Kilton, Oct. 30, 1794.

HALLAY ?, Jerusha and Hiram Newhall, int. Nov. 1, 1779.

HANCOCK, Artemas of Templeton and Phebe Whitney, Jan. 5, 1812.

HAPGOOD, Eunice of Shrewsbury and Ebenezer Hartshorn, April 20, 1767. In Shrewsbury.

HARRINGTON (see Herington, etc.), Abram (s. Daniel and Sarah, a. 43) and Fanny Moore, Dec. 3, 1845.

Betsey of Orange and William Fletcher, int. April 7, 18[33].

George W. and Julia Pratt, both of Royalston, Dec. 11, 1842.*

HARRIS, Elener of Hollis and Job Harris, int. Jan. 19, 1764.

Gilbert D. (s. Jonathan G. and Lucy, a. 24) and Marcy Stratton, Aug. 20, 1849.

Job and Elener Harris of Hollis, int. Jan. 19, 1764.

Richard and Celia Sprague of Petersham, int. Oct. 18, 1806.

Thomas of Warwick and Eunice Lampson, int. Sept. 8, 1780.

HARTSHORN, Ebenezer and Eunice Hapgood of Shrewsbury, April 20, 1767. In Shrewsbury.

HARVEY, Sally and Amos Partridge of Chesterfield, int. June 27, 1783.

HARWOOD, Benjamin M. and Harriet Drake, Oct. 4, 1841.

David and Rebecca Ann Reed of Brattleborough, int. July 23, 1816.

David and Lois Kelton, April 2, 1823.

* Intention not recorded.

HARWOOD, Jonathan and Olive Muzze of Jamaica, Vt., int. Jan. 30, 1808.
Olive and Freeman R. Sibley, Feb. 20, 1834.
Phebe and Amos Blodget, Jan. 13, 1814.
Prudence of Oxford and Amos Sibley, int. June 9, 1809.
Seth K. and Caroline Drake, Oct. 23, 1831.
Stephen and Olive Morse, Dec. 30, 1801.
Stephen and Martha Bullard, May 16, 1827.
Stephen and Elizabeth Kendall, March 1, 1804.

HASAY (see Hasy, Heasy), Samuel and Silance Chub, Oct. 12, 1775.

HASEY, Zaccheus and Abigail Sargent, both of Hubbardston, May 30, 1781.*

HASKELL, Loring and Sally Lincoln of Oakham, int. Dec. 20, 1818.

HASKINS, Rane of N. Salem and Thomas Fairbank, int. April 13, 1804.
Stephen and Susanna Rice of Hardwick, March 6, 1789. In Hardwick.

HASY (see Hasay, Heasy), Esther and Paul Church, June 16, 1774.

HAVEN, Asa and Lucy R. Smith of New Salem, int. Sept. 19, 1820.
Capt. Chauncy and Urania Thompson of Swansey, N. H., int. Aug. 20, 1825.
Daniel and Sally Gilbart of Brookfield, int. March 7, 1805.
Dea. John and Mrs. Martha Waite of Royalston, April 27, 1778. In Royalston.
Eunice and Abner Sawyer, April 3, 1792.
Eunice (d. Jotham and Hannah, a. 27) and James G. Smith of Phillipston, May 26, 1847.
John Jr. and Martha Death, Sept. 8, 1777.
John and Nabbie Fay, Feb. 10, 1784.
John Jr. and Rachel Sargent of Fitzwilliam, N. H., int. April 2, 1810.
John and Anna Fay, March 5, 1823.
Jotham and Hannah Taft of Heath, int. Oct. 9, 1812.
Keziah and William Young, Jan. 18, 1780.
Levi and Mary Smith, Jan. 5, 1803.
Lydia and Matthias C. Mayo, June 22, 1841.
Mercy and Ezra Sherman of Cambridge, N.Y., Feb. 21, 1819.
Patty and John Hill 2d, Oct. 27, 1812.
Rhoda and Samuel Young, Feb. 26, 1772.

* Intention not recorded.

ATHOL MARRIAGES. 135

HAVEN, Rhoda and Volentine Randall of Stratton, Vt., March 3, 18[08].
Sally and Joseph Beal, Aug. 31, 1807.
Samuel and Dorothy Godard, Dec. 23, 18[07].
Samuel S. and Anna Stevens of Petersham, Feb. 25, 1841. In Petersham.
Susanna and Levi Young, Aug. 22, 1804.
Susannah and Stephen Smith, July 23, 1766.
William of Newport and Rebekah Jacobs, int. June 27, 1781.

HAYNES, Huldah of Sudbury and Maltire Eaton, Dec. 31, 1778. In Sudbury.

HEASY ?, Mary and Luke Robbins, Dec. 8, 1774.
Zachius and Nabby Lumbard, March 16, 1777.

HEMENWAY (see Hemingway), Ethan of Barre and Harriot Tyler, Oct. 17, 1827.
Lovicy of Barre and John L. Ellis, int. Feb. 23, 1811.
Lucy A. of Bredport, Vt., and Amos Drury, int. Jan. 23, 1822.

HEMMINGWAY (see Hemenway), Joel of Lancaster, N.H., and Esther Houghton of Petersham, Jan. 21, 1807.*
Mary F. and John Briggs Jr., both of Orange, Nov. 25, 1841.*

HEMMINWAY, Martha of Royalston and Edward Holman Jr., Dec. 21, 1786. In Royalston.

HENSHAW, John P. and Mary Green of Stoddard, N.H., int. April 5, 1823.

HERINGTON (see Harrington), Margery of Marlborough and Benjamin Warrin, int. May 5, 1766.

HERRINGTON, Millisent of Orange and Isaac Hill, int. April 11, 1795.

HEWET, Robey and Calvin Morton, int. April 12, 1804.

HEYWARD, Frederick L. of Royalston (s. Lyman and Maria, a. 21) and Emeline Dyer, Nov. 29, 1849. In Royalston.

HEYWOOD, Wid. Catherine and Neil McLane, July 30, 1848.

HILDRETH, Daniel and Hannah Rugg of Hindsdale, N.H., int. Aug. 13, 1814.

HILL, Aaron of Sterling and Hannah Godard, Oct. 28, 1801.
Asa and Anna Ballard, June 20, 1820.

* Intention not recorded.

HILL, Caroline (d. Aaron and Hannah, a. 27) and James Stratton 2d, Dec. 15, 1848.
Danford and Charlotte Morse, July 22, 1827.
Deborah L. and Alonzo Mann of Royalston, April 26, 1842. In Royalston.
Dolly and Alfred Tucker of Ware, April 6, 1841.
Elizabeth and Josiah Flint of Royalston, April 10, 1827.
Emory and Rhoda Twichell, Dec. 6, 1821.
Fidelia (d. Aaron and Hannah, a. 37) and David Southwick Brock, Nov. 19, 1844.
Hannah and Adam Prouty of West Boylston, Oct. 6, 1828.
Isaac and Millisent Herrington of Orange, int. April 11, 1795. [Married April 8 in C.R.]
John and Susanna Perminter, Feb. 8, 1795.
John 2d and Sarah Ryant of Sturbridge, int. Dec. 5, 1800.
John 2d and Patty Haven, Oct. 27, 1812.
John and Dolly Smith, Nov. 30, 1837.
Jonathan J. and Nancy Dyer, Jan. 31, 1838.
Levina [Lavina in int.] and David Wheeler of Petersham, Nov. 11, 1795. In Petersham.
Lucy and Ezra Thayer of Orwell, Vt., Jan. 13, 1800.
Mary and Simeon Young, int. Feb. 13, 1786.
Moses Jr. and Abigail Kilton, Nov. 7, 1793.
Phebe and Paul Wheeler of Royalston, int. Sept. 14, 1803.
Ruth and Joel Drewry, June 12, 1793.
Sally of Sturbridge and Samuel Morse, int. Feb. 16, 1794.

HINDS, Mrs. Nancy B. and Lewis R. Howe, both of Orange, Dec. 22, 1836.*
Sabrina W. (d. Hiram and Amanda, a. 17) and John Bowen, July 8, 1849 ?.

HOAR, Harriet of Westminster and Andrew S. Chubb of Phillipston, Aug. 29, 1843.
Timothy and Lydia Bouker, Jan. 21, 1819.

HODGES, Ardilisa and Levi Blodgett, Aug. 16, 1816.
Simeon W. of Norton and Emeline Babbitt of Petersham, June 27, 1841.*

HODSKIN, Clarissa of Pelham and Absolom Lord, int. March 15, 1816.

HOLBROOK, Candace and Benjamin Estabrook, May 23, 1831.
Enos of Keene, N. H., and Mary Kendall, March 10, 1822.

* Intention not recorded.

ATHOL MARRIAGES. 137

HOLBROOK, Rhoda of Swansey, N. H., and Nathan Cheney Jr., int. Oct. 28, 1826.

HOLDEN, Amos P. and Clarissa Battle, May 20, 1838.
Anderson of South Orange and Orator Meachum of Petersham, Jan. 27, 1839.*
Hannah of Orange and Ebenezer Knight, June 7, 18[08].
Josiah (s. Simeon and Polly, a. 26) and Betsey Cheney, both of Orange, March 31, 1846

HOLMAN, Edward Jr. and Martha Hemminway of Royalston, Dec. 21, 1786. In Royalston.
John and Salla Field, Oct. 23, 1788.
Lydia and John Beul [Beal in int.] of Royalston, May 10, 1789. In Royalston.
Noah and Ruth Stockwell of Royalston, June 3, 1795. In Royalston.
Oliver of Petersham and Anna Morse, Nov. 15, 1808.
Sally and Isaac Norcross Jr. of Royalston, June 14, 1797.
Sarah G. of Petersham and Plummer Prouty of Spencer, June 30, 1842.*
Stephen and Hannah Fuller, Sept. 5, 1799.

HOLMES (see Holms), Aminta of Winchester, N. H., and Thurston Andrews, int. Nov. 25, 1821.
Dr. Jacob and Thankful Jones of Westminster, int. April 29, 1809.
Sally of Templeton and George Fitts, int. May 3, 1809.

HOLMS (see above), Lucy and Ephraim Willard, both of Petersham, Feb. 18, 1801.*

HOLT, Daniel L. of Hardwick and Sophronia Briggs, June 30, 1840.
Martha S. and William Bronsdon, April 22, 1840.
Sophia L. (d. Ebenezer and Arethusa) and Isaac Turner of Townsend, April 25, 1844.

HOOKER, Sarah and Moses Marbel, Oct. 10, 1775.

HORR, Susan G. (d. Timothy and ———, a. 21) and Matthew Cheney, May 24, 1846.

HOUGHTON, Esther of Petersham and Joel Hemmingway of Lancaster, N.H., Jan. 21, 1807.*
Martha of Bolton and William Fowler, int. April 12, 1817.

* Intention not recorded.

ATHOL MARRIAGES.

HOW (see Howe), Abel and Hannah Bradbury [Needham in c.r.], both of Petersham, Dec. 3, 1778.*
Hannah of Warwick and John Rhodes of Dummerston, N.Y., June 5, 1778.*
John [of Timpleton in int.] and Hannah Newton, Dec. 13, 1769.
Nathan of Hilsborough, N. H., and Mary Wait, Aug. 15, 1793.
Thomas and Mary Ellis of Royalston, int. May 22, 1779.
See Stow.

HOWARD, Artemas and Susanna Ward, Nov. 29, 1827.
Cynthia P. and Charles Farr, March 27, 1838.
Emily M. (d. Simon and Lucy, a. 22) and George Farr, April 30, 1846.
Joel R. of Warwick (s. Joel and Lucy, a. 24) and Elizabeth Stockwell, Sept. 30, 1845.
Lemuel of Orange and Lydia Kelton, Nov. 26, 1801.
Leonard and Mary Dewing, both of Orange, April 16, 1836.*
Lucy Ann and Norris Davis of Orange, Oct. 30, 1831.
Mary and Elisha J. Pitts of Orange, Nov. 20, 1823.
Mary and Ira Oaks, Oct. 7, 1834.
Ruth and Lewis I. Whitney, July 18, 1824.
Simeon Jr. and Mary Lovering, May 21, 1826.
Simeon and Phebe Hadley of Hardwick, int. Sept. 6, 1828.

HOWE (see How), Lewis R. and Mrs. Nancy B. Hinds, both of Orange, Dec. 22, 1836.*
Mary A. of South Orange and David H. Gregory of Princeton, Dec. 15, 1841.*

HOYT, Salmon B. of Deerfield (a. 28) and Rebecca Humphreys, May 16, 1847.

HUBBARD, Lucia of Chester, Vt., and Lucius Field, int. Aug. 27, 1813.
Maria of Royalston and David Dexter, int. Oct. 18, 1835.

HUIT, Preserved and Jeremiah Twichel, Feb. 5, 1818.

HUMFREY (see Humphreys, Humphry), James and Esther, Wiswell, Oct. 9, 1751. c.r.

HUMPHREY, Arethusa and Rev. John Walker of Greenfield, N. H., Feb. 13, 1813.
Esther and Jabez Ward, Nov. 29, 1787.
Frances W. and Dea. ? William H. Williams, May 12, 1822.
Henry and Sophronia Parker of Hubbardston, int. May 15, 1836.

* Intention not recorded.

ATHOL MARRIAGES. 139

HUMPHREY, James Jr. and Lucy Brigham of Fitzwilliam, N. H., int. Oct. 13, 1793.
Lois and Levi Stratton, Dec. 19, 1795.
Lois Wiswell and Moses Oliver, Nov. 23, 1780.
Samuel and Lois Morton, Dec. 29, 1763.
Sarah Evens of Orange and Eliel Smith, int. Sept. 18, 1795.

HUMPHREYS, Ann R. and Samuel Sweetser Jr., Dec. 7, 1823.
Caroline and Ebenezer Brock, Sept. 15, 1841.
Charles and Jane Jones, Oct. 9, 1830. In Templeton.
Clarissa and Spencer Field of Boston, April 28, 1829.
Esther and Hiram H. Allen of Amherst, July 14, 1841.
James Jr. and Sally Kendell, [June] 17, 1823.
Lucy B. and Fenno Thorp, Feb. 23, 1840.
Maria A. (d. James and Sarah, a. 23) and Charles A. Bullock of Fitchburg, June 3, 1847.
Mary T. and Joseph Batchelder Jr. of Greenfield, N.H., May 20, 1819.
Rebecca (d. John F. and Betsey, a. 23) and Salmon B. Hoyt of Deerfield, May 16, 1847.

HUMP[H]RY (see above), Lydia and Asa Lord, Aug. 15, 1785.

HUNT, Abigail P. (d. Luther and Deborah) and Edwin C. Rice of Orange, Sept. 3, 1843.
Gustavus A. M. of Petersham (s. Luther and Deborah) and Hannah C. Peabody, July 4, 1843.

HUTCHENS, Moses and Susannah Thayer [of Richmond in int.], Sept. 9, 1779.

HUTCHINS, Jerushe and Abner Smith, Dec. 11, 1771.

HUTCHSON, Jacob and Mary Clark of Medfield, int. Nov. 7, 1778.

INGALS, Joseph of Surrey, N. H., and Lucy Knapp of Petersham, Sept. 23, 1800.*

JACKSON, Anna and Charles Baker, Jr., Nov. 25, 1779.*
Hannah W. and John Orcutt, both of Orange, Nov. 30, 1842.*
Nabby of Petersham and Robert Bradish, Sept. 23, 1793. In Petersham.
Nathan of Petersham and Betsy Stevens of Gerry, July 1, 1800.*

JACOBS, John and Bulah Moor, int. March 7, 1778.
John Jr., of Royalston and Sally Godard, Oct. 10, 1804.

* Intention not recorded.

ATHOL MARRIAGES.

JACOBS, Joseph and Sarah Bragg of Royalston, May 17, 1792. In Royalston.
Joseph and Elizabeth Townsend, Nov. 15, 1796.
Lydia and David Daniels Baker, Sept. 15, 1802.
Rebekah and William Haven of Newport, int. June 27, 1781.
Whitman and Mrs. ? Rebeca Gro ? of Abington, Conn., int. May 8, 1773.

JAQUES, Stephen (s. Jeremiah and Mary, a. 35, widr.) and Susan B. Twichell, Dec. 9, 1847.

JENKINS, Mercy F. of Barre and Ira Ellis, int. Oct. 1, 1823 [1825 ?].

JENNINGS, Lyman of Ewing and Hannah F. Kelton, Nov. 21, 1843.
Susan of Ewing (d. Abna and Patienc, a. 32) and Silas Drury of Wendell, Sept. 7, 1847.

JOHNSON, Chloe of Mendon and Ezra Fish, June 27, 1798. In Mendon.
Esther of Orange and Joseph Lord, Jan. 7, 1786. In Orange.
Patty of Orange and Moses Forrester, int. Aug. 2, 1808.
Sally of Orange and Joseph Richardson, int. Dec. 2, 1809.
William of Chesterfield, N. H., and Lois Marsh, May 28, 1800.

JONES, Abigail of Weston and John Hadley, June 16, 1785. In Weston.
Amos Jr. and Lephe Estabrook of Holden, int. April 12, 1800.
Frederic and Maria Sweetser, Dec. 1, 1832.
James of Wensor, Vt. and Christianna H. Field, Feb. 16, 1819.
Jane and Charles Humphreys, Oct. 9, 1830. In Templeton.
John of Hope, Me., and Luisa Estabrook, Feb. 4, 1826. At Vernon, Vt. c.r.
Lydia and Robert Thompson of Royalston, int. May 21, 1802.
Obidiah [of Northfield in int.] and Mary Oliver, Aug. 2, 1781.
Otis of Angelica, N.Y., and Harriet Stockwell, Oct. 30, 1831.
Prescott and Jane Moore of Cambridge, Jan. —, 1798. In Cambridge.
Susanna of Royalston and Joseph Godard, int. Nov. 29, 1810.
Thankful of Westminster and Dr. Jacob Holmes, int. April 29, 1809.
Theodore and Marcia Estabrook, Aug. 29, 1819.

KELLOGG, Dwight H. of Amherst and Margaret Lucena Kelton, Sept. 12, 1843.

ATHOL MARRIAGES. 141

KELTON (see Kilton), Benjamin and Mary Russel of Barre, Oct. 26, 1786. In Barre.
Calvin Jr. and Belinda Ellinwood, int. April 10, 1829. [Married May 21, C.R.]
Frances A. and Fisher A. Wilder of Greenville, Ind., April 28, 1839.
George and Lydia Graves, Aug. 28, 1760.
George O. (s. Jonathan and Dolly, a. 41) and Delia Baker, Sept. 3, 1846.
Hannah F. (d. John and Electa) and Lyman Jennings of Ewing, Nov. 21, 1843.
Hannah L. and Lyman Kendell, Oct. 3, 1824.
James and Sally Capron, April 27, 1788.
John and Electa Morton, Oct. 25, 1815.
Jonathan [Jr. in int.] and Dolly Cuting, Sept. 10, 1789.
Lois and David Harwood, April 2, 1823.
Lydia and Lemuel Howard of Orange, Nov. 26, 1801.
Margaret Lucena (d. Calvin and Hepzibah) and Dwight H. Kellogg of Amherst, Sept. 12, 1843.
Mary and Dea. Joseph Emerson of Wendell, Sept. 11, 1817.
Samuel and Susanna Ward, March 18, 1818.

KENDAL (see Kendall, Kendell, Kindal, Kindall, Kindell), Timothy and Rebekah Graves, July 15, 1775.

KENDALL, Ann and Joshua Young, Nov. 20, 1825.
Anna and Joel Morton, June 25, 1800.
Calvin and Abigal Bacheler of Royalston, June 27, 1793. In Royalston.
Calvin Jr. and Lydia L. Wetherell of Swanzey, N. H., int. April 23, 1831.
Elizabath and Pelog Stratten, Nov. 29, 1769.
Elizabeth and Stephen Harwood, March 1, 1804.
Esther and Reuben Smith of Orvil, Feb. 12, 1789.
Hannah and James Oliver, Sept. 30, 1801.
Jane Oliver and Edward Raymond Jr., Oct. 30, 1783.
Joel and Sally Raymond, Nov. 5, 1787. In Royalston.
Joel and Wid. Anna Crosby, Dec. 31, 1822.
John and Mrs. Susannah Smith of Gerry, Feb. 21, 1796. In Phillipston.
Capt. John and Wid. Rebeccah Whitmore of Royalston, Sept. 12, 1827.
John Jr. and Cynthia Garfield, Nov. 30, 1837.
Jonathan and Anne Oliver, Jan. 23, 1765.
Levi and Sally Newell, Oct. 22, 1786.
Lois and Freeborn Raymond, July 16, 1789.

KENDALL, Maria and Russell Smith, Aug. 21, 1839.
Mary and Enos Holbrook of Keene, N. H., March 10, 1822.
Molly and David Twichel of N. Salem, Sept. 3, 1800.
Nancy and Clark Thompson, Aug. 25, 1840.
Olive and Eleazer Graves Jr., March 13, 1787. In Royalston.
Polly and Aaron Wright of Fitzwilliam, N. H., Dec. 29, 18[07].
Rebecca L. and Abel Lord, int. May 30, 1799.
Rebecka and Josiah Wilder Jr. of Templeton, Sept. 30, 1807.
Samuel and Molly Taylor, May 1, 1788.
Samuel of Orwell, Vt., and Hannah Morse, Jan. 23, 1801.
Seth and Deborah Stratton, March 10, 1756.
Seth and Olive Blanden of Royalston, int. Dec. 21, 1799.
Seth and Polly Blanden of Royalston, int. Oct. 20, 1804.
Sinda and John Crosby, Oct. 1, 1794.
Susanna and Abijah Smith of Orwell, April 24, 1791.

KENDELL (see above and Kindal, etc.), Joel Jr. and Rebecca Chase of Keene, N. H., int. Oct. 11, 1828.
Jonathan and Sally Orcutt, April 27, 1824.
Lydia S. and Ezekiel G. Davis of Grafton, Oct. 4, 1827.
Lyman and Hannah L. Kelton, Oct. 3, 1824.
Sally and James Humphreys Jr., [June] 17, 1823.

KIDDER, Jonathan Jr. of Wendell and Nancy Rice Lewis, Dec. 2, 1818.
Nancy and Manson J. Woodward, May 22, 1839.

KILTON (see Kelton), Abigail and Moses Hill Jr., Nov. 7, 1793.
Calvin and Hepsibah Woodward, April 8, 1800.
Fanny and John Fairbank Jr., July 16, 1780.
Lois and Howard Manley, June 7, 1814.
Mary and Joshua Grant of Partridgefield, int. May 7, 1785.
  "Mary Kilton appeared May 11, and forbid the band."
Mary and Samuel Hale, Oct. 30, 1794.

KIMBALL, Mary of Peterborough, N. H., and Luna [?] B. Richardson, int. Nov. 10, 1833.

KIMPLAN, William and Katerine Oliver of Rutland, int. Feb. 12, 1764.

KINDAL (see Kendall, etc., and below), Mary and Jacob Rich, Aug. 4, 1774.

KINDALL, Anna and Thomas Atkins, both of Gerry, Oct. 24, 1799.*

* Intention not recorded.

ATHOL MARRIAGES. 143

KINDALL, Hannah and Reuben Graves, July 8, 1778.
Lydia and Earll Cutting, Dec. 10, 1784.

KINDELL, Jesse Jr. and Elizebeth Raymond, Oct. 12, 1780.

KING, Emily (d. Isaac and Polly, a. 19) and William G. Fay, Oct. 21, 1846.
Lucretia E. (d. Isaac and Polly, a. 22) and Charles S. Bruce, April 9, 1846.

KINSLEY, Abiel of Orange and Olive Fairbank, Aug. 27, 1797.
Malinda of Montague and Joshua Morton Jr., int. Oct. 30, 1802.

KNAPP, Lucy of Petersham and Joseph Ingals of Surrey, N. H., Sept. 23, 1800.*

KNEELAND, Leonard and Sylvia Goddard of Orange, int. Nov. 2, 1833.

KNIGHT, Ebenezer Jr. and Esther Sprague, Jan. 5, 1786.
Ebenezer and [Wid.] Hannah Holden of Orange, June 7, 18[08].
Isaac and Lucy Whipple of New Braintree, int. Oct. 2, 1802.
Samuel and Patty Whipple, Dec. 12, 1806.

KNIGHTS (see Nights), Isaac and Patty Walker, Jan. 23, 1777.
Nancy of Phillipston and George Sprague, June 1, 1826.

KNOWLES, Mehetabel and Caleb Thompson of New Sal[em], Nov. 7, 1784.

KNOWLTON, Clarinda and Joseph C. Weeks, both of Oakham, Sept. 22, 1831.*
Stilman and Emily Thorp, Dec. 29, 1831.

LAMB, David of Framingham and Lydia Barret, Nov. 13, 1795.
Elianor of Phillipston and Franklin Peirce, int. Oct. 27, 1817,
Elizabeth and John H. Morse, July 22, 1818.
Hannah of Gerry and Jacob Ball, Jan. 16, 1806.
Mary H. and Francis W. Lovering of Philipston, in year ending April 1, 1834.

LAMPSON, Asa [of Roxbury, Canada, in int.] and Rachel Ball, Dec. 1, 1762.
Betty of Unity, N. H., and Abraham Ball, int. May 26, 1793.
Daniel and Martha Morton, Jan. 17, 1773.
Eunice and Thomas Harris of Warwick, int. Sept. 8, 1780.

LANG[?], Enoch of Eaton, N. H., and Eliza Bancroft, Feb. 24, 1833.

* Intention not recorded.

LARRIBEE, Artemas B. of Barnard, Vt., and Susanna G. Stratton, June 16, 1840.

LAWATER, Stephen and Dolly Wheeler of Gardner, Oct. 3, 1798. In Gardner.

LEALAND, Mary of New Salem and Benjamin Fish, int. Nov. 4, 1813.

LEANARD, Moses [of Roxbury, Canada, in int.] and Rhoda Smith, May 17, 1762.

LEE, Angeline M. and John M. Twichell, April 7, 1842. Dup.
Henry and Wid. Nancy Felton, June 21, 1821.
William D. Jr. and Sarah H. Munsell, June 7, 1841.

LEWES, Mercy and Simon [Samuel in int.] Mellen of Westminster, Jan. 7, 1808.

LEWIS (see Lowis), Anna and William Guild of Dedham, Nov. 9, 1819.
Betsy and John Bryant, May 2, 1821.
Eunice (d. Hiram and Phebe, a. 32) and Nelson Simonds of Templeton, Oct. 21, 1848.
Harriet (d. Hiram and Phebe, a. 21) and Bradey B. Drake, April 2, 1846.
Hiram and Mary Fry of Royalstone, int. Sept. 8, 1814.
Hiram and Phebe Frye, May 23, 1822.
Hiram Jr. and Hannah H. Whitney, Oct. 10, 1841.
John and Sarah Wiman of Winchendon, int. Oct. 25, 1810.
Mary and Orrin Powers of Troy, Wis., Oct. 1, 1839.
Nancy Rice and Jonathan Kidder Jr. of Wendell, Dec. 2, 1818.
Phebe and William Bronsden of Phillipston, March 2, 1829.
Thomas and Sarah Addison of Greenfield, N. H., int. Jan. 16, 1816.
Thomas Jr. of Harvard and Sally Carroll, Oct. 14, 1823.
[Luce in int.] William Jr. and Sarah Margit, March 25, 1778.

LINCOLN, Alanson of Petersham and Laura Graves, Sept. 9, 1818.
Charles O. of Wendell and Mary Bullard, Sept. 13, 1838.
Gooding of Dover, Vt., and Abigail Presson, Oct. 9, 1825.
Sally of Oakham and Loring Haskell, int. Dec. 20, 1818.
Senaca W. of Deerfield and Evelina S. Gilmore, May 28, 1843.
Sumner J. of Brookfield (s. Ivers and Sarah, a. 22) and Nancy Angelia Clapp, Aug. 4, 1846.
Thomas and Allis Mann of Petersham, Jan. 6, 1803.

LINCOLN, William R. of Westboro' (s. Ivers and Sarah, a. 31, widr.) and Elizabeth Patrick, June 21, 1849.

LITTLE, Rufus of Sudbury, Vt., and Unice Goodale, Feb. 14, 1797.

LITTLEFIELD, George T. of Chelsea (s. Thomas and Lucinda, a. 26) and Ann Thorp, Nov. 29, 1849.

LIVERBOO, [Leberveau in Templeton v.r.] Lewis and Susan Dodge of Templeton, int. June 3, 1825.

LOMBARD (see Lumbard), Elizabath and Moses Smith, April 29, 1773.
Thankful and Samuel Wier of Walpole, N. H., Sept. 9, 1795.

LONGLEY, John and Olive Adams of Winchendon, June 15, 1820.

LORD, Aaron and Hannah Graves, Oct. 3, 1793.
Abel and Rebecca L. Kendall, int. May 30, 1799.
Abel and Adaline Fay, May 25, 1842.
Abigail and John Wood of Royalston, Nov. —, 1836.
Abigail Scot and Abijah Ellis of Orange, May 28, 1788.
Absolom and Clarissa Hodskin of Pelham, int. March 15, 1816.
Asa and Lydia Hump[h]ry, Aug. 15, 1785.
Cyroll C. and Betsey L. Bryant, March 19, 1833.
Gardner and Nancy Young, March 4, 1813.
Gardner and Sally Smith of Phillipston, int. Feb. 11, 1815.
Hannah and Joel Bryant of Petersham, Feb. 3, 1801.
James A. and Rosella Young, both of Templeton, Dec. 7, 1848.*
Joseph and Esther Johnson of Orange, Jan. 7, 1786. In Orange.
Jotham and Julia Allen of Orange, int. March 18, 1806.
Leonard ? and Asaph Oliver, Jan. 6, 1803.
Leonard ? and Stephen Stratton, Sept. 18, 1811.
Luther of Orange and Martha Stratton, April 7, 1812.
Mary of Putney and Aaron Smith, int. March 17, 1770.
Persis and Moses Dexter, both of Orange, April 13, 1837.*
Rhoda and Joshua Myrick, Jan. 28, 1798.
Stephen and Mary Mortin, April 1, 1760.
Stephen and Sarah Marble, both of Oringe, Dec. 12, 1790. C.R.
Thomas and Leonard Smith, Nov. 6, 1760.
Thomas Jr. and Desire Ward of Orange, int. Sept. 17, 1800.
Thomas B. (s. Justin C.) and Marianne Partridge, Sept. 19, 1844[?].
William and Mary Preston, Sept. 22, 1760.

* Intention not recorded.

LOUD, Edward of Fitzwilliam, N. H., and Sally Conant, Feb. 15, 1825.

LOVE, Robart and Mary Cutting, May 20, 1778.

LOVELL, Sarah of Sutton and Josiah Waite, March 15, 1775. In Sutton.

LOVERING, Asenath and Benjamin M. Twichell, Nov. 5, 1820.
Francis W. of Phillipston and Mary H. Lamb, in year ending April 1, 1834.
Levi and Sally Eames of Holliston, Jan. 29, 1802.
Lucy of Templeton and William H. Ward, int. Dec. 2, 1817.
Mary and Simeon Howard Jr., May 21, 1826.

LOWIS (see Lewis), Presella of Barry and Zerah Greenleaf, Aug. 30, 1801.

LUMBARD (see Lombard), Hannah and David Young, Sept. 30, 1784.
Mehetable and Lynds Smith, Oct. 9, 178[8 ?].
Nabby and Zachius Heasy [Hosay?], March 16, 1777.

LYNDS [Lind in int.], Lydia of Worcester, and Asa Smith, March 1, 1770. In Worcester.

LYON, Mary Ann of Phillipston and Abraham Oaks Jr., int. Aug. 21, 1829.
Mehitabel of Royalston and Barnabas Mendall, int. April 1, 1811.

MacBRIDE, Charlotte and Asahel Burt of Westmoreland, N. H., Nov. 14, 1802.

MackBRIDE, Jenne and Christopher Wiar, int. March 6, 1779.

McCLALLAN, Harrington and Fanny Town, March 26, 1818.

MACLALLEN, Jonathan and Lydia Ward, May 20, 1804.

McMASTER, Jenne of Palmar and Ebenezar Parsons, int. March 22, 1779.

McLANE, Neil and Catherine Heywood (widow), July 30, 1848.

MALLARD, Elvira of Gill and Amos Cheney, int. Nov. 13, 1825.

MANDELL, Mary of Barre and Nathaniel Babbit, March 3, 1778. In Barre.

MANLEY, Aden and Miriam Dewing of North Brookfield, int., Dec. 18, 1816.
Betsey and Alpheus Thayer of Brattleborough, March 19, 1817.
Howard and Lois Kilton, June 7, 1814.

MANN, Allis of Petersham and Thomas Lincoln, Jan. 6, 1803.
Alonzo of Royalston and Deborah L. Hill, April 26, 1842. In Royalston.
Hannah and John Briggs, int. May 24, 1823.
Wid. Lydia and James Sanderson, both of Petersham, Aug. 27, 1815.*
Priscilla A. of Petersham (d. Thomas and ———, a. 21) and David A. Ellinwood, Dec. 9, 1846.
William of Newsalem and Abigail Cook, in year ending April 1, 1834.

MANNING, Isable and Artemas Stone of Fitzwilliam, N. H., Sept. 20, 1797.
Patty and Joshua Robins of Stratton, Vt., Feb. 1, 1801.

MANSFIELD, Abigail M. of Bath, Me. (d. Andrew and Sarah, a. 21) and Ebenezer M. Chipman of Salem, Feb. 24, 1846.
Amos and Betsey Fisk of Wendell, between April 30, 1795 and April 30, 1796. In Wendell. [Int. Aug. 16, 1795.]

MARBEL [Marble in int.], Moses and Sarah Hooker, Oct. 10, 1775.

MARBLE, Elizabeth and John Sanders, Dec. 3, 1761.
Hannah and Joseph Bucknum Jr., Nov. 23, 1758.
Lucy of Petersham and Luther Seaver, int. June 24, 1783.
Mary of Orange and Melvin Adams, int. Nov. 21, 1825.
Moses and Lydia Barret of Berre, June 7, 1788.
Paul of Orange and Polly Adams, April 26, 1823.
Sarah and Stephen Lord, both of Oringe, Dec. 12, 1790. C.R.
Silas and Keterine Newton of Marlborough, int. Sept. 1, 1764.

MARGIT, Sarah and William Lewis [Luce ?] Jr., March 25, 1778.

MARSH, Lois and William Johnson of Chesterfield, N.H., May 28, 1800.
Mehitable of Barre and Paul Church, Jan. 18, 1797.
Mehitable and Reuben Young, April 12, 1807.
Sarah and George W. Wadkins, Oct. 23, 1825.
Thaddeus and Mary Carriel, May 5, 1819.

MARTIN, Mary of Templeton and Samuel Dunton, int. Oct. 21, 1780.

* Intention not recorded.

MASON, George of Warwick and Hannah Fay, May 12, 1814.
Nancy and William Fernald of Milton, N. H., June 16, 1842.
Welcome and Sabrina Childs, Dec. 14, 1809.

MATHEWS, Fanny R. and Shade[?] A. Earl, both of North Brookfield, May 24, 1835. In North Brookfield.*

MAYHEW, Sally of Barre and Luke Robbins, March 11, 1802.

MAYNARD, Betsy of Stow and William Bigelow, int. Jan. 13, 1809.

MAYO, Esther K. of Orange and Thomas H. Ward of Princton, Oct. 27, 1835.*
Martha A. (d. Simeon and Martha, a. 24) and John A. Brock of Worcester, April 4, 1848.
Matthias C. and Lydia Haven, June 22, 1841.

MAZRO, Francis of Petersham and Anne Frederick, April 12, 1784.

MEACHAM, James C. and Nancy Hale of Winchester, N. H., int. Feb. 6, 1836.

MEACHUM, Emeline S. (d. William and Mary, a. 19) and John O. Morey, May 6, 1847.
Orator of Petersham and Anderson Holden of South Orange, Jan. 27, 1839.*
William of New Salem and Polley Stratton, Sept. 11, 1811.
William of Petersham and Mary Ann Stephens, May 6, 1835.

MELLEN, Simon [Samuel in int.] of Westminster and Mercy Lewes, Jan. 7, 1808.

MENDALL, Barnabas and Mehitabel Lyon of Royalston, int. April 1, 1811.

MENDELL, Barnabas and Ruth Chamberlain of Dana, int. June 26, 1819.

MERRIAM, Evelina (d. Asaph and Anna G., a. 20) and James C. Partridge of Burlington, Ia., Aug. 26, 1845.
Lansford of Newsalem and Susan Young, May —, 1836.

MILLER, Asa and Sally Oliver, Aug. 19, 1828.
Esther and Ellsworth Sawyer of Royalston, Oct. —, 1836.
Isaac Jr. of Keene, N. H., and Asenath Drury, April 22, 1832.
Thomas and Mary Ann Bryant, Dec. 4, 1837.

MILLS, Eunice and Benajah Woodbury of Royalston, Oct. 25, 1798.

* Intention not recorded.

ATHOL MARRIAGES. 149

MOODY, Lyman B. of Amherst (s. David and Achsah, a. 29) and Catharine Spooner, March 29, 1848.

MOOR (see Moore, More), Bulah and John Jacobs, int. March 7, 1778.

[Moore in int.] Lydia and Ephraim Cadey Jr., March 31, 1774.

MOORE, Eunice and Joshua Mordock of Granville, N. Y., Feb. 7, 1787. In Royalston.

Fanny (d. Jonathan and Olive Harwood, a. 36) and Abram Harrington, Dec. 3, 1845.

Hannah of Cambridge and Samuel Switcher, Oct. 24, 1792. In Cambridge.

Jane of Cambridge and Prescott Jones, Jan. —, 1798. In Cambridge.

Rev Josiah and Rebecca W. Sturtevant of Plymouth, int. April 8, 1831.

Mary and James Clemence Jr. of Petersham, May 27, 1772. In Petersham.

MORDOCK (see Murdock), Joshua of Granville, N. Y. and Eunice Moore, Feb. 7, 1787. In Royalston.

MORE (see Moor, Moore), Joshua and Deborah Townsend, Jan. 14, 1800.

William and Polly Dunbar of Orange, int. April 10, 1811.

MOREY, John O. (s. Osborn and Eliza, a. 23) and Emeline S. Meachum, May 6, 1847.

MORRISON, Daniel E. of Orange and Mrs. Almira Crowl, Nov. 2, 1840.

MORSE, Anna and Oliver Holman of Petersham, Nov. 15, 1808.
Betsy of Ashby and John Crosby, int. Aug. 27, 1808.
Catherine and Hiram Young, June 15, 1837.
Charlotte and Danford Hill, July 22, 1827.
Cushing B. (s. Paul and Sally, a. 27) and Julia E. Munsel, Nov. 25, 1847.
George and Mary S. Proctor, Nov. 6, 1835.
Hannah and Samuel Kendall of Orwell, Vt., Jan. 23, 1801.
James E. (s. Joseph and Olive, a. 28) and Sarah B. Bancroft, Nov. 15, 1844.
John H. and Elizabeth Lamb, July 22, 1818.
Laban and Esther Fish, April 16, 1838.
Levi and Lucy A. Cummings, May 31, 1843.

ATHOL MARRIAGES.

MORSE, Olive and Stephen Harwood, Dec. 30, 1801.
Olive of Putney, Vt., and Jeremiah Morton, int. Oct. 6, 1828.
Polly and Zacheus Presson of Royalston, Dec. 18, 1803.
Samuel and Sally Hill of Sturbridge, int. Feb. 16, 1794.
Samuel and Deborah Stratton, Jan. 29, 1799.
Samuel Jr. and Ruth Drury, April 12, 1827.
Sumner R. and Nancy Stratton, April 25, 1833.
Sumner R. (s. Paul and Salley, a. 40, widr.) and Mary T. Stratton, May 31, 1839.
William Jr. and Charlotte Morton, Sept. 25, 1793.
William and Sally Drury, Nov. 23, 1839.

MORTIN (see Morton), Abagail and James Stratton Jr., Dec. 26, 1750.
Benjamin and Mary Dexter, Sept. 28, 1760.
Lydia and Robart Bradish, Oct. 29, 1754.
Mary and Stephen Lord, April 1, 1760.

MORTON (see above), Abner and Sopha Goddard, May 14, 1764.
Allice and Bela W. Putnam of Greenwich, Dec. 5, 1830.
Calvin and Robey Hewet, int. April 12, 1804.
Charlotte and William Morse Jr., Sept. 25, 1793.
Daniel and Lecte Fairbank, June 14, 1792.
Dolle and Benjamin Powers, July 26, 1774.
Electa and John Kelton, Oct. 25, 1815.
Fanny and Lynds Smith, Oct. 13, 1833.
Gerusha and Levi Fletcher, March 13, 1783.
Hannah and Samuel Morton, Sept. 10, 1795.
Jeremah and Alice Ford, Nov. 30, 1766.
Jeremiah and Olive Morse of Putney, Vt., int. Oct. 6, 1828.
Jerusha and Jonas Bradish, Nov. 29, 1757.
Joel and Anna Kendall, June 25, 1800.
Lt. Joel and Wid. Phebe Wood of Petersham, int. April 18, 1829.
Joshua and Azubah Graves, Feb. 1, 1774.
Joshua and Rebekah Rich, int. Aug. 18, 1785. [married at Royalston, Nov. 3. C.R.]
Joshua Jr. and Malinda Kinsley of Montague, int. Oct. 30, 1802.
Dr. Joshua and Mrs. Asubah Williams of Dana, int. April 1, 1816.
Lois and Samuel Humphrey, Dec. 29, 1763.
Lydia and John Sanderson of Petersham, Feb. 11, 1812.
Martha and Daniel Lampson, Jan. 17, 1773.
Moses and Maryann A. Fay, both of Orange, Aug. 30, 1829. C.R.
Olive and Edward Smith Jr., Oct. 24, 1813.

MORTON, Phinehas and Huldah Brown of Petersham, int. March 18, 1800.
Reuben and Judith Coles [Coates?], March 27, 1777.
Richard and Thankful Eaton of New Salem, int. Jan. 12, 1782.
Sally of Newsalem, and Bartholomew Woodward, int. Jan. 14, 1815.
Samuel Jr. and Esther Goddard, Aug. 23, 1773.
Samuel and Hannah Morton, Sept. 10, 1795.
Submit and Caleb Smith, Nov. 18, 1762.

MOULTON, Proctor of Prescott (s. Nathan and Polly, a. 42, widr.) and Augustus (*sic*) A. Goodnow of New Salem, Nov. 8, 1848.*

MUNSEL, Julia E. (d. Elisha and Polly, a. 22) and Cushing B. Morse, Nov. 25, 1847.

MUNSELL, Sarah H. and William D. Lee, Jr. June 7, 1841.

MURDOCK, Betsy and Abijah Thayer, both of Petersham, Jan. 1, 1802.*

MUZZE, Olive of Jamaica, Vt., and Jonathan Harwood, int. Jan. 30, 1808.

MYRICK, Elvira and Gideon Sibley, Sept. 23, 1823.
Joseph P. and Sarah L. Averell of Milford, N.H., int. Aug. 30, 1834.
Joshua and Rhoda Lord, Jan. 28, 1798.
Joshua and Patty Pierce, July 12, 1801.
Nathaniel of Harwick and Wid. Susanna Taylor, Oct. 23, 1794.

NASON, Jonas B. of Boston and Caroline Gennison of Orange, Dec. 19, 1839.*

NEEDHAM, see Bradbury.

NEWELL, Meriam and William Brown of Gerry, int. Aug. 10, 1794.
Sally and Levi Kendall, Oct. 22, 1786.

NEWHALL, George and Mary Woods of Wendell, int. Sept. 6, 1823.
Hannah and Erastus Danforth, April 6, 1815.
Hiram and Jerusha Hallay ?, int. Nov. 1, 1779.
Jerusha and Abraham Nutt Jr., Oct. 3, 1793.
Jonathan and Susanna Graves, Oct. 24, 1799.

* Intention not recorded.

NEWHALL, Joshua and Polly Cutting, April 24, 1791.
Lucy and Nehemiah Ward, April 8, 1816.
Mary and Hasey Floyd Sprague of Gerry, May 8, 1788.
Sally and Stephen Fessendon of Rutland, April 16, 1801.
Samuel and Betsy Fish, May 28, 1826.
William of Vernon, Vt., and Clarissa Phillips, Jan. 18, 1807.

NEWTON, Elizabath and James Stockwill, Dec. 6, 1769.
Hannah and John How, Dec. 13, 1769.
Keterine of Marlborough and Silas Marble, int. Sept. 1, 1764.
Step[h]en (s. Stephen and Catharine, a. 22) and Mary Dyer, March 14, 1848.

NICHOLS, Asa and Mary Derby, both of Westminster, Jan. 16, 1806.*
Elijah and Sally Church, Nov. 29, 1797.

NIGHTINGALE, Rev. Crawford of Springfield (s. Samuel and Elizabeth, a. 29) and Mary H. Williams, May 13, 1846.

NIGHTS (see Knights), Ebenezer and Mary Baley of Stow, int. Sept. 2, 1772.

NORCROSS, Isaac Jr. of Royalston and Sally Holman, June 14, 1797.
Levi of Templeton and Wid. Molly Drury, int. June 28, 1823.
Nancy of Templeton and Samuel Wiley, int. Sept. 15, 1827.

NUTT, Abraham Jr. and Jerusha Newhall, Oct. 3, 1793.
Abraham Jr. and Hannah Brown of Chesterfield, N.H., int. Jan. 10, 1796.
James and Susannah Cochran of Blandford, —— —, 1770. In Blandford.
Jerusha and David Pike of Boston, Jan. 19, 1823.
Susannah and Moses Ball, Feb. 18, 1762.

NYE, Hannah E. (a. 23) and Abner W. Twichell, Oct. 21, 1846.

OAK (see below), Cinthia and Joel S. Hale, Dec. 23, 1819.
Ira and Mrs. Lucy Fay, Sept. 3, 1839.

OAKES, Betcey and Abijah Underwood, Aug. 18, 1801.

OAKS (see above), Abraham Jr. and Mary Ann Lyon of Phillipston, int. Aug. 21, 1829.
Ira and Mary Howard, Oct. 7, 1834.
Mariann A. (d. Abraham and Mary A., a. 15) and Phelps P. Gilmore, July 4, 1847.

*Intention not recorded.

ATHOL MARRIAGES. 153

OLDHAM, John and Sybil Adams of New Salem, int. Dec. 2, 1818.

OLIVER, Aaron and Lucy Smith, Jan. 19, 1774.
Aaron and Susan Whitcomb, Dec. 5, 1830.
Ann L. [Anne Durham in int.] and Hezekiah Goddard of Orange, Aug. 15, 1784. In Orange.
Anne and Jonathan Kendall, Jan. 23, 1765.
Asaph and Leonard Lord, Jan. 6, 1803.
Calvin H. and Dolly Wood, March 26, 1805.
Elizabeth and Phinehas Alden [Allen in int.] of Jameca, Vt., Feb. 18, 1796.
Eunice H. of Pelham and Daniel Stratton, int. April 12, 1828.
Franklin and Emily Eaton Woodard, int. Aug. 26, 1832. [Married Sept. 12. C.R.]
George and Rhoda Young, Nov. 28, 1799.
George Esq. and Deborah White of Warwick, int. Aug. 8, 1818.
Hannah and George Web Felton of Petersham, Sept. 12, 1785.
Isabel and Ruggles Ware [Ward ?], Nov. 2, 1780.
Isabella and James Caldwell, Jan. 15, 1751.
James and Hannah Kendall, Sept. 30, 1801.
James Jr. and Minerva Fay, Sept. 20, 1827.
Jemima and Josiah Ford, May 27, 1773.
John Jr. and Sally Ward, Sept. 23, 1790.
Katerine of Rutland and William Kimplan, int. Feb. 12, 1764.
Lois W. and Wilder Stephens of Warwich, Nov. 19, 1795.
Mary and Peter Fissington, Nov. 16, 1761.
Mary and Obidiah Jones, Aug. 2, 1781.
Meribah and Zebina Sanders of Sudbury, Vt., Jan. 3, 1793.
Moses and Lois Wiswell Humphrey, Nov. 23, 1780.
Moses W. and Betsey Fisher, int. Sept. 19, 1829. [Married Oct. 5, C.R.]
Rachel and Benjamin Bridges, Oct. 10, 1790.
Sally and Asa Miller, Aug. 19, 1828.
Thomas and Lois Young, April 26, 1838.
Tirzoh and Aaron Smith, Nov. 19, 1778.
William and Anna Forbes of Rutland District, Dec. 7, 1767. In Barre.

ORCUT, Mary H. of Templeton and Joseph Proctor, int. Dec. 29, 1810.

ORCUTT, David and Lucretia Baldwin of Phillipston, int. Nov. 15, 1823.
John and Hannah W. Jackson, both of Orange, Nov. 30, 1842.*

* Intention not recorded.

ORCUTT, Jonathan of Templeton and Allice Graves, Nov. 9, 1806.
Martha of Ewings Grant and Prescott Foskett of Orange, April 20, 1836.*
Sally and Jonathan Kendell, April 27, 1824.

OSGOOD, Mary [wid.] and Jabez Ward, March 27, 1817.
Mary Ann and Dana Rich of Phillipston, Jan. 17, 1826.
Samuel M. (s. Elihu and Ruth, a. 28, widr.) and Jane Thorp, Nov. 4, 1846.

PAGE, Mercy of Hardwick and Nathaniel Graves, int. April 12, 1777.

PAIN, Barnabas and Lois Woods of Orange, int. Dec. 21, 1788.

PAINE, Hannah of Greenwich and Goodell Godard, int. Dec. 10, 1818.
Mary and Isaac Shepardson of Royalston, int. April 28, 1793.

PARKER, Joseph P. and Eliza H. Stone of Petersham, April 6, 1842. In Petersham.
Nancy of Royalston and Nathan Godard, May 24, 1803.
Ruth of Gerry and Joshua Doane, Oct. 5, 1801.
[Of Oxford in int.], Sarah and Ephraim Cady Jr., March 4, 1776.
Sophronia of Hubbardston and Henry Humphrey, int. May 15, 1836.

PARKS, Catharine of Gerry and Samuel Goddard of Royalston, June 29, 1790.*

PARMENTER (see Perminter), Zilpha and Amos S. Piper, both of Ewings Grant, May 3, 1837.*

PARSONS, Ebenezer and Jenne McMaster of Palmer, int. March 22, 1779.

PARTRIDGE, Amos of Chesterfield and Sally Harvey, int. June 27, 1783.
Elizabeth M. and William L. Sargent of Barre, June 11, 1840.
James C. of Burlington, Ia. (s. Ezekiel and Anna M., a. 23) and Evelina Merriam, Aug. 26, 1845.
Marianne (d. John H.) and Thomas B. Lord, Sept. 19, 1844[?].
Susan H. and Merrick E. Ainsworth, April 28, 1842. Dup.

PATRICK, Elizabeth (d. Samuel and Abigail, a. 26) and William R. Lincoln of Westboro', June 21, 1849.

* Intention not recorded.

ATHOL MARRIAGES.   155

PEABODY, Calvin of Petersham and Hannah Twichell, Jan. 9, 18[21 or 22].
Hannah C. (d. Isaac K. and Sally) and Gustavus A. M. Hunt of Petersham, July 4, 1843.
Isaac K. and Clarissa Gay, Jan. 1, 1822.
Kitteridge and Sally Twichel, May 4, 1814.

PECK, Rebecka of Royalston and Salma Alger of Northfield, Dec. 1, 1808.*
Rutina of Royalston and Hugh Foster, int. Feb. 14, 1818.
Vilroy A. of Orange and Prentice H. Pond of Franklin, July 9, 1837.*

PECKHAM, Abigail of Petersham and Phineas Pratt, int. Dec. 16, 1785.
Alfred of Templeton and Hannah Ann Ball, Jan. 12, 1841.
Rebeccah and David Amsden, both of Petersham, Dec. 8, 1818.*

PEIRCE (see Pierce) Eleanor and Levi B. Clark of Boston, Nov. 24, 1822.
Franklin and Elianor Lamb of Phillipston, int. Oct. 27, 1817.
James and Mary Wood, Nov. 19, 1787.
Mary and Benjamin Davis of Holden, Jan. 18, 1816.
Patty and James Young, Jan. 20, 1812.
Sarah and Moses Stockwell, Aug. 15, 1768.
Susan H. of Petersham and Moses P. Ball, int. March 11, 1825.
William Jr. and Hannah Brown, both of Royalston, June 9, 1819.*

PERMINTER (see Parmenter), Oliver of Molberough, N.H., and Vina Fay, April 4, 1793.
Susanna and John Hill, Feb. 8, 1795.

PERRY, Clarissa and David Goddard of Orange, March 29, 1829.
William and Katherine E. Sawyer, April —, 1835.

PHILLIPS, Aaron I. and Susan Walker, Nov. 17, 1833.
Betsey and Joshua Stratton, Sept. 8, 1825.
Clarissa and William Newhall of Vernon, Vt., Jan. 18, 1807.
Mary of Gerry and Adinijah Ball, Feb. 28, 1788.
Nathaniel and Mary Baley, April 29, 1784.

PIERCE (see Peirce), Adaline of Chesterfield, N. H., and Freeman Chase, int. May 9, 1833.
Wid. Eleanor and Joseph Rich Jr., March 9, 1831.
Ezubah and Enos Twichel Jr., Sept. 25, 1793.
Gilbert and Mary Ann Stimson, April 2, 1840.

* Intention not recorded.

PIERCE, Jonas of Royalston and Fanny Earl, April 20, 1826.
Patty and Joshua Myrick, July 12, 1801.
Seraphinia and Samuel Young of Acton, Oct. 29, 1808.

PIERSE [Rice in Royalston V.R.], William of Royalston and Polly Anger, Sept. 13, 1784. In Royalston.

PIKE, David and Joanna Chany, Oct. 26, 1786.
David of Boston and Jerusha Nutt, Jan. 19, 1823.
Dorcas and Aaron Blanshard, int. July 23, 1784.
Elizabeth and Jonas Goss, Nov. 11, 1766.*

PIPER, Amos S. and Zilpha Parmenter, both of Ewings Grant, May 3, 1837.*
Emily E. and John S. Banks, both of Ewings Grant, April 18, 1838.*
John and Sarah Wellington, both of Templeton, Aug. 1, 1784.*
Silvanus and Sally Sawtle, both of Gerry, June 14, 1810.*

PITTS, Elisha J. of Orange and Mary Howard, Nov. 20, 1823.

POND, Prentice H. of Franklin and Vilroy A. Peck of Orange, July 9, 1837.*

POOR, Marcy and Amos Bucknam, May 20, 1767.

POWERS, Benjamin and Dolle Morton, July 26, 1774.
Benjamin of Petersham and Anna Raymond, Nov. 1, 1786.
Mary of Petersham and Jotham Bigelow, int. July 9, 1771.
Orrin of Troy, Wis., and Mary Lewis, Oct. 1, 1839.
Sarah A. of Petersham and Freeborn Raymond, int. Jan. 18, 1777.

PRATT, Julia and George W. Harrington, both of Royalston, Dec. 11, 1842.*
Mary and Solomon Fay, Sept. 3, 1761.
Pamelia of Charlton and Rev. John V. Wilson, int. Aug. 23, 1834.
Phineas and Abigail Peckham of Petersham, int. Dec. 16, 1785.
Sally and Lemuel Whitney of Warwick, int. Aug. 18, 1804.

PRESON (see below), Perciulls and Martha Fessondon, int. Sept. 8, 1793.

PRESSON, Abigail and Gooding Lincoln of Dover, Vt., Oct. 9, 1825.
Zacheus of Royalston and Polly Morse, Dec. 18, 1803.

PRESTON (see above), Mary and William Lord, Sept. 22, 1760.
Oliver and Mina Rich of Phillipston, int. Sept. 6, 1816.

* Intention not recorded.

ATHOL MARRIAGES. 157

PRIEST, Calvin of Northfield and Susanna Wesson, Aug. 6, 1798.
PROCTOR, Harriet H. and Samuel Ellsworth of Greenwich, Sept. 15, 1840.
Joseph and Mary H. Orcut of Templeton, int. Dec. 29, 1810.
Mary S. and George Morse, Nov. 6, 1835.
PROUTY, Adam of West Boylston and Hannah Hill, Oct. 6, 1828.
Plummer of Spencer and Sarah G. Holman of Petersham, June 30, 1842.*
PUTNAM, Bela W. of Greenwich and Allice Morton, Dec. 5, 1830.
Pliney of Sutton and Eliza Gray, Nov. 29, 1827.
RANDALL, Volentine of Stratton, Vt., and Rhoda Haven, March 3, 18[08].
RAYMOND (see Reymond), Abigail and Thomas Townsend, Feb. 15, 1795.
Abigail and Luther Smith, Sept. 14, 1805.
Anna and Joshua Bullard, June 15, 1775.
Anna and Benjamin Powers of Petersham, Nov. 1, 1786.
Anna and Amos Caruth, Dec. 17, 18[07].
Edward Jr. and Jane Oliver Kendall, Oct. 30, 1783.
Elizebeth and Jesse Kindell Jr., Oct. 12, 1780.
Elizabeth and Silas Stow Jr. of Gerry, Dec. 24, 1812.
Freeborn and Mary Young, Aug. 18, 1763.
Freeborn and Sarah Powers of Petersham, int. Jan. 18, 1777.
Freeborn Jr. and Lucinda Graves, Nov. 5, 1787. In Royalston.
Freeborn and Lois Kendall, July 16, 1789.
Freeborn Jr. and Jane Rich of Gerry, March 10, 1801.
Lucinda and John Twichel of New Salem, Dec. 22, 1813.
Lydia and Allen Reynolds of Orwell, Vt., Feb. 21, 18[08].
Mary of Royalston and Jonathan Wheeler, int. Dec. 6, 1822.
Molley and Alpheus Ward, March 7, 1782.
Patty and Nahum Ward, June 21, 1792.
Ruth and Josiah Goddard, Nov. 8, 1774.
Sally and Joel Kendall, Nov. 5, 1787. In Royalston.
Sarah and David Chase of Royalston, Nov. 29, 1786. In Royalston.
Sullivan of Royalston and Anna Wheeler, Jan. 25, 1825.
William and Lydia Ward, July 6, 1781.
William and Sophia Ward, int. Nov. 16, 1782.

* Intention not recorded.

ATHOL MARRIAGES.

REED, Rebeccah Ann of Brattleborough and David Harwood, int. July 23, 1816.

REYMOND (see Raymond), Susanna and Rufus Walker of Hubbardton, Vt., Feb. 21, 1796.

REYNOLDS, Allen of Orwell, Vt., and Lydia Raymond, Feb. 21, 18[08].
Tertius of Warren, Ct. and Elisa Talbot, int. May 16, 1829.

RHODES, John of Dummerston, N.Y., and Hannah How of Warwick, June 5, 1778.*

RICE, Alanson of Greenwich and Sophia Chamberlain, Jan. 7, 1817.
Edwin C. of Orange and Abigail P. Hunt, Sept. 3, 1843.
Jonas and Olive Stimpson, March 31, 1825.
Somantha of New Salem and Franklin Adams, Jan. 3, 1842. In New Salem.
Susanna of Hardwick and Stephen Haskins [Watkins ?], March 6, 1789. In Hardwick.
Uriah [of Warwick c.r.] and Unice Church [of Petersham, c.r.], Sept. 7, 1780.*
Wiliam of Royalston and Polle Anger, int. Sept. 10, 1784.
See Pierse.

RICH, Almeda and Albert Farr, Jan. 15, 1849.
Asiah and Asohel Sanders, May 26, 1783.
Benjamin and Nabby Day, both of Phillipston, Oct. 4, 1821.*
Cynthia of Phillipston and Charles Bruce, int. Aug. 23, 1829.
Dana of Phillipston and Mary Ann Osgood, Jan. 17, 1826.
Deborah and Chester Brigham [Bingham ?] of Chesterfie[ld], Sept. 23, 1786.
Frederick and Salina Cook, Nov. 13, 1839.
Jacob [of Warwick in int.] and Mary Kindal, Aug. 4, 1774.
Jane of Gerry and Freeborn Raymond Jr., March 10, 1801.
Joseph Jr. and Wid. Eleanor Pierce, March 9, 1831.
Joseph Jr. and Mrs. Mary L. Day of Gardner, May 4, 1842. In Gardner.
Mina of Phillipston and Oliver Preston, int. Sept. 6, 1816.
Rebeccah and Edmond Wilbor, April 3, 1827.
Rebekah and Joshua Morton, int. Aug. 18, 1785.
Salome and Lyman Brown of Hubbardston, int. April 27, 1836.
Thankful and Thomas Stratton, April 5, 1784.
Zaccheus Jr. and Lydia Brown, Nov. 7, 1781. [Int. Oct. 13, 1782 ?.]

* Intention not recorded.

ATHOL MARRIAGES. 159

RICHARDS, William (s. William and Susan, a. 21) and Laura A. Cummings, Oct. 27, 1846.

RICHARDSON, Alice [of Royalston in int.] and Abner Graves, Feb. 12, 1768.
Azubah of Templeton and Levi Stockwell, Aug. 23, 1787. In Templeton.
Betsey H. and George Smith, in year ending April 1, 1834.
Caroline of Petersham and Elisha Stratton, May 23, 1786. In Petersham.
Charles and Lydia Barret of Ashby, int. Aug. 25, 1814.
Esther of Brookfield and Nathaniel Stratton, May 15, 1792. In Brookfield.
Hannah and Nathaniel Graves Jr., June 16, 1774.
Joseph and Sally Johnson of Orange, int. Dec. 2, 1809.
Josiah [Isaiah ?] of Petersham and Esther Bigelow, July 3, 1783. In Petersham.
Josiah of Leominster and Reliance Crocker Crosby, int. March 1, 1808.
Luna[?] B. and Mary Kimball of Peterborough, N.H., int. Nov. 10, 1833.
Lysander and Amanda Baker of Orange, int. July 26, 1831.
Nathaniel of Peterborough, N.H., and Emeline Young, Oct. 31, 1830.
Timothy and Sarah Easty, Dec. 31, 1767. In Royalston.
Warren of Plymouth and Lucretia Ward, Oct. 9, 1822.
Wyman and Arathusa Southick, Aug. 13, 1827.

RIDER, Mary and Robert Young Jr., June 6, 1776.
Seth and Deborah Chase of Petersham, int. March 22, 1776.

ROBBINS (see Robins), Luke and Mary Heasy ? Dec. 8, 1774.
Luke and Sally Mayhew of Barre, March 11, 1802.
Phinehas and Anna Calhoon of Petersham, April 18, 1793. In Petersham.

ROBERTS, Abraham and Hannah Whitney, both of Warwich, Nov. 13, 1777.*
Ruben of Amherst and Hannah Goddard, Aug. 4, 1841.

ROBINS (see Robbins), Chloe and Peter Sanderson of Phillipston, June 12, 1814.
Joshua of Stratton, Vt., and Patty Manning, Feb. 1, 1801.

ROBINSON, Mary of Nottingham West and George Talbot Jr., int. Oct. 1, 1825.

* Intention not recorded.

ROBY, Louisa Ann and George Bryant, Oct. 24, 1841.

ROGERS, Abel [of Petersham, c.r.] and Sarah Young, Oct. 11, 1769.
Elizabeth of Petersham and Asa Stratton, int. Nov. 23, 1821.

ROOT, Charles S. of Greenwich (a. 26) and Rowena S. Bassett, Feb. 3, 1847.
Penelope and Elihu Smith, March 17, 1805.

ROSS, Abigail and Bridgeman Stephens, both of Petersham, May 25, 1819.*

RUGG, Hannah of Hindsdale, N.H., and Daniel Hildreth, int. Aug. 13, 1814.

RUGGLES, Lemuel and Lydia Brigham of New Brantree, int. Dec. 25, 1779.

RUSSEL, Mary of Barre and Benjamin Kelton, Oct. 26, 1786. In Barre.

RUSSELL, Hannah M. and Jesse C. Davenport of Petersham, April 5, 1841.

RYANT, Sarah of Sturbridge and John Hill 2d, int. Dec. 5, 1800.

SANDERS (see Saunders), Asahel and Asiah Rich, May 26, 1783.
Benjamin and Hannah Young, Dec. 2, 1762.
John and Elizabeth Marble, Dec. 3, 1761.
Zebina of Sudbury, Vt. and Meribah Oliver, Jan. 3, 1793.

SANDERSON, Albert and Louisa Young, int. Sept. 1, 1833.
Benjamin and Hannah Young, Aug. 18, 1763. c.r.
James and Wid. Lydia Mann, both of Petersham, Aug. 27, 1815.*
John of Petersham and Lydia Morton, Feb. 11, 1812.
Peter of Phillipston and Chloe Robins, June 12, 1814.

SARGENT, Abigail and Zaccheus Hasey, both of Hubbardston, May 30, 1781.*
Ezra of Putnam Co., Ga., and Maria Ellenwood, Dec. 12, 1824.
Rachel of Fitzwilliam, N.H., int John Haven Jr., int. April 2, 1810.
William L. of Barre and Elizabeth M. Partridge, June 11, 1840.

SAUNDERS (see Sanders), Franklin of Westminster and Alice Barrett, Oct. 30, 1831.

SAWTELL (see Sawtle), Abigail and Thomas Carcless, both of Templeton, Aug. 16, 1783.*

* Intention not recorded.

SAWTELL, Eunice of Phillipston and Abel Bigelow, int. Oct. 13, 1828.
Ruth and Calvin Goss, both of Gerry, June 3, 1790.*
SAWTLE (see above), Salley and Silvanus Piper, both of Gerry, June 14, 1810.*
SAWYER, Abner and Eunice Haven, April 3, 1792.
Ellsworth of Royalston and Esther Miller, Oct. —, 1836.
Hannah of Templeton and James Badger, int. Jan. 13, 1800.
Jabez of Wendell and Jemima Caruth of Gerry, Feb. 23, 1798.*
Katherine E. and William Perry, April —, 1835.
Sylvester of Royalston and Esther Bigelow, June 27, 1843.
William of Stoneham and Betsey P. Chase, Oct. 27, 1841. In Royalston.

SEAVER, Jane R. and Stillman Stockwell, June 4, 1839.
Luther and Lucy Marble of Petersham, int. June 24, 1783.

SHATTUCK, Polley and Theadore Bates, both of Templeton, Sept. 1, 1785.*

SHAW, Sarah of Lecester and David Goddard, int. Nov. 10, 1769.

SHEPARDSON, Eli [Eri in Royalston v.R.] and Elvira S. Bemis, both of Royalston, Jan. 5, 1843.*
Isaac of Royalston and Mary Paine, int. April 28, 1793.

SHERMAN, Ezra of Cambridge, N.Y., and Mercy Haven, Feb. 21, 1819.
Jason Jr. of Barre and Polly Stow of Gerry, Oct. 17, 1809.*
Mercy and Henry Taft of Caroline, N.Y., June 9, 1825.

SHUTE, Susa of Templeton and John Coalman Jr., March 18, 1784.

SIBLEY, Amos and Prudence Harwood of Oxford, int. June 9, 1809.
Elisha [of Hardwick in int.] and Elizebeth Twitchel, Nov. 1, 1781.
Freeman R. and Olive Harwood, Feb. 20, 1834.
Gideon and Elvira Myrick, Sept. 23, 1823.
Mary and Dr. Christopher C. Wheaton of Royalston, June 2, 1835.
Sumner and Clarissa Barns of Gill, int. Nov. 6, 1830.
Willard and Luthera Barry, Oct. 19, 1842.

* Intention not recorded.

SIMONDS, Mary Isabella (d. Stillman and Elizabeth, a. 19) and David A. Hale of New York, Sept. 3, 1849.
Nelson of Templeton (s. James and Hannah, a. 42, widr.) and Eunice Lewis, Oct. 21, 1848.
Zebodee of Concord, N.Y. and Nancy Giles, Aug. 26, 1821.

SKINNER, Benjamin C. and Mary R. Stockwell, Oct. 8, 1840.

SMITH, Aaron and Mary Lord of Putney, int. March 17, 1770.
Aaron and Tirzoh Oliver, Nov. 19, 1778.
Abigail and Ichabod Dexter, Aug. 2, 1759.
Abijah of Orwell and Susanna Kendall, April 24, 1791.
Abner and Jerushe Hutchins, Dec. 11, 1771.
Adin H. and Louisa M. Adams of Orange, March 2, 1843.
Asa and Lydia Lynds of Worcester, March 1, 1770. In Worcester.
B. Ellsworth of Amherst and Mary W. Allen, May 5, 1841.
Betsy and Jonathan Clement of Richfield, N.Y., Aug. 7, 1806.
Caleb and Submit Morton, Nov. 18, 1762.
Caleb and Abigail Baker of Northampton, int. Feb. 1, 1789.
Dolly and Abner Graves Jr., June 12, 1806.
Dolly and John Hill, Nov. 30, 1837.
Ebenezer of Newsalem and Ruth Goddard, March 22, 1825.
Edward Jr. and Olive Morton, Oct. 24, 1813.
Eliel and Sarah Evens Humphrey of Orange, int. Sept. 18, 1795.
Elihu and Rebekah Bigelow of Royalston, int. June 8, 1798.
Elihu and Penelope Root, March 17, 1805.
Elisha [Elihu in Royalston v.r.], and Rebecca Bigelow of Royalston, Nov. 29, [17—] [1798]. In Royalston.
Elizabeth [wid. ?] and William Stratton, March 2, 1780.
Ephraim and Zeruiah Wood, Aug. 14, 1776.
Gamaliel and Maria Charlotte Aldrich, Nov. 24, 1842. c.r.
George and Betsey H. Richardson, in year ending April 1, 1834.
Giles and Mehitable Fairbank, April 3, 1794.
Henry of Swansey, N.H., and Eunice Davis of Orange, Dec. 17, 1840.*
James G. of Phillipston (s. Nathaniel and Betsey, a. 26) and Eunice Haven, May 26, 1847.
Jonathan and Hannah Taylor, Dec. 17, 1795.
Joshua and Hannah Fish, Jan. 8, 1799.
Lafayette (s. Ebenezer and Ruth, a. 20) and Amelia E. Goddard, Nov. 27, 1845.
Leonard ? and Thomas Lord, Nov. 6, 1760.
Lucy and Aaron Oliver, Jan. 19, 1774.
Lucy R. of New Salem and Asa Haven, int. Sept. 19, 1820.

* Intention not recorded.

ATHOL MARRIAGES. 163

SMITH, Luther and Abigail Raymond, Sept. 14, 1805.
Luthera A. (d. Eben and Ruth, a. 20) and James L. Hagar, Jan. 1, 1849.
Lydia and John Drury, July 3, 1765.
Lydia of Warwick and Isaiah Sterns, int. March 17, 1798.
Lydia and Daniel Ward, Nov. 30, 1815.
Lynds and Fanny Morton, Oct. 13, 1833.
Lynds and Mehetable Lumbard, Oct. 9, 178[8 ?].
Martha and Joseph Dexter, Dec. 9, 1756.
Mary of Weston and Jonathan Fisk, Feb. 23, 1774. In Weston.
Mary and Levi Haven, Jan. 5, 1803.
Moses and Elisabeth Lombard, April 29, 1773.
Nathaniel Jr. of Phillipston and Betsy Godard, May 11, 1819.
Reuben of Orvil and Esther Kendall, Feb. 12, 1789.
Rhoda and Moses Leanard, May 17, 1762.
Russell and Maria Kendall, Aug. 21, 1839.
Sally and Philemon Fairbanks, June 19, 1779. In Bolton.
Sally of Phillipston and Gardner Lord, int. Feb. 11, 1815.
Solomon and Tabetha Briggs, Dec. 27, 1780.
Stephen and Susannah Haven, July 23, 1766.
Submit and John Dickerson of Orwell, Vt., Feb. 8, 1800.
Mrs. Susannah of Gerry and John Kendall, Feb. 21, 1796. In Phillipston.

SOUTHICK, Arathusa and Wyman Richardson, Aug. 13, 1827.

SPAULDING, Benjamin Goodridge and Abigail Dyer, int. Nov. 18, 1802.
Levi of Lyndsborough, N.H., and Clarry Goddard, March 3, 1796.

SPEAR, Joseph O. and Lydia H. Crossman, March 21, 1844.
Silas Jr. and Harriet White, both of Orange, April 21, 1840.*

SPENCER, Wealthy and Stillman Stockwell, June 21, 1835.

SPOONER, Alden and Dolly Flagg of Lancaster, int. Oct. 1, 1820.
Catharine (d. Asa and Dolly, a. 27) and Lyman B. Moody of Amherst, March 29, 1848.

SPRAGUE, Celia of Petersham and Richard Harris, int. Oct. 18, 1806.
Ephraim S. and Sarah T. Wheeler of Fitzwilliam, N.H., int. Sept. 4, 1829.
Esther and Ebenezer Knight Jr., Jan. 5, 1786.
George and Nancy Knights of Phillipston, June 1, 1826.

* Intention not recorded.

SPRAGUE, Hasey Floyd of Gerry and Mary Newhall, May 8, 1788.
I[s]rael and Ruth Fisk of Templeton, Oct. 16, 1783. In Templeton.
Joseph and Mehitable Chamberlain of Dana, int. Aug. 20, 1819.
Joshua of Petersham and Lois Stoc[—] of Gerry, May 26, 1791.*
Sally Stockwell and Joel Stratton, Feb. 24, 1822.

STEARNS (see Sterns), Samuel and Lydia Clemonts, Sept. 7, 1796.

STEBBINS, Josiah of Winchester, N. H., and Abigail Stratton, int. July 27, 1797.
Rowena L. and Stephen Devenport, Feb. 8, 1844.

STERNS (see Stearns), Isaiah and Lydia Smith of Warwick, int. March 17, 1798.

STEPHENS (see Stevens), Bridgeman and Abigail Ross, both of Petersham, May 25, 1819.*
Mary Ann and William Meachum of Petersham, May 6, 1835.
Wilder of Warwich and [Wid.] Lois W. [Wiswell in c.r.] Oliver, Nov. 19, 1795.

STEVANS (see above) [Stevens in int.], Jacob and Dolly Davis of Concord, March 28, 1797. In Concord.

STEVENS, Abel of Gardner and Clarissa Stratton, May 8, 1811.
Anna of Petersham and Samuel S. Haven, Feb. 25, 1841. In Petersham.
Betsy of Gerry and Nathan Jackson of Petersham, July 1, 1800.*
Charles H. of Manchester, N.H. (s. Charles B. and Julia A., a. 28) and Dolly F. Campbell, Sept. 7, 1846.
Harriet N. (d. Isaac and Eunice B., a. 18) and Dr. George D. Colony, May 23, 1849.
Samuell of Thetford, Vt., and Mary Bancroft, Jan. 31, 1836.

STIMPSON (see Stimson), John of N. Salem and Tila Wilmarth, Aug. 19, 1802.
Olive and Jonas Rice, March 31, 1825.

STIMSON (see above), Mary Ann and Gilbert Pierce, April 2, 1840.

STOCKWELL (see Stockwill), Abagal and Benjamin Woodbury, Aug. 15, 1768.
Ammi and Susan Day, April 14, 1837. In Winchendon.
Betsy of Royalston and Seth Twichel, May 14, 1822.
Cyrus and Ruth Bancroft of Ewings Grant, Dec. 3, 1835.

* Intention not recorded.

ATHOL MARRIAGES. 165

STOCKWELL, Dolly of Sutton and Simeon [Simon ?] Stockwell, Dec. 29, 1799. In Sutton.
Elizabeth (d. John and Betsy, a. 18) and Joel R. Howard of Warwick, Sept. 30, 1845.
Emmons and Elvira Wood of Royalston, int. Aug. 25, 1831.
Freeland and Minerva P. Ball, in year ending April 1, 1834.
Hannah and Daniel Bigelow, April 29, 1827.
Harriet and Otis Jones of Angelica, N.Y., Oct. 30, 1831.
John and Betsy Briggs, Nov. 30, 1815.
Joseph of Royalston and Dorothy Drury, April 26, 1821.
Leah and Benona Twichel, int. Jan. 1, 1792.
Levi and Azubah Richardson of Templeton, Aug. 23, 1787. In Templeton.
Lois of Gerry and Joshua Sprague of Petersham, May 26, 1791.*
Mary and Kimball Cole of New Market, N.H., March 17, 1842.
Mary R. and Benjamin C. Skinner, Oct. 8, 1840.
Moses and Sarah Peirce [of Royalston, C.R.], Aug. 15, 1768.
Noah and Polly Briggs, Sept. 29, 1807.
Peter and Sally Turner, April 10, 1800.
Ruth of Royalston and Noah Holman, June 3, 1795. In Royalston.
Sally of Royalston and Chester Twitchell, int. May 24, 1823.
Sally of Royalston and George W. Drury, int. Feb. 24, 1827.
Sarah of Chesterfield and William Bates, int. April 26, 1777.
Sarah (d. Noah and Polly, a. 26) and Amos Drury of Wendell, May 5, 1847.
Simeon and Dolly Stockwell of Sutton, Dec. 29, 1799. In Sutton.
Stillman and Wealthy Spencer, June 21, 1835.
Stillman and Jane R. Seaver, June 4, 1839.
Sylvestre and Polly Fay, int. Aug. 12, 1832. [Married, Sept. 4, C.R.]
Ziba and Hannah Town, April 21, 1785. In Templeton.

STOCKWILL (see above), James and Elizabath Newton, Dec. 6, 1769.
Jesse and Annis Grout of Templeton, April 3, 1782.

STONE, Abigail T. and Abner Stratton, Jan. 1, 1806.
Artemas of Fitzwilliam, N.H., and Isable Manning, Sept. 20, 1797.
Eliza H. of Petersham and Joseph P. Parker, April 6, 1842. In Petersham.
Hannah of Rutland and Benjamin Dexter, int. Oct. 10, 1769.
Hannah of Framingham and Nathan Underwood, int. Jan. 11, 1819.
Nathan and Nancy Willard of Peterham, int. Dec. 19, 1810.
Ursula of Dana (d. John B. and Olive, a. 23) and Dexter Aldrich, April 12, 1849.

* Intention not recorded.

ATHOL MARRIAGES.

STOW, Polly of Gerry and Jason Sherman Jr. of Barre, Oct. 17, 1809.*
Silas Jr. of Gerry and Elizabeth Raymond, Dec. 24, 1812.
[How ?] Thomas and Mary Elliss of Royalston, June 22, 1779. In Royalston.

STRATTEN, (see Stratton), Pelog and Elizabath Kendall, Nov. 29, 1769.
Stephen and Martha Graves, Sept. 24, 1767.

STRATTON (see above), Abel and Betcy Batchelor of Fitchburg, int. Aug. 22, 1801.
Abigail of Pequioge and Henry Chase of Nichewaug, Dec. 29, 1746. In Petersham.
Abigail and Josiah Stebbins of Winchester, N.H., int. July 27, 1797.
Abigail and Josephus Bardwell of Williamston, Feb. 25, 1816.
Abigail and Asa W. Twichell, Nov. 24, 1842.
Abner and Abigail T. [Tufts, c.r.] Stone, Jan. 1, 1806.
Abner G. and Ophelia Barton, July 7, 1842.
Amos T. (s. Abner and Abigail, a. 31) and Eleanor Stratton, Jan. 3, 1849.
Andrew and Lois Ward, Oct. 2, 1817.
Ann and Mason Ainsworth of Barre, April —, 1836.
Asa and Susanna Giles of N. Salem, int. Aug. 15, 1807.
Asa and Elizabeth Rogers of Petersham, int. Nov. 23, 1821.
Betsey and Elisha Field of New Salem, Oct. 6, 1812 [1811 ?].
Betsy and Benjamin Cook Jr., May 29, 1828. Dup.
Clarissa and Abel Stevens of Gardner, May 8, 1811.
Daniel and Eunice H. Oliver of Pelham, int. April 12, 1828.
David and Sally Wadsworth of Grafton, int. May 5, 1810.
David and Rachel Dike, Sept. 25, 1825.
Deborah and Seth Kendall, March 10, 1746.
Deborah and Samuel Morse, Jan. 29, 1799.
Dolly and Samuell Cobb, Sept. 9, 1835.
Ebenezer and Hannah Wilder of Sterling, int. March 19, 1802.
Eleanor (d. Jonathan and Esther, a. 26) and Amos T. Stratton, Jan. 3, 1849.
Elias and Wid. Joanna Brooks, March 25, 1796.
Elisha and Caroline Richardson of Petersham, May 23, 1786. In Petersham.
Elizabeth and Benjamen Toundson, Oct. 5, 1769.
Elizabeth and William Townsend, Feb. 7, 1805.
Hannah and Benjamin Fairbank, Nov. 25, 1787.
Hannah and Reuben Stratton, May 20, 1835.

* Intention not recorded.

ATHOL MARRIAGES. 167

STRATTON, Hannah and Chester Crawford, April —, 1837.
Harriet and Edward F. Ward of Orange, May 24, 1842.
Jabez and Mari Dudley of Sutton, int. March 8, 1800.
James Jr. and Abagail Mortin, Dec. 26, 1750.
James and Susanna Ward of New Salem, int. Feb. 10, 1818.
James and Sally Ward of Orange, int. Sept. 8, 1827.
James 2d (s. Walter and Lucy, a. 27), and Caroline Hill, Dec. 15, 1848.
Joel and Sally Stockwell Sprague, Feb. 24, 1822.
Jonathan and Ruth Foster of No. Salem, Nov. 10, 1788.
Jonathan and Esther Fay, March 8, 1821.
Joseph and Dolly Wheeler of Petersham, May 23, 1793. In Petersham.
Joseph Jr. and Martha West of Templeton, int. Oct. 14, 1826.
Joshua and Betsey Phillips, Sept. 8, 1825.
Laura and George L. Dike, Sept. 29, 1833.
Laura W. and Daniel Davis, July 6, 1842.
Lemira D. and Prescott Giles of New Salem, int. Oct. 17, 1829.
Levi and Lois Humphrey, Dec. 19, 1795.
Lois and Stephen Foster of Sullivan, N.H., May 14, 1834.
Lucy and Enos Twichel of Brockport, N.Y. [June] 19, 1826.
Lucy A. (d. Walter and Lucy, a. 20) and Merrill D. Fuller of Phillipston, May 31, 1848.
Marabah and Stephen Batchelor, April 28, 1774.
Marcy (d. Joseph, a. 22) and Gilbert D. Harris, Aug. 20, 1849.
Martha and Luther Lord of Orange, April 7, 1812.
Mary and Moses Wood of South Hadley, Aug. 10, 1817.
Mary Alzina of Phillipston and Albert Thorp, int. May 3, 1832.
Mary T. (d. Abner and Abigail, a. 41) and Sumner R. Morse, May 31, 1849.
Molly and Bezaleel Gleason of Hubbardston, March 17, 1795.
Nancy and Sumner R. Morse, April 25, 1833.
Nancy and George W. Ward, Sept. 22, 1841.
Nathaniel and Esther Richardson of Brookfield, May 15, 1792. In Brookfield.
Polly and William Meachum of New Salem, Sept. 11, 1811.
Reuben and Hannah Stratton, May 20, 1835.
Sally and Levi Derby, Jan. 14, 1810.
Sally and Curtiss Gould, March 9, 1825.
Sarah M. (d. Joel and Sally, a. 19) and Levi G. Fessenden of Fitchburg, Oct. 22, 1849.
Stephen and Leonard Lord, Sept. 18, 1811.
Susanna G. and Artemas B. Larribee of Barnard, Vt., June 16, 1840.

STRATTON, Thomas and Thankful Rich, April 5, 1784.
Walter and Lucy Dudley of Petersham, int. Aug. 26, 1815.
William and [Wid.] Elizabeth Smith, March 2, 1780.
Zebulan and Jerusha Bradish of Winchendon, June 9, 1780. In Winchendon.

STRONG, Solomon and Sally Sweetser, Nov. 20, 1803.

STURTEVANT, Rebecca W. of Plymouth and Rev. Josiah Moore, int. April 8, 1831.

SWEETSER (see Switcher), Abigail and Joel Wood of Westminster, Dec. 9, 1818.
Caroline and Gen. Ebenezer L. Barnard of Worcester, May 23, 1838.
Hannah A. (d. Samuel and Anna, a. 23) and William B. Washburn of Orange, Sept. 6, 1847.
Maranda and James Goldsbury of Warwick, Jan. 3, 1827.
Maria and Frederic Jones, Dec. 1, 1832.
Sally and Solomon Strong, Nov. 20, 1803.
Samuel Jr. and Ann R. Humphreys, Dec. 7, 1823.
William S. of Paxton and Eliza P. Wheaton of Warwick, May —, 1836.*

SWITCHER (see above) [Sweetser in int.], Samuel and Hannah Moore of Cambridge, Oct. 24, 1792. In Cambridge.

TAFT, Anna of Royalston and Capt. Adonijah Ball, int. Dec. 26, 1818.
Hannah of Heath and Jotham Haven, int. Oct. 9, 1812.
Henry of Caroline, N.Y., and Mercy Sherman, June 9, 1825.

TALBERT, Josiah and Lydia Goodale of Templeton, int. July 1, 1815.

TALBOT, Elisa and Tertius Reynolds of Warren, Ct., int. May 16, 1829.
George and Betty Ward of Hanneker, N.H., int. April 11, 1789.
George Jr. and Mary Robinson of Nottingham West, int. Oct. 1, 1825.

TAYLER (see Taylor), Rufus and Mary Goddard, Dec. 8, 1763.
Rufus and Susanna Goddard, int. March 10, 1774.

TAYLOR (see above), Hannah and Jonathan Smith, Dec. 17, 1795.
Lois and David Bigelow, June 3, 1779.
Lucius and Mercy Bryant, Nov. 28, 1833.

* Intention not recorded.

ATHOL MARRIAGES.   169

TAYLOR, Molly and Samuel Kendall, May 1, 1788.
Wid. Susanna and Nathaniel Myrick of Harwick, Oct. 23, 1797.

TENNY, Charles R. and Silence L. Bryant, Dec. 3, 1843.

TENNEY, Lydia E. of Royalston and James P. Barr of Ware, May 19, 1842.*

THAYER, Alpheus of Brattleborough and Betsey Manley, March 19, 1817.
Abijah and Betsy Murdock, both of Petersham, Jan. 1, 1802.*
Eunice S. and Charles R. Cleveland of Hardwick, Sept. 21, 1842.
Ezra of Orwell, Vt., and Lucy Hill, Jan. 13, 1800.
[Thare in int.], Susannah [of Richmond in int.] and Moses Hutchens, Sept. 9, 1779.

THOMAS (see Thompson), Eunice of Berry and Roger Walker, int. May 31, 1795.
Foxwell N. and Nancy Wilder of Winchendon, int. Aug. 15, 1817.

THOMPSON (see Thomson), Caleb of New Sal[em] and Mehetabel Knowles, Nov. 7, 1784.
Caroline and Rodolphus Cobb, int. Jan. 4, 1836.
Clark and Nancy Kendall, Aug. 25, 1840.
[Thomas ?] Eunice of Barre and Rogers Walker, June 1, 1796. In Barre.
Robert of Royalston and Lydia Jones, int. May 21, 1802.
Sally of Swansey, N.H., and Horace Drury, int. Dec. 29, 1827.
Urania of Swansey, N.H., and Capt. Chauncy Haven, int. Aug. 20, 1825.

THOMSON (see above), Polly [Patty in int.] and Willard Varnum, Sept. 9, 1779.

THORP, Albert and Mary Alzina Stratton of Phillipston, int. May 3, 1832.
Ann (d. Eliphalet and Ruth, a. 23) and George T. Littlefield of Chelsea, Nov. 29, 1849.
Emily and Stilman Knowlton, Dec. 29, 1831.
Fenno and Lucy B. Humphreys, Feb. 23, 1840.
Jane (d. Eliphalet and Ruth, a. 23) and Samuel M. Osgood, Nov. 4, 1846.
Lydia (d. Eliphalet and Ruthe, a. 25) and Samuel Babcock of Milton, Dec. 4, 1844.

TOTMAN, L. Maria of Hardwick (d. Levi and Elizabeth, a. 29) and Addison P. Barber of Amherst, Sept. 21, 1848.*
Lucretia of Petersham and Miles Cobb of Hardwick, Jan. 31, 1827.*

* Intention not recorded.

ATHOL MARRIAGES.

TOWN (see Towne), Ephraim and Huldah Gail, both of Warwick, Dec. 18, 1777.
Fanny and Harrington McClallan, March 26, 1818.
Hannah and Ziba Stockwell, April 21, 1785. In Templeton.

TOWNE (see above), Elijah and Molly Ballard, Jan. 26, 1786. In Royalston.

TOUNDSON, Benjamen and Elizabeth Stratton, Oct. 5, 1769.

TOWNSEND, Abigail D. and Joseph W. Goddard of Royalston, April 9, 1833.
Benjamin and Polly Goddard, May 12, 1802.
Deborah and Joshua More, Jan. 14, 1800.
Elizabeth and Joseph Jacobs, Nov. 15, 1796.
Elizabeth and Edward Drury, March 17, 1835.
Harriet and John S. Drury, Aug. 16, 1836.
James and Elvira Twichell of Walpole, N.H., int. March 1, 1832.
James and Lydia H. Davis of South Orange, Sept. 25, 1839.
Lysander F. and Clarissa Chase, int. Oct. 24, 1829. [Married, Nov. 18, c.r.]
Lysander F. and Lucy Collar of Orange, June 23, 1839.
Mary (d. William and Elizabeth, a. 23) and William I. Goddard, Nov. 9, 1845.
Thomas and Abigail Raymond, Feb. 15, 1795.
Col. Thomas and Ann Godard of Petersham, int. Aug. 31, 1827.
William and Elizabeth Stratton, Feb. 7, 1805.

TRAIN, David and Hannah Bates, int. April 22, 1774.
Isaac and Elizebeth Comming, Sept. 17, 1779.
Jonathan and Marcy Baits, Sept. 12, 1770.

TUCKER, Alfred of Ware and Dolly Hill, April 6, 1841.

TURNER, Isaac of Townsend and Sophia L. Holt, April 25, 1844.
John and Almira K. Emory, both of South Orange, Nov. 21, 1839.*
Sally and Peter Stockwell, April 10, 1800.
Sally of Royalston and Jacob Bancroft, Aug. 28, 1833.

TUTTLE, Maria and James Ball, Dec. 2, 1819.

TUZADRICK [Fradrick in Sutton v.r.], Prince and Anne Augustus of Sutton, Nov. 16, 1780. In Sutton.

TWICHEL (see Twichell, Twitchell), Abagail and Joseph Fay, June 3, 1773.

* Intention not recorded.

ATHOL MARRIAGES. 171

TWICHEL, Alfred and Olive Wilmarth, Oct. 3, 1802.
Bala and Sally Bishup, Sept. 2, 1792. In Richmond.
Benona and Leah Stockwell, int. Jan. 1, 1792.
Benoni and Zilpah Woodward, Feb. 13, 1800.
David of N. Salem and Molly Kendall, Sept. 3, 1800.
Enos and Relief Fairbanks, Dec. 1, 1772.
Enos Jr. and Ezubah Pierce, Sept. 25, 1793.
Enos of Brockport, N.Y., and Lucy Stratton, [June] 19, 1826.
Esther and George Gabyer, Jan. 16, 1777.
Evi [Eri?] and Irene Whitney of Petersham, Jan. 1, 1817.
Francis and Sally Fish, Feb. 12, 1809.
Jeremiah and Preserved Huit, Feb. 5, 1818.
John of New Salem and Lucinda Raymond, Dec. 22, 1813.
Josiah and Hannah Crosbey, June 9, 1789.
Martha and Amos Bullard, March 12, 1812.
Meriam and Moses Chase, June 6, 1797.
Metilda and Ephraim Fairbank, May 26, 1802.
Relief and Ebenezer Doane of Petersham, Jan. 11, 1815.
Sally and Kitteridge Peabody, May 4, 1814.
Sarah and Jonathan Ward, Nov. 26, [1777].
Seth Jr. and Hulday Eaton of New Salem, int. June 9, 1780.
Seth Jr. and Phebe Goddard, May 13, 1790.
Seth and Betsy Stockwell of Royalston, May 14, 1822.
Sylvia and Abel Whitney of Orange, July 15, 1810.

TWICHELL (see Twitchel, Twitchell, etc.], Abner W. (s. Alfred and Hannah, a. 21) and Hannah E. Nye, Oct. 21, 1846.
Asa W. and Abigail Stratton, Nov. 24, 1842.
Benjamin M. and Asenath Lovering, Nov. 5, 1820.
Caroline (d. Samuel D. and Abigail, a. 26) and Simon Barrous of New Bedford, Dec. 25, 1845.
David Marshall of Warwick and Somantha Cook, March 9, 1842.
Doratha and Edward Ward, both of Warwick, Nov. 26, 1778.*
Elvira of Walpole, N.H., and James Townsend, int. March 1, 1832.
Hannah and Calvin Peabody of Petersham, Jan. 9, 18[21 or 22].
Hannah and Collins Andrews, Oct. 1, 1827.
Harriet A. (d. Benjamin M. and Asenath, a. 23) and James S. Fay, May 31, 1848.
Huldah and Enoch Wyman of Winchendon, int. July 23, 1831.
John M. and Angeline M. Lee, April 7, 1842. Dup.
Letsey P. (d. Seth and Betsey, a. 19) and Lemuel Fales Jr. of Claremont, N.H., May 13, 1847.
Lucetta and Levi Young Jr. of Petersham, Jan. 6, 1841.

* Intention not recorded.

ATHOL MARRIAGES.

TWICHELL, Mary Ann and Clark Ellis, March 29, 1840.
Parna and Josiah Willard, April 13, 1823.
Releaf and Moses Ball, Sept. 4, 1816.
Rhoda and Emory Hill, Dec. 6, 1821.
Sally and Henry Whitney, Dec. 28, 1820.
Susan B. (d. Alfred and Hannah, a. 16) and Stephen Jaques, Dec. 9, 1847.

TWITCHEL, Elizebeth and Elisha Sibley, Nov. 1, 1781.

TWITCHELL (see Twichel, Twichell), Abner and Hannah Brown of New Salem, Aug. 16, 1785. In Orange.
Chester and Sally Stockwell of Royalston, int. May 24, 1823.

TYLER, Harriot and Ethan Hemenway of Barre, Oct. 17, 1827.

UNDERHILL, Henry B. of Warren (s. Abraham and Mary, a. 25) and Harriet Y. Fish, Feb. 18, 1847.

UNDERWOOD, Abijah and Betcey Oakes, Aug. 18, 1801.
Charles (s. Nathan and Hannah ?, a. 26) and Lucy Ward, April 11, 1849.
Harriet A. (d. Nathan and Hannah A., a. 24) and Francis Ward, Dec. 26, 1844.
Joshua and Lucy Underwood of Framingham, int. March 4, 1816.
Lucy of Framingham and Joshua Underwood, int. March 4, 1816.
Nathan and Hannah Stone of Framingham, int. Jan. 11, 1819.

VARNUM, Willard and Polly [Patty ?] Thomson, Sept. 9, 1779.
Willard and Hannah Walcup, Feb. 15, 1781.

WADE, Mercy of Glossister and Josiah Wood, int. Sept. 2, 1776.

WADKINS (see Watkins), George W. and Sarah Marsh, Oct. 23, 1825.

WADSWORTH, Sally of Grafton, and David Stratton, int. May 5, 1810.

WAIT (see below) Eunice and Paul Wheeler, Oct. 9, 1794.
Mary and Nathan How of Hilsborough, N.H., Aug. 15, 1793.

WAITE (see above), Josiah [Joshua ?] and Sarah Lovell of Sutton, March 15, 1775. In Sutton.
Mrs. Martha of Royalston and Dea. John Haven, April 27, 1778. In Royalston.

WALCUP [Walkup in int.] Hannah and Willard Varnum, Feb. 15, 1781.

WALKER, Elias of Royalston and Rhoda Drury, Jan. —, 1835.
Rev. John of Greenfield, N.H., and Arethusa Humphrey, Feb. 13, 1813.
Lois and John Day, Aug. 26, 1795.
Patty and Isaac Knights, Jan. 23, 1777.
Rogers and Eunice Thompson [Thomas ?] of Barre, June 1, 1796. In Barre. [Negroes ?].
Rufus of Hubbardton, Vt., and Susanna Reymond, Feb. 21, 1796.
Susan and Aaron I. Phillips, Nov. 17, 1833.

WARD, Alpheus and Molley Raymond, March 7, 1782.
Anna and Jonas Fay, Jan. 19, 1815.
Betty of Hanneker, N.H., and George Talbot, int. April 11, 1789.
Daniel and Lydia Smith, Nov. 30, 1815.
Desire of Orange and Thomas Lord Jr., int. Sept. 17, 1800.
Edward and Doratha Twitchell, both of Warwick, Nov. 26, 1778.*
Edward F. of Orange and Harriet Stratton, May 24, 1842.
Francis (s. Daniel and Lydia S., a. 26, married) and Harriet A. Underwood, Dec. 26, 1844.
George W. and Nancy Stratton, Sept. 22, 1841.
Jabez and Esther Humphrey, Nov. 29, 1787.
Jabez and [Wid.] Mary Osgood, March 27, 1817.
Jonathan and Sarah Twichel, Nov. 26, [1777].
Lois and Andrew Stratton, Oct. 2, 1817.
Lucretia and Warren Richardson of Plymouth, Oct. 9, 1822.
Lucy (d. William H. and Lucy ?, a. 26) and Charles Underwood, April 11, 1849.
Luseba and Samuel Clark, May 2, 1821.
Lydia and William Raymond, July 6, 1781.
Lydia and Jonathan Maclallen, May 20, 1804.
Lydia S. and John G. Brown, April 4, 1838.
Molly of Orange and Josiah Fay, Sept. 18, 1798.
Nahum and Patty Raymond, June 21, 1792.
Nancy M. (d. Daniel and Lydia) and B. Dexter Washburn of Orange, April 9, 1844.
Nathan and Maria Godard of Orange, int. April 20, 1816.
Nehemiah and Lucy Newhall, April 8, 1816.
Patty and David Dike, June 17, 1801.
[Ware ?] Ruggles and Isabel Oliver, Nov. 2, 1780.
Sally and John Oliver Jr., Sept. 23, 1790.
Sally of Orange and James Stratton, int. Sept. 8, 1827.
Silvanus and Hannah Goddard of Petersham, int. Nov. 22, 1775.
Sophia and William Raymond, int. Nov. 16, 1782.
Susanna of New Salem and James Stratton, int. Feb. 10, 1818.

* Intention not recorded.

WARD, Susanna and Samuel Kelton, March 18, 1818.
Susanna and Artemas Howard, Nov. 29, 1827.
Thomas H. of Princeton and Esther K. Mayo of Orange, Oct. 27, 1835.*
William H. and Lucy Lovering of Templeton, int. Dec. 2, 1817.

WARDEN, John of Worcester and Narcissa Davis of Orange, June 14, 1837.*

WARE, see Ward.

WARREN (see Warrin), Benjamin and Perny Fairbank, Feb. 2, 1792.
Daniel and Elizabeth Foster of Royalston, Sept. 20, 1789. In Royalston.

WARRIN, Benjamin and Margery Herington of Marlborough, int. May 5, 1766.

WASHBURN, B. Dexter of Orange (s. Joseph) and Nancy M. Ward, April 9, 1844.
William B. of Orange (s. Asa and Phebe, a. 27) and Hannah A. Sweetser, Sept. 6, 1847.

WATKINS (see Wadkins), Stephen and Susanna Rice of Hardwick, int. Jan. 25, 1789.

WAYMATH, Joseph, " a Transient Person," and Wid. Elizabeth Young, int. May 6, 1807.

WEEKS, Joseph C. and Clarinda Knowlton, both of Oakham, Sept. 22, 1831.*

WELLINGTON, Sarah and John Piper, both of Templeton, Aug. 1, 1784.*

WELMARTH (see Wilmarth), Susanna and Thomas Fairbank, Aug. 17, 1808.

WESSON, Anna and Joseph Brown of Orange, alias Ewinshire, int. June 18, 1802.
Josiah and Nabby Batchelor of Fitchburg, int. Sept. 20, 1803.
Susanna and Calvin Priest of Northfield, Aug. 6, 1798.
Rev. William B. of Hardwick and Azubah Graves, Nov. 5, 180[7].

WEST, Paul of New Braintree and Abigail Burbank, Nov. 5, 1795.
Martha of Templeton and Joseph Stratton Jr., int. Oct. 14, 1826.

* Intention not recorded.

WETHERELL, Lydia L. of Swanzey, N.H., and Calvin Kendall Jr., int. April 23, 1831.

WHEATON, Dr. Christopher C. of Royalston and Mary Sibley, June 2, 1835.
Eliza P. of Warwick and William S. Sweetser of Paxton, May —, 1836.*

WHEALLER (see Wheeler), James and Sarah Bates, int. Feb. 13, 1779.

WHEELER (see Whealler), Anna and Sullivan Raymond of Royalston, Jan. 25, 1825.
David of Petersham and Levina Hill, Nov. 11, 1795. In Petersham.
David Jr. and Augusta E. Whipple, int. Feb. 21, 1835.
Dolly of Petersham and Joseph Stratton, May 23, 1793. In Petersham.
Dolly of Gardner and Stephen Lawater, Oct. 3, 1798. In Gardner.
Jesse G. and Harriet Foskett of Orange, int. Oct. 8, 1829. [Married, Feb. 25, 1830, C.R.]
Jonathan and Mary Raymond of Royalston, int. Dec. 6, 1822.
Jonathan and Wid. Hannah Fisher, int. Oct. 15, 1830.
Margaret and Ephraim Goodale, Nov. 25, 1802.
Mary (d. Johathan and Hannah) and Hollon Farr, Oct. 17, 1849.
Paul and Eunice Wait, Oct. 9, 1794.
Paul of Royalston and Phebe Hill, int. Sept. 14, 1803.
Rachel and Clemant Bryant, Nov. 27, 1806.
Sarah T. of Fitzwilliam, N.H., and Ephraim S. Sprague, int. Sept. 4, 1829.
Sina and Nathan Whitney of Royalston, May 16, 1805.
Zacheus Jr. and Betsy Dexter of Orange, int. Oct. 31, 1803.

WHIPPLE, Augusta E. and David Wheeler Jr., int. Feb. 21, 1835.
Lucy of New Braintree and Isaac Knight, int. Oct. 2, 1802.
Patty and Samuel Knight, Dec. 12, 1806.

WHITCOMB, Louisa of Phillipston and Joel Drury Jr., int. April 6, 1835.
Susan and Aaron Oliver, Dec. 5, 1830.

WHITE, Deborah of Warwick and George Oliver Esq., int. Aug. 8, 1818.
Harriet and Silas Spear Jr., both of Orange, April 21, 1840.*
Nathan and Lydia Wilder of Winchendon, int. Oct. 11, 1814.

* Intention not recorded.

176 ATHOL MARRIAGES.

WHITE, Sarah and Nahum Fay, Oct. 18, 1804.
Wid. Tabitha of ———— and John Fairbanks, Dec. 15, 1796. In Leominster.
William and Lucy Woodard, Nov. 28, 1805.

WHITMORE, Elisha of Royalston and Tabatha Axdail, Aug. 13, 1782. In Royalston.
Wid. Rebeccah of Royalston and Capt. John Kendall, Sept. 12, 1827.

WHITNEY, Abel of Orange and Sylvia Twichel, July 15, 1810.
Deborah (d. William K.) and Lyman Fox, Aug. 20, 1848.
Elbridge W. of Petersham and Sophia Ann Billings, Oct. 20, 1841.
Hannah and Abraham Roberts, both of Warwick, Nov. 13, 1777.*
Hannah H. and Hiram Lewis Jr., Oct. 10, 1841.
Henry and Sally Twichell, Dec. 28, 1820.
Irene of Petersham and Evi [Eri ?] Twichel, Jan. 1, 1817.
Lemuel of Warwick and Sally Pratt, int. Aug. 18, 1804.
Lewis I. and Ruth Howard, July 18, 1824.
Nathan of Royalston and Sina Wheeler, May 16, 1805.
Phebe and Artemas Hancock of Templeton, Jan. 5, 1812.
Susanna K. and Silas Fry, May 16, 1840.
William K and Mary Ann Billings, April 2, 1843.

WIAR, Christopher and Jenne MackBride, int. March 6, 1779.

WIER, Samuel of Walpole, N.H., and Thankful Lombard, Sept. 9, 1795

WIGGINS, Harriot N. (d. James and Sarah, a. 23) and Joseph Bartlett, Nov. 3, 1845.

WILBOR, Edmond and Rebeccah Rich, April 3, 1827.

WILD, Rachel of Brantree and Aseph Fanton, int. Oct. 13, 1780.

WILDER, Ann M. and John Boutell, int. Oct. 24, 1834 [1835 ?].
Artemas of Petersham and Lucy Ellenwood, March 13, 18[08].
Fisher A. of Greenville, Ind., and Frances A. Kelton, April 28, 1839.
Hannah of Sterling and Ebenezer Stratton, int. March 19, 1802.
Josiah Jr. of Templeton and Rebecka Kendall, Sept. 30, 1807.
Lydia of Winchendon and Nathan White, int. Oct. 11, 1814.
Nancy of Winchendon and Foxwell N. Thomas, int. Aug. 15, 1817.

WILEY, Joseph of Hubbardston and Susanna Drury, March 24, 1803.
Samuel and Nancy Norcross of Templeton, int. Sept. 15, 1827.

* Intention not recorded.

WILKINSON, George and Rhoda Woodard, in year ending April 1, 1834.

WILLARD, Ephraim and Lucy Holms, both of Petersham, Feb. 18, 1801.*
Josiah and Parna Twichell, April 13, 1823.
Levi of Decatur, Ga., and Sarah P. Allen, May —, 1835.
Nancy of Petersham and Nathan Stone, int. Dec. 19, 1810.

WILLIAMS, Mrs. Azubah of Dana and Dr. Joshua Morton, int. April 1, 1816.
John K. and Esther Ebit of Petersham, int. July 1, 1822.
Mary H. (d. William H. and Frances, a. 19) and Rev. Crawford Nightingale of Springfield, May 13, 1846.
Dea ? William H. and Frances W. Humphrey, May 12, 1822.

WILLMARTH (see Welmarth, Wilmarth) Diana (d. Hannah) and Albigence P. Bryant of Templeton, June 4, 1846.

WILLSON (see Wilson) Loring and Maria Burrougs of Alstead, N.H., int. Oct. 5, 1834.

WILMARTH (see Willmarth), Olive and Alfred Twichel, Oct. 3, 1802.
Tila and John Stimpson of N. Salem, Aug. 19, 1802.

WILSON (see Willson), Rev. John V. and Pamelia Pratt of Charlton, int. Aug. 23, 1834.

WIMAN (see Wyman), Sarah of Winchendon and John Lewis, int. Oct. 25, 1810.

WISWELL, Esther and James Humphrey, Oct. 9, 1751. c.r.

WITT, Aurelia D. and Harden Doane, Aug. 30, 1819.
Elvira Brigham (d. David and Polly, a. 25) and George Willard Babbitt, Oct. 22, 1844.
Levi and Lurana Foster of Orange, Nov. 29, 1795. In Orange.

WOOD (see Woods), Dolly and Calvin H. Oliver, March 26, 1805.
Elijah and Sally Farrar, May 29, 1800.
Elvira of Royalston and Emmons Stockwell, int. Aug. 25, 1831.
Joel of Westminster and Abigail Sweetser, Dec. 9, 1818.
John of Royalston and Abigail Lord, Nov. —, 1836.
Josiah and Mercy Wade of Glossister, int. Sept. 2, 1776.
Mary, (d. Kimbal and Mary) and James Peirce, Nov. 19, 1787.
Moses of South Hadley and Mary Stratton, Aug. 10, 1817.

* Intention not recorded.

WOOD, Wid. Phebe of Petersham and Lt. Joel Morton, int. April 18, 1829.
Susanna and Edward Dike, Feb. 22, 1803.
Zeruiah and Ephraim Smith, Aug. 14, 1776.

WOODARD (see Woodward), Emily Eaton and Franklin Oliver, int. Aug. 26, 1832.
Lucy and William White, Nov. 28, 1805.
Philinda and David Young Jr., Aug. 23, 1822.
Rhoda and George Wilkinson, in year ending April 1, 1834.

WOODBURY, Benajah of Royalston and Eunice Mills, Oct. 25, 1798.
Benjamen [Benajah ?] and Abagal Stockwell, Aug. 15, 1768.
Elizabeth of Royalsto- and John Burbank, June 15, 1788.
James of Royalston and Susanna Goddard, Jan. 28, 1802.

WOODS (see Wood), Lois of Orange and Barnabas Pain, int. Dec. 21, 1788.
Mary of Wendell and George Newhall, int. Sept. 6, 1823.

WOODWARD (see Woodard), Abijah and Betcey Oakes, Aug. 18, 1801.
Amos of Royalston and Caty Goddard, int. July 7, 1783.
Bartholomew and Sally Morton of Newsalem, int. Jan. 14, 1815.
Hepsibah and Calvin Kilton, April 8, 1800.
Joseph and Sibbel Goddard, July 3, 1765.
Manson J. and Nancy Kidder, May 22, 1839.
Zilpah and Benoni Twichel, Feb. 13, 1800.

WRIGHT [Capt.] Aaron of Fitzwilliam, N.H., and [wid.] Polly Kendall, Dec. 29, 18[07].

WYATT, Joshua and Ruth Cook, both of Petersham, June 13, 1833.*

WYMAN (see Wiman), Enoch of Winchendon and Huldah Twichell, int. July 23, 1831.

YOUNG, Abner and Lucy Estabrook, Jan. 15, 1818.
Albert F. and Sarah G. Barber, Aug. 27, 1843.
Anna and Moses Fish, May 8, 1823.
Arathusa and Jacob Carter, Nov. 28, 1816.
David and Hannah Lumb[ard], Sept. 30, 1784.
David Jr. and Philinda Woodard, Aug. 23, 1822.
Wid. Elizabeth and Joseph Waymath, "a Transient Person," int., May 6, 1807.

* Intention not recorded.

ATHOL MARRIAGES. 179

YOUNG, Emeline and Nathaniel Richardson of Peterborough, N.H., Oct. 31, 1830.
Fanny of Orwell, Vt., and Joshua Young, int. May 16, 1829.
Hannah and Benjamin Sanders, Dec. 2, 1762.
Hannah and Samuel Dike, Aug. 14, 1803.
Hannah L. and Charles Crosby, April 21, 1819.
Hiram and Catherine Morse, June 15, 1837.
James and Patty Pierce, Jan. 20, 1812.
Joab and Sally Dike, Sept. 5, 1833.
Joel and Sarah Ball, Feb. 23, 1797.
Joseph and Sophia Field, Sept. 29, 1817.
Joshua and Ann Kendall, Nov. 20, 1825.
Joshua and Fanny Young of Orwell, Vt., int. May 16, 1829.
Levi and Susanna Haven, Aug. 22, 1804.
Levi Jr. of Petersham and Lucetta Twichell, Jan. 6, 1841.
Lois and David Drury, March 5, 1805.
Lois and Thomas Oliver, April 26, 1838.
Louisa and Albert Sanderson, int. Sept. 1, 1833.
Lucy R. and Dr. Earl Cushman of Orwell, Vt., Sept. 11, 1834.
Mary and Freeborn Raymond, Aug. 18, 1763.
Mary and Ira Baker of Orange, Dec. 1, 1831.
Wid. Mehitable and Artemas Church of Templeton, int. April 5, 1832.
Nancy and Gardner Lord, March 4, 1813.
Polly (d. Joel and Sally, a. 38) and Samuel Clark, April 23, 1846.
Reuben and Mehitable Marsh, April 12, 1807.
Rhoda and George Oliver, Nov. 28, 1799.
Robert and Elisabeth Gray of Pelham, int. Nov. 24, 1764.
Robert Jr. and Mary Rider, June 6, 1776.
Rosella and James A. Lord, both of Templeton, Dec. 7, 1848.*
Sally and Joel E. Drury of Wendell, Nov. 16, 1831.
Samuel and Rhoda Haven, Feb. 26, 1772.
Samuel and Lois Cotting of Petersham, int. Nov. 21, 1778.
[Dr. in int. and c.r.] Samuel of Acton and Seraphinia Pierce, Oct. 29, 1808.
Sarah and Abel Rogers, Oct. 11, 1769.
Simeon and Mary Hill, int. Feb. 13, 1786.
Susan and Lansford Merriam of Newsalem, May —, 1836.
William and Keziah Haven, Jan. 18, 1780.

* Intention not recorded.

ATHOL DEATHS.

ATHOL DEATHS.

To the year 1850.

ADAMS, Gilman, s. Timothy and Deidamia, Dec. 31, 1812. [a. 5. c.r.]
Hannah, d. Thomas and Marthow, April 23, 1810, a. 23. G.S.3.
Timothy, h. Deidamia, Oct. 6, 1813, [a. 42, c.r.].
Timothy, h. Laura, April 10, 1835.

ALDRICH, Moses (married), July 24, 1845, a. 62 y. 3 m. 4 d. Bowel complaint. Born in Richmond, N.H. Harness maker.

ALLEN, James, May 7, 1823, a. 39. G.S.3.
John Frederick, s. John and Elvira Eunice, Sept. 8, 1841, a. 1 y. 3 m. 8 d. Scalded.

ALLERD, Mary, w. Andrew, June 13, 1776. c.r.

AMSDEN, ———, ch. Festus F. and Mary, May 20, 1849. Dysentery. [ch. Frederick H. and M. L., May 19, a. 1 y. 6 m. G.S.2.]

ANDREWS, Alonzo, twin s. Collin and Hannah, April 24, 1829, a. 1 y. 1 m. 16 d.

BABBITT, Francis Fairbank, twin s. Pliny H. and Lydia T., July 29, 1844, a. 6 m. 29 d. Teething and Dysentery.
Franklin Pliney, twin s. Pliny H. and Lydia T., July 30, 1844, a. 6 m. 30 d. Teething and Dysentery.
Harriet Newell, d. Thomas and Nancy W., Nov. 28, 1835, a. 2 y. 4 m. 17 d.
Susan A., w. George W., Nov. 20, 1843, a. 29 y. 4 m. 12 d. Consumption. Buried in Hinsdale, N.H. Dup.

BACHELLOR, Meranda Augusta, ch. ———, Sept. 10, 1831, a. 5 y. c.r.

BACKLEY [Buckley ?], ———, wid. ———, Feb. 12, 1849, a. 73.

BACON, Mrs. Betsy, March 7, 1842; a. 39. G.S.1.

BAKER, Ira, July 24, 1843, a. 36. G.S.2.

BALL, Adonijah, d. at Saratoga on his way home from Crown Point. He went out a listed soldier from Perquage in the year 1760, s. Isaac and Rachel. C.R.
Adonijah Jr., h. Anna, May 31, 1828. [a. 37. Killed by fall of a rock under which he was at work, G.S.3.]
Adonijah, s. Moses and Susanna, Dec. 17, 1833, a. 61.
Almira R. H., d. James and Maria, Oct. 16, 1831, a. 3 y. 2 m. G.S.2.
Eunice, w. Absolom, Feb. 16, 1835, a. 53. G.S.1.
Isaac, March 21, 1789. In old age. C.R.
Jacob, May 29, 1817, a. 46 y. C.R.
James (single), Aug. 2, 1847, a. 79.
James W., s. James and Maria, April 27, 1823, a. 2 y. 6 m. 21 d.
Mary, w. Adonijah, Oct. 27, 1822, a. 55 [56, C.R.] G.S.3.
Moses, s. Adonijah and Mary, June 7, 1795, a. 1 y. 8 m. 4 d.
Moses, Nov. 15, 1820, a. 80 y. C.R.
Rachel, w. Isaac, Oct. 12, 1779. C.R.
Samuel Collins, s. Adonijah and Mary, Aug. 17, 1831, a. 31 y. 10 m. 7 d.
Susanna, w. Moses, Oct. 25, 1815, [a. 76, G.S.3.].
———, ch. Jacob's w., Oct. 26, 1809, a. 7 y. C.R.
———, ch. Adonijah, June 7, 1795, a. about 2 y. C.R.
———, ch. Addonijah Jr., Aug. 19, 1821, a. 16 m. C.R.

BALLARD, Abigail, d. Joshua and Anne, Nov. 1, 1794, a. 10 y. 1 m. 3 d.
Anna, wid. Joshua, Nov. 25, 1843, a. 87 y. 5 m. 8 d. Lung fever. Dup.
Daniel, Feb. 22, 1806, a. 20 y. at [Herwhut ?] while a school master. C.R.
Elizabeth, w. Elijah, Jan. 4, 1817, [a. 29, C.R.].
Hepsibah, wid. John, June 3, 1811, [a. 83, C.R.].
John Jr., s. John and Hipzibah, Oct. —, 1776, at Fort George. C.R.
John, Feb. 17, 1804, a. 76 y. C.R.
William Morse, s. Elijah and Elizabeth, April 9, 1818, a. nearly 3.
———, s. John and Hipzabah, March 15, 1753. C.R.

BANCROFT, Jacob, (widr.), Oct. 7, 1848, a. 85.
Joshua Abburn, March 30, 1844, a. 22 y. 5 m. 21 d. Buried in Erving. Tanner.
Mrs. ———, —— —, 1832. C.R.

BARBER, George M. S., s. John P. and Ellen ?, Sept. 9, 1849, a. 2. Dysentery.

BARNES, ———, inf. ———, March 2, 1846, a. 1 m. 2 d.

ATHOL DEATHS.

BARRELL, ———, ch. John, Oct. 6, 1803, a. 13 m. c.r.
———, ch. John, Nov. 5, 1803. c.r.

BARRET [Basset ?], ———, w. John, Sept. 18, 1848, a. 81.
Lydia, d. John and Naomy, Nov. 6, 1803, a. 5 y. 7 m. 23 d.
Nancy, d. John and Naomy, Oct. 4, 1803, a. 1 y. 2 m.
Oliver, s. John, Aug. 8, 1846, a. 47.

BARTLETT, ———, d. Joseph, Sept. 10, 1846, a. 14 d.

BASSET (see Bassett), Sylvia, d. Jacob, Aug. 10, 1849, a. 44. Dysentery.
———, ch. Jacob, Nov. 17, 1819, a. 5 y. c.r.

BASSETT (see above), Chloe, Aug. 26, 1845, a. 58. g.s.1.
Wid. Jemima, Jan. 1, 1853.

BATES, William Jr., s. William and Mercy, Feb. 29, 1776. c.r.

BEARD, Porter, s. Edward and Hannah, Oct. 25, 1849, a. 3 d.

BERT[?], ———, ch. Asahel, Jan. 14, 1807. c.r.

BIDAL[?], ———, d. Isaac and Hannah, Dec. 6, 1780. c.r.

BIGELOW (see Biglow), Abel, h. Eunice, Oct. 7, 1841. [1840, a. 53, g.s.2.].
David, Dec. 7, 1837, a. 83. g.s.3.
Esther, d. Abel and Hannah, Feb. 27, 1820, a. nearly 3.
Hannah, w. Abel, Dec. 30, 1827, [a. 36, g.s.3.].
Hannah, w. Daniel, Aug. 12, 1849, a. 49. Consumption.
Louis, wid. David, Sept. 22, 1839, a. 83. g.s.3.
Lucena, d. Abel and Hannah, July 2, 1844, a. 18 y. 10 m. 8 d. Consumption.
Roena, d. Abel and Eunice, June 22, 1845, a. 15 y. 4 m. 25 d. Consumption.
Solon, s. Abel and Eunice, Dec. 5, 1841, a. 3 y. 6 d.
William, h. Elizabeth, s. David and Louis ?, Jan. 22, 1827. [a. 47, g.s.3.]
William, s. Abel and Hannah, March 26, 1844, a. 16 y. 3 m. 2 d. Consumption.

BIGLOW (see Bigelow), Persis, d. Jotham and Mary, April 1, 1776. c.r.
Jonathan, s. Jotham and Mary, April 10, 1776. c.r.
———, s. Noah and ———, Feb. 4, 1775. c.r.
———, s. Jotham and Mary, March 2, 1776. c.r.
———, inf. David and wife, Feb. —, 1799. c.r.
———, ch. Daniel, Jan. —, 1834, a. 9 m. c.r.

ATHOL DEATHS.

BISHOP, Jane, w. Tony, Nov. 27, 1804, a. 50. G.S.1.

BLAKE, Charles W., s. Thomas H. and Eunice W., Feb. 6, 1843. a. 5 m. G.S.2.
Ella G., d. Bradley B. and Harriet, Feb. 25, 1849, a. 8 m. G.S.1.
Fred B., s. Thomas H. and Eunice W., Oct. 1, 1845, a. 20 m. G.S.2.

BLANCHARD, Mariam, Jan. 22, 1819, a. 17 y. In a consumption, C.R.
———, inf. of Moses and ———, March 20, 1795. C.R.

BILLINGS, Mary Ann, d. Israel, July 21, 1842, a. 5.
Mary Ann T., d. Erastus and Abigail R. E., July 2, 1842, a. 4 y. 6 m. G.S.2.

BLISS, Persis, w. Stephen W., Jan. 15, 1844, a. 31 y. 5 m. 1 d. Consumption.
Joseph W., s. Stephen W. and Persis, Sept. 5, 1838, a. 1 m. 2 d.

BOUTELL, Martha E., d. James and Martha, Sept. 4, 1849, a. 2. Dysentery. [M. Evelina, d. James and Martha H. (Ward), a. 2 y. 6 m., G.S.2.]
——— [Ellen M., G.S.2.], d. John and Maria, June 7, 1844, a. 2 m. 11 d. Lung fever.

BOWKER, Miss Lucy, Aug. 5, 1820, a. 19 y. 11 m. 9 d. G.S.3.

BOYDEN, Amos, father Elbridge, April 1, 1837.
Ellen Louisa, d. Elbridge and Louisa [A., G.S.2.], July 20, 1843, a. 8 y. 2 m. 10 d, [a. 7 y. 8 m. 10 d., G.S.].

BRADISH, Mr. Robert, June —, 1792, a. 80 y. C.R.

BREDGES, ———, ch. Benj. and ———, April 9, 1791, a. 2 d. C.R.

BRIANT, ———, ch. John, July 26, 1823, a. 1 y. 6 m. C.R.

BRIGGS, Adaline G., w. Moses, Sept. 18 [17 ?], 1849, a. 43 [48 ?, G.S.2.] Dysentery.
Dolly [Polly ?] wid. Isaac, July 9, 1842.
Isaac, s. Moses and Adaline G., Aug. 24, 1835, a. 2 y. 3 m. G.S.2.
Isaac, h. Polly, July 13, 1837, [July 12, a. 75. G.S.3.].
Dea. James, Aug. 6, 1793, a. 74. G.S.3.
Levi, Jan. 22, 1835, a. 31. G.S.3.
Polly, wid. Elder Isaac, July 9, 1842, a. 78. G.S.3.
Rhoda, d. Isaac and Polly, July 20, 1815, a. 23 y. 5 m. 4 d.
Sally, d. Isaac and Polly, March 27, 1816, in 28th y.
———, wid., Sept. 11, 1819. C.R.

BROCK, David H. H., s. David S. and Elizabeth B., March 2, 1842, a. 2 y. 1 m. 7 d.
Elizabeth, w. David S., July 1, 1844, a. 30 y. 5 m. 1 d. Consumption. Born in Northbridge.
Esther L., d. Isaac Z. and Esther, Feb. 20, 1846 [1845 ? G.S.6], a. 27 d. Fever.
Hannah E., d. David S., Aug. 28, 1845, a. 2 m. 10 d. Sore mouth.
Louisa [w. Isaac Z.], May 8, 1838, [a. 19, G.S.3.].
Mary E., d. David S. and Elizabeth B., April 5, 1839, a. 2 y. 1 m. 24 d.

BRONSDON, ———, [Jane G.S.], d. William [and Martha], Sept. 7, 1846, a. 1, [a. 10 m. G.S. ?]. Dropsy on brain.

BROOKS, George E., [Edward, G.S.2.], (married), s. John and Pauh, Nov. 1, 1847, a. 24. Fever.
Jonas, h. Joanna, Dec. 20, 1786.
Moses Austin, s. John and Puah, Dec. 26, 1831, a. 11 y. 11 m. G.S.2.
———, w. Joel, Sept. 5, 1846, a. 76. Disease of heart. Buried in Petersham.

BROWN, Allen, s. Nathaniel and Huldah, Aug. 13, 1803.
Henrietta [Agnes], Oct. 1 [6 ?], 1844, a. 6 m. 4 d, [8 d. G.S.1.].
Lydia [Mariah, d. John G. and Lydia S. ?], July 31, 1839, a. 6 d., [a. 5 w. G.S.2.].
———, Mr. ———, Feb. 18, 1798. a. 64 y. on a visit to his daughter. C.R.

BRUCE, Charles (married), April 26, 1845, a. 36 y. 2 m. 19 d. Born in Lancaster.
Ezekiel, s. Ezekiel and ———, bap. Sept. 14, 1776. C.R.

BRYANT, Clement, Feb. 15, 1837, a. 52. G.S.2.

BUCKLEY, Mrs. Abigail, Feb. 13, 1849. a. 73 y. C.R.

BUCKMAN, Darius, April 25, 1833, [a. 28. G.S.3.].

BUCKNAM, Calvin, July 29, 1821. a. 26 y. One of the poor. C.R.
Mr. Joseph, April 10, 1774. C.R.
Rhoda, d. Joseph and Hannah, Nov. 2, 1776. C.R.
———, d. Joseph and Hannah, May 1, 1759. a. 1 d. C.R.
———, s. Joseph and Hannah, April 7, 1773. C.R.
———, ch. wid. Susanna, Sept. 15, 1808, a. 18 m. C.R.

BULLARD, Amos, Feb. 27, 1825, [a. 48. G.S.3.].
Daniel Franklin, s. Daniel and Polly, March 31, 1842, a. 3 y. 1 m. 23 d.
Ebenezer, a child belonging to Dea. John and Susannah Haven, Aug. 23, 1777. C.R.
Polly, w. Amos, Aug. 6, 1809, [a. 22, C.R.]

BURBANK, Abigail, d. Thomas and Abigail, April 20, 1795, a. 5 y. 3 m. 16 d.
Betsy, d. Thomas and Abigail, April 6, 1795, in 11th y.
Daniel, s. Thomas and Abigail, April 20, 1795, in 14th y.
Mr. ———, April 21, 1794. C.R.

BURBECK, George R., s. John and Hephzibah, Sept. 27, 1835, a. 4. G.S.2.
Hepsabeth, w. John, Sept. 8, 1849, a. 59, [58. G.S.2.]. Dysentery.

CADY, ———, d. Ephraim and Sarah, Feb. 8, 1777. C.R.

CADEY, Lucy, d. Ephraim and Mercy, Oct. 26, 1775. C.R.
Lydia, w. Ephraim Jr., June 7, 1774. C.R.
Mercy, w. Ephraim Jr., Feb. 17, 1773. C.R.
———, s. Barachi and Elisabeth, Oct. 28, 1774. C.R.

CAPRON, Sally, d. Ephraim and Sally, Aug. 5, 1791, a. 2 y. 5 m.
Sally, w. Ephraim, March 5, 1792.
William, s. Ephraim and Lucy, Oct. 21, 1799, a. 4 y. 4 m. 19 d.
———, ch. Eph. and ———, Sept. 2, 1791. a. 2½ y. C.R.

CARPENTER, ———, s. Caroline, Oct. 25, 1846, a. 14 d.

CARTER, Edwin Y., s. Jacob and Arathusa, Jan. 19, 1818, a. 8 m.

CHAPLIN, Ebenezer, M. D., (married), s. Rev. Ebenezer, May 14, 1844, a. 67 y. 10 m. 26 d. Appoploxy. Born in Millbury.

CHASE, Benjamin F., s. Freeman and Adelin, Sept. 24, 1849, a. 3 y. 10 m. Dysentery.
Clarissa, d. Ebenezer and Barsilva, March 3, 1804, in 3 d. y.
Clark, s. Moses and Meriam, Sept. 6, 1804, a. 1 y. 11 m. 12 d.
Elizabeth Ann, d. Freeman and Adaline, Oct. 4, 1836, a. nearly 1.
Ephraim F., s. Moses and Miriam, Oct. 19, 1832, a. 18 y. 9 m. G.S.3.
Freeman, s. Moses and Meriam, Aug. 9, 1808, a. 3 y. 7 m.
Meriam, w. Moses, Oct. 23 [20 G.S.], 1838, [a. 62, G.S.3.].
Royal, s. Moses and Meriam, Sept. 26, 1801, a. 1 [2, G.S.3] y. 4 m. 6 d.

CHASE, Stilman, s. Moses and Meriam, Sept. 8, 1804, a. 6 y. 1 m. 22 d.

CHENEY, Elizabeth, d. Samuel F., June 25, 1846, a. 18. Consumption.

Royal Whelock, s. Amos and Elvira, March 16, 1829, a. 1 y. 10 m.

CHURCH, Charlotte, d. Nehemiah, Sept. 17, 1845, a. 23 y. 10 m. 25 d. Typhus fever. Born in Hinsdale, N.H., and buried there.

Esther, w. Dea. Paul, Dec. 25 [18, C.R.] 1790, in 40th y. G.S.3.

Paul, s. Paul and ———, Oct. —, 1789. C.R.

Dea. Paul, Dec. 2, 1820 ? [1826, C.R.], a. 79. G.S.3.

CLAPP, Harriot Shipley, d. Samuel and Nancy B., March 8, 1833, a. 1 y. 11 m. 11 d.

Samuel A. (married), s. Samuel Jr., June 6, 1848, a. 26. Consumption. Painter.

CLARK, Anna, d. S., Sept. 20, 1849, a. 11 m. Dysentery.

Clarence F., s. James E. and Sylve C., Aug. 27, 1849, a. 1 y. 8 m. Dysentery.

David, s. Benjamin and Mehitable, Jan. 16, 1790, a. 11 y. 8 m.

George W., s. Joseph W. and Mary E., Oct. 9, 1845, a. 1 m. 4 d. Sore mouth.

James W., s. James E. [and Sylvia C.], Aug. 2, 1845, a. 16 d.

Jonathan, s. Benjamin and Mehitable, Feb. 4, 1786, a. 1 y. 10 m. 23 d.

Sarah, [Wid. ———], Dec. 19, 1833, a. 76. G.S.3.

———, [Lucian E. G.S.2.], twin s. James E., May 17, 1846, a 2 d.

———, [Lucius E. G.S.2.], twin s. James E., May 21, 1846, a. 6 d.

CODA, Mary, w. John, Aug. 10, 1847, a. 91. G.S.1.

CODY, Mrs. ———, Aug. 11, 1847, a. 90.

COLEMAN, Samuel, s. John and Martha, March 8, 1771. C.R.

COMMINS (see Cummings), David, s. Joseph and Elisabeth, March 24, 1776. C.R.

Nathan, s. Joseph and Elizabeth, March 30, 1776. C.R.

CONANT, Laura A., d. George W. and Laura, Aug. 21, 1849. Stillborn.

Laura A., w. George W., Oct. 27, 1849, a. 30. Dysentery.

COOK, ———, inf. d. Benjamin and Betsey, March 18, 1829, a. 14 [15, C.R.] d.

COOK, Benjamin (married), May 13, 1843, a. 79 y. 3 m. 19 d. Dropsy on chest.
Oscar M., s. Jacob S., Sept. 28, 1845, a. 4 m. 24 d.
———, [Smith M., G.S.2], inf. J. S., Sept. 30, 1846, a. 28 d. Dysentary.
———, [Elizabeth J., G.S.2], w. Jacob S. [Smith], Nov. 4, 1846, a. 25. Typhoid fever.

CRAWFORD, Albert B., s. Chester and Hannah, July 1, 1839, a. 16 m. G.S.3.
Daniel E., s. Daniel and Laura, Oct. 8, 1849, a. 2. G.S.2.
Laura, w. [Daniel], Sept. 29, 1849, a. 38, [44, G.S.2.]. Dysentery.
Laura E., d. Daniel and Laura, Jan. 22, 1846, a. 2 y. 3 m. 24 d. Croup.

CROSBY, Cindea, w. John, April 9, 1806.
Hannah, wid. Joseph, May 30, 1803, [a. 70, C.R.].
Jonathan, May 26, 1822, a. 59 y. C.R.
Joseph, h. Hannah, ——— ——, ———.
Lucenda, w. John, April 9, 1806, a. 36 y. C.R.
Maria Frances, d. Jonathan and Anna, Jan. 8, 1817, in 6th y.
Phebe Stevens, d. Jonathan and Anna, Aug. 9, 1800.
William s. Jonathan and Anna, Jan. 22 [15, C.R.], 1807.
———, ch. Stephen and ———, buried Jan. 7, 1792. C.R.
———, inf. Jonathan, April 3, 1811, a. 4 d. C.R.

CUMMINGS (see Commins), Almira, d. Samuel Jr. and Maria, April 24, 1849, a. 19. Consumption.
Chandler, s. John, Oct. 12, 1849, a. 16. Dysentery.
———, twin d. John, Sept. 17, 1844, a. 19 d. Soar mouth.
———, twin d. John, Sept. 19, 1844, a. 21 d. Soar mouth.

CUSHING, ———, wid. Lucy, Dec. 10, 1813, a. 74 y. C.R.

CUTTING, Ensign George, at Rutland, on his way home from a journey, Dec. 29, 1765. C.R.
George, Jan. 6, 1778. C.R.
George, Oct. 13, 1794, a. 17 y. C.R.
Jemima, sister to George, Nov. 20, 1759. C.R.
Mary, d. William and Lucy, Nov. 1, 1839, a. 31. G.S.1.
Oliver, s. George and Judith, Dec. 19, 1771. C.R.
William P., Jan. 4, 1845, a. 41. G.S.1.

DAILY, Patrick, July 16, 1846, a. 36. Killed by blasting rock. Born in Ireland and buried in Worcester.

ATHOL DEATHS. 191

DANFORTH, John, h. Hannah, Nov. 2, 1803, in 36th y.
Sally, Feb. 6, 1807, a. 11 y. C.R.

DAVENPORT, Seveno R., s. David B. and Martha R., July 21, 1845, a. 1 m. 1 d. Fits.

DAVIS, Philetus Ansbury, s. Norris and Lucy Ann, Feb. —, 1836, a. 9 m. about.
Rebecca, May 8, 1801, a. 18 y. Black Jaundice. C.R.
———, inf. Roswell, March 14, 1813. C.R.
———, inf. Ezekiel G. and Lydia, Jan. 10, 1842, on day of birth.

DERBY, Harriot, d. Abraham and Demarious, Oct. 21, 1809, a. 1 y. 11 m. 18 d.

DEXTER, Mr. Daniel, Feb. 26, 1781. C.R.
Hepzibath, w. Benjamin Jr., Dec. 24, 1799.
Simion, s. Benjamin and Hannah, March 1, 1773. C.R.
———, d. Benjamin and Hannah, Aug. 28, 1774. C.R.

DICKENSON, Ebenezer, Feb. 8, 1830, a. 36 y., of Amherst. C.R.

DIKE, David, h. Patty, July 1, 1838.
Hannah, w. Samuel, d. William and Kezia Young, ——— ———, ———. [Nov. 1, 1807, a. 25. C.R.]
John, May 13, 1825, a. 80 y. C.R.
John Loren, s. John and Aurilla, Aug. 17, 1831, a. 2 y. 13 d.
Jonathan, April 27, 1800, a. 25 y. C.R.
Lusetta, d. Samuel and Hannah, Dec. 16, 1817, [a. 18, C.R.].
Mary Ann, Nov. 19, 1826, a. 16 y. C.R.
Patty H., d. David and Patty, March 6, 1809, a. 3 y. lacking 7 days.
Widow Sarah, Dec. 14, 1776. C.R.
Sarah, w. John, July 2, 1817, a. 69 y. C.R.
Susanna, w. David, Oct. 31, 1800.

DOAN, Benjamin S., s. Austin and Hannah, Sept. 20, 1849, a. 4. Dysentery.
George U., s. Austin and Hannah, Sept. 2, 1849, a. 2. Dysentry.

DRAKE, Ellen T., d. Brad B. and Harriet, Feb. 27, 1849, a. 8 m. Dysentery.
———, d. Mr. ———, Aug. 10, 1832. C.R.

DREWRY (see Drury), Amos, Oct. 2, 1822, a. 23 y. C.R.
Lidea, June 26, 1818, a. 29 y. C.R.
Lucy, w. Capt., Oct. 11, 1825. C.R.

DREWRY, Lydia, w. John, Aug. 10, 1822, a. 76 y. C.R.
Rhoda, Jan. 12, 1812, a. 21 y. C.R.
Samuel, April 15, 1819, a. 13 y. In a consumption. C.R.

DRURY (see Drewry), Asa, s. John and Lydia, Sept. 6, 1777. C.R.
Charles B., s. David and Belsey, Oct. 5, 1846, a. 6 m. G.S.1.
Electa, d. John and Lydia, Sept. 15, 1777. C.R.
John, s. John and Lydia, Aug. 17, 1777. C.R.
John, h. Lydia, April 26, 1831.
Ruth, wid. Joel, March 22, 1848, a. 78.
———, inf. s. David, Oct. 26, 1844. Dysentary.

DUNMORE, Ezra, s. Silvenus and Jaine, Sept. 22, 1804, a. 5 m. lacking 4 d.
Eliza, d. Silvenus and Jaine, Feb. 8, 1809, a. 2 y. 4 m. 24 d.

DUNTON, Abigail, w. Ebenezer, Sept. 5, 1776. C.R.
Nehemiah, s. Ebenezer and Abigail, July 11, 1776. C.R.
Persis, d. Ebenezer and Abigail, Aug. 31, 1776. C.R.

DUTTON, Rebeccah, Jan. 13, 1813, a. 39 y. C.R.

DWIER, John, Dec. 11, 1846, a. 35. Killed by blasting. Born in Ireland and buried in Fitchburg.

DYER, Ambrose, s. Shebna and Mary, Dec. 16, 1782, a. 16 d.
Olive, April 20, 1826. C.R.
Samuel, March 28, 1807, a. 26 y. C.R.
Sarah, d. Shebna and Mary, May 11, 1786, a. 16 d.
Shebney, April 19, 1808, a. 66 y. C.R.
———, ch. James, March 7, 1810. C.R.
———, ch. James, Sept. 17, 1813. C.R.
———, wid. June 1, 1818, a. 73 y. C.R.

EGGLESTON, Lucy H. W., w. Rev. A. B., Aug. 29, 1819. G.S.1.

ELLENWOOD (see Ellinwood), Eliza Crombie, d. James and Rebecca, Aug. 22, 1829, in 17th y.
James, March 16, 1826, a. 44 y. C.R.
Lusaby, d. James and Rebecca, Feb. 20, 1821, a. 1 y. 8 m. 3 d.
———, ch. Daniel, Feb. 4, 1816, a. 1 y. C.R.

ELLINWOOD (see Ellenwood), Austin, s. Daniel and Dorothy, Feb. 4, 1816, a. 1 y. 2 m. 25 d.
Dr. Daniel, h. Lucy, April 29, 1794, [in 42d. (44th ?) y., G.S.3.].
Daniel, h. Dorothy, Feb. 15, 1831, [a. 54, G.S.3.].
Eliza A., w. Austin, May 12, 1842, a. 25. G.S.5. }
Eliza Farnsworth, w. Austin, May 12, 1842. }

ATHOL DEATHS. 193

ELLINWOOD, Lucy, wid. Dr. Daniel, March 23, 1838, a. 81. G.S.3.
Rhoena, d. Daniel and Dorothy, May 11, 1829, a. 22 y. 28 d.
Capt. Thomas, June 6, 1840, a. 39. G.S.3.

ELLIS, Chester, s. Clark and Mary Ann, March 27, 1843, a. 6 m. 29 d.
Fanny M. [Maria], w. Seth E. Jr., Jan. 13, 1846, a. 27 y. 2 m. 18 d. Dropsy on Brain. Born in Orange.

ESTABROOK, Candace, Aug. 15, 1837.
Rev. Joseph, D.D., April 18, 1830, [a. 71 y. 1 m. 14 d. G.S.2.].

ESTERBROOK, Lucy [Cushing], w. Rev. Joseph, Aug. 9, 1828, [a. 65, C.R.].

FAIRBANK (see Fairbanks, Farbank), Doritha [Dolle in dup.], d. John and Releef, Aug. 27, 1790, a. 29 y. 3 m. 13 d. In Charlemont. Dup.
Hannah, w. Thomas, Dec. 11, 1800.
Harriot, d. Reuben and Lucinda, Dec. 4, 1811, a. 2 y. 7 m. 11 d.
John, Feb. 9, 1817, in 86th y. G.S.3.
Rane, w. Thomas, Feb. 19, 1807.
Releef, w. John, Oct. 29 [30, C.R.], 1795, a. 69. G.S.3.
Samuel, s. John and Releef, June 3, 1777, a. 20 y. 3 m. 13 d. Dup.
Silas, s. Benjamin and Hannah, Aug. 31, 1809, a. 19 y. 6 m. 6 d.
Thomas, March 23, 1816, [a. 79, C.R.].
———, d. Thomas and Hannah, July 13, 1780. C.R.

FAIRBANKS, Ephraim (married), s. John, Dec. 23 [30, G.S.2.], 1844, a. 79 y. 1 m. 21 d. Disease of heart.
Matilda, wid. Ephraim, April 19 [18, G.S.2.], 1848, a. 79.

FARBANK (see above), Jonathan, July 28, 1823. C.R.
Susanna, Jan. 29, 1821, a. 91. C.R.

FARR, Clarissa, d. Amariah and Clarissa, May 17, 1816, a. 1 y. 8 m. 17 d.
———, ch. Amariah, Sept. 14, 1832. C.R.

FAY, Abigail, d. Joseph and Abigail, March 21, 1810, a. 24 y. 5 m. Spotted Fever.
Abigail, wid. Joseph, Sept. 25, 1827. [Sept. 26, 1826, a. 74. G.S.3. and C.R.]
Almena, d. Seth, Feb. 24, 1823, a. 17 m. C.R.
Betsey, d. Josiah and Molly, Feb. 21, 1816, a. 2 y. 25 d.
Emily E., w., William G., Jan. 10, 1849, a. 21. Fever.
Jonas (married), Oct. 28, 1849, a. 61. Stomach disease.

ATHOL DEATHS.

FAY, Joseph, h. Abigail, Jan. 20, 1825, [a. 83, G.S.3.].
Josiah, h. Molly, March 10, 1834. [a. 60, G.S.4.] [60 on day of death, C.R.]
Josiah, s. Jonathan Ward and Mary L., May 5, 1835, a. 9 m. 13 d.
Lucinda. d. Joseph, July 2, 1849, a. 53. Consumption.
Martha Clement, d. Jonathan Ward and Mary L., Dec. 11, 1841, a. 1 y. 11 m.
Mary, w. Solomon, Dec. 6, 1836, a. 86. G.S.1.
Nahum, h. Sarah, Aug. 28, 1810, [a. 33, C.R.].
Nahum, Aug. 18, 1823, a. 18 y. In Petersham. He cut his throat. C.R.
Polly, d. Solomon and Mary, Sept. 19, 1787, a. 2 y. 25 d.
Sabra, d. Solomon and Mary, June 6, 1786, a. 2 y. 11 m. 4 d.
Sabra, d. Artemas and Delight, Sept. 25, 1804, a. 6 y. 11 m.
Solomon, h. Mary, Nov. 22, 1814, [a. 80, C.R.].
Vienna [d. Solomon and Mary ?], April 23, 1795.
———, ch. Artemas, Sept. 22, 1804, a. 2 y. C.R.
———, inf. of Nayam, Feb. 21, 1808. C.R.
——— [Mary B., G.S.4.], w. James S., May 13, 1847, a. 38. Consumption.

FELT, Elijah (married), March 19, 1849, a. 50. Dropsy.

FELTON, Miss Aurelia S., Sept. 2, 1819, a. 30. G.S.3.
Daniel Jr., s. Daniel and Lois, June 25, 1779. C.R.
David, s. Daniel and Lois, Aug. 71, 1779, a. nearly 2.
David H., March 19, 1819, a. 26. G.S.3.
Lloyd, s. Daniel and Lois, June 25, 1779, a. 1 m. 20 d.

FIELD, Lucius H., s. Lucius and Lucia, May 8, 1815, a. 8 m. 7 d. G.S.3, [a. 7 m., C.R.].
———, inf. s. Zachariah and Abigail, May 28, 1818 [1813 ?, C.R.], a. 1 hour. G.S.3.
———, ch. Elihu and Lucy Stratton, Aug. 11, 1827, a. 2. C.R.

FISH, Chloe, w. Ezra ?, Nov. 15, 1833, a. 56. G.S.1.
Ezra (married), March 31, 1848, a. 77.
Francis, s. Samuel and Betsy, Sept. 30, 1802, a. 1 y. 10 m. 14 d.
Henry (married), Sept. 11, 1846, a. 41. Typhoid fever.
Horatio [Horatio K., G.S.] (married), March 30, 1848, a. 29. [a. 26, G.S.1.]
Lucy, d. Ezra and Chloa, Aug. 29, 1803, a. 9 m. 17 d.
Marian, d. Benjamin and Mary, June 19, 1816, a. 20 m. 3 d. G.S.1.
Samuel, July 23, 1834, a. 65. G.S.1.
Simeon, March 9, 1825, a. 77. G.S.1.
Tabitha, wid. Simeon, Feb. 21, 1835, a. 85. G.S.1.

ATHOL DEATHS. 195

FISHER, Maranda, d. Oliver M. and Hannah, Sept. 13, 1831, a. 5. G.S.3.

FISK, ———, s. Mr. and w., June 23, 1795, a. 17 y. C.R.

FITTS, Sally, w. George [Esq.], Oct. 16, 1812, [a. 26, G.S.3.].
Sally Luann, d. George and Sally, Dec. 27, 1812, a. 5 m. 6 d.
———, ch. George, Dec. 28, 1812. C.R.

FLETCHER, Betsey, w. William, Aug. 8, 1844, a. 32 y. 6 m. 26 d. Consumption. Born in Orange.
James S., s. William [and Betsey], Sept. 21, 1844, a. 1 y. 6 m. 27 d. Consumption.
Joanna, Feb. 2, 1827, a. 72 y. C.R.

FLINT, Elizabeth Ann, d. Josiah and Elizabeth, July 7 [8, C.R.], 1830, a. 1 y. 2 m. 21 d.
Hannah Elizabeth, twin d. Josiah and Elizabeth, March 14, 1828, a. 2 m.

FORD, Mercy, d. Josiah and Jemima, Oct. 28, 1780. C.R.

FORESTOR, ———, ch. Moses, Sept. 23, 1808, a. 20 d. C.R.

FOSTER, Elmon J. [s. Daniel and Hannah J. ?], Sept. 18, 1841, a. 16 d. G.S.2.
Hopestill, s. Edward and Deborah, Nov. 18, 1776. C.R.
James, s. Edward and Deborah, Nov. 22, 1776. C.R.
Dea. James, June 18, 1787, in 88th y. G.S.3.
John W. (married), Sept. 8, 1849, a. 50. Consumption. Buried in Phillipton.
Lydia d. Edward and Deborah, Nov. 21, 1776. C.R.
Martha How, d. Asa W. and Elmira, Sept. 5, 1827, a. 2 m. 10 d.
William Henry, s. Asa W. and Elmira, Aug. 14, 1841, a. 12 y. 11 m. [Killed by the kick of a horse, G.S.6.]
———, ch. John W. and Dorinda, Aug. 20, 1849, a. 3. Dysentery. Buried in Phillipston.

FRY (see Frye), Ana, w. Job, Oct. 1, 1849, a. 43 y. 6 m. Dysentery.
Barzillat, s. Silas and Susannah K., March 15, 1841, a. 5 w. G.S.3.
Job, s. Job, Aug. 28, 1844, a. 2. Dysentary.
Martha Jane, d. Job and ———, Nov. 5, 1841, a. 1 y. 2 m. 21 d.

FRYE (see above), Florella, w. Job, Aug. 7, 1833.

GARFIELD, George, Jan. 26, 1837, a. 58. G.S.3.
Luke Jones, eldest s. George and Patty G., instantly killed by fall of a tree June 10, 1819, a. 11 y. 9 m. 9 d. G.S.3.

ATHOL DEATHS.

GARFIELD, Wid. Lydia, April —, 1834, a. 80 y. c.r.
Moses, March 23, 1843, a. 77.
Reuben, March 11, 1831 [1830, a. 77, c.r.].

GATES, Betsy, w. John, d. Seth and Lucy Fay, June 25, 1843, a. 23. Consumption. Dup.
John Fay, s. John and Betsy, May 31, 1843, a. 1 y. 6 m. 6 d. Consumption. Dup.

GEROLD, ———, ch. Mr. ———, Aug. —, 1832. c.r.

GILES, Alban, Nov. 21, 1825, a. 21 y. c.r.
Elmira Stratton, w. Prescott, —— —, 1844, a. 37. G.S.1.
S., Oct. 28, 1849. Cholera Infantum.

GLAZIER, Isaac (married), May 5, 1847, a. 47. Consumption. Carpenter.

GODARD (see Goddard), Ebenezer, Nov. 18, 1762, in 49th y. G.S.1.
Elijah, s. E. and Mehitable, Oct. 5, 1817, [a. 13, c.r.].
Franklin, s. Walter and Hannah, May 27, 1827, a. 18 y. 4 m. 13 d.
Hollis, s. Elijah and Mehitable, Aug. 2, 1808, a. 13 y. 6 m. 21 d.
Hannah, d. Elijah and Mehitable, Oct. 14, 1808, a. nearly 3.
Molly, d. James and Betta, June 29, 1810, in 36th y.
Polly, d. Walter and Hannah, May 7 [8, c.r.], 1827, a. 16 y. 8 m. 18 d.

GODDARD (see Godard), Benjamin, s. Ebenezer and Sibbil, Nov. 6, 1771. c.r.
Betty, w. James, May 30, 1807.
David, Oct. 7, 1777. He was killed att Still Water. c.r.
David, s. Edward and Ruth, Feb. 13, 1795. In 18th y.
David, s. Josiah, April 6, 1844, a. 32. Consumption. Born in Wendell, buried in Leominster. Preacher.
Ebenezer, Aug. 15, 1822, a. 71 y. c.r.
Electa, Oct. 9, 1818, a. 20 y. c.r.
Ellen F., d. Ephraim and Laura, Sept. 22, 1849, a. 1 y. 5 m. Dysentery.
Elmer, s. Joseph and Lucy, 2d wife, Aug. 8, 1841, in 19th y.
Ephraim (married), Nov. 24, 1849, a. 79 [78, G.S.2.]. Schymus Stomach.
Hannah, d. James and Bette, Aug. 29, 1777. c.r.
Henry, s. Josiah and Ruth, Aug. 16, 1777. c.r.
James, h. Betty, Feb. 22, 1809, [a. 68, c.r.].
Jonathan, s. David and Margit, Nov. 28, 1811, a. 55 y. 11 m. 5 d.
Josiah [Esq.], h. Ruth, Oct. 23, 1801, [a. 55, c.r.].

ATHOL DEATHS. 197

GODDARD, Lucinda, w. Eber, July 18, 1834, a. 31. G.S.2.
Lucy, w. Joseph, May 24, 1802, [a. 29, C.R.].
Mary, w. Nathaniel, Feb. 1, 1767. C.R.
Patty, March 28, 1796, in 24 y. C.R.
Sally, d. widow, April 10, 1795, a. 18 y. C.R.
Wid. Sarah, Sept. 21, 1824, a. 81 y. C.R.
———, ch. James and Bette, Sept. 26, 1768. C.R.
———, s. Ebenezer and Hannah, May 3, 1776, a. 2 h. C.R.
———, widow, Nov. 28, 1798, a. 94 y. C.R.
———, ch. Elijah and wife, Jan. 22, 1801, a. 3 d. C.R.
———, inf. of Elijah, March 20, 1808. C.R.
———, ch. Dea., Oct. 14, 1808, a. 3 y. C.R.
———, second w. Joseph, June 8, 1809, a. 30 y. C.R.
———, inf. Dea., Aug. 6, 1809, a. 3 d. C.R.
———, ch. Luther, Feb. 14, 1822, a. 4 m. C.R.

GOODALE, ———, w. Ephraim, Aug. 11, 1803, a. 20 y. C.R.

GOODELL, John, s. John, Feb. 6, 1849, a. 36. Nervous fever.

GOULD, Idelia A., d. Nahum C. and Sophronia, Aug. 3, 1832, a. 3 m. 11 d. G.S.3.
Jacob Orlando, s. Curtis and Sally, April 17, 1833, a. 4 y. 4 m. 25 d.
Naham C., s. N. C. and S., June 5, 1834, a. 6 m. G.S.3.
Sally, w. Curtice ?, Oct. 8, 1848, a. 48. Consumption.
William, Feb. 12, 1839, a. 73. G.S.3.
———, ch. wid., Jan. —, 1834, a. 7 m. C.R.

GOVE ?, ———, d. Peter and Sarah, April 18, 1764. C.R.

GRADY, James, June 8, 1846, a. 45. Killed by blasting rock. Born in Ireland and buried in Worcester.

GRAVES, Lieut. Abner, March 26, 1830, [a. 89, G.S.3.].
Abner (married), June 27, 1849, a. 68 [69, G.S.2.]. Fever.
Alice, w. Lieut. Abner, Oct. 3, 1823, [a. 84, G.S.2.].
Eleazer, s. Eleazer and Sarah, Sept. 24, 1756. C.R.
Eleazer, h. Olive, ——— —, — [Nov. 9, 1822, a. 63, G.S.3.].
Elezar, Jan. 25, 1795, a. 84 y. C.R.
Elijah, s. Eliazer and Sarah, Aug. 6, 1773. C.R.
Elijah, s. Eleazer Jr. and Olive, Jan. 1, 1804, a. 14 y. 2 m. 14 d.
Hannah, w. Nathaniel Jr., March 29, 1775. C.R.
Hannah, w. Nathaniel, Feb. 13, 1783, in 75th y. G.S.3.
Jesse, s. Eleazer Jr. and Olive, Feb. 23, 1801, in 3d y.
Judith, widow ———, June 7, 1807, a. 43[?] y. C.R.

GRAVES, Lois, d. Eleazer Jr. and Olive, Aug. 30, 1804, a. 4 y. 1 m. 10 d.
Molly, June 11, 1823, a. 84 y. c.r.
Nancy, d. Eleazer Jr. and Olive, Sept. 1, 1804, in 11th y.
Nathaniel, Aug. 31, 1796, in 90th y. g.s.3. [88, c.r.]
Olive, w. Eleazer Jr., April 23, 1809, [a. 49, c.r.].
Samuel, s. Eleazer and Sarah, Nov. 8, 1759, at Crown Point. (This young man a Listed Soldier to Crown Point.) c.r.
Sarah, w. Eleazer, Sept. 26, 1766. c.r.
Sarah, d. Eleazer and Sarah, Jan. 31, 1772. c.r.
———, ch. ? Eleazer and ———, Nov. 14, 1791. c.r.

GRAY, Charles, s. Alexander and Elvira, Aug. 15, 1835, a. 1 y. 8 m. 21 d.
Saphira Allen d. Thomas and Milley, Oct. 22, 1809.
Thomas, s. Alexander and Elvira, July 25, 1832 [1835 ? c.r.], a. nearly 5.
Thomas, Dec. 14 [13 ?], 1847, [a. 79, g.s.2.]. Old age.
———, ch. Thomas, Oct. 21, 1809, a. 6 m. c.r.

GREEN, Charlotte, March 3, 1826, a. 18 y. Girl of color. c.r.

GROVES, ———, ch. Eleazer and wife, Feb. 23, 1801. A fever Nerves. c.r.

GUILD, Sally, w. Curtis, Oct. 9, 1848, a. 48. g.s.6.

HADLEY. ———, ch. Samuel, Nov. 18, 1819, a. 7 m. c.r.
———, w. Samuel, Oct. 2, 1820. c.r.

HAGER, Aaron (married), Jan. 15, 1846, a. 77 y. 7 m. Born in Petersham. Pensioner.

HALE, Dameris, 2d w. Sam., Nov. 26, 1793. c.r.
Mary, 3d w. Samuel, Oct. 28, 1797.
Polly, d. Samuel, April 5, 1795, a. 10 y. c.r.
Samuel, May 26, 1799. c.r.
———, ch. Sam. and ———, Jan. 19, 1792, a. 9 m. c.r.
Mrs. ———, w. Samuel, April 8, 1792, a. 36 y. c.r.
———, ch. Samuel, April 28, 1795, a. 8 y. c.r.

HANSHAW, John P., Feb. 19, 1825, a. 26 y. c.r.

HAPGOOD, Josephine [Josephine E. g.s.2.], d. Lyman W., Feb. 8, 1847, a. 5 [and 4 m., g.s.]. Croup.

HARRICK (see Herrick), Sally, w. Silas, Jan. 10, 1812, a. 31 y. c.r.

HARWHICH, ———, ch. David, Sept. 11, 1823, a. 1 y. 6 m. C.R.

HARWOOD, Abigal, wid. Stephen, June 10, 1838, in 89th y. G.S.1.
Adeline, d. Seth K. and Caroline, June 25, 1840, a. 5 y. 2 m.
Elizebeth, w. Stephen, June 10, 1826, a. 53 y. C.R.
George W., s. David and Lois, drowned in Millers River, Aug. 25, 1840, a. 12. G.S.1.
Harriet, d. Seth and Caroline, Sept. 8, 1840, a. 1 y. 4 m. 15 d.
Harriet Adaline, d. Seth K. and Caroline, Aug. 1, 1843, a. 2 y. 3 m. 11 d. Scarlet fever. Dup.
Hattie A., d. Seth K. and Caroline C., Sept. —, 1844, a. 2. G.S.1.
Elizebeth, w. Stephen, June 10, 1826, a. 52. G.S.3.
Martha, wid. Stephen, Sept. 30, 1837, a. 52. G.S.3.
Olive, w. Stephen, Sept. 7, 1802, a. 26. G.S.3.
Rebeccah Ann, w. David, May 16, 1822, a. 26. G.S.1.
Stephen, h. Elisabeth, Sept. 25, 1835, [a. 62, G.S.3.].
Stephen K., s. Seth K. and Caroline, June 9, 1840, a. 7 y. 18 d.

HASEY? (see Heasey), Mrs. Sarah, wid. ———, Dec. 18, 1798, a. in 81st y. G.S.3.

HAVEN, Daniel, Feb. 27, 1807, a. 28 y. C.R.
Grace, d. John and Susanna, Jan. 1, 1754, a. 6 y. 5 d.
Grace, d. Dea. John and Susannah, Aug. 23, 1777. C.R.
Dea. John, July 12, 1807, a. 81 y. C.R.
Mr. John, Nov. 8, 1831. In Dummerston, Vt.
John (married), Sept. 8, 1849, a. 65. Liver complaint.
Jonathan, s. Jonathan and Hannah, Aug. 31, 1769. C.R.
Jonathan, Dec. 24, 1769. C.R.
Lydia, d. John and Susannah, Dec. 23, 1767. C.R.
Martha, w. John June 20, 1822, a. 66 y. C.R.
Mary d. Jonathan and Hannah, Sept. 8, 1770. C.R.
Moses, s. Simon and Ruth, June 3, 1769. C.R.
Mr. Richard, Aug. 3, 1770. C.R.
Samuel, April 24, 1808 [a. 28, C.R.]
Susannah, w. Dea. John, Sept. 2, 1777. C.R.
———, the widow, Nov. —, 1790, in the 91 y. of her age. C.R.
———, only s. Asa, Aug. 26, 1791, a. 16 y. C.R.
———, ch. widow, May 5, 1807, a. about 1 y. C.R.
———, and ———, twins of Asa and Lucy R., Jan. 17, 1828 on day of birth.

HAZE, ——— (married), April 7, 1846, a. 40. Killed by falling of a bank on Railroad excavation. Born in Ireland and buried in Worcester.

ATHOL DEATHS.

HEADLEY, ch. John and ———, Nov. 17, 1788, a. 1 h. c.r.

HEASEY (see Hasey), ———, d. Samuel and Silence, Aug. 17, 1776. Child. c.r.

HEASY, Abigail, w. Zaccheus, Sept. 23, 1778. c.r.

HERRICK (see Harrick), Sally, w. Silas, April 25, 1833, a. 28. g.s.3.
Silas Milton, s. Silas and Sally, Sept. 24, 1811, a. 9 m. 10 d. g.s.3.

HEWIT, Samuel, a Soldier belonging to Taunton; he died att. Lieut. William Oliver, Dec. 17, 1762. c.r.

HEYWOOD, Charles, s. Alpheus and Lucretia ?, Aug. 9, 1833, a. 2 y. 3 m. g.s.1.
George A., s. Alpheus and Lucretia, Nov. 3, 1842, a. 7 m. Dysentary.
Myra F., d. Alpheus and Lucretia, Nov. 11, 1842, a. 2 y. 4 m. 29 d. Dysentary.
Myra F., d. Alpheus and Lucretia, April 1, 1848, a. 4 y. 2 m. g.s.1.

HILL (see Hills), Abijah, Sept. 7, 1838, a. 51.
Abijah, s. John C. and Dolly, June [July ?] 13, 1843, a. 3 y. 2 m. 6 d. Scarlet fever.
Charlotte, w. Danford, April 10, 1832.
Danford, widr. Charlotte, Aug. 28, 1834, [a. 30, g.s.3.].
Hannah, w. Aaron, April 28, 1849, a. 72. Fever.
Huldah Maria, d. Danford and Charlotte, Aug. 15, 1842, a. 14 y. 7 m.
John, s. Moses and Lucy, Aug. 23, 1777. c.r.
Wid. Lucy, Nov. 16, 1826, a. 81 y. c.r.
Moses, Nov. 15, 1820, a. 80 y. c.r.
Otis Willard, s. Emory and Rhoda, April 15, 1835 [*sic*].
Rhoda, w. Emory, April 4, 1835.
Samuel, s. Moses and Lucy, Aug. 9, 1777. c.r.
Sarah Luann, d. Danford and Charlotte, Oct. 6, 1836, a. 6 y. 11 m. 1 d.
——— The widow, Sept. 16, 1794, in an advanced age. c.r.
———, w. John, Jan. 14, 1800. c.r.
———, w. A., Oct. 23, 1832, a. 28 y. c.r.
———, ch. Danforth, [prob. Dec. 18, 1832]. c.r.
———, s. Jonathan J., Sept. 8, 1845, a. 9 m. 9 d. Dysentery.

HILLS (see above), ———, ch. Asa and Anna, March 29, 1824, a. 1 w. C.R.

HINDS, Amanda, d. Hiram D. and Amanda, March 30, 1848, a. 2 y. 3 m.
Eliza Ellemanda, d. Hiram D. and Ellemanda, Dec. 30, 1831, a. 1 y. 8 m. 4 d. At Hubbardston.
William Lloyd Garrison, s. Hiram D. and Ellemanda, June 14, 1837, a. 3 m. 4 d.

HOAR, Lucy Ann [Lucy B. in dup.], d. Timothy and Lydia, Jan. 31, 1827, a. 4 y. 13 d.
Lydia B., w. Timothy, Sept. 11, 1848, a. 54. Consumption.
———, ch. Timothy, April —, 1834, a. about 2 y. C.R.

HODGE, ———, s. Asa S., July 15, 1846, a. 6 d.

HOLBROOK, Polly, w. Adin, Sept. 1, 1849, a. 59. Dysentry.

HOLLAND, Hannah, w. John, Dec. 24, 1771. C.R.
Ruben, s. Hugh and Elizabeth, Sept. 28, 1756. C.R.

HOLMAN, Zilpah, Dec. 28, 1810. C.R.
———, Mrs., Nov. 19, 1802. C.R.

HOLMES, Catharine, d. Jacob and Thankful, Aug. 1, 1813, a. 3 y. 21 d.
———, inf. Dr. Jacob and Thankful, Dec. 26, 1823. C.R.

HOLT, Ebenezer, h. Arethusa, July 3, 1835, [a. 47, G.S.1.].
———, ch. ———, April —, 1834, a. 4 m. C.R.

HOOKER, Jacob, Aug. 13, 1781. C.R.
Widow Mary, Dec. 6, 1806, a. 90 y. C.R.

HORN, Eliza, d. Timothy and Lydia, ——— —, 1834, a. 2. G.S.2.
Lucy A., d. Timothy and Lydia, ——— —, 1827, a. 4. G.S.2.
John (married), Nov. 12, 1849, a. 44. Consumption. Born in Ireland.
Patrick, s. John and Bridget, Aug. 23, 1849, a. 2. Dysentry.
Susan, d. John and Bridget, Sept. 5, 1849, a. 7. Dysentery.
———, s. John and Bridget, Sept. 2, 1849, a. 1 d.

HOUGHTON, Levi, s. Benj. Sept. 4, 1819, a. 4 y. C.R.
———, ch. Benj., Aug. 31, 1819, a. 2 y. C.R.

HOW, John Perkins, s. Perkins and Nancy, Jan. 13, 1803, a. 8 m. 1 d.

ATHOL DEATHS.

HOWARD, A. H. ?, Sept. 4, 1849, a. 8. Dysentery.
Charles, s. Simeon Jr. and Mary, Sept. 30, 1838, a. 4 y. 6 m.
Charles P., s. Simeon and Mary, Sept. 1, 1837, a. 3 y. 5 m. G.S.1.
Elizabeth, w. Joel, May 20, 1849, a. 22 [21, G.S.2.]. Dysentery.
Emily, d. Simeon and Lucy, May 19, 1822, a. 2 y. 2 m. 23 d.
Lucy, w. Simeon, Oct. 1, 1826 [a. 47, G.S.1. [49, C.R.]].
Lydia, [d. Lemuel and Lydia ?], March 4, 1816, [a. 1 y. 6 m. 2 d.?].
Phebe, wid. Simeon, Jan. 19, 1831, [a. 37, G.S.1.].
Prudence Putnam, d. Simeon and Lucy, Aug. —, 1810, a. 1 y. 3 m.
Seth, s. Simeon and Phebe, Sept. 2, 1829, a. 23 d.
Simeon, h. Phebe, Sept. 25, 1830, [a. 55, G.S.1.].

HO———, Ebenr, July 3, 1835, a. 47 y. C.R.

HOR—ICH, ———, ch. David, Oct. 13, 1817, a. 6 d. C.R.

HOYT, Ana, w. Ebenezer, Dec. 1, 1848, a. 73. Buried in Deerfield.

HUDSON, Ebenezer, s. Esra and Relief, June 22, 1770. C.R.
Ebenezer, s. Ezra and Relief, Oct. 13, 1777. C.R.
Liberty, s. Ezra and Relief, Sept. 22, 1777. C.R.

HUMFREY, Sarah, d. James and Esther, Aug. 26, 1756, a. 2 y. 8 m. 8 d. at Dorchester. C.R.

HUMPHREY (see Humphreys), Anna Richards, d. John and Hannah, Sept. 16 [17, C.R.], 1801, a. 2 y. 2 m. 23 d.
Azubah, d. Samuel and Lois, Nov. 11, 1785, a. 15 y. 8 d.
Calvin [s. Thomas and Esther], Nov. 29, 1773, a. 6 y. 1 m. 23 d.
Clarissa, d. Mary and John, March 6, 1792, a. 2 y. 3 m. 12 d.
Esther, d. Samuel and Lois, Sept. — [23, C.R.], 1776, a. 2 y. 4 m.
Esther, wid. Rev. James, March 5, 1822, a. 94. G.S.2.
Euseba, wid. Royal, ——— —, 1833, [Jan. 20, a. 69, G.S.2.].
Rev. James, May 8, 1796, [a. 74. First minister of Athol, settled 1750, G.S.2.].
James, h. Lucy [s. Rev. James and Esther], May 23 [24, G.S.], 1836, [a. 72, G.S.2.].
John, h. Hannah, Jan. 24 [25 ?], 1837, [a. 81, G.S.2.].
John F., h. Betsey, May 5, 1829, [a. 40, G.S.2.].
Jonas, s. Samuel and Lois, Feb. 19 [15, C.R.], 1773, a. 5 m. 4 d.
Lucy Morse, d. James Jr. and Lucy, Jan. 20, 1814, a. 9 y. 3 m. 6 d.
Mary, w. John, Jan. 21, 1792, [a. 36, G.S.3.].
Mary Tileston, d. John and Hannah, Aug. 20, 1825, a. 30 y. 1 m. 15 d.
Otis, s. Royal and Euseba, A᠎ 8, 1800, in 3d y.

HUMPHREY, Otis, s. Royal and Euseba, Oct. 7, 1803, a. nearly 2 m.
Samuel, July 20, 1814. c.r.
Susanna Payson, d. Samuel and Lois, March 6, 1784, in 20th y.
———n, s. Rev. James and Esther, Nov. 20, 1773, a. 6 y. 6 m. G.S.3.
———, ch. Royal and ———, June —, 1793. C.R.
———, Father James, March 8, 1803, a. 74 y. C.R.
———, Mother James, Jan. 12, 1803, a. 67 y. C.R.

HUMPHREYS (see Humphrey), George W., s. John W. and Sophia ?, Sept. 1, 1833, a. 3 m. 27 d. G.S.2.
Helen Anganette, d. Heney, Aug. 28, 1844, a. 7 m. 22 d. Dysentary.
Horatio Willard, s. James Jr. and Sarah, Aug. 15, 1837, a. 5 y. 3 m. 7 d.
John W. (married), s. James, April 25, 1845, a. 43 y. 8 m. 16 d. Consumption.
Liza H., d. John H. [Harvey] and Urana B., Sept. 29 [27, G.S.2.], 1849, a. 1 y. 6 [9 ?] m. Dysentery.
[Dr.] Royal (widr.), March 30, 1848, a. 86 y. 6 m.
———, ch. Dr. Oct. 6, 1803, a. 15 m. C.R.

HUNT, ———, inf. d. Luther Jr., Aug. 25, 1847.

HUTCHINS, Prudence, d. Edward and ———, Sept. 28, 1776. C.R.

JACOBS, Helen Louisa, d. Loring and M. H., Nov. 10, 1833 [1853 ?] a. 5 y. 4 m. 5 d. G.S.2.
Mary Agnes, d. Loring and M. H., Aug. 30, 1848, a. 5 w. 6 d. G.S.2.
Pallatiah, s. John and Bulah, Sept. —, 1788, a. 3.
Roxy, d. John and Bulah, Jan. 1, 1801, a. 3 y. 3 m. 15 d.
———, ch. John, Dec. 29, 1800. C.R.

JENNISON, Austin, Sept. 3, 1844, a. 32 y. 1 m. 28 d. Buried at Prescott, Mass. G.S.2.

JOHNSON (see Jonson), Henry (widr.), Dec. 14, 1846, a. 64. Found dead in bed. Born and buried in Petersham.
Mrs. Lucy [between March 11, 1831 and May 5, 1831], a. 42 y. C.R.
Lucy, w. Henry, March —, 1846, a. 55.
Mary Sprague, d. William and Nancy, Nov. 20, 1843, a. 26 y. 8 d. Bleeding at Lungs.
Myra L., d. George W. and Hannah F., Aug. 23, 1848, a. 3 m. 24 d. G.S.1.

ATHOL DEATHS.

JONES, Edwin, s. Prescott and Jane, Oct. 1, 1813, a. 2 y. 2 m. 15 d.
Jane, wid. Prescott, May 26, 1835, [a. 66, G.S.3.].
Prescott, h. Jane, April 19, 1828, [a. 57, G.S.3.].
Sarah, d. Amos and Lydia, April 1, 1795, a. 10 y. 1 m. 20 d.
[Mrs.] Sarah, Feb. 5, 1815, [in 65th y., G.S.3.].
William Augustus, s. Prescott and Jane Nov. 4, 1813, a. 8 y. 14 d.

JONSON (see Johnson), ———, s. Enock ?, Aug. 25, 1848. Dysentery.

KELTON (see Kilton), Abigail, wid. Thomas, Sept. 24, 1842.
Calvin, h. Hepzibah, Sept. 16, 1842, [a. 68, G.S.2.].
Dolly, w. John, Jan. 22, 1848, a. 77.
George, Aug. 16, 1813, a. 86 y. C.R.
John W., h. Electa, March 16, 1828, [a. 39, C.R.].
Jonathan (widr.), April 23 [24, G.S.1.], 1849, a. 83. Fever.
Jonathan, Nov. 21, 1804, a. 74 y. C.R.
Wid. Lidea, March 5, 1821, a. 82 y. C.R.
Margaret, d. Calvin and Hepzibah, Jan. 3 [1, C.R.], 1814, a. 10 y. 9 m. 15 d.
Samuel, June 26, 1821, a. 29. G.S.3.
Thomas, May 5, 1829, a. 65 y. C.R.
———, ch. James, Oct. 3, 1779. C.R.
———, w. James, July 4, 1824, a. 60 y. C.R.

KENDALL (see Kendell, Kindall), Abigail [Batcheller], w. Calvin, Feb. 2, 1845, a. 70 y. 4 m. 25 d. Disease of heart. Born in Royalston.
Abigail B., d. Calvin Jr. and Lydia, Aug. 22, 1835, a. 2 y. 1 m. 17 d.
Abigail Balch, d. Joel and Sall, Feb. 10 [13, C.R.], 1829, [a. 29, G.S.3.].
Alfred [W.], s. Wyman, June 18 [16 ?], 1849, a. 18. Consumption.
Anna, d. Jesse and Elisabeth, Aug. 30, 1777, a. 2 y. 3 m. 26 d.
Anna, d. Joel and Sall, Feb. 1, 1813, [a. 18, C.R.].
Wid. Anna, Nov. 3, 1824, a. 82 y. C.R.
Deborah, d. Seth and Deborah, Nov. 28, 1763. C.R.
Deborah, wid. Seth, Oct. 22, 1791.
Elizabeth, wid. Dea. Jesse, June 22 [20], 1813, [in 81st y., G.S.3.].
Francis, s. Amos and ———, Sept. 23, 1777. C.R.
Francis E., s. Joel and Sally, Jan. 17, 1822, a. 18. G.S.3.
Francis Evens, s. Lyman and Hannah, Oct. 24, 1825, a. 1 m. 28 d.
Jane Rebecca, d. Joel and Rebecca, July 4, 1835, a. 5 y. 6 m. 9 d.
Jane Rebecca, d. Joel and Rebecca, Oct. 19, 1837, a. 6 m. 28 d.
Dea. Jesse, April [14], 1797, [in 70th y., G.S.3. 61, C.R.].

KENDALL, Joel, h. Sall, May 22, 1834, [a. 72, G.S.3.].
Joel Chase, s. Joel and Rebecca, Jan. 22, 1842, a. 2 y. 2 m. 13 d.
Jonathan, h. Anna, July 8, 1817, [a. 74, C.R.].
Joseph, s. Joel and Rebecca, Dec. 15, 1832, a. 11 m. 11 d.
The widow Lidea, Oct. —, 1791. C.R.
Lucy, d. Seth and Olive, Nov. 8, 1802, a. 27 d.
Maria Sterling, d. Lyman and Hannah, July 7, 1835, a. 1 y. 7 m. 16 d.
Molle, d. Jonathan and Anna, Aug. 19, 1777. C.R.
Olive, w. Seth, Oct. 31, 1802, [a. 27 y., C.R.].
Raymond, March 29, 1819, a. 19 y. C.R.
Royal, s. Seth and Olive, Oct. 9, 1802, a. 1 y. 11 m. 7 d.
Sally, d. Jona., July 28, 1795, a. 12 y. C.R.
Sally, w. Joel, Jan. 25, 1822, a. 55. G.S.3.
Seth, h. Deborah, July 5, 1790.
Seth Jr., Sept. 9, 1806, a. 36 y. 4 m. 9 d. "By a flash of Lightning." Dup.
Stephen, s. John and Susanna, Oct. 31 [Nov. 1, C.R.], 1799, a. 8 m. 15 d.
Susan, d. John, Feb. 2, 1822, a. 2 y. 3 m. C.R.
Susanna, w. John, —— —, ——. [June 1, 1827, a. 53, C.R.]
Thomas, June 24, 1824, a. 28 y. C.R.
Timothy, h. Rebeckah, Oct. 20, 1805, [a. 64, C.R.].
———, d. Jonathan and Anna, Dec. 28, 1765, a. about 2 w. C.R.
———, ch. Calven, May 27, 1820, a. 4 y. C.R.

KENDELL (see above), Mary Elizabeth, d. Albert and Caroline, April 7, 1842, a. 2 y. 8 m. G.S.3.

KEYES, Henry L., s. Seth, April 27, 1846, a. 1 y. 1 m. 2 d. Consumption on lungs. Born in Conway.

KIDDER, Harriet Jane, d. John and Maria E., June 24 [21, G.S.2.], 1843, a. 5 m. 13 d. Scarlet fever.
Joseph, s. Jonathan and Nancy R., Feb. 27, 1842, a. 21 d.
Nancy R., w. Jonathan, Aug. 18, 1845, a. 46 y. 1 m. 2 d. Consumption.
Sylvia, d. Jonathan and Nancy R., Aug. 14, 1840, a. 10 y. 9 m. 21 d.

KILTON (see Kelton), James, s. James and Sally, Oct. 9, 1799, a. 1 y. 3 m. 28 d.
Jane, Nov. 2, 1829, a. 69 y. C.R.
John, s. Jonathan and Margeret, April 28, 1778. C.R.
Lucas, s. Jonathan and Margeret, March —, 1778, in the Southern army. C.R.

ATHOL DEATHS.

KILTON, Margret, w. Jonathan, Dec. 14, 1817, [a. 82, c.r.].
Reuben, s. George and Lydia, June 22, 1777. C.R.
———, s. Jonathan and Margeret Kilton, Feb. 1, 1777. C.R.

KIMPLAND, Jemima, w. William, June 10, 1762. C.R.
———, s. William and Caterine, Aug. 20, 1773. C.R.

KINDALL (see Kendall) Rebeckah, w. Timothy, June 1, 1776.

KING, Ira [Jno ?], April 6, 1848, a. 80.
Mary E., d. Isaac and Polly, July 10, 1823, a. 8 m. 11 d. At New Salem ?.

KNEELAND, Lucy W., d. Leonard and Sylvia, Jan. 25, 1842, a. 7 y. 7 m. 21 d. Scarlet fever.

KNIGHT (see Knights, Night), Ebenezer, May 18, 1814, a. 91 y. C.R.
Isaac, Jan. 15, 1809, a. 56 y. C.R.
Mary, w. Ebenezer, Jan. 27, 1772. C.R.
———, w. Isaac, May 30, 1801. C.R.
———, ch. Abraham, May 27, 1805, a. 4 y. C.R.
———, w. Ebenezer, Sept. 20, 1807, a. 78 y. C.R.
———, ch. Isaac and wife, Feb. 1, 1801, a. 9 m. Consumption. C.R.

KNIGHTS (see above), Lucy, d. Ebenezer and Mary, Aug. 17, 1772. C.R.
Submit, d. Ebenezer and Mary, May 18, 1772. C.R.
———, ch. Isaac and ———, March 8, 1792. C.R.

KNOWLTON, Charles Henry, s. Stillman and Lydia, Feb. 20, 1842, a. 13 y. 6 m. 13 d.
Lydia, w. Stillman, Jan. 28, 1831.

LAMB, Rebeckah, Oct. 24, 1818. C.R.

LANE, Annis, Aug. 15, 1825, a. 18 [19, G.S.1.], of Swansy, N.H. C.R.
William, s. Alvinza, Aug. 19, 1842. Dup.

LARRIBEE, Susanna Giles, w. Artemas B., d. Asa and Susanna Stratton, Oct. 30, 1841, a. 26 y. 6 m. 15 d.

LAWRENCE, Mrs. ———, Aug. 21, 1849, a. 26.

LEE, George H., s. William D. Jr. and Sarah, April 28, 1846, a. 4 y. 4 m. 5 d. Croup.

ATHOL DEATHS. 207

LEE, George Henry, s. William D. and Lydia H., Dec. 20, 1836, a. 22 y. 1 m. 27 d.
Harriet Chastine, d. William D. and Lydia H., July 1, 1835, a. 5 y. 1 m. 4 d.
Harriot M., d. William D. and Lydia H., Oct. 15, 1819, a. 1 y. 6 m. G.S.3.
Harriet Maria, d. William D. and Lydia H., Oct. 15, 1820, a. 2 y. 6 m. 20 d. [Perhaps same as above.]
Henry, s. Henry and Nancy, Sept. 12, 1825, a. 3 m. 15 d.
Henry (married), July 29, 1845, a. 59 y. 1 m. 18 d. Bowel complaint. Born in Marlborough, and died in Hospital at Worcester.
Jonathan, April 17, 1833, in 75th y. G.S.1.
Samuel, s. Henry and Nancy, April 30 [May 1, C.R.], 1834, a. 2 y. 5 m. G.S.1.
William Dexter, s. William D. and Lydia H., Sept. 2, 1815, a. 2 y. 5 m. 25 d.

LEWIS, Abijah, at Cambridge in the Army, s. William and Mary, May 29, 1776. C.R.
Hiram G., s. Hiram Jr. and Hannah, Sept. 24, 1849, a. 2 y. 12 d. Dysentery.
Olive, w. Thomas, Aug. 10, 1814, [a. 51 y. C.R.].
Rice, Jan. 30, 1816, a. 16 y. C.R.
Sally, d. William and Sarah, Jan. —, 1792, a. about 18 m.
Sally, w. William, May 3, 1827, a. 70 y. C.R.
Samuel, twin s. William and Sarah, Jan. 30, 1816, in 17th y.
Sarah, w. William, May 3, 1827.
Thomas, March 20, 1814, a. probably 80 y. C.R.
William, Oct. 30, 1802, a. 83 y. C.R.
William, widr. Sarah, Oct. 11, 1829, [a. 66, C.R.].
———, ch. Wm., Jan. 1, 1805, a. 10 m. C.R.
———, the widow, Feb. 22, 1805, a. 86 y. C.R.
———, [Cordelia A.], d. Hiram and Hannah, H., Sept. 9, 1846, a. 2 y. [3 d., G.S.2.].

LINCOLN, Arianna G., w. Eustus M., —— —, 1837. G.S.2.
Henry Clay, s. Amasa, July 30, 1845, a. 16 [and 5 m., G.S.2.]. Drowned in Chickopee River in Springfield.
Otis Lysander, s. Amasa and Zilpha, Nov. 27, 1815, a. 1 y. 11 m. 6 d.
Zilpha, w. Amasa, June 10 [9, G.S.], 1836, [a. 51 y. 6 m., G.S.2.].
———, w. Thomas, July 20, 1805. C.R.

LINES, ———, ch. Wm. Jr., Jan. 12, 1793. C.R.

LOMBARD (see Lumbard), James Jr., s. James and Thankfull, May 15, 1774. C.R.
James, Feb. 15, 1812, a. 80 y. C.R.
Janny, d. James and Thankfull, Sept. 3, 1778. C.R.
Wid. Thankfull, Dec. 28, 1818, a. 85 y. C.R.

LONGLEY, John, h. Olive, Aug. 27, 1835, [a. 42, C.R.].

LORD, Lt. Aaron, Aug. 8, 1798, in 32d y. G.S.3.
Abel, s. Thomas and Leonard, July 26, 1770. C.R.
Abel, Oct. 3, 1799. C.R.
Absalom, May 16, 1846, a. 56. Chronic Rheumatism.
Cyrell C., Sept. 21, 1847, a. 58.
Hannah, d. William and Mary, Aug. 21, 1765. C.R.
Hiram, s. Absalom and Clarissa, June 18 [27, C.R.], 1830, a. 7 m.
John, s. Stephen and Mary, Aug. 22, 1774. C.R.
Leonard ? Smith, wid. Capt. Thomas, —— —, 1821, a. 77. G.S.1.
Nancy Young, w. Gardner, Jan. 25, 1814, [a. 25, C.R.].
Nancy Young, d. Gardner and Nancy, Aug. 14, 1833, a. 19 y. 7 m.
Rhoda, d. Thomas and Leonard, Jan. 30, 1766. C.R.
Stephen, s. Stephen and Mary, Jan. 26, 1764, a. 3 y. 7 m. 11 d.
Sumner Young, s. Gardner, March 13, 1823, a. 7 y. Scalde. C.R.
Capt. Thomas, a soldier in the French and Indian and Revolutionary Wars, —— —, 1810, a. 84. G.S.1. [Dec. 3, a. 75, C.R.]
——— —, inf. Thomas, March 1, 1811. C.R.

LUCAS, James, Oct. 13 [14], 1822, a. 80, [84, C.R.] G.S.3.

LUCUS, Mary, April 26, 1817, a. 75 y. C.R.

LUMBARD (see Lombard), Salle, d. James and Thankfull, Sept. 13, 1777. C.R.

McMANEY, Margaret C., w. James, Sept. 4, 1849, a. 19. Buried in Worcester.

McMANY, ———, d. James and Margarett, Sept. 19, 1849, a. 5 m. Buried in Worcester.

MALLORY, Elisabeth, w. Charles, July 12, 1849, a. 29. Fever.
Elisabeth, d. Charles and Elisabeth, July 27, 1849, a. 14 d.

MANLEY, Betsey, w. Obed, Oct. 11, 1841.

MARBLE, Hannah, April 26 [28], 1812, [a. 29 y. C.R.].
Wid. Lidia, Dec. 21, 1826, a. 79 y. C.R.

ATHOL DEATHS. 209

MARBLE, Moses, Oct. 18, 1796, a. 51 y. C.R.
Robert, Feb. 17, 1791, in the 84 y. C.R.

MARS, Silvia Gordon, w. Rev. John N., Dec. —, 1838, a. 29. G.S.2.

MARSH, Amos A., s. Peter H. and Sally, Feb. 23, 1846, a. 1 y. 9 m. 20 d. Croup. Buried in Barre.
Emma Louisa, d. Hiram and Sabra Ann, July 10, 1844, a. 1 y. 2 m. 27 d. Cholera Morbus. Born in East Windsor, Vt.
Julia J., d. Peter and Sally, Feb. 26, 1846, a. 3 y. 3 m. 26 d. Born and buried in Barre.
———, s. Peter H. and Sally, Dec. 16, 1845, a. 2 d.

MARVEL, Abijah, s. Silas and Katarine, Sept. 13, 1768. C.R.

MATHEWS, Emily, R., w. Nelson, Oct. 20, 1849, a. 32. Dysentery.

MAYHEW, Emerson, Aug. 31, 1819, a. 33. G.S.3.
Miss Sally, Jan. 29, 1825, a. 32. G.S.3.

MAYO, Emerson, Aug. 31, 1819, a. 33 y. C.R.
Sally, Jan. 29, 1825, a. 32 y. C.R.

MEACHAM, Francis Orator, s. Orator and Anderson, March 27, 1842, a. 10 m. 3 d. G.S.6.
Mary Ann, w. William, March 11, 1843, a. 27. G.S.6.
Mary Elizabeth, d. William and Mary, March 22, 1840, a. 2 y. 10 m. G.S.6.
William, Aug. 8, 1845, a. 55. G.S.6.

MEACHUM, Polly, w. William, Dec. 1, 1833, a. 41. G.S.3.
———, wid. ———, April 7, 1849, a. 57.

MELLER [Mellen ?], John, Feb. 1, 1848, a. 21.

MENDALL, Wid. Mary, Oct. 28, 1822, a. 71 y. C.R.

MENDEL, Mehetable, w. Barnabus, Oct. 11, 1811, a. 30 y. C.R.

MENDELL, Barnabas, July 8, 1833, a. 55. G.S.2.
Mary, Oct. 28, 1811, a. 70. G.S.2.
Paul, Jan. 7, 1807, a. 50. G.S.2.

MERIAM, Salmon N., Jan. 26, 1843.

MILES, ———, inf. Clough K., Feb. 10, 1827, a. 1 d. C.R.

MILLER, Joseph Henry, s. Thomas and Mary [Mary Ann, G.S.3.], Oct. 12, 1842, a. 1 y. 10 m. 6 d.
———, ch. Joseph, Feb. 1, 1824, a. 3 y. C.R.
———, ch. John, Jan. 27, 1829, a. 3 w. C.R.

MOOR, Jane, Feb. 24, 1813, a. 19 y. C.R.

MOORE, Anna, w. Samuel, Dec. 28, 1828, [a. 62, G.S.2.].
Caroline L., d. Joseph P., Sept. 22, 1844, a. 5 m. 23 d. Inflamation of Brain.
Daniel, s. Chandler Wright and Susan, ——— —, 1846, in 1st y. G.S.1.
Daniel, s. Chandler Wright and Susan, ——— —, 1847. G.S.1.
Daniel, s. Daniel, Oct. 9, 1848, a. 24. Fever.
Henry Kirk, s. Peter and Lucy H., May 28, 1842, a. 3 y. 10 m. 1 d. G.S.2.
John (married), March 27, 1845. Fits. Born in Orange and buried there. [a. 56, G.S.1.]
Octavo M., d. Joseph P. and Susa, July 4, 1849, a. 3. Dysentery. [a. 2 y. 4 m. 11 d., G.S.2.]
Permelia, d. Jonathan and Caroline, Sept. 22, 1849, a. 22. Dysentery.
Samuel, Sept. 17, 1841, [a. 76, G.S.2.]. Dup.
———, s. William, Sept. 26, 1846, a. 10. Croup.
———, s. Chandler W., Oct. 5, 1846, a. 5 m. Dysentary.
———, d. William, Nov. 9, 1846, a. 11. Croup.

MORSE, Abigail, d. William Jr. and Charlotte, Dec. 23, 1809, a. 16.
Alma R., d. William and Phila, Sept. 17, 1837, a. 14. G.S.3.
Anne, w. Samuel, Dec. 28, 1828, a. 62 y. C.R.
Charles, s. William and Phila, June 19 [20, C.R.], 1830, a. 2 y. 5 m. 19 d.
Charles, s. William and Sally, Sept. 9, 1848, a. 6 m.
Mrs. Charlotte, Dec. 18, 1832, a. 64 y. C.R.
Denison, s. Joseph and Jemima, Aug. 14, 1773. C.R.
Eleanor A., d. Samuel and Ruth, Aug. 25, 1834, a. 2. C.R.3.
Henry F., s. Henry, Jan. 12, 1849, a. 28. Consumption.
Joseph, Sept. 18, 1777. He was killed in the fight att Still Water. C.R.
Mary, wid. William, Feb. 6, 1830, [a. 88, C.R.].
Nancy, w. S. [Sumner] R., April 19, 1848, a. 37.
Paul, Jan. 25, 1841, a. 61. G.S.3.
Phila, w. William, June 7, 1835 [a. 35, G.S.3.]
Phila Jane, d. William and Phila, April 29, 1833, a. 10 m. 5 d.

ATHOL DEATHS.

Morse, Reuben, s. Samuel and Deborah, Oct. 31, 1799, a. 17 d.
Reubin, s. Samuel and Deborah, Oct. 7 [8, c.r.], 1801, a. 1 y. 21 d.
Sally, d. Wm. and ———, April 4, 1795, a. 9 y. c.r.
Sally, w. Samuel, Dec. 16, 1797.
Sally, d. Paul and Sally, Sept. 11, 1805, a. 1 y. 8 m. 24 d.
Sally, w. Paul; Aug. 29, 1838, a. 54. g.s.3.
Sally, d. William and Phila, Aug. 11, 1842, a. 18 y. 4 m. 17 d.
Sarah, d. widow, June 25, 1819, a. 17 y. c.r.
Sumner, s. Paul and Sally, March 10, 1808, a. 1 y. 4 m. 10 d. [16 m. 13 d., g.s.3.]
William Jr., June 5, 1810, a. 43 y. c.r.
William, Nov. 25, 1826, a. 87. g.s.3. [Perhaps same as below.]
William, Dec. 2, 1826, a. 88 y., who lived with his wife 63 y. c.r.
William, h. Mary, Nov. 29, 1827.
———, ch. Samuel, March 20, 1795. c.r.
———, ch. Samuel and wife, Dec. 9, 1797. c.r.
———, inf. of Samuel, Nov. 1, 1799. c.r.
———, w. Wm., June 7, 1835, a. 35 y. c.r.
———, s. Levi Jr., Jan. 18, 1847, a. 1 m. 6 d. Found dead in bed.
———, inf. William Jr., Feb. 15, 1847.
———, ch. William and Sally, Sept. 5, 1847, a. 6 m.

MORTON, Wid. Alice, Feb. 24, 1814, [a. 75 y., c.r.].
Anna, w. Joel, March 2. 1828, [a. 54 y., c.r.].
Austine J., March 8, 1833, a. 6 m. g.s.2.
Azubah, Nov. 3, 1814, a. 23 y. c.r.
Azubah third, w. Joshua, Nov. 30, 1823, a. 62 y. c.r.
Benjamin Freeman, s. Reubin and Judath, Jan. 22, 1802, a. nearly 6.
Betsey, d. Rhuben and ———, April 9, 1795, a. 10 y. c.r.
Electa, w. Daniel, March 9, 1845, a. 77 y. 8 m. 23 d. Lung fever.
Esther, d. Lemuel and Esther, Oct. 20, 1778. c.r.
Fanny Almeda, d. Daniel and Electa, Oct. 15, 1810, a. 5 y. 8 m. 15 d.
Gadweight [Gad Wait, c.r.], s. Martin and Jerusha, March 18, 1770, a. 2 y. 3 d.
Gilbert, July 27, 1799. c.r.
Hannah Graves, d. Daniel and Electa, March 28, 1814, a. 12 y. 15 d.
Huldah, wid. [Phinehas], May 12 [11, g.s.1.], 1825, a. 60 y. c.r.
Jeremiah, h. Alice, Nov. 30, 1781, [a. 48, g.s.3.].
Joel (married), Feb. 10, 1845, a. 74 y. 4 m. 29 d. Dropsy.
John, s. Jeremiah and Alice, Jan. 13, 1816, in 39th y. [41st y., g.s.3.]
Joshua Jr., s. Joshua and Azubah, Dec. 28, 1777. c.r.
Dr. Joshua, Feb. 13, 1827, in 83d y. g.s.1.
Julius, s. Abner and Sophia, Sept. 23, 1773. c.r.

ATHOL DEATHS.

MORTON, Widow Lidea, Oct. 1, 1804, a. 93 y. C.R.
Lydia, d. Joshua and Azubah, Sept. 29, 1776. C.R.
Margerett, Feb. 3, 1825, a. 87 y. C.R.
    "In Oct. 1, 1738, the first female born in this Town. C.R."
Mary, d. Phinehas and Huldah, Aug. 7, 1803, a. 2 y. 3 m. 14 d.
Noah, March 17, 1798, a. 79 y. C.R.
Noah, Feb. 16 [18, C.R.], 1827, a. 23. G.S.1.
Olive Fairbanks, d. Daniel and Electa, Dec. 18, 1813, a. 19 y. 10 m. 4 d.
Phinehas, h. Huldah, Dec. 21, 1810, [a. 59, C.R.].
Rebecca, w. Joshua, Oct. 5, 1813, a. 55 y. C.R.
Reubin, h. Judath, July 30, 1835.
Rhoda, d. Hannah, now w. Samuel ———, June 28, 1803, a. 18. C.R.
Wid. Rhoda, Feb. 9, 1819, a. 97 y. C.R.
Leut Richard, Jan. 1, 1772. C.R.
Samuel, Jan. 3, 1793[4 ?] in the 85 y. C.R.
Socrates, s. Dr. J. and ———, March 29, 1795. C.R.
Thomas, s. Samuel and Lydia, Nov. 20, 1756. C.R.
——— (Mr. or Mrs. ?), Jeremiah, Nov. 30, 1781. C.R.
———, ch. Dr. and Rebecca, May 4, 1788, a. 57 d. C.R.
———, inf. ch. Dr. Joshua and ———, Dec. 22, 1794. C.R.
———, inf. Dr., Dec. —, 1795. C.R.
———, ch. Dr., June 1, 1798. C.R.
———, ch. Phinehas, Aug. 13, 1803. C.R.
———, w. Ruben, Aug. 21, 1803, a. 50 y. C.R.
———, ch. Dr., Sept. 22, 1804, a. 5 y. C.R.

MOULTON, Wesley Asbury, s. Aaron and Elenor, Dec. 26, 1836, a. 3 y. 6 m. 19 d.

MUZZY, Miss Sarah, Jan. 23, 1816, a. 22. G.S.1.

MYRICK, [Merick in [C.R.], Rhoda, w. Joshua, Nov. 27, 1798.
Thomas E., [Thomas Eaton Mireck in C.R.], drowned July 27, 1820, a. 13. G.S.3.

NEWHALL, Chaney, s. Joshua and Polly, Feb. 13, 1796, a. 1 y. 8 m. 5 d.
George, s. Joshua and Polly, March 31, 1842, a. 50 y. 5 d.
George, h. Mary, ——— —, ———. At Amherst.
Hiram, s. Hiram and Jerusha, June 4, 1795, in 15th y. [14th y., C.R.]
Hiram Esq., Sept. 21, 1816, [a. 78 y. C.R.].

NEWHALL, Jerusha, w. Hiram, Sept. 16, 1807, a. 50 y. C.R.
Joshua, July 14, 1825, [a. 55., G.S.I.].
Lucy, d. Hiram and Jerusha, Oct. 11, 1793, a. 1 y. 7 m. 8 d.
Lucy Maria, d. Samuel and Betsey, Nov. 30, 1842, [1841, G.S.I.], a. 2 y. 2 m. 15 d.
Mary, w. George, March 10, 1835, [a. 43 y. 26 d. G.S.I.].
Olive, d. Hiram and Jerusha, June 15, 1795, in 6th y.
Sarah, w. Hiram, June 24, 1778.
———, ch. Joshua, Feb. 14, 1795, a. about 2 y. C.R.

NEWTON, ———, inf. Ward, Sept. 21, 1827, a. 5 w. C.R.

NICHOLS, ———, Mr. Nov. 30, 1795, a. 75 y. C.R.

NICKERSON, Harrison, s. Col. Nathan and Hannah, Sept. 9, [8, C.R.], 1822, a. 2 y. 4 m. G.S.I.

NIGHT (see Knight), Isaac, Nov. 7, 1800, a. 19 y. C.R.
Lucy, d. Isaac, Oct. 19, 1800. C.R.

NORTON, Jonathan, Feb. 20, 1811, a stranger at the widow Morton's, aged, as he said, 80. C.R.

NUTT, Grace, w. Abraham, Nov. 11, 1756. C.R.
Jerusha, w. Abraham Jr., April 28, 1795.
———, inf. ch. Abraham and Grace, Aug. 1, 1752. C.R.
———, inf. ch. Abraham and Grace, ———, 1756. C.R.
———, d. Abraham and Sarah, Aug. 9, 1760, a. 1 d. C.R.
———, widow, Aug. 15, 1808, a. 82 y. C.R.

NYE, Samuel, Feb. 15, 1848, a. 26.

OAKS, Joanna, w. Abraham, Nov. 9, 1841.
Lucy [2d], w. Ira, Aug. 4 [5], 1841, [a. 39. G.S.2.].
Mary A. S., d. Abraham and Mary Ann, Oct. 7, 1831, a. 13 m. G.S.2.
Mary, w. Ira, April 24, 1838, a. 36. G.S.2.
Sirley, s. Ira and Mary, April 19, 1838, a. 11 d. G.S.2.
———, ch. John, Nov. 15, 1813, a. 2 y. C.R.

OLDS, Chloe I., d. Warren and Harriet, Sept. 5, 1849, a. 8. Dysentery.

OLIVER, Aaron, s. Capt. John, one of the first settlers of Athol, ———, [Jan. 3, C.R.], 1826, a. 77. G.S.I.
Aaron, s. James and Hannah, Aug. 17, 1831, a. 27 y. 3 m. 15 d.
Mrs. Ann, w. Leut William, Nov. 9, 1778. C.R.

OLIVER, Calvin H., —— ——, ——. [Jan. 29, 1824, a. 43, C.R.]
Charles s. Rhoda, —— ——, [Feb. 13, C.R.], 1826, a. 14 [13, C.R.].
    G.S.1.
Cinda, d. James and Hannah, Oct. 26 [25, C.R.], 1809, a. 3 y. lacking 4 d.
Cornwell, s. George and Rhoda, Dec. 26, 1804, a. 2 y. 2 m. 13 d.
Daniel, s. William and Anna, June 2, 1760. C.R.
Daniel, s. Robart and Lydia, Jan. 14 [Feb. 13, C.R.], 1774, in 13th y.
Deborah White, 2d w. George, —— ——, 1830, a. 51. G.S.1.
Frank, s. Franklin and Emily E., Oct. 14, 1800 ?, a. 2 y. 1 m. 1 d. G.S.2.
Franklin, s. Franklin, and Emily Eaton, Oct. 14, 1840, a. 2 y. 1 m. 1 d.
George, eldest s. Aaron, —— ——, 1842, a. 67. G.S.1.
George Sidney, s. James and Minevia, —— ——, 1843. G.S.2.
Hannah, wid. James, Sept. 9, 1849, a. 69. Dysentery.
James Jr., s. William and Anna Jr., Sept. 13, 1777. C.R.
Lieut. James, Jan. 28 [25, C.R.], 1790, in 64th y. G.S.3.
James, h. Hannah, May 7, 1829, [a. 51, C.R.].
James Durham, s. Robart and Lydia, Jan. 4, [3, C.R.] 1774, in 9th y.
Jenny, d. William and Ann, June 5, 1766, at Rutland. C.R.
Jenny, d. William and Anna Jr., Sept. 3, 1777. C.R.
John, Dec. 23, 1811, a. 87 y. C.R.
John, s. John and Mary, Dec. 23, 1811, a. 45 y. 21 d.
Lucinda, d. James and Hannah, July 20, 1814, a. 8 m. 11 d.
Lucy Smith, wid. Aaron, —— ——, 1835, a. 84. G.S.1.
Mary, April 6, 1812. [Wid. ——, a. 83, C.R.]
Moses, h. Lois, July 1, 1792, [in 39th y., G.S.3.].
Nancy, d. James and Hannah, Feb. 22, 1818, a. 6 m. 16 d.
Rachel, d. John and Mary, June 28, 1766, in 11th y.
Rhoda [Young, 1st] w. George, Aug. 14, 1815, [a. 38, G.S.1.].
Rosella A., d. James and Minerva ?, —— ——, 1835. G.S.2.
Sarah, d. Moses and Lois, June 14, 1794, a. 3.
Sydney, s. James and Minerva, Sept. 14, 1843, a. 5 m. Fits. Dup.
William, s. Robart and Lydia, June 13, 1766, a. 2 y. 6 m. 23 d.
William, s. Robart and Lydia, Jan. 13, 1774, in 8th y.
William A. Aug. 11, 1831. C.R.
——, child Aaron and ——, May 17, 1795. C.R.
——, ch. widow Lowis Wiswel, June 14, 1795, a. 3 y. C.R.
——, inf. George, July 21, 1815, a. 4 d. C.R.
——, ch. James, Feb. 22, 1818, a. 6 m. C.R.

ORCUTT, Abner G., (married), s. Jonathan, Oct. 15, 1844, a. 30 y. 7 m. 10 d. Consumption.
Abner Graves, s. Jonathan and Alice, April 13 [12, C.R.], 1813, [a. 4, C.R.].
Adeline, d. Jonathan and Alice, Sept. 22, 1831.
Alice, wid., Jonathan, Aug. 8, 1842.
Alice R., d. Jonathan and Alice, Dec. 8, 1830, [a. 20, C.R.].
Azubah, d. Capt. Jonathan and Alice, Feb. 7 [8 C.R.], 1827, a. 15, G.S.3.
Jonathan, h. Alice, Oct. 8, 1841.

OSBORN, Fredrick A., s. Andrew B. and Mary, Aug. 22, 1849, a. 2 y. 1 m. Dysentery.

OSGOOD, Adaline, d. David and Polly, May 28 [29, C.R.], 1817, in 6th y.
David, h. Molly, March 3, 1815, [a. 34, C.R.].

PACKARD, ———, wid. ———, April 22, 1849, a. 81.

PAGE, Martha, wid. Dea. Nathaniel, Feb. 15, 1816, [63, C.R.].
Dea. Nathaniel, Jan. 6, 1816, [a. 79 y. C.R.].

PARKER, Lydia w. Joseph P., Dec. 22, 1841.

PARMETER, Vina, w. Oliver, April 25, 1795. C.R.

PARTRIDGE, Elizabeth, w. Ziba, June 10, 1848, a. 82. G.S.1.

PEABODY, Sally, w. Kitteridge [Isaac K., C.R.], July 28, 1821, [a. 27, C.R.].

PEBODY, John, Nov. 15, 1806, a. 18 y. C.R.

PERRY, Tyler, March 25, 1836.

PERY [Perry ?], Caleb (married), Oct. 22, 1849, a. 76. Brain Feaver.

PETTS, ———, Mr. or Mrs. ? ———, Dec. 30, 1803, a. 72 y. C.R.

PHELEPS, ——— Mr., Jan. 2, 1810, a. 83 y. C.R.
———, ch. Jonas A. and Abigal, Oct. 27, 1848.

PHILLIPS, Leander, s. Jonas A. and Abigail B., Nov. —, 1849, a. 4 d. G.S.2.
Samuel, April 19, 1796, in 48 y. C.R.
William J., s. Jonas A. and Abigail B., Dec. 25, 1846, a. 1 m. G.S.2.

PHILLIPS, ———, child Nathaniel and ———, April —, 1795. C.R.
———, s. Jonas A., Dec. 25, 1846, a. 1 m.

PIERCE, Franklin, h. Eleanor, Aug. 13, 1830.
Joel Meri———, ———, ———. G.S.3.
Joseph, h. Eleanor, March 12, 1835, [a. 78, C.R.].
Mary, w. James, d. Kimbal and Mary Wood, Nov. 2, 1788, a. 22 y. 3 m. 10 d.
William Crawford, s. Franklin and Eleanor, June 2, 1818, a. 4 m. 5 d.

PIKE, Lucinda, w. William, Oct. 4, 1849, a. 60.

POWERS, Mrs. Rebecca, Nov. 28, 1829, a. 93 y. C.R.

PRESSON, Mary, d. Percide [Perside, C.R.] ? and Martha, Feb. 3, 1809, a. 23 d.

PROCTOR, Anne Maria, d. Joseph and Mary H., July 11, 1828, a. 16 y. 4 m. 26 d.
Charles, s. Joseph and Mary H., Feb. 22, 1816, a. 2 m. 17 d.
Joseph, h. Mary H., ——— —, ———. [Perhaps same as next below.]
Joseph Esq., Aug. 6, 1822, a. 56. G.S.3.
Mary Ann, d. Wid. Mary, July 11, 1828, a. 16 y. C.R.
Mary H., wid. Joseph, July 9, 1840, a. 51. G.S.3.
———, inf. Joseph Esq., March 2, 1819, a. 2 d. C.R.

PROUTY, Frances M., d. Adam and Hannah, Sept. 9, 1829, a. 2 m. 25 d.
George C., s. Adam and Hannah, July 29, 1832, a. 7 m. 15 d.
George P., s. Adam and Hannah, March 25, 1837, a. 8 m. 23 d.
Hannah, w. Adam, Oct. 19, 1844, a. 40 y. 2 m. 23 d. Typhus fever. Born in Sterling.

PUTNAM, Bela W., h. Alice, April 12, 1842, [a. 36 y. 9 m., G.S.5.].
Joel Morton, s. Bela W. and Alice, killed by a kick from a horse, ——— —, ———.

RANDALL, Adison F., s. Capt. Stephen and Lois, Oct. 6, 1822, a. 21 m. G.S.1.
Alexander H., s. Capt. Stephen and Lois, Sept. 27, 1822, a. 4 y. 4 m. G.S.1.
Asa L., s. Capt. Stephen and Lois, May 12, 1812, a. 8 m. 10 d. G.S.1.
———, ch. ———, May 11, 1812, a. 8 m. C.R.

RAYMOND, Wid. Abigail, Dec. 21, 1814, a. 84 y. C.R.
Elizabeth, July 17, 1813, a. 34 y. C.R.

RAYMOND, Freeborn F., s. Freeborn Jr. and Jain, Sept. 23, 1808, a. 1 y. 10 m. 21 d.
Lois, w. Freeborn Jr., June 6, 1800.
Lucinda, w. Freeborn Jr., April — [12], 1788, [in 20th y., G.S.3.].
Mary, w. Freeborn, May 15, 1777. C.R.
Nathan, s. Edward and ———, June 23, 1776. C.R.
Wyman G., Sept. 24, 1827, a. 39 y. C.R.
———, ch. Freeborn, Feb. 24, 1792, a. 6 m. C.R.
———, ch. Freeborn and ———, Sept. 23, 1794. C.R.
———, ch. Freeborn and wife, July 19, 1800, a. 5 y. C.R.

RAYNER, ———, s. J. S., April. 5, 1847, a. 20 d.

RICE, Ellen M., d. James M. and Clara ?, Sept. 5, 1849, a. 1 y. 10 m. 13 d. Dysentry.
Lucinda Faustina, d. Jonas and Olive, Oct. 23, 1841, a. 3 y. 1 m. 10 d.
Nancy, w. Samuel, Oct. 24 [25, C.R.], 1807.
Persis, d. Adonijah and Tamar, Feb. 6, 1777. C.R.
Rachel, w. Uriah, Sept. 7, 1777. C,R.
———, ch. Aaron, May 29, 1847, a. 2 m.

RICH, Hannah, d. David and Hannah, Oct. 27, 1799.
Jonathan, ——— ———, 1776, d. at York. He went out in the Militia a soldier. C.R.
Joseph, (widr.), Jan. 30 [29, G.S.2.], 1849, a. 77.
Maria, w. Joseph, April 17, 1846, a. 72 y. 9 m. 22 d. Dropsy of Heart. Born in Littleton.
Nellie, w. Joseph, Aug. 14, 1841, a. 44. G.S.2.
Recta, d. Joseph [and Maria], Sept. 11, 1847, a. 47. Consumption.
———, ch. David and wife, Sept. 10, 1799, a. 5 m. C.R.
———, Wid. Zacheus, March 22, 1817, a. 77 y. C.R.

RICHARDSON, Charles Orwell, s. Wyman and Arethusa, Sept. 26, 1840, a. 10 m. 13 d.
Hamilton, twin s. Lysander and Amanda, Sept. 15, 1839, a. 4 m. G.S.1.
Hannibal, twin s. Lysander and Amanda, Sept. 15, 1839, a. 4 m. G.S.1.
Hosea B., s. Lysander and Amanda, Jan. 4, 1841, a. 6. G.S.1.
Ruben, Sept. 8, 1825, a. 41 y. C.R.
———, ch. Isaiah, ———, April 1, 1791, a. 9 m. C.R.
———, the widow, Jan. 4, 1798. C.R.
———, inf. s. L., Aug. 28, 1844. Dysentary.

RIPLEY, ———, d. S. F., Feb. 24, 1847, a. 1. Consumption.

ROBBINS (see Robins), Lucy, d. Luke and Mary, Jan. 23, 1792, a. 4 y. 1 m. G.S.3.
Luke, March 21, 1836, a. 86. G.S.3.
Mary H., w. Luke, March 27, 1800, a. 45. G.S.3.

ROBINS (see above), Abigail, d. Luke and ———, June 2, 1795, a. 10 ? y. C.R.
Martha, d. Luke, May 26, 1795, a. 15 ? y. C.R.

ROBINSON, ———, wid. ———, Oct. 3, 1846, a. 68. Typhoid fever. Buried in Springfield.

RUGGLES, Lydia H., w. Samuel, Aug. 22, 1827, a. 74. G.S.1.
Nansy, d. Samuel and Lydia, May 25, 1781. C.R.
Samuel, Nov. 29, 1829, a. 78. G.S.1.
———, s. Samuel and Lydia, May 20, 1777. C.R.

SANBURN, William A., s. William B. and Merriam R., Nov. 12, 1845, a. 3 m. G.S.1.

SANDERS, Cloe, d. John and Elizabeth, Sept. 16, 1776. C.R.
Elizabeth, d. John and Elizabeth, Feb. 13, 1774. C.R.
Samuel Groves, s. Benjamin and Hannah, Oct. 25, 1776. C.R.

SAWIN, ———, inf. Emory, ——— [1849 ?], a. 1 d.

SAWTELL, Richard, July 31, 1838, [a. 87, G.S.3.].
Susanna, d. Henry and Sarah, April 27, 1780. C.R.
Sarah, wid. Richard, March 5, 1846, a. 89 y. 25 d. Born in Petersham.

SAWYER, Jonathan W., ——— —, 1827. G.S.1.
Sally, d. Nathaniel and Sally, Aug. 30, 1840, a. 23. G.S.3.
———, only child Abner, Jan. 26, 1795, a. 2 y. C.R.

SCOT, Jacob, s. Samuel and Sarah, Sept. 24, 1756. C.R.
Mary, d. Samuel and Sarah, Oct. 14, 1756. C.R.
Sarah, d. Samuel and Sarah, Oct. 22, 1756. C.R.

SEDGER, William D., h. Arethusa, Sept. 27, 1838. In London, Eng.

SHATTUCK, Phebe, d. C. J., Aug. 27, 1847, a. 2.

SHEPPARD, Tyler, Sept. 12, 1849, a. 21. Dysentery. Buried in Townsend, Vt.

SIBLEY, Emaly [Emily, G.S.3.], d. Pearley and Polly, April 29, 1815, a. 2 y. 2 m. 6 d.

SIBLEY, George Perley, only s. Willard and Luthera, Oct. 11, 1847, a. 13 m. G.S.1.
Maria, d. Gideon and Elvira, Sept. 10, 1828, a. 1 y. 10 m. 25 d. [2 y. 7 m., C.R.]
Pearley, s. Pearley and Polly, Dec. 1, 1802, a. 5 m. 7 d.
Pearley, s. Pearley and Polly, Aug. 28, 1808, in 5th y. [4 y. 10 m., G.S.3.]
———, s. Willard, Oct. 11, 1847, a. 1 y. 2 m.

SIMONDS, Charles W., April 10, 1839, a. 3 y. 15 d. [s. Stillman and Elizabeth R. ?]
Henry, s. Lucius, Dec. 15, 1846, a. 3. Croup.
Joseph H., s. Lucius B. and Ann E., Dec. 15, 1846, a. 3. G.S.2.
Sarah T., d. Alben and Sarah, Sept. 5, 1849, a. 2 y. 5 m. Dysentery. [Sarah Jennette, d. Albert G., a. 5 m., G.S.2.]

SMITH, Dea. Aaron, March 9, 1798, a. 83 y. C.R.
Abigail, w. Aaron, May 13, 1769. C.R.
Asa, h. Lydia, Sept. 19, 1815 [a. 75, G.S.1, [74, C.R.]].
Charles, s. Luther and Abigail, March 1, 1826, a. 18, [17, G.S.1.].
Edward, s. Edward of New Salem, Jan. 18, 1814, [a. 24, C.R.].
Elisha Lord, s. Aaron and Tirzah, Oct. 12 [13 ?] 1802, a. 3 y. 7 m. 7 d.
Ephraim, Oct. 11, 1793, in the 82 year of his age. C.R.
George (married), s. Luther and Abigail R., Aug. 9, 1844, a. 34 y. 3 m. 27 d. Fever. Founder.
Hipzibah, d. Ephraim and Martha, Dec. 9, 1771. C.R.
Horace, s. Horace I., Sept. 12, 1849, a. 2. Dysentery.
Jonathan, Nov. 2, 1823, a. 51 y. C.R.
Joshua (married), April 3, 1846, a. 77 y. 10 m. 17 d. Consumption.
Lemira, d. Joshua and Hannah, May 16, 1806, a. 2 y. 27 d.
Lois, d. Aaron and Tirzah, Dec. 26, 1802, a. 5 y. 7 m. 21 d.
Lucy, d. Joshua and Hannah, Aug. 12, 1835, a. 29 y. 5 m. 1 d.
Luther (married), Aug. 30 [29, G.S.], 1844, [a. 60, G.S.1.]. Fever.
Lydia L., wid. Capt. Asa, Sept. 10, 1836, a. 91. G.S.1.
Martha, w. Ephraim, Dec. 18, 1775. C.R.
Mary C., w. Adin H., Jan. 22, 1842.
Moses, Dec. 6, 1776, at Ashby [?] upon his way from the army at York. C.R.
Moses, s. Mrs. Stratton, March 10, 1792, a. 18 y. C.R.
Olive F. [M. ?], w. Edward, [d. Daniel and Electa Morton], Dec. 18, 1813, [a. 20. G.S.3.].
Pamelia, d. Asa and Lydia, April 21, 1774. C.R.
Polly, d. Joshua and Hannah [Hannah F. G.S.1.], March 7 [6, G.S., 8, C.R.], 1803, a. 1 y. 1 m. 1 d.

SMITH, Rhoda, June 29, 1803, a. 18 y. c.r.
Sally Freeman, d. Nathaniel and Arathusa, March 10, 1809, in 3d y.
Stilman, s. Luther and Abigail, Nov. —, 1823, a. 8 y. 8 m.
Submit, w. Caleb, Dec. 13, 1783, a. 41 y. 1 m. 1 d.
Theodore H., s. Lynds and Fanny M., May 13, 1842, a. 11 m.
———, ch. Dea. Aaron and Mary, May 7, 1771, a. ½ h. c.r.
———, s. Dea. Aaron and Mary, March 19, 1775. c.r.
———, w. Elder [?], Sept. 11, 1802. c.r.
———, ch. Capt. Aaron and wife, Nov. 26, 1802. c.r.
———, ch. Joshua and Hannah, May 16, 1806, a. 2 y. c.r.
———, ch. Luther, Nov. 18, 1823, a. 8 y. 8 m. c.r.
———, wid. ———, July 19, 1849, a. 86. Old age.

SPOONER, Byron Flagg, s. Alden and Dolly, May 20, 1838 [*sic*].
Dolly, w. Asa, Oct. 20, 1845, a. 61. Bilious Cholic. Born in Winchendon.

SPRAGUE, Francis Henry, s. Ephraim S. and Sarah T., Oct. 19, 1841, a. 7 y. 4 m. 1 d
James Thompson, s. Ephraim S. and Sarah T., Oct. 24, 1841, a. 3 y. 10 m. 10 d. At Barre.
Phebe, w. Israel, June 13, 1782.

STEARNS, Lydia, w. Samuel, July 10, 1817.
Prosper, Oct. 18, 1823, a. 19 y. c.r.
Samuel, widr. Lydia, Dec. 3, 1817, [a. 51, c.r.].
———, ch. Saml., at Abner Stratton's, Sept. 4, 1818. c.r.

STEPHENS, Mrs. ———, July 3, 1789, was killed with the lightning. c.r.

STEVENS, Marcia, d. Isaac and Eunice Backus, June 27, 1841, a. 15 y. 3 m. 21 d. g.s.2.
Timothy, s. Jacob and ———, April 17, 1781. c.r.

STIMPSON, Abner Twichell, s. John and Tyla, Sept. 19 [21, c.r.], 1822, a. 3 y. 5 m. 3 d.
James Humphreys, s. John and Tyla, June —, 1824, a. 4 m.
Olive, d. Elias and ———, Feb. 15, 1795. a. 15 y. c.r.
Olive, Jan. 26, 1805, a. 20 y. c.r.
———, Mr., Oct. 23[?], 1801, a. 77 y. Died instantly. c.r.
———, ch. John, June 11, 1824, a. 3 m. c.r.
———, w. John, Oct. 20, 1846, a. 62. Consumption.

STOCKWELL, Elmer, [Elener] [?], April 6, 1828, a. 24 y. At Worcester. c.r.

ATHOL DEATHS. 221

STOCKWELL, Elijah, s. Ephraim and Sarah, Feb. 7, 1776. c.r.
Emmons, s. John and Catarine, Sept. 22, 1777. c.r.
Ephraim, s. Ephraim and Sarah, Oct. 1, 1764. c.r.
Jemima, w. Noah, Jan. 10, 1837, a. 82. g.s.3.
Josiah, —— —, ——. g.s.3.
Lydia, d. Ephraim and Sarah, Jan. 17, 1776. c.r.
Lawson, s. Simon and Dolley, Sept. 12, 1803, a. 3 y. 6 m. 16 d.
Lucy Ann, d. Joseph and Dorathy, Sept. 16, 1840, a. 10 y. 2 m. 28 d.
Marcy, d. Noah and Jamima, May 22, 1801, a. 9. g.s.3.
Nancy, d. Noah, Aug. 4, 1845, a. 20 y. 13 d. Consumption.
Noah, h. Polly, Sept. 9 [19], 1839, [a. 93, g.s.3.].
Noah, (married), s. Noah, Feb. 9, 1846, a. 61 y. 7 m. Consumption. Born in Sutton.
Phebe, d. Ephraim and Sarah, April 7, 1769. c.r.
Polly, Sept. 17, 1803, a. 22 y. c.r.
Rebecca, d. Noah, May 27, 1801, a. 18 y. Scarlet fever. c.r.
Sarah, d. Ephraim and Sarah, Dec. 29, 1775. c.r.
Wealthy, w. Stillman, Oct. 9, 1838, a. 38. g.s.3.
———, child Noah and wife, May 22, 1801, a. 10 y. Scarlet fever. c.r.
———, ch Simon, Sept. 12, 1803. c.r.
———, ch. Elisha, April 7, 1848, a. 4.

STONE, Nancy, d. Nathan, Aug. 12, 1844, a. 30 y. 6 m. 18 d. Suicide.
Nathan, school master, Sept. 19, 1765. c.r.
Paul, s. John and Susannah, Sept. 29, 1776. c.r.
Seneca, s. Nathan and Nancy, Feb. 27, 1813, a. 1 m. 15 d.
Seth, May 27, 1827, a. 74 y. c.r.
Timothy, s. John and Susannah, Sept. 25, 1776. c.r.
———, ch. Mr. and w., Sept. 12, 1791, a. about 4 m. c.r.
———, [George F., g.s.2.], s. Clark L., Jan. 16 [15, g.s.], 1847, a. a. 6 m. Inflamation of Bowels.

STOW, Anna, d. John and Hannah, Nov. 20, 1773. c.r.
Jonathan, s. John and Hannah, July 5, 1776. c.r.
Lydia, d. John and Hannah, Nov. 3, 1773. c.r.
Nathaniel, s. John and Hannah, Dec. 27, 1773. c.r.
Ruth, d. John and Hannah, Aug. 26, 1777. c.r.

STOWEL, ———, ch. the widow, Nov. 21, 1802, a. 3 y. c.r.

STOWELL, Charlotte A., d. Ira and Abigail, Jan. 1, 1838, a. 4 y. 6 m. g.s.3.

ATHOL DEATHS.

STRATEN (see Stratin, Straton, Stratton, Stretton), Mr. James, Oct. 22, 1775. C.R.

STRATIN, Asa, s. James and Abagail, Feb. 16, 1779. C.R.

STRATON, Elias, Feb. 11, 1806. C.R.
―――, ch. Jona. and ―――, Aug. 20, 1790. C.R.

STRATTEN, James, s. James and Abagail, July 1, 1785, a. 21 y. C.R.

STRATTON (see above and Stretton), Abel, s. Peleg and Elizabeth, Feb. 11, 1829, in 54th y.
Abel, h. Susan, s. Abel, Jan. 18, 1844, a. 34 y. 3 m. 7 d. Consumption. Born in Petersham.
Abigail, w. Ebenezer, Jan. 30 [29], 1801, [a. 31, C.R.].
Abijah, s. Ebenezer and Abigail, Aug. 1, 1830, a. 33 y. 2 m. 11 d.
Alexander A., ――― ―, 1835, a. 24. G.S.1.
Asa, h. Susanna, July 15, 1835.
Asa Alexander, s. Asa and Susanna, Aug. 15, 1835, in 24th y.
Carolina, w. Elias, Feb. 21, 1829, [a. 71, G.S.3.].
Charles, s. wid. Feb. 2, 1826, a. 17 y. C.R.
Clark M., s. Joseph and Alice, April 1, 1846, a. 4 m. 29 d.
Cyrus W., s. Ruben and Hannah, Feb. 23, 1849, a. 3 y. 9 m. G.S.2.
Ebenezer, h. Hannah, Sept. 14, 1835, [a. 76, G.S.6.].
Elizabeth, w. William, Feb. 4, 1821, in 67th y. G.S.1.
Elizabeth, w. Peleg, July 30, 1831.
Esther Ward, w. Jonathan, July 18, 1843. Consumption. [a. 44, G.S.6.]
Ira, s. Wm. and ―――, Feb. 26, 1795, a. 7 y. C.R.
Jabez, h. Mari, Oct. 4 [5], 1816, [a. 47, C.R.].
Jacob, s. Joseph and Dolly, Sept. 20, 1808, a. 4 y. 1 m. 27 d.
James, July 31, 1792, in 63d y. G.S.3.
James Edward, s. James and Susannah, Oct. 18, 1841, a 22 y. 2. m. 25 d.
Jerusha, d. Zebulon and Jerusha, June 10 [19 ?], 1795, a. 4 y. 9 m. G.S.3.
Jesse, s. Peleg and Elizabeth, Sept. 13, 1787, a. 4 y. 17 d.
Joel, h. Sally, Feb. 6, 1837, while on a journey for his health in the State of Georgia.
Joseph, h. Dolly, April 13, 1834, [a. 66, C.R.].
Levi, April 7, 1821, a. 49. G.S.3.
Lydia, d. Levi and Lois, Nov. 21, 1814, a. 18 y. 7 m. 3 d.
Martha, w. Stephen, Nov. 15, 1810, [a. 66, C.R.].

STRATTON, Martha [W.], w. Joseph, Aug. 17, 1841, [a. 36, G.S.6.].
Miss Mary, Dec. 14, 1839, a. 36. G.S.3.
Mary, wid. Jabez, Oct. 23 [22, G.S.], 1848, a. 76 [77, G.S.6.].
Nancy, d. Stephen and Martha, Sept. 5, 1810, a. 36 y. 2 m. 2 d.
Racheal, w. David, June 22, 1844, a. 42 y. 3 m. 17 d. Consumption.
Sarah, w. David, Jan. 17, 1825, a. 37 y. C.R.
Stephen, s. Stephen and Martha, May 15, 1784, in 6th y.
Stephen, s. Stephen and Martha, Sept. 5, 1801, in 18th y.
Col. Stephen, widr. Martha, March 31 [April 1, C.R.], 1814, [a. 71, G.S.3.].
Susan, d. Abel and Susan, May 12, 1844, a. 5 m. 4 d. Consumption. Dup.
Susanna Giles, w. Asa, —— —, 1842, a. 56. G.S.1.
Susannah, w. James, May 8, 1824, [a. 37, C.R.].
Wilder, s. Ebenezer and Hannah, Oct. 8, 1806, a. 3 y. 5 m. 26 d.
William, May 9, 1805, in 70th y. G.S.1.
Zebulon, s. Zebulon and Jerusha, June 13, 1795, a. 7 y. 2 m. G.S.3.
——, ch. Peleg, Jr., Sept. 20, 1815. C.R.
——, inf. David, June 30, 1819, a. 1 h. C.R.
——, ch. Peleg Jr., Oct. 23, 1819, a. 3 y. 9 m. C.R.
——, ch. Ruben, Feb. 24, 1849, a. 3.
——, w. Elias, Oct. 4, 1795, a. 62 y. C.R.
——, infant ch. Ebenezer and ——, Jan. 19, 1801. 1 minute old. C.R.
——, ch. Jabez, Sept. 20, 1810, a. 6 w. C.R.

STRETTON (see above), Frances, s. Joseph and Alice, June 5, 1849, a. 3 d.

SULLIVAN, Roger, Aug. 31, 1847, a. 24. Killed on Railroad.

SWEETSER, Ann R. [Anna, G.S.], w. Samuel Jr., Aug. 11, 1835, [a. 34, G.S.2.].
Ann [Anna, G.S.2.] E., d. Samuel, Nov. 4, 1844, a. 7. Typhus fever.
Charles Humphrey, s. Samuel Jr. and Ann R., April 14, 1835, a. 6 y. 2 m. 14 d.
Maria Ann, d. Samuel and Nancy M., Sept. 6 [7, G.S.2.], 1847, a. 1 y. 6 m.
Mary, d. Samuel and Hannah, March 26, 1818, a. 24. G.S.2.
Nancy Maria, w. Samuel, March 29, 1847, a. 33. Consumption.
Samuel, h. Hannah, July 27, 1842.
Samuel, (widr.), April 29, 1847, a. 48. Consumption.

TAFT, Polly, Aug. 14, 1802, a. 9 y. C.R.

TAYLOR, David, s. Rufus and Mary, Oct. 16, 1793. C.R.
Mary, w. Rufus, June 1, 1773. C.R.
Rufus, Feb. —, 1783. C.R.
Susannah, d. Rufus and Mary, Oct. 19, 1773. C.R.

THAYER, ———, wid. ———, Feb. 20, 1825, a. 92 y. C.R.

THORP, Eli, s. Eliphalet and Ruthy, Dec. 23, 1836, a. 20 y. 6 m. 3 d.
Fenno F., s. Fenno and Lucy B., Sept. 4, 1849, a. 6 y. 2 m. Dysentery.
Hannah, d. Ira and Catharine, Aug. 17, 1815, a. 1 m. 7 d.

TOLBERT, ———, ch. Mr. and wife, Jan. 29, 1803. C.R.

TOTTMAN, Samuel, May 28, 1807, a. 50 y. C.R.

TOWNSEND, Abigail, d. Thomas and Abigail, Sept. 13, 1802, a. 7 m. 8 d.
Abigail, wid. Thomas, June 7, 1830, [a. 58, C.R.].
Almira, d. Thomas and Abigail, July 28, 1809, on day of birth.
Ann [Anna, G.S.], w. Col. Thomas, May 22, 1839, [a. 35, G.S.2.].
Benjamin, s. Benjamin and Elisabeth, July 18, 1783, in 7th y. (Perhaps same as next.)
Lieut. Benjamin, July 18, 1783, in 42d y. G.S.3.
Benjamin, s. Thomas and Abigail, Sept. 30, 1814, a. 19 y. 3 m. 8 d.
Benjamin, s. William and Elizabeth, April 12, 1819, a. 1.
Clarissa, 1st w. Lysander F., Jan. 13, 1838.
Dana, s. Thomas and Abigail, Sept. 19, 1802, a. 2 y. 7 m. 3 d.
Elizabeth, w. William, April 1, 1822, [a. 43, C.R.].
Lucy, 2d w. Lysander F., Nov. 14, 1840. Killed by the over turning of a wagon in Orange.
Thomas, h. Abigail, July 23, 1816, [a. 46, G.S.3.].
Thomas, s. William and Elizabeth, Aug. 18, 1825, a. 5 y. 5 m. 27 d.
William, s. William and Elizabeth, Jan. 3, 1832, a. nearly 26.
William, widr. Elizabeth, Dec. 25, 1834.
———, ch. Capt. T., July 7, 1810, a. 4 h. C.R.

TRAIN, Molley, d. Jonathan and Marcy, Jan. 5, 1776. C.R.
———, ch. Jonathan and Mercy, July 25, 1771, a. 2 w. C.R.

TWICHEL (see Twichell, Twitchel, Twitchell), Abner, Feb. 15, 1825, a. 71 y. C.R.

TWICHEL, Azubah, d. Enos Jr. and Azubah, Sept. 16, 1804, a. 2 y. 5 m. 6 d.
Benoni, Aug. 29, 1819, a. 74 y. C.R.
Calvin, s. Seth and Phebe, Jan. 12, 1795, a. 4 m. 23 d.
Enos, h. Releif, July 25, 1812, [a. 62, C.R.].
Jeremiah, senior, Oct. 6, 1810, [a. 68, C.R.].
John, March 1, 1802, a. 48 y. C.R.
Joseph, s. David and Sarah, May 11, 1769, in 19th y.
Josiah, Sept. 30, 1826, a. 59 y. C.R.
Widow Martha, April 5, 1810, a. 55 y. C.R.
Relief, wid. Enos, Aug. 16, 1835.
Sally, July 5, 1790, a. 22 y. C.R.
Sarah, twin d. David and Sarah, Oct. 28, 1756. Nitchawoog. C.R.
Sarah, d. David and Sarah, Oct. 20, 1765, a. 7 lacking 2 days.
Seth, s. Seth and Phebe, June 4, 1794, in 2d y.
Seth, h. Phebe ?, Nov. 7, 1802, [1803 ?, C.R.].
Willard, s. Josiah and Hannah, Sept. 5, 1803, a. 6 m. 24 d.
———, ch. Josiah, Nov. 25, 1790. C.R.
———, inf. of Benana ?, Sept. 13, 1792. C.R.
———, The widow, Feb. 23, 1793[4 ?]. C.R.
———, child Seth, June 5, 1795, a. 2 y. C.R.
———, ch. widow, Sept. 23, 1802, a. 6 y. C.R.
———, ch. Josiah, Sept. 5, 1803, a. 9 m. C.R.
———, ch. Lemuel, Oct. 9, 1804. C.R.
———, ch. Wm., Sept. 18, 1805. C.R.
———, ch. Alford, Dec. 17, 1817, a. 3 m. C.R.
———, ch. Samuel, Sept. 10, 1819, a. 16 m. C.R.
———, ch. Jeremiah, Oct. 8, 1823, a. 1 y. 1 m. C.R.
———, ch. Chester, Aug. 12, 1828, a. 2. C.R.

TWICHELL, Charles, s. Alfred 2d and Hannah, July 16, 1839.
Chester, h. Sally, Sept. 8, 1840.
David Goddard, s. Seth and Phebe, Dec. 6, 1838, a. 48 y. 1 m. 21 d. Dup.
Emma I., d. Uriah, Sept. 8, 1849, a. 2. Dysentery.
Mary L., d. Uriah, Sept. 7, 1849, a. 4. Dysentery.
Permelia Earl, d. Abner G. and Hannah, Feb. 18, 1848, a. 11 m.
Wid. Rhoda [wid. Jeremiah ?], Dec. 18, 1832, a. 94.
Miss Sally, May 13, 1839, a. 47. G.S.2.
Sally Luann, Feb. 13, 1839, a. 6. G.S.3.
Sybel, May 10, 1840, a. 41. G.S.3.
———, ch. Chester, Apri, —, 1845, a. 6 d. Buried in Orange.

TWITCHEL, David, s. Dea. David and Sarah, April 17, 1776. C.R.
Hariot L., d. Frances and Sally, Sept. 10, 1828, a. 9 y. C.R.
Jane, April 14, 1807. C.R.
Marian, Nov. 5, 1827, a. 48 y. C.R.
Widow Sarah, June 10, 1812, a. 90 y. C.R.

TWITCHELL (see above), Hannah A., w. Abner, Dec. 14, 1848, a. 25.

UNDERWOOD, Nathan (married), Sept. 6, 1848, a. 53. Suicide.

VARNUM, Patty, w. Willard, April 15, 1780. C.R.

WAIT, Sophronia, d. Joseph and Hannah, Jan. 20, 1848, a. 20.
———, d. Mr. ——— and w. May —, 1795, a. about 17 y. C.R.

WALLINGFORD, Ezekeal, killed by Indians, Aug. —, 1746. G.S.I.

WARD, Ambrose, s. Walter, Oct. 13, 1819, a. 8 y. C.R.
Beriah, Oct. 23, 1773. C.R.
Beriah, Jan. 22, 1826, a. 24 y. Senior class, college. C.R.
Esther, w. Jabez, Oct. 11 [6, C.R.], 1813, [a. 46, C.R.].
Henry, s. Jabez and Esther, June 10, 1814, a. 25 y. 10 m. 19 d. [23 y., C.R.]
Lucena, w. Francis S., Jan. 3, 1844. At Phillipston.
Lucina, d. Francis S. and Harriet A. ?, June 3, 1844, a. 21. G.S.2.
Lucy, w. William H., Jan. 2, 1829, [a. 40, G.S.3, [41, C.R.]].
Lyman, s. Jabez and Esther, March 28, 1818, a. 11 y. 1 m. 25 d.
Widow Margeret, Aug. 26, 1777. C.R.
Mary, w. Jonathan, July 6, 1777. C.R.
Persis Diana, d. Daniel and Lydia, Jan. 27, 1843, a. 16 y. 2 m. 28 d.
Polly, d. Alpheus and Molley, July 6, 1817, in 27th y.
———, ch. Jabez, March 26, 1809, a. 13 m. C.R.
———, ch. Walter, July 13, 1822. C.R.

WARNER, Ichabod Porter, July 19, 1777. In the Pest house of Small Pox. C.R.

WARREN, Louisa (single), Aug. 16, 1846, a. 70. Cancer.
Sarah (single), July 9, 1847, a. 38. Cancer.

WELCH, ———, Aug. 9, 1846, a. 32. Killed while blasting rock. Buried in Worcester.

WELSH, ———, Oct. 13, 1845, a. 33. Drowned. Born in Ireland and buried in Springfield.

WESSON, Josiah (widr.), June 15, 1843, a. 76.
Wid. Mary, May 1, 1812, a. 78 y. C.R.
Nabby, w. Josiah, Dec. 20, 1833, a. 57. G.S.3.

WESTON, ———, Mrs., April —, 1802. C.R.

WETHERBY, Caleb, s. John and Mary, Sept. 12, 1775. C.R.

WHEATON, Christopher C., M.D., Sept. 24, 1848, a. 46. Amherst Coll., 1828. G.S.1.

WHEELER, Eunice, w. Paul, July 4, 1801.
Franklin, s. Jonathan, Sept. 11, 1849, a. 3 y. 11 m. Dysentery.
Harriet A., Aug. 27, 1834, a. 2. G.S.1.
Jesse G., Sept. 9, 1835, a. 29. G.S.1.
Jonathan, s. Jonathan and Hannah, Oct. 8, 1836, a. 3 m. G.S.3.
Lucinda, d. Paul and Eunice, Jan. 30, 1802, a. 1 y. 1 d.
Margaret, d. Jonathan and Hannah, May 17, 1842, a. 10 m. 5 d.
Mary Raymond, 1st w. Jonathan, April 30, 1830.
Mercy, July 6, 1813. C.R.
Polly, w. Jona., May 7, 1830, a. 38 y. C.R.
Silence, w. Zacheus, Sept. 9, 1829, a. 78. G.S.3.

WHIPPLE, Samuel, Sept. 19, 1775. C.R.

WHITE, Ephraim, March 15, 1815, a. 51 y. A stranger. C.R.
Nathan, Feb. 17, 1817, a. 32. G.S.3.

WHITNEY, Francis A., s. [d. ?] Elbridge W. and Sophia A., Sept. 17, 1846, a. 8 m. 12 d. G.S.2.
Isaac Henry, s. Moses and Tabitha, Oct. 1, 1804.
Mr. Jonas, April 7, 1776. C.R.
Lucy, d. Chandler and Martha, Aug. 19, 1843, a. 16 y. 7 m. Consumption.
Martha, w. Chandler, Jan. 8, 1848, a. 52. G.S.2.
Mary [W.] d. William K., [and Deborah], Sept. 6, 1846, a. 16. Typhus fever.
Patty, w. C. H., Jan. 8, 1848, a. 47.
———, ch. Moses, Oct. 1, 1804, a. 2 y. C.R.
———, ch. Saml., Feb. 7, 1817, a. 1 y. C.R.
———, [Frances A., above ?], inf. d. Whipple, Sept. 18, 1846. Dysentary.

WIDGER, James B. [s. Thomas and Elisabeth], of Lynn, Jan. 18, 1843, [a. 21, G.S.2.].

WILCOCKS, Seth, July 12, 1825. A stranger. C.R.

WILEY (see Wyley, Wylie), Samuel, June 13, 1847, a. 41. Typhoid fever.

WILKINSON, Mrs., ———, May 5, 1831. C.R.

WILLARD, Ephraim, h. Lucy, April 23, 1804, [a. 37, G.S.3.].
Ephraim, June 16, 1836, a. 62. G.S.3.
Horatio, April 28, 1831, [a. 30, G.S.3.].
Wid. Lucy, June 16, 1836.
Mrs. Mary, Jan. 3, 1829, a. 89 y. in Hartland Vt. of cancer. At the age of 6 years she resided in this Town, Athol, & was taken captive by the Indians & carried to ——— where she remained a prisoner two [?] years when she was returned to her country. C.R.

WILLIAMS, Alfred, s. Elbridge and Harriot, Dec. 24, 1834, a. 3 m. 24 d. G.S.3.
Marietta, w. William H., Dec. 4, 1820.
———, w. Dr., Jan. —, 1821. C.R.

WILSON, Francis, Dec. 19, 1803, a. 24 y. A stranger. C.R.

WOOD (see Woods), Alpheus, Feb. 24, 1825, a. 69 y. C.R.
Frederic H., s. Joel and Abby M., Aug. 1, 1836, a. 9. G.S.2.
Josephus, s. wid. Abagail, March 11, 1849, a. 16 [and 6 m. 20 d., G.S.2.] Diabetus.
Kimball, Sept. 22, 1805, a. 63 y. C.R.
Mary, w. Kimball, March 22, 1805, [March 21, a. 62, C.R.].
Oliver, s. Kimbal and Mary, Aug. 29, 1778, a. 14 d.
Sarah, w. E. G., Feb. 9, 1848, a. 37.
Susanna, d. Kimbal and Mary, Oct. 22 [21, C.R.], 1776, a. 4 y. 6 m. 20 d.

WOODBURN, Maj. Thomas, April 5, 1807, a. 38 [37, C.R.]. G.S.3.

WOODS (see Wood), William, the father of Thomas, was buried June 28, 1770. C.R. [Died June 27.]

WOODWARD, Abijah, h. Elizabeth, June 27, 1815, [a. 53, C.R.].
Bartholomew, h. Sally, March 6, 1827, [a. 42, G.S.3.].
C. Clarence, s. George W. and Electa M., Sept. 9, 1849, a. 7 m. G.S.2.

ATHOL DEATHS.

WOODWARD, George C., s. George W. and Electa, Sept. 9, 1849, a. 7 m. Dysentery.
James Manson, s. Manson and Nancy, May 30, 1843, a. 9 m. 26 d. Scarlet fever.
Sally, w. Bartholomew, Dec. 20, 1827, [a. 38, G.S.3.].
Wallis Watson, s. Manson J. and Nancy, May 30, 1843, a. 9 m. 26 d. Scarlet fever.
———, inf. Bartholomy, Nov. 25, 1815, a. 3 d. C.R.

WYLEY (see Wiley), Susanna, w. Joseph, Aug. 22, 1806. C.R.

WYLIE (see Wiley), Mary E., d. Samuel and Nancy, Nov. 4, 1849, a. 5 y. 5 m. 23 d. Dysentery.

YOUNG, Abner, Nov. 22, 1841, a. 49. G.S.2.
Amasa, s. William and Kezia, Aug. —, [16, C.R.], 1804, a. 10 [20?, C.R.]
Anna, d. Robert and Sarah, April 28, 1763. C.R.
Anna, d. Robert and Elizabeth, Sept. 2, 1769. C.R.
Anne, w. Joshua, Feb. 2, 1827, a. 23 y. C.R.
Wid. Betsy, Feb. 23, 1825, a. 95 y. C.R.
Caroline, d. Abner and Lucy, ——— —, ———. [Dec. 5, 1824, a. 2, C.R.]
David, h. Hannah, ——— —, ———. [Probably same as next.]
David, Feb. 13, 1841, a. 85. G.S.1.
Eunice, d. William and Kezia, Dec. 31, 1789, a. 13 d.
Hannah, wid. David, June 1, 1842, a. 77.
Harriot, d. James and Patty, March 25, 1814, a. 1 y. 5 m. 11 d.
Hiram (married), Sept. 27, 1849, a. 36. Dysentery.
Isabel M., May 21, 1832, a. 22. G.S.1.
James, s. James and Patty, Aug. 15 [16, C.R.], 1826, a. 1 y. 5 m. 26 d.
Jarvis, s. Joseph and Sophia, July 30, 1835, [July 29, 1836, dup.] a. 13 m. G.S.3. [1 y. 26 d., C.R.]
John, s. Samuel and Rhoda, Aug. 16, 1777, in 5th y.
John, s. Joel and Sarah, Sept. 27, 1803, a. 4 y. 6 m. [a. 3, C.R.]
Jonathan, s. Joel and Sarah, Sept. 22 [20, C.R.], 1803, a. 1.
Joseph E., s. Abner and Lucy, Jan. 29, 1826, a. 1 y. C.R.
Joseph E., s. Abner and Lucy, March 15, 1827, a. 4½ m. C.R.
Josephine, d. Abner and Lucy, July 1, 1838, a. 1 y. less 5 d.
Keziah, w. William, Oct. 13, 1803, [a. 43, C.R.].
Levi, s. Samuel and Rhoda, Aug. 18, 1777, in 3d y.
Lois, w. Samuel, ——— —, ———. [Nov. 26, 1808, a. 54., C.R.]
Mary, w. David, Feb. 28, 1819, a. 32 [28, C.R.]. G.S.1.

YOUNG, Nathaniel, Jan. 9, 1811, a. 24 y. C.R.
Polly, d. William and Kezia, March 25 [24, C.R.], 1805, a. 24 y. 11 d.
Rhoda, w. Samuel, Sept. 10, 1777.
Robert, Nov. 20, 1796. C.R.
Royal, s. William and Kezia, April 13, 1805, in 18th y.
Ruben, Nov. 5, 1822, a. 36, [Oct. 6, G.S.1. At Belchertown. C.R.].
Samuel, widr. Lois, Dec. 5, 1831.
Sarah, w. Robert, Jan. 18, 1761. C.R.
William, s. William and Kezia, Jan. 6, 1809, a. nearly 23.
William, widr. Keziah, April 21, 1810, [a. 62, C.R.].
———, inf. Joel and wife, April 13, 1801, a. 1 d. C.R.
———, ch. David Jr., Feb. 19, 1820, a. 1 y. C.R.
———, inf. Joshua, Jan. 29, 1827, a..2 d. C.R.
———, inf. Joshua, Oct. 10, 1831. C.R.

UNIDENTIFIED.

———, Titus, a Negro belonging to James and Esther Humphrey, Nov. 7, 1773, a. 3 y. 6 m. wanting 2 d. C.R.
———, Stephen, a Negro Boy of Rev. J. Humphrey, Jan. 20, 1793. C.R.
———, ———, an Irish child, Aug. 23, 1847.
Six men, Oct. 27, 1847, Killed by falling of R. R. bridge.
Unknown man, March 18, 1848, a. 29. Born in Ireland.
———, ———, male, Oct. 2, 1849, a. 25. Killed in Railroad Accident. Born in Ireland, buried in Worcester.

www.ingramcontent.com/pod-product-compliance
Lightning Source LLC
Chambersburg PA
CBHW071949160426
43198CB00011B/1609